CROSSED CURRENTS

CROSSED CURRENTS

⚓

Navy Women from WWI to Tailhook

JEAN EBBERT
MARIE-BETH HALL

Foreword by
Capt. Edward L. Beach, USN (Ret.)

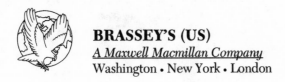

BRASSEY'S (US)
A Maxwell Macmillan Company
Washington • New York • London

Copyright © 1993 Brassey's (US)

Brassey's (US)

Editorial Offices
Brassey's (US)
8000 Westpark Drive
First Floor
McLean, Virginia 22102

Order Department
Brassey's Book Orders
c/o Macmillan Publishing Co.
100 Front Street, Box 500
Riverside, New Jersey 08075

Brassey's (US) is a Maxwell Macmillan Company. Brassey's (US) books are available at special discounts for bulk purchases for sales promotions, premiums, fund-raising, or educational use through the Special Sales Director, Macmillan Publishing Company, 866 Third Avenue, New York, New York 10022.

Library of Congress Cataloging-in-Publication Data

Ebbert, Jean
    Crossed currents : Navy women from WWI to Tailhook / Jean Ebbert,
  Marie-Beth Hall; foreword by Edward L. Beach.
        p. cm.
    Includes bibliographical references and index.
    ISBN 0-02-881022-8
    1. United States. Navy—Women. I. Hall, Marie-Beth. II. Title.
VB324.W65E23 1993
359'.0082—dc20   92-39963

10 9 8 7 6 5 4 3 2 1
Printed in the United States of America

To
The Women of the U.S. Navy

CONTENTS

⚓

[Handwritten annotations:]

write up starting w/

(1) Exit in (WW 2)

(2) The Korean Conflict

(3) The Vietnam part

(4) Today . . . .

(5) My conclusion

12 pages limit

PART FOUR
Modern Navy Women

FOREWORD

by Capt. Edward L. Beach, USN (Ret.)

Only in recent years have women begun to attain their rightful and full participation in national and world affairs. Women have always had to work in one way or another; but only recently have they really been counted as full-fledged citizens of the United States (read members of the human establishment) with all the perquisites and responsibilities thereof. In the United States, the right to vote was granted by the Nineteenth Amendment in 1919 and ratified in 1920. Many women today are handling full careers in some aspect of our industrial world; and, significantly, the two-salaried family has evolved into a recognized and probably long-lasting phenomenon.

Since the U.S. Navy was formed, women have served it in many unofficial ways as the married partners of naval personnel. Officers' wives since time beyond memory have been doing what they could to make things better for their husbands' ships and their crews; but not until the "great" war did our Navy officially employ women on their own to do a job. For World War I the naval position of Yeoman (F) (miscalled "yeomanette" by some) was created, and thousands of women were enlisted. The job was on shore and clerical, much of it in the Navy Department in Washington, D.C., and its announced (and true) purpose was to make more male yeomen available for sea duty as the fleet expanded. The need was so great and the employment of women so fast once Secretary of the Navy Josephus Daniels (more famous for abolishing the naval officers' wine mess) made the breakthrough decision that for a time not much thought was given to their technical status or to the obligation the Navy had assumed toward them.

All Yeomen (F) were released to inactive duty when the war ended. Surprisingly, our Navy of 1919 had no idea that another war would bring a repetition of the same dire need for women. Quite the contrary, after the World War I experience, the Navy created restrictions that had to be circumvented during the hectic years of 1941 and 1942. When the emergency came, these were swept aside. Women were again called to service, this time in both officer and enlisted grades.

For this second time around, however, women owed much to the Yeomen (F) of World War I. The evolution of women's aspirations and the thoughtful understanding of the problems involved in once again going on active naval duty went essentially hand in hand. The U.S. Navy and the women of America in general were fortunate that some of those former Yeomen (F)—capable, hard working, and wise—were available to take the helm from the very beginning.

A new day had dawned. The Women Accepted for Volunteer Emergency Service (WAVES) by deliberate design took in some of the highest-class professional women in the country: college presidents, professors, and some of the very few women in high industry or management positions. When the war ended, these women did not just go away, as had happened before and as apparently a number of high-ranking male naval officers expected. Thus, they encountered the "crossed currents" in the title of this long-awaited book. No doubt an outgrowth of and similar to the development of the status of women throughout the country and the world, the fact is that women had to fight every inch of the way for their recognition in the Navy, just as they had to for recognition in all other strata of civilization in the first half of this century. These particular women saw their chance and their duty and made the most of it.

Crossed Currents is the chronicle of their battle, ending with the most objective analysis of the "Tailhook" incident that I have yet come upon. Of course that is told from the point of view of the women involved, but the authors are professional in every sense of the word. Until a better story is told, we would do well to pay attention to what they saw and how they tell it.

Although the major part of the battle is already won, for the Navy, sex and sexual customs as well as the primordial sexual urge are at the bedrock of what must still be done. The authors of this book—Navy women both, one an officer and both married to captains in the Navy— take pains to separate their focus on the attendant problems from the sometimes prurient interest in sex that sells books and movies. The problem is there, most surely, and maybe even the temptation; but they chose to concentrate on the real story: the Navy's needs, how women met those needs (and still retained the biological difference with which they were born), and how the women about whom they write dedicated their lives (in some cases had to give them) in the struggle to be accepted for what they could do for our Navy.

Although the Tailhook affair was traumatic and its ramifications have not all yet been seen, from the point of view of where our culture is going it can be said that it was essentially a good thing that it happened, in the same way as this can be said about Pearl Harbor. The damage was great in both cases, but just as Pearl Harbor galvanized us and shook the world, Tailhook showed the Navy and the whole country the unacceptable side of the traditional ways in which men and women have managed their inherent biological differences. It is not at all too much to say that Tailhook shook the Navy.

The authors of this book at the outset announce that they had a big story to tell without dwelling in detail on the offbeat things that must have happened. But neither would they ignore the inevitable problems when men and women are thrown together, without lengthy preconditioning, in as recondite and strenuous a calling as the naval service. In fact, they have obviously viewed what has gone on so far as an essential part of that very preconditioning that is so necessary.

All the same, Ebbert and Hall have not shied away from full descriptions, often with citations, of some of the less-than-supportive reactions of men who may have felt themselves threatened by the advent of women into their otherwise all-male bastion. Likewise, the occasional misbehavior, sexual or otherwise, male or female, is not overlooked. There have been numerous "illegitimate" pregnancies, as well as occasional legitimate courtships and marriage; and when it happened, what *is* special is how wisely the Navy dealt with its pregnant officers and sailors. Whenever possible, married couples were collocated (assigned duties in the same localities). Pregnancy, however, in or out of marriage, used to result in immediate discharge of the woman; now there are only a few weeks of maternity leave, and marriage is not a factor. But sex, consensual or not, is not permitted on board ship. Married couples, collocated or not, cannot be assigned to the same ship. And the authors quite frankly admit that the "burning question" of homosexual or lesbian individuals has not yet been entirely solved.

Regarding the relatively frequent examples, early on, of seniors having difficulty in accepting the presence of women, in nearly every case the story shows that even the greatest misogynist, once having experienced what women could do for him in mutual areas of responsibility, almost always became thoroughly converted. Initial resistance in some cases was pronounced, but often such men did not realize that they were in fact out of their depth. In almost every case of such confrontation, their female antagonist was an outstanding woman and had been more than once the foremost woman in her field when she decided, for whatever reason, to sign up in the Navy.

Because of limitations on the number of female officers allowed, many very high-caliber women settled for enlisted status, and as a consequence male officers sometimes greatly underestimated them and were neatly outmaneuvered by them. As Ebbert and Hall point out, however, women seldom announced success with a blare of trumpets and clash of cymbals. Instead, they tended to savor quietly the moment when their intransigent boss(es) not only accepted defeat but (in a manner of speaking) praised them for it.

The term *WAVE* became obsolete when women were fully integrated into the Navy. WAVES, as the acronym implies, were volunteers for emergency service. But after World War II, contrary to the situation after World War I when Yeomen (F) were all discharged or sent to the inactive reserve, the WAVES were converted into the regular Navy. There have been female officers and female sailors—enlisted women—ever since, and of recent years their strengths and responsibilities have waxed. They have come a long way since the day when a senior male officer roared that he wanted nothing to do with women (in the Navy) because they were "no good" (in the Navy). Today, we have women commanding ships, flying aircraft, even making tailhook landings on aircraft carriers just as effectively as their male counterparts. We have them handling boats and anchor gear, working in the engine rooms, and operating lathes in the ship's machine shops. The only thing yet prohibited by law is crewing on a combat ship. But women Marines and women in the Army have been in combat; and all, in all services, are trained in some combat skills. As one Marine sergeant explained it, "You never can tell what might happen, and if they are out there, even in the rear lines, they have got to know how to protect themselves."

It has been historically noted that fundamental change is usually very slow to come, even extremely lengthy in its beginning stages. When, as is said, "its time has come," things do move faster and faster as each succeeding event fuels the next. Women have been around as long as men, but only in recent years has the true subordinacy of their status been challenged. Their ascendancy in the Navy is only one of a number of changes in our culture in which they figure. As they are fond of saying, if women in the city can be killed by bombs dropped by an enemy aircraft, why can they not shoot back? If they can help manufacture munitions, which they do, can they not actually use those munitions?

The sea change has long been coming. We are seeing its culmination, and we have only one or two steps yet to take. Symbolized by accepting women in combat, which is likely, we are seeing a total change in men's attitudes toward women and women's attitudes toward themselves and men. *Crossed Currents* gives us the best picture yet of this sea change. Spartan women were said to be as militant as their men: "Bring me back this shield," one is said to have told her son, "or come back dead upon it." Women of the United States—in a larger sense, women of the Western world—are not thinking of emulating that Spartan mother, but they are looking their men in the eye and saying, unmistakably, "We are different because of biology, but in the things that count we are as good as you are, even though we may do some things a little differently."

The only problem now is to discern the problems of the future and maintain undiminished—even improved—abilities to handle them. Although the Navy was not created to be the vehicle of social change, that mandate has been laid on it by our society's highest authority. It is still up to our Navy to maintain the purpose for which it was built, even as the world changes and that purpose evolves.

Women from now on will be a full-fledged part of our Navy, and that is a permanent change. As that proceeds we shall have to accept in both sexes all the changes and differences that go along with it. Some of the changes are deep-seated and deeply cultural, and their evolution has not ended.

What has happened and is continuing, for the story is going on even as we write, can only be epitomized by the well-known French aphorism, "Vive la différence!" That, at least, will never change; the U.S. Navy is learning to live with it.

PREFACE

⚓

In the U.S. Navy today there are about sixty thousand women, including two thousand in the Nurse Corps. They constitute about 10 percent of its active-duty force and include jet pilots, rear admirals, commanding officers of ships and aircraft squadrons, and graduates of the Naval Academy. They have repaired damaged hulls in the Persian Gulf and engineered policy in the Pentagon. They serve in every kind of unit, in every kind of job except those from which they are excluded by law. Despite these restrictions, they have climbed close to the pinnacles of the naval profession. Yet naval historians have largely ignored these women and their predecessors. A reader can peruse book after book on modern U.S. naval history and find no mention that nearly twelve thousand women in addition to nurses served in the Navy in World War I. World War II WAVES are better known, but even respected historians have managed to include one or more errors in the few paragraphs they allot these women. Although the Nurse Corps was established in 1908, and although Navy nurses have served in combat zones since World War I and been prisoners of war, they too have thus far been neglected by historians and biographers.

The authors decided to fill part of this void in the history of the U.S. Navy by offering a one-volume chronicle that begins with the Yeomen (F) of World War I and concludes in the present day. We have not included the history of Navy nurses in this book, chiefly because we believe that they deserve to have their own separate, full-length book. For simplicity's sake and unless otherwise indicated, when we refer to women in the Navy we mean those other than nurses. We intend this book to serve as a general text that will acquaint a wide audience with this nearly unknown aspect of twentieth-century American history. We also hope that it will be a starting point for further research into naval, feminist, and social history.

We have observed that whenever women enter a field dominated by men (or vice versa), popular interest focuses on the sexual frontier between male and female. This is not the story we have chosen to tell. Rather, our account focuses on the Navy's recruitment of women not for their charms but rather for their abilities. Our emphasis is on the Navy's struggle to accept change and women's struggles to be accepted by the Navy.

Both authors have long-standing ties with the Navy and bear it deep affection. We are both married to retired naval officers. Marie-Beth Hall is the daughter of a naval officer and the mother of two more. Jean Ebbert is a former naval officer and the author of books and articles about the Navy and for thirteen years was a Naval Academy information officer. We write, then, from the viewpoint of well-informed observers, sympathetic both to the Navy's ambivalence about women and to its women's impatience with that ambivalence. Ours is not a particularly feminist stance. Nonetheless, we are women of our time whose sensibilities have been challenged by feminist thought. While we have tried to show the genuine professional concerns that lie beneath some of the Navy's cautious attitudes and decisions about women, we have also described inequities the service has imposed on women.

We drew our story from documents in widely dispersed archives, a handful of little-known memoirs, newspaper and magazine stories, occasional articles in professional journals, and scores of personal interviews. When we began our work in 1982, these were the only sources. Since then, the amount of published material on women in the military has grown. Landmark developments include the publication in 1982 of *Women in the Military,* by Maj. Gen. Jeanne Holm, in 1988 of *Sound Off,* by Dorothy and Carl J. Schneider, and in 1989 of Judith Stiehm's *Arms and the Enlisted Woman* as well as the founding in 1983 of *Minerva,* a quarterly report on women and the military. These works mark the beginning of an interest that goes beyond the journalistic to the genuinely historical. However, they deal with the women serving in all the armed forces, and most deal with single themes and cover limited periods. We believe that it is time for separate histories of women's service in each of the armed forces.

Here is one such history, the story, stretching now over nearly three-quarters of a century, of how the U.S. Navy opened its ranks to women other than nurses and of how women struggled to gain acceptance. The Navy's acceptance was reluctant, driven more by need than by anything else. Need and reluctance were recurring themes, but so were innovations, commitment, and the Navy's pride in its women. Even when many of its officials privately and sometimes publicly deplored the recruitment of women, once the Navy bowed to necessity and began opening gangways, it tried to do so well. For most Navy women, their struggle was marked by loyalty to and affection for the Navy, pride in their service to the country, as well as puzzlement and sometimes anger that struggle was necessary at all. Even when Navy policies and programs strongly supported progress for women, some Navy men opposed it. Expressions of their opposition ranged widely from apathy to sexual assault. The best-known example of the latter occurred at the infamous Tailhook Convention in 1991, producing sensational coverage in newspapers and television from coast to coast. The revelations of the next twelve months led to serious repercussions in the Navy: the secretary of the Navy resigned, the careers of several admirals were derailed, and Congress held up the promotions of all officers who might have any involvement with the convention.

The story then is of two currents, crossing and recrossing, sometimes conflicting, sometimes converging. One current is the Navy's gradual inclusion of women, often grudging yet sometimes handled with verve and distinction, and its attempt to acknowledge changing realities without losing traditional values. The other current is that of the women's struggle to find acceptance within a male-dominated profession.

As any sailor knows, where currents cross, the waters are troubled.

ACKNOWLEDGMENTS

⚓

We began our research in January 1982 and completed the manuscript in June 1992. During that period we received help from many, many people, in particular those named here. To the following we are much indebted for their interest and encouragement: the late Capt. Joy Bright Hancock; Lt. Comdr. Nonna Cheatham and Capts. Elizabeth Wylie and Georgia Sadler, all retired Navy; Dr. Harold D. Langley, director of Naval History, Smithsonian Institution; the late Capt. Paul Ryan, USN (Ret.) of the Hoover Institution at Stanford University; Dr. Linda Grant DePauw of George Washington University; Dr. Margaret C. Devilbiss; Mr. Paul Stilwell, director of the U.S. Naval Institute's oral history program; Dr. D'Ann Campbell of Indiana University; and Ms. Carolyn Becraft.

Many persons facilitated our work in archives and libraries, most notably Drs. Ronald Spector and Dean Allard of the Naval Historical Center, as well as staff members Martha Crawley, Regina Akers, and Drs. Edward Marolda and Lynne Dunne; Mr. John Vajda and the staff of the Navy Department library; Ms. Patricia Williams and the staff of the Times-Journal library; Ms. Evelyn Cherpak, curator of the Naval Historical Collection at the Naval War College; Ms. Charlotte Palmer Seeley and Dr. George Chalou of the National Archives; and the staff of the library of the Center for Naval Analyses.

The files of the Navy Department office known as Op-01(W) have been an invaluable source. For making them available to us, as well as for helping us to find other information and understand processes and events that we might otherwise have overlooked, we offer the deepest thanks to Capts. Julie DiLorenzo, Kathleen Bruyere, and Martha Whitehead, Lt. Comdrs. Maureen Davidovich and Donna Looney, and Petty Officers Joseph Keenan, Patricia Sandt, and Beth Snyder.

We are particularly indebted to Capt. John V. Hall, USN (Ret.), and to novelist and historian Capt. Edward L. Beach, USN (Ret.), for critical review and discussion, and to Capt. Leigh Ebbert for his support and professional advice.

Four sources of information merit special mention. Beyond what we specifically cite in our notes and references, we depended on each for certain periods and/or perspectives. The first is Eunice Dessez's *The First Enlisted Women,* the only published book-length treatment of the Yeomen (F) of World War I. A former Yeoman (F), Dessez recounts details and reflects attitudes reported nowhere else. Another former Yeoman (F), Capt. Joy Bright Hancock, USN (Ret.), wrote the memoir *Lady in the Navy,* uniquely valuable because of its author's monumental career, ranging from 1917 to 1953 and culminating in her position as the first assistant chief of naval personnel for women. A mainstay of our research on the WAVES is *History of the Women's Reserve,* published by the Navy Department as part of a huge, multivolume history of U.S. Naval administration in World War II. While an official history, it provides an objective look at the Navy's administration of the Women's Reserve. A fourth source to which we owe more than our citations could indicate is *Women in the Military,* by Maj. Gen. Jeanne Holm, USAF (Ret.). Published shortly after we began our own research (and updated in 1992), it soon became one of our major resources. Holm brings unique insight and perspective to many developments, particularly those between 1950 and 1972.

Finally, to all the women and men of the U.S. Navy, past and present, who gave so generously of their time, energy, and memories—this book is our thanks to you.

PART ONE

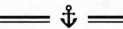

Yeomen (F) in World War I

1

America's First Enlisted Women

" I said, 'Let me see the appropriation bill. . . . It does not say . . . any-where that a yeoman must be a man.' "

— JOSEPHUS DANIELS

In World War I nearly twelve thousand women served in the U.S. Navy. Speed, simplicity, and brevity characterized the entire experience. They were recruited and enlisted quickly, chiefly because the idea that women might serve in the Navy was so inconceivable that no law against it existed. They wore hastily designed uniforms and were given the same titles and pay as Navy men for the same jobs. The Navy enlisted them to do clerical work ashore so that more men could be sent to sea. These women received no formal Navy training (many did not need it, as they were already experienced workers; and, in any event, the Navy was not pre-pared to give them any). Their service was brief—less than two years for most—and generally unmarred by struggle with the vast institution whose urgent call for help they had answered so promptly. Their struggle with the Navy, and the Navy's struggle to acknowledge their contribu-tions, came only after the war ended.

The First Enlisted Woman

On March 21, 1917, Loretta Perfectus Walsh enlisted in the U.S. Naval Reserve.[1] Educated at a parochial school in her hometown of Olyphant, Pennsylvania, and at the Scranton Lackawanna Business College in Scranton, Pennsylvania, she was working as a civilian clerk at a Navy recruiting station in Philadelphia when an opportunity arose to join the

Navy. Except for nurses, she was the first female member of any armed force of the United States. She fell ill while on recruiting duty and was discharged for disability in 1919. She entered a government hospital in Denver and was later transferred to a private sanatorium, where she died in 1925. She was buried in Olyphant.

To the women with whom she had served, Loretta Walsh epitomized their place in history: She was the first of the first enlisted women, and they wanted her service and theirs to be remembered. They sought to re-inter her in Arlington National Cemetery, where the War Department had granted her, as a veteran, a single plot. Then they asked for a larger plot to accommodate a monument commemorating all the U.S. Navy women who had served during the war. When this attempt failed, they chose to erect the monument over her grave in Olyphant. With considerable assistance from fellow American Legionnaires, they completed the monument and dedicated it in October 1937. The women made no further effort to secure a national memorial. To this day, the only monument to Walsh is the one above her grave in Olyphant.

How was it that Loretta Walsh served in the Navy at all? Why in 1917 did this conservative institution that had only recently accepted a handful of female nurses take into its ranks women who would serve in other roles? The story is not altogether clear, for during the war little effort was made to document it and in succeeding decades it was all but forgotten.

Does a Yeoman Have to Be a Man?

In the spring of 1917, Secretary of the Navy Josephus Daniels had some particularly acute concerns. The country was about to go to war, and he was not sure how he could keep the Navy operating. In the four years since he had taken office much had been accomplished to strengthen the service, but much more needed to be done. The innovations owed something to Daniels's shrewd choice of Franklin Roosevelt as assistant secretary of the Navy, for Roosevelt was popular with high-ranking naval officers and powerful members of Congress, whereas Daniels was not. They made an effective team. Although the Naval Act of 1916 (Public Law 241) authorized a substantial buildup of Navy forces over the next three years, Daniels was still worried about manpower. Where would he find men to serve in the Navy's growing number of ships? Where would he find men to train their crews? Aside from the numbers needed in ships, where would he find enough men with sufficient training and experience to perform the myriad jobs ashore?

The Navy Department whose efficiency he and Roosevelt had improved still required staggering numbers of records to be kept; letters and orders to be written, copied, and filed; contracts to be drafted and copied; and maps and charts to be updated. To keep this immense and growing bureaucracy afloat, telephone operators, messengers, and clerical workers were needed by the hundreds.

The Navy Department already employed large numbers of women as clerks in the Civil Service. To increase their numbers was perhaps one way of finding clerical help. However, as Daniels later recalled,

> There was no appropriation to pay civilians for the work that was immediately necessary. Every bureau and naval establishment appealed for clerks and stenographers. How could they be secured at once? The Civil Service Commission could not furnish a tithe of the number required, even if there had been money to pay them.[2]

Furthermore, civil servants were not under full military control: They could not be deployed as swiftly and flexibly as uniformed persons, nor were they subject to military discipline. But what if the women were *not* civilians? What if the thousands of working women employed throughout the nation were invited to enlist in the Navy? This novel idea surfaced officially on March 7, 1917, when Rear Adm. L. C. Palmer, chief of the Bureau of Navigation (the office within the Navy Department in charge of personnel matters), wrote to Daniels asking if women could be enrolled.[3]

Exactly who originated the idea is not known. Lt. Comdr. Frederick Payne, a Navy recruiter in Philadelphia, later claimed he had recommended to the Navy Department that women be enlisted in order to spur male enlistments. His claim was never substantiated, nor was it ever refuted. In any event, Daniels seized upon the idea. He had long held advanced views on the rights and roles of women and supported their right to vote. (In 1920 his wife would be a delegate to an international convention of suffragettes.) Now, he saw, enlisting women in the Navy could help avert a manpower crisis.

Could he legally enlist women? The 1916 legislation said that "all persons who may be capable of performing special useful service for coastal defense" could be enrolled in the Naval Coast Defense Reserve Force. Daniels triumphantly announced to his advisors, "It does not say . . . anywhere that a yeoman must be a man." To Palmer he wrote, "Nothing can be found which would prohibit the enrollment of women.

On the contrary, it is believed their enrollment was contemplated." On March 19, 1917, the Bureau of Navigation notified the commandants of all naval districts to enroll women "in the ratings of Yeoman, Electrician (radio), or in such other ratings as the Commandant may consider essential to the District organization."[4]

Daniels had made no mention of women as potential members of the reserve forces in his cover letter forwarding the draft of the 1916 Naval Act to Senator Benjamin R. Tillman, chairman of the Senate Committee on Naval Affairs. Nor had the possibility of female enrollments arisen during hearings preceding the act's passage. Regardless of who may have contemplated what, the Navy now set upon a historic course.

The Call to Colors

The Navy's announcement that it would enroll women to serve as more than just nurses was broadcast over the radio, and copies of the Bureau of Navigation's letter to naval district commandants probably appeared on bulletin boards at some recruiting stations. No record has been found of what navy recruiters thought about this unprecedented step; evidently some failed to take it seriously. But the women who got the word—and many recall hearing very early—took it seriously enough.[5] On March 29, 1917, the *New York Times* reported on page 1:

> Many applications were received at the naval recruiting station yesterday from women who were anxious to see active service in some capacity, but because no official order had been received from Washington, none was accepted. Women who went to the offices said they had been told that Secretary Daniels had made the announcement that women might be enrolled as clerks or nurses. They were indignant when informed that no authority had been received here. Several of them left their names and addresses.

The Navy Department was already receiving many inquiries from women as well as men anxious to be enrolled in the Naval Reserve. Throughout the months of February, March, and April 1917, the Navy received letters from doctors, meteorologists, gunners, accountants, and others. Women were told to address their applications to the commandant of their local recruiting district. Members of Congress were also asking the Navy Department about this idea of enlisting women. Between March 3 and April 10, the department received letters on the subject from, among others, Representatives John J. Eagan, Halvor Steenerson, Franklin W. Mondell, and Fred L. Blackmon. To each the Department replied that the law permitted the enrollment of women, adding that "at present a few women are being enrolled for clerical work. Applicants should be referred to the nearest Naval District Headquarters." Meanwhile, the Navy's Bureau of Medicine and Surgery had drafted a circular relating to "physical examinations for women for enrollment in the Naval Coast Defense Reserve Force."[6]

The Navy's step to recruit women attracted little public attention. Here and there the metropolitan dailies—the *Baltimore Sun*, *Washington Post*, and *New York Times*—noted the secretary's announcement and the enrollment of individual women. But these news items seldom appeared on front pages and apparently elicited neither editorial comment nor letters from readers. Nor did Daniels accompany his decision with fanfare. Perhaps he saw no reason; he was, after all, only responding to necessity. Or perhaps he suspected a public outcry, in which case he had good reason to announce the enrollment of women as quietly as possible. There is no record of protests from Navy men, for they were busy putting the Navy on a war footing. If they grumbled, they did so privately.

But by women the announcement was received with perceptible excitement. In the final ten days of March 1917, one hundred women enlisted, even though war would not be declared until April 6. On May 28 the *New York Times* reported that a total of 725 women had enlisted.

Answering the Call

There were various motives for the women to enlist, among which patriotism appears to have been the chief. Public sentiment had been aroused by German submarine attacks on American shipping. The memory of the *Lusitania*'s sinking two years earlier still fueled outrage. The idea of taking up arms against the "Huns" was popular. For some women, patriotism was deeply personal: Their brothers, fathers, husbands, or sweethearts were already in uniform. One woman, for example, had recently lost her father, a merchant seaman: German submarines sank his ship, even before the nation was at war.

Many responded quickly, like Phyllis Kelley. In March 1917 she held an excellent job as secretary to the president of the Dodge Brothers Motor Company in Boston. Yet when she heard a radio announcement inviting women to enlist in the Naval Reserve at the Boston Navy Yard, she acted promptly: "On my lunch hour I drove to the Navy Yard, was interviewed, enrolled, and sworn in at once, and assigned for duty the following day." Another woman recalled postponing her trip to the recruiting office for forty-eight hours but wondered if it was right to delay even that long. In New York, more than a hundred women applying for enlistment besieged the Cable Censor's Office after it was learned that new regulations regarding cable messages going overseas would greatly increase that office's workload.[7]

Family solidarity was evidently a factor in some enlistments. Two and sometimes three sisters enlisted together. Even though recruits were supposed to be at least eighteen years old, exceptions were made if an applicant's parents approved. One woman enlisted at the age of fifteen and served with her mother, who also enlisted, at the New York Cable Censor's Office. Birth certificates were not checked too carefully, and at least one fourteen-year-old enlisted, Thelma Franklin of Florida. She revealed her true age years later while applying to the Civil Service.

Political considerations may have influenced some women's decisions to enlist. In 1917 women had not yet gained the right to vote in national elections, although some states permitted them to vote in state and local campaigns. Some well understood that women serving in Navy uniform would heighten the demand for women's suffrage. This understanding was implicit in a postcard that Daniels received on March 21, 1917:

> I am sure your proposal to recruit women in the U.S. Navy will meet with great success. The women in this country are eager to do everything they can to help the government—and they are also anxious to become citizens of the U.S.A. I hope you will help women to get the vote and women will show what they can do. "Women are people."[8]

The card, postmarked New York City, was signed "Anxious."

Finally, a few women saw in the Navy's offer a chance for steady employment at decent wages, in fact the same wages as men who held identical jobs. For Dollie Purvis, it was purely a matter of survival. Her Navy husband had gone to sea, and without his paycheck "I began to get hungry. I heard the Navy was taking women and I thought, well, at least I'd get fed regularly."[9]

Some parents objected to their daughters' desire to enlist. Patriotism and the prospect of steady employment at a good wage were all very well, but to many substantial and respectable parents, letting their daughters join the Navy was simply unthinkable because sailors did not enjoy the best of reputations.

Eventually more than 11,880 women would enlist. The greatest number in service at any one time, on December 1, 1918, was 11,275, roughly 2 percent of the Navy's active-duty strength at war's end.[10] One chronicler wrote that they

> came from all walks of life . . . daughters of rich parents, of Cabinet Officers, Senators, Representatives; mothers, wives, sisters and daughters of Army, Navy and Marine Officers; as well as many relatives of enlisted men of the service. Women of international repute came from all parts of the world and stood side by side with poor, shabbily dressed girls from tenement houses, each waiting her turn to file an application. . . . Many wanted to be sent to sea and to foreign shores.[11]

Daniels, of course, had every reason to be pleased with this large and ready response to his bold stroke. Of the women who enlisted he said, "When the Navy Department asked for recruits . . . it was only a question of which ones to choose, so many responded—clear-eyed, eager, wonderful women, ready for any task allotted them. . . . They worked unceasingly, untiringly."[12] The Navy's appeal was widespread; women came from all over the nation. New York contributed the largest number, 2,324. Washington, D.C., was next, with 1,874,[13] then Massachusetts with 1,324. Contributions from other states and U.S. possessions ranged from 1 (New Mexico) to 1,071 (Virginia). Even two British subjects enlisted.[14]

The number of women to enlist was the greatest number in service at any one time. The response was from around the U.S. and even this ?

The Women Arrive

Procedures varied as Navy recruiters tried to adapt their accustomed enlistment routines to accommodate women. Usually a woman was interviewed first. Stenographers and typists were tested for their skills. Those who passed muster were then given rather perfunctory physical examinations by medical officers assisted by Navy nurses. The healthy women were sworn in. They took the same oath as men:

> I, . . . do solemnly swear [or affirm] that I will bear true faith and allegiance to the United States of America, and that I will serve them honestly and faithfully against all their enemies whomsoever; and that I will obey the orders of the President of the United States, and the orders of the officers appointed over me, according to the Rules and Articles of the Government of the Navy.

The new reservist was then handed her identification card and instructed to wait for orders.

Some women were enrolled as yeoman first, second, or third class, while others were designated as landsman, a level below seaman.* Such inconsistencies appeared before procedures and qualifications became standardized. A few women with outstanding qualifications were enrolled in the highest rating, chief yeoman. Other ratings were master-at-arms third class and mess attendant third class. At least two experienced telegraphers, Abby Putnam Morrison and Marion Taylor, who had graduated from a course for wireless operators at Hunter College in New York City, were enrolled as electricians first class. But by far the overwhelming majority were enlisted as yeomen.

The Navy had never before needed to note in its records whether a member was male or female. Thus it was not long before Navy orders sending yeomen to serve in ships inadvertently included women. One woman ordered to a ship was Joy Bright, the spunky, redheaded daughter of a New Jersey businessman. The orders came while she was serving at the Philadelphia Navy Yard. Her commanding officer there

> had never approved of women being attached to the Navy in a military capacity so when I presented these orders to him, he was blunt. "Carry them out." Upon reporting [for shipboard duty] I was told in no uncertain terms that the Navy had no intention of ordering women to sea for duty in combat ships. . . . I returned to my [former] job.[15]

After several similar episodes, the Navy took the precaution of putting an F after the name of every woman on its rolls. Thus women became known as Yeomen (F). If spoken hurriedly or indistinctly, this sounded like "yeomanette." Since that name also seemed appropriate, it was used by many who knew neither the proper term nor its origin. Others objected strenuously to this usage. Rear Adm. Samuel McGowan, the Navy's paymaster general, was particularly outspoken: "They must not be called yeowomen or yeomanettes. These women are as much a part of the Navy as the men who have enlisted. They do the same work and receive the same pay as men of the same rating. They are yeomen."[16] Daniels later explained that he "never did like this 'ette' business . . . if a woman does a job she ought to have the name of the job, so we put in parentheses (F)."[17]

Most enlisted women lived at home and commuted to their duty stations. The Navy was hard put to find either funds or means to transport them to distant duty stations, nor did it have housing available in which to lodge them. However, because its greatest need was for women in its

---

Rates are levels of proficiency reached, such as second or first class; *ratings* are occupational specialties, such as yeoman and radioman.

main offices, the Navy did transport a sizable number of Yeomen (F) to Washington, D.C., where approximately two thousand served. This resulted in financial hardship for women who had to find housing and outfit themselves in uniforms.

> In groups of ten, sometimes less, the First Enlisted Women from Boston, Chicago, New York, Norfolk and Philadelphia were ordered to Washington, D.C., for further assignment. Many of these recruits had never been away from their families. Some were inconvenienced because they had only the clothes on their backs. An uninformed Recruiting Officer had told them they would receive a $100 clothing allowance as soon as they reached Washington. As a matter of fact, it took from a week to ten days for the Disbursing Office to open their pay accounts.[18]

The situation was better at Mare Island Navy Yard in San Francisco Bay, where a large group of enlisted women was assigned to the medical department. There the Navy was able to remodel a Marine barracks to accommodate fifty-five women, who lived two to a room and were transported to their work in a two-car train, the Powder Puff Special.

The Yeomen (F) Pull Their Oar

No matter how skilled and qualified as stenographers and typists, the Yeomen (F) still faced formidable challenges. They had to familiarize themselves with *The Bluejacket's Manual* and *Naval Regulations* and with the nomenclature of Navy ships. In the evenings, after their regular work was done, some received special instruction in naval terminology. They performed the same clerical tasks they had as civilians, but the subject matter was new; if that made the work more difficult at first, it also made it more satisfying, for it was related directly to the war effort. Also, wearing a Navy uniform added a dash of glamor that appealed to more adventurous women.

The many women who had business training and/or experience met the Navy's need for clerks who could go straight to work and be relied upon to handle competently whatever was put before them. The service could spare no time to train them. A woman was shown her desk and the work that was to be done, then the man who had been doing it was sent off to sea. Similar confidence was placed in the abilities of Yeomen (F) who held college degrees. In a time when very few women even attended college, any female who graduated could be counted upon to learn quickly anything she needed to learn. These women, had they been men, would have been eligible for commissions. ⌡

⌐Yeomen (F) performed many different kinds of duties. For instance, one verified bills presented to the Navy Department for costs incurred in ship repairs, while another worked as a draftsman. One worked in Norfolk with patrol boat crews of the Fifth Naval District, and at least two traveled through their home states as recruiters. In Hawaii thirty Navy women worked at the Naval Intelligence Office, at the navy yard, and at the Cable and Postal Censor's Office. In Seattle several women bacteriologists who enlisted as Yeomen (F) trained Navy nurses.[19]

Right from the beginning, Yeomen (F) established themselves as the "voice" of the Navy, replacing Marines and sailors as telephone switchboard operators.

> . . . [From] 1917 to 1920, Naval officers returning from sea duty received the shock of their lives when they picked up the telephones and heard a friendly female voice say, "Good morning." . . . The speed, alacrity and superior performance with which the calls were handled, established women as permanent operators of the switchboards in the Naval telephone system.[20]

One group of Yeomen (F) worked on munitions in Newport, Rhode Island. Secretary Daniels described them as "particularly efficient. . . . Prior to their employment, 175 men produced 5,000 primers a week; in July 1918, 340 women made 55,000 a week . . . six times the output of a man was the average for the women."[21] (Daniels did not say whether the men's production figure was taken from a wartime period, when all production would have risen. Still, a sixfold increase says a great deal about the women's ability and devotion, and Daniels must have relished it.) Other Yeomen (F) worked as translators, fingerprint experts, and camouflage designers. In addition to their regularly assigned duties, many were ordered after the close of regular business hours to theaters and other public places to promote the sale of war bonds. Five enlisted women in the Navy's Bureau of Medicine and Surgery are reputed to have served with hospital units in France.[22] ⌡

Wearing the Navy Blue

The Navy was quick to ensure that the Yeomen (F) would be suitably uniformed. On April 17, 1917, less than a month after Daniels's announcement, the Navy added a new chapter to its *Uniform Regulations.* The chief items were a single-breasted, belted coat or jacket with a patch pocket on each hip, and a skirt with a hemline four inches above the wearer's anklebone. The jackets and skirts were navy blue serge for winter and white duck for summer. Under the jacket was worn a plain, long-sleeved white shirtwaist; a regular Navy neckerchief was added when the shirt's collar was unbuttoned and folded back. An ankle-length blue serge cape could be worn over the winter uniform. Hats were straight-brimmed, made of navy blue felt or white straw. The uniform could be modified according to the work being done. A picture of Yeomen (F) assembling primers at a munitions factory in Bloomfield, New Jersey, shows them with the familiar "crackerjack" jumper worn by generations of sailors, with V-necks flowing into large square collars trimmed with three rows of white piping. In Hawaii, two Yeomen (F) on duty at the Cable and Postal Censor's Office were specifically instructed not to wear uniforms, because the work they were doing was so secret that their connection to the Navy could not be revealed.

The uniform turned out to be a success. It looked authentic Navy while reflecting current fashion. But officially describing uniforms and actually outfitting the women in them were two different things. In mid-June the Navy asked contractors to bid on the uniforms, specifying that they "must be out in one week after the contract is given out." Delays in meeting the contract, compounded by mismeasurements on the part of Navy tailors unaccustomed to fitting uniforms to female figures, meant that some Yeomen (F) waited as long as five months to receive their uniforms.

To circumvent the delay, some women supplied their own uniforms. Navy practice for men was to issue them their uniforms, then deduct the cost from their pay, which included a uniform gratuity. The same practice was invoked for the women (blue suits, $7.50; white suits, $6.75; winter capes, $25; hats, $4.50). When one Yeoman (F) found her pay docked for the uniform she had supplied herself, she protested all the way up the chain of command and won. On June 19, 1917, Secretary Daniels directed her commanding officer to remove the charge. Meanwhile, the comptroller of the treasury was deliberating whether the uniform gratuity could be paid in cash to women who had supplied their own uniforms. On October 6, 1917, he ruled that such a payment was not authorized. A Navy Supply Corps officer at the receiving ship in New Orleans objected to this ruling. He wrote to Daniels on August 22, 1918, that there were "over a hundred yeomen (female) at this station and each recruit is required to purchase a complete outfit of uniforms immediately after enrollment." On September 3 Daniels replied,

As the Department has now prescribed a regulation uniform for female yeomen and they are authorized to wear same the Department is of the opinion that the payment in cash of the authorized allowance for uniform gratuity to female yeomen who supply themselves with the prescribed uniform is legal, and those who are supplied uniforms by the Department are entitled to a credit for uniform gratuity on account of same.[23]

Discipline

Yeomen (F) were expected to meet the Navy's standards of discipline. The Bureau of Navigation advised senior officers against court-martialing women, commenting that those found unsatisfactory might be discharged; a better solution would be to find some work they could perform. Almost without exception the women met disciplinary standards, and apparently naval officers and petty officers had little or no trouble providing leadership to work forces that now included women. At least one Yeoman (F) was court-martialed, a proceeding of which Daniels took a dim view. He wrote to the offender's commanding officer, "The Department considers it inadvisable to try female yeomen by courtmartial, as in contravention to public policy. Accordingly, the proceedings and sentence in the above-named case are hereby disapproved." To his diary he confided, "She left when sick and [her commanding officer] did not like it. She was jerked up without time for advice. I overruled the action. Cannot deal with women as with men."[24] Daniels here touched upon issues with which the Navy would deal again and again as it struggled to absorb women into its ranks. First, how much advice and leadership did women need as they struggled to adapt to the Navy? Second, how was the Navy to steer a course that treated women in a manner acceptable to the public, yet consistent with its own standards of discipline that must, in the interest of morale, be applied equally to all hands?

A Measure of Value

The idea of commissioning some Yeomen (F) arose and was discussed quite seriously. Rear Admiral McGowan officially recommended Yeoman (F) Sue Dorsey for a reserve commission. Her responsibilities included maintaining the performance records for fifteen hundred pay officers, and she had the authority to assign them to various posts.

But neither Dorsey nor any other Yeoman (F) ever received a commission, for the war ended before the idea could be further explored.[25] That it even arose is a measure of how valuable women's service was to the Navy.

Mustering Out

Enlistments for naval reservists were four years. Thus when the Armistice ending the war was signed on November 11, 1918, Yeomen (F) were still obliged to remain on duty. They had plenty to do, for even though the shooting had stopped the Navy had to bring back from overseas and release thousands of sailors whose enlistments had expired, a huge chore requiring a large clerical force.

Also important was properly celebrating the men's return from war. The Yeomen (F) Battalion took part in the festivities. The battalion, formed in January 1918, consisted of four companies of enlisted women stationed in Washington, D.C. It was led by a male reserve officer. On specified weekdays after working hours, Yeomen (F) would meet on the Ellipse just south of the White House. There they would learn the intricacies of marching and close-order drill. Secretary Daniels took great pride in this, pronouncing them "proficient in drill and handsome in appearance." The battalion marched on New York City's Fifth Avenue in the Victory Loan March of 1919, and it was among the units in the line of march to welcome home the Forty-Second ("Rainbow") Division of the U.S. Army. The battalion also formed the guard of honor at Union Station in Washington when President Wilson returned from the Paris Peace Conference on February 22, 1919. Their final appearance as a unit was on July 30, 1919, when they passed in review for Daniels and Assistant Secretary Roosevelt.

Meanwhile, Yeomen (F) in Philadelphia were learning the rudiments of drill from Marines at the navy yard, chiefly so that they could participate in liberty bond parades on Broad Street. Joy Bright recalled,

> We learned hardly more than "forward march," "halt," and the necessity of maintaining straight lines, and keeping in step. No instructions were ever given to the effect that we were not to break step for any obstacles that might be in the way, but sometimes there was sharp provocation for changing direction. . . . For example, the time . . . we marched behind beautiful, high-spirited horses that had not been housebroken. After a particularly shabby parade performance, our

instructor gave us explicit instruction: "You don't kick it, you don't jump over it, you step in it."[26]

⌐As the Navy's wartime activities wound down, Congress saw no reason to keep paying reservists it no longer needed. The Naval Appropriations Act of 1919 said quite pointedly that "female members, except nurses, of the Naval Reserve Force and in the Marine Corps Reserve shall, as soon as practicable, and in no event more than 30 days after the approval of the Act, be placed on inactive duty." Release of Yeomen (F) continued throughout 1919 and 1920, indicating that the Navy's need for them extended considerably beyond thirty days. For example, Yeomen (F) helped prepare for the first transatlantic flight, which the Navy accomplished in the spring of 1919. Those released from active duty were continued on inactive status with retainer pay of twelve dollars a year until their enlistments expired. However, not all returned to civilian life. Fifty-seven Yeomen (F) died in service, most of them from the influenza epidemic of 1918.[27]

The War Ends and the Struggle Begins

Had it not been for Rear Adm. Charles McVay, chief of the Bureau of Ordnance, the Navy might have dismissed the Yeomen (F) out of hand. Believing that there would never again be a need to reenlist any of these women or enlist any women other than nurses, the Navy at first thought to give them "ordinary" or "good" discharges. Because such discharges were given to men who were not recommended for reenlistment, the women regarded this as a slur. So did McVay; he and others who had been impressed by (and grateful for) the women's contribution persuaded Navy officials to grant them honorable discharges instead. Without such discharges, they would have been ineligible for certain veterans' benefits. That they gained any benefits and any recognition owes more to their own struggle than to help from the Navy.

Following the war two circumstances combined to help Yeomen (F) in this struggle. The first was that many of them remained in government service, a milieu in which the relationship between lobbying and legislation is fully appreciated. The second was the formation of the American Legion, which former Yeomen (F) joined in great numbers. Continuing government service and association with a powerful veterans' organization created a nexus from which sprang leadership and action.

Helen O'Neill: Service in and out of Uniform

The Naval Appropriations Act of 1919 allowed the secretary of the Navy to give temporary civilian appointments in the Navy Department to reservists whose "conduct, services and efficiency have demonstrated the desirability of their retention." Yeomen (F) had proved so valuable as clerks and administrative assistants that many were offered temporary Civil Service appointments that, in numerous cases, became permanent. As late as 1957 it was estimated that as many as a hundred former Yeomen (F) were still working for the Navy as civilians.

One of them was Helen O'Neill. Tall, graceful, fair-skinned and red-haired, her dignified bearing lightened by a quick smile and exceptional fluency, she impressed all who met her. At home in Boston before the war (her family lived across the street from Joseph and Rose Kennedy), she had been an excellent student expected to enter Radcliffe College. But O'Neill, although a dutiful daughter, was inclined to follow her own path. "I thought the young men and women in the business offices were having a wonderful time, so I said I'd rather go to Burdett Business College."[28] She completed the two-year course in just under twelve months, then worked for some months in Boston. She also took the examination for the Civil Service, which at that time paid higher wages than the private sector. Soon she was offered a job in the Navy's Hydrographic Office in Washington:

> I was the first female in the chart section, but they didn't keep me busy enough. I got myself transferred to the Hydrographer's Office, but still wasn't busy enough, and moved to the Office of the Chief of Enlisted Personnel. Two male Chief Yeomen and I reviewed all his correspondence. When the Navy began enlisting women I applied right away and they enrolled me as a Chief Yeoman, since I was doing the same work as the two male chiefs. That office expanded greatly during the war, and I supervised men, but I never had any trouble with any of them.[29]

After being released from active duty O'Neill reverted to her Civil Service status and resumed her career in the Navy Department. This was interrupted by World War II, when she was called to put on a military uniform once more. She was one of a group of former Yeomen (F) whose leadership and initiative, sparked by the camaraderie of wartime service, created in 1926 a network of considerable historic import. Something of their staunchness is captured in a portrait that the Navy commissioned in 1925 for a display of naval uniforms at the Sesquicentennial Exhibition in Philadelphia. O'Neill and two other former Yeomen (F) posed in turn for the portrait, wearing tailor-made uniforms identical to those they had worn only a few years earlier. It is believed to be the only painting of Yeomen (F) in authentic uniform. For most of the 1970s the Navy had no idea where the portrait was; it had disappeared after some old Navy Department buildings were demolished in 1970. Thanks largely to the efforts of O'Neill, in 1981 a Navy seaman named Michelle Hughes was able to report its whereabouts at the Navy's Recruit Training Command in Orlando, Florida, where it still hangs.

The American Legion and Women Veterans

Like male veterans, former Yeomen (F) wished to maintain their wartime camaraderie, and many of them enthusiastically joined the American Legion. In Washington, D.C., where many like Helen O'Neill had served and then chosen to remain, about a thousand formed the first all–Yeoman (F) post and the second of all legion posts to be organized. Named the Betsy Ross Post, it was soon renamed USS *Jacob Jones* Post No. 2, in honor of the first U.S. Navy destroyer lost in the war. Other posts composed wholly or overwhelmingly of women veterans were established soon after the war in New York, Connecticut, Pennsylvania, Virginia, Massachusetts, and Illinois.

In smaller towns and cities where women veterans were less numerous, many joined with male veterans in forming legion posts. One former Yeoman (F), living twenty-five miles east of Cleveland, would later report ruefully to her former colleagues that the local legion post did not want women members. Inevitably, in the "mixed" posts women were in the minority. Many nonetheless attained high local, regional, and national legion offices.[30]

From the beginning, the importance of the legion to its women members was clearly demonstrated. In 1924 Representative John McKenzie of Chicago introduced a bill to provide adjusted compensation for war veterans that specifically excluded women other than nurses from its provisions. Already indignant that former Yeomen (F) had not been invited to testify at hearings for the bill, members of the Jacob Jones Post sought and gained help from the legion's legislative committee. With its support and guidance, Helen O'Neill, now commander of that post and accompanied by its legislative officer, visited Senator David Walsh of Massachusetts, a member of the Naval Affairs Committee. When they explained to him the extent of the services the Yeomen (F) had performed during the war, "it put quite a different complexion on the whole thing."[31]

O'Neill also spoke to McKenzie, who said his original intention had been to exclude all reservists from receiving benefits. However, he had been unsuccessful because a few male reservists had performed distinguished services; some had even served overseas. Still wanting to keep the cost of funding the bill's provisions as low as possible, he had then focused on the women reservists as one group he could exclude. During committee hearings, McKenzie had argued that women reservists had received "fair compensation" and that there was no reason to pay money to women who as Yeomen (F) had "made more money than they've ever made in their lives." However, when O'Neill advised him that the women would not take such discrimination lightly, the bill's wording was changed to include them. O'Neill recalled, "McKenzie's assistant later told me the congressman said he could see my red hair getting redder all the time."[32] If Congress had excluded them, it would have had to reckon with the legion, a consequence that congressmen had already learned was politically undesirable. President Calvin Coolidge signed the bill, the Adjusted Compensation Act, on May 19, 1924.

Meanwhile, former Yeomen (F) (not supported by any Navy officials) were testifying to the Senate Naval Affairs Committee that their service was being denigrated by the wording of the proposed Naval Reserve Act of 1925 (43 Statute 1080), which would limit membership in the Naval Reserve to "male citizens of the United States." Senator Tasker Oddie of Nevada was so impressed with their testimony that he proposed to strike the word *male.* But Senator James Wadsworth of New York noted that allowing women into the Naval Reserve might open the way to allowing them into the Army Reserve as well. None of his colleagues supported Oddie; perhaps they shared Wadsworth's implied assumption that women in the reserve would be an absurdity. Finding no support and unwilling to hold up passage of the bill, Oddie withdrew his proposal. Thus the word *male* remained and was carried over into the Naval Reserve Act of 1938, which would have serious consequences only a few years later when the Navy faced another alarming manpower shortage and found—as Josephus Daniels had not—that the law denied it the option of enlisting women.

The National Yeomen (F)

Former Yeomen (F) needed no further lessons in how easily their historic contributions might be overlooked. Determined to organize, they had a preliminary meeting in New York in 1925. At the legion's eighth annual convention in Philadelphia in August 1926, the members of Legion Post No. 50 (an all-woman post) hosted a meeting of former Yeomen (F). They formed the National Yeomen (F) (NYF), and elected Cecelia Geiger of Philadelphia as its first commander. When her two-year term expired, she was succeeded by Helen O'Neill. Among her other contributions to the NYF, O'Neill designed its crest, an anchor superimposed over two crossed quills, which resembles the Navy's rating badge for yeomen.

In 1936, more than six hundred NYF members, representing every state, as well as Puerto Rico, Hawaii, and Alaska, petitioned Congress to grant their organization a charter. Public Law 676-74 granted the charter on June 15 of the same year. Among other provisions, the charter directed the secretary of the Smithsonian Institution to permit the NYF to deposit its "collection, manuscripts, books, pamphlets and other materials for history." As a result, the division of naval history at the Smithsonian's Museum of American History has a complete file of *The Notebook*, a newsletter that the NYF issued quarterly from 1926 to 1985. Without this collection, much of the history of the Yeomen (F) would have been lost, for the Navy's own records of them are meager.

*The Notebook*s reveal that Yeomen (F) clearly understood the historical significance of their service, and they feared historical neglect. The September 1929 issue asked members to send in reminiscences of their service: "Say it in your own words, just let it be true. . . . Let's put this wonderful story of ours in black and white for future generations." From 1935 until its demise half a century later, the NYF repeatedly asked the federal government to issue a postage stamp commemorating its members' service. The request was never granted. A comment in *The Notebook* of September 1968 is typical:

> Again come the disheartening letters from the Post Office Department, saying "Our Citizens Stamp Advisory Committee gave very serious consideration to your request, but . . ." and now, after they have turned us down for our 50th anniversary, they advise that "since the anniversary year has passed apparently it will be necessary to wait for another significant date to further pursue the proposal. . . ." But the unkindest cut of all came when the Women Marines were honored with a Stamp to mark their 25th ANNIVERSARY!

In *The Notebook* of December 1985, NYF commander Anne Kendig announced the organization's demise: "The average age of our members is between 85 and 90 years, and traveling to places of our annual and other meetings has become difficult, if not impossible for some of us. Much as we dislike to admit to infirmities of age, we must face reality." The NYF's cash assets, plus generous contributions from some of its remaining two hundred members, were used to establish the Smithsonian Yeoman (F) Memorial Fund. Administered by the Smithsonian's curator for naval history, the fund is to be used to prepare exhibits and publications featuring the Yeomen (F) and to support historical research focused on them.

As of 1987, about a dozen former Yeomen (F) lived in the U.S. Naval Home in Gulfport, Mississippi. One of them wrote in *The Notebook* in 1980, as she was about to take up residence there, "Little did I think, when I enlisted in 1918, that the Navy would do so much for me in my 'old age.' . . . Yes, I am grateful to Secretary of the Navy Josephus Daniels, who made it possible for us to serve our country."

In a time of need, the U.S. Navy called on women to take the place of men it needed elsewhere. The women responded and did the job they were asked to do: They freed the men for duty at sea. They had little trouble meeting the Navy's requirements, despite a lack of formal Navy training, and the Navy had little trouble absorbing this influx of nearly twelve thousand women, for it was seen as a wartime emergency measure of short duration and little consequence. The women were not even allowed to enlist in the Navy's peacetime reserves.

The women viewed their contribution in a different light. Having been treated as equals during the war—at least in terms of pay and responsibility within a given rating—they were unwilling to be treated as inferiors after the war. They resented attempts to deny them honorable discharges and the benefits of the Adjusted Compensation Act. They were able to forestall those attempts, but lacking support from the Navy, they failed to prevent Congress from excluding women from the Naval Reserve. Exclusion was an ungrateful gesture that would later hamper the Navy when once again it needed to take in women.

The most significant point about the Yeomen (F) was simply that they served well. Thanks to the vision and daring of Josephus Daniels and to the efforts of the Yeomen (F) themselves, no longer could the idea of women other than nurses serving in the Navy be described as impossible or inconceivable. Never again could anyone say it could not be done, for it had been done.

PART TWO

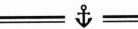

WAVES of World War II

2

Once Again,
a Time of Need

"I simply have not got enough Navy to go around."
— President Franklin Roosevelt

The first struggle women had with the Navy in World War II was simply to be allowed into it. Had it not been for the Naval Reserve Act of 1938, which precluded women from the Naval Reserve, the Navy might have been able to bring women into its ranks six months earlier than it did. As it was, in the days immediately following Pearl Harbor, the Navy was forced into a legislative battle in order to do what Josephus Daniels had done twenty-five years earlier with the stroke of a pen. This time it was the Army that led the way to put women in uniform; a bill to create the Women's Auxiliary Army Corps (WAAC) preceded a similar Navy bill by six months. Since the Navy's idea of the nature of its women's program differed from the Army's, it had the added burden of convincing Congress to allow it to pursue a different path.

Not that the Navy was at all eager to have women other than nurses in its ranks; one observer noted that it would rather have had monkeys than women.[1] But like it or not, the Navy could not fight the war without women, and so it struggled to launch its program in proper style.

Darkening Horizons

Throughout the 1930s Japan, Germany, and Italy greatly strengthened their armed forces and began using military might to expand their respective spheres of influence. Other world powers viewed these aggressions with alarm but refrained from military intervention until September 1939, when Germany invaded Poland. Great Britain and France declared war on Germany, but by June of 1940 German forces had overrun most of Europe and France had collapsed.

Within a week of the fall of Paris, Congress passed the so-called Two-Ocean Navy Act (Public Law 76-757) authorizing the construction of 257 additional ships, an increase of 70 percent. In an attempt to bolster beleaguered Great Britain two other important steps were taken. In September 1940 the United States traded fifty old U.S. Navy destroyers to Great Britain in return for ninety-nine-year leases on British naval and air bases in Bermuda and the Caribbean, and in March 1941 Congress approved the Lend-Lease Act (Public Law 77-11) allowing the United States to lend arms, munitions, and supplies to Great Britain.

To the U.S. Navy fell most of the burden of carrying out these mandates. Navy crews refurbished and reactivated the fifty old destroyers before turning them over to British crews. To protect the flow of crucial supplies to Great Britain against German submarines, U.S. Navy ships began to escort convoys of merchant ships as far as Iceland—and paid the price: On September 4, 1941, the USS *Greer* was attacked; on October 17 the USS *Kearny* was also attacked; and on October 31 the USS *Reuben James* went down with 115 of her crew of 160. Thus, three months before the Japanese attack on Pearl Harbor that precipitated America's formal entry into armed conflict, the U.S. Navy was in a shooting war. It was painfully shorthanded. In his annual report to Congress for fiscal year 1941, Secretary of the Navy Frank Knox emphasized the urgency of the Navy's need for manpower. Numbers of regular officers had been reassigned from auxiliary ships to combatants and from shore stations to duty at sea, with reserve or retired officers replacing them. In addition, enlistments had more than doubled in the previous fiscal year, from thirty-eight thousand to almost eighty thousand. But nowhere in the secretary's report to Congress was there any hint that the Navy might have to call upon women to meet its manpower crisis. Nearly a quarter of a century had passed since women other than nurses had worn Navy uniforms. The contributions of the Yeomen (F) were scarcely remembered, even though former Assistant Secretary Franklin D. Roosevelt was now president and had in his employ a secretary, Marguerite ("Missy") LeHand, who was a former Yeoman (F).

The Army Leads the Way

On September 1, 1939, President Roosevelt appointed Gen. George C. Marshall Army chief of staff. Within a month, Marshall directed his subordinates to prepare plans for a corps of women to serve in Army uniform. They submitted a report recommending that under no circumstances were women in any such corps to be given full military status. They might serve *with* the Army but certainly not *in* it. The War Department showed no interest in the report.[2]

But someone else was thinking about women in the armed services and had been for decades. Representative Edith Nourse Rogers of Massachusetts had served in Congress since 1925. In World War I she had joined the Women's Overseas League and gone abroad with that organization, then returned to work with the American Red Cross, caring for disabled veterans at Walter Reed Hospital. Presidents Harding and Coolidge had appointed her as their personal representative for disabled veterans. In this capacity she had visited every military hospital in the nation and seen some of the inequities experienced by women who had served overseas with the military in World War I. Because they lacked full military status, they were not entitled to the same benefits as male veterans. She was determined that if women were again to serve as part of the armed forces, they would do so under circumstances that would guarantee them the same protection as male service members.

In May 1941 Rogers advised Marshall that she was about to introduce legislation that would allow the Army to accept women under circumstances that she considered equitable. Marshall responded enthusiastically, but determined opposition within the War Department and in Congress delayed the passage of Public Law 554, which established the WAAC, until May 1942. As the word *auxiliary* suggests, the women would serve not in the Army, but with it. This compromise was the price exacted by the War Department and Congress in exchange for the legislation's passage. Later events would prove the auxiliary concept unsound, leading to the establishment of the Women's Army Corps (WAC) in July 1943.[3]

The Navy's Reluctant Acceptance

At this time in the Navy's Bureau of Aeronautics there was a group of forward-looking naval aviators. Naval aviation was still young and its potential yet to be realized. Its fast-developing technology had attracted the more daring and innovative officers. They were less prone than many to go by the book, for in naval aviation they were writing the book. They had been convinced for some time that the Navy would eventually need women. Led by Capt. Arthur Radford, the bureau's head of training, this group had thought hard about how women could most effectively be brought into the Navy. Former Yeoman (F) Joy Bright Hancock, who had been working as a civilian in the bureau since the mid-1920s, later recalled that their discussions centered on how to organize women into "groups for administrative purposes so they would be the least disrupting to the Navy when they were brought in. . . . They were coming in eventually, so let's get something down in the way of planning that would be workable immediately in the way of housing, and discipline, and utilization."[4] Comdr. Ralph Ofstie, a naval aviator returned from duty in London to serve in the bureau, had brought back information about women in the Royal Navy, popularly known as WRENS. Hancock was sent to see how Canada was going about organizing its female navy members.

More than once, the Bureau of Aeronautics had asked the Bureau of Naval Personnel,* headed at this time by Rear Adm. Chester Nimitz, to draft and present to Congress legislation that would permit women to serve in the Navy. Nimitz's position was well known: He had no intention of bringing in women.

However, public interest was building. From the moment WAAC legislation was introduced in October 1941, the Navy Department had received numerous inquiries as to when similar legislation for the Navy would be forthcoming. In response, the head of the Naval Reserve reluctantly explored the question. He concluded that the Civil Service would be able to supply any extra personnel that might be needed. Then, on December 9, 1941, Representative Rogers telephoned Nimitz to ask if the Navy was interested in having a bill similar to the WAAC legislation introduced in Congress. Nimitz replied cautiously, suggesting that she formally request the views of Secretary of the Navy Frank Knox. Her call drove home the point made by the inquiries received throughout the previous two months: The question of women had to be addressed.[5]

Three days later, Nimitz contacted all Navy Department bureaus asking them to assess their need for a Navy counterpart to the WAAC.

---

*In May 1942 the personnel functions of the Bureau of Navigation were taken over by the newly formed Bureau of Personnel. This reorganization took place near the end of events described in this chapter, but the newer name is used throughout.

According to the official naval history of World War II, with some notable exceptions, the bureau responses were negative, revealing widespread failure to appreciate either the imminence or the full extent of personnel shortages. The Office of the Judge Advocate General, the Bureau of Medicine and Surgery, and the Bureau of Yards and Docks all reported that they had no need for women. The Bureau of Supplies and Accounts replied that the establishment of a women's auxiliary did not appear to be "desirable," while the Bureau of Ordnance and the assistant secretary of the Navy indicated that the Civil Service would be able to furnish them any additional workers they might need.

The result of the Bureau of Naval Personnel's survey of its needs was marginally positive: Its officer division suggested that three women officers might be usefully employed, while its chief clerk foresaw that labor would be in short supply and that the Civil Service might not be able to meet the Navy's need for more workers. But this bureau considered any arrangement similar to the WAAC inadvisable, since such a corps of women would not be under the Navy's discipline or control.

The Office of the Chief of Naval Operations responded enthusiastically. Its vastly expanded wartime communications network could not be run by civilian workers. Because of the hours they worked (around the clock) and the secrecy of the messages they handled, communications personnel had to be under military discipline and control. Accordingly, the chief of naval operations (CNO) recommended that a women's reserve be built up without delay.

The Bureau of Aeronautics pounced on the opportunity to offer its views. Drawing upon its own extensive research, it prepared an impressive reply that outlined specifically the many kinds of skilled and technical work that women could perform in naval aviation. It went even further, suggesting policies that, as the official Navy history later reported, "anticipated most of the major aspects of the subsequent organization of the Women's Reserve."[6]

Outside Washington, responses to questions about the possible employment of women followed a similar pattern. Most offices and districts showed little interest, although the commandant of the Eleventh Naval District, headquartered in San Diego, reached conclusions similar to those of the CNO. He believed that both enlisted and commissioned women could be used in communications, specifically in coding. The commandant of the Twelfth Naval District, headquartered in San Francisco, was both positive and specific: 66 women officers and 362 enlisted women could be employed. The Naval Operating Base at Norfolk, Virginia, estimated it could use 233 enlisted women. Many of those queried were quite concerned about barracks for women, which may have influenced their judgment on the question of women's employment. In any event, by late spring more than 1,000 enlisted and 150 officer billets for women were identified throughout the Navy.[7] The days that followed Pearl Harbor found the Navy struggling to accept yet one more unwelcome reality: It needed women *in* uniform.

In or With

The law establishing the Women's Reserve of the Navy (WR) was passed and signed after seven months of disagreement among the Navy, the executive branch, and the Congress as to whether women should serve in the Navy or, like the WAAC, merely with it. Secretary of the Navy Frank Knox acted promptly on the recommendations of those Navy officials who strongly endorsed accepting women as Navy members. For flexibility of assignment, for discipline and control, as well as for the convenience of having all women reservists blanketed within existing legislation, the secretary proposed simply that an additional title be added to the Naval Reserve Act of 1938. He suggested the establishment of a women's auxiliary reserve as a branch of the Naval Reserve; appointments and enlistments in this auxiliary would be made only in time of war and were to expire no later than six months after the war's end. On February 2 Knox sent this proposal to the director of the Bureau of the Budget for approval. The director turned down the proposal seventeen days later, commenting that if the Navy proposed legislation more like that already cleared for the establishment of the WAAC—that is, for women to serve with the Navy rather than in it—he would offer no objection. But such legislation was unacceptable to Knox.[8]

How long the stalemate might have continued no one can say. The Bureau of Naval Personnel, with its long-standing resistance to women in the Navy, had no reason to be displeased with this state of affairs. For as long as the budget director would not accept Knox's proposal and Knox would not accept a naval version of the WAAC, the bureau need make no move. It could take the position that the matter was being resolved by higher authority.

The Bureau of Aeronautics, however, sought and found a fresh initiative. It turned, appropriately enough, to a woman for help. Dr. Margaret Chung of San Francisco, a physician and surgeon, had long been interested in aviation, particularly naval aviation. One of her hobbies was collecting relics of famous airplanes. She had many naval aviator friends

who referred to themselves as "the sons of Mom Chung." Having learned
of the stalemate, she asked Representative Melvin Maas of Minnesota,
who had served in the aviation branch of the U.S. Marine Corps in World
War I and was one of her "sons," to introduce legislation independently
of the Navy. On March 18 he did just that, while as a result of Maas's
prodding Senator Raymond E. Willis of Indiana introduced an identical
bill. Not surprisingly, these two bills repeated almost verbatim the language of the legislation proposed by Knox in February. It was reported
that when Rear Adm. Randall Jacobs, Nimitz's successor, heard about
this end run, he roared, "Who did this?"[9]

Although Representative Carl Vinson of Georgia, chairman of the
House Naval Affairs Committee, was "anything but enthusiastic about
putting women in uniform," the committee nevertheless reported favorably on the Maas bill on April 16. The House passed it the same day and
sent it to the Senate. The Willis bill, however, encountered resistance.
The Senate Naval Affairs Committee objected strenuously to it on the
grounds that it differed from the WAAC legislation. Most of the furor
emanated from the committee's chairman, Senator David Walsh of
Massachusetts. Nearly nineteen years earlier he had agreed to include
former Yeomen (F) among the veterans who would receive adjusted
compensation for wartime service, but now he opposed the idea of
women in the Navy. Others on the committee evidently shared his views,
for they declared that a woman's place was in the home (never mind that
many civil servants were women or that women were working in aircraft
factories and shipyards as welders and riveters), and that serving in the
armed forces would destroy their femininity and compromise their future
as mothers.[10]

The Navy Calls upon Distinguished Women

By the spring of 1942 it was clear that women would soon be entering the
Navy, although under exactly what conditions was still being debated.
The legislative logjam would continue until midsummer. Meanwhile
Navy officials wished insofar as possible to tailor the women's component
to their own requirements. If they must do this thing, then they wanted
to do it right—or at least, their way. But administration policy for women
was an uncharted sea—to whom could they turn for guidance on these
matters? Fortunately, they had a precedent. For some time they had been
seeking help from the academic community in finding men with suffi-

cient scientific and mathematical skills to operate the Navy's increasingly sophisticated machinery and to administer its increasingly technical programs. Perhaps the nation's women educators could help them now.

After consulting Dr. Virginia Gildersleeve, dean of Barnard College, the Navy called Dr. Elizabeth Reynard of the Barnard faculty to serve as special assistant to Rear Admiral Jacobs. Reynard was already noted for her studies on women's abilities and the types of work for which they might be particularly suited. Her performance as Jacobs's assistant confirmed the Navy's expectations about the caliber of help it could expect from women educators, and within weeks of her appointment she was able to form the Women's Advisory Council to meet with Navy officials. Chaired by Gildersleeve, the council included some of the nation's most distinguished women, many of whom had done graduate work at Columbia: Dr. Meta Glass of Sweet Briar College; Dr. Lillian Gilbreth, a national authority on efficiency in the workplace; Dr. Ada Comstock, president of Radcliffe College; Harriet Elliot, dean of women at the University of North Carolina; Dean Alice Lloyd of the University of Michigan; Mrs. Malbone Graham, a noted lecturer from the West Coast; and Mrs. Thomas Gates, wife of the president of the University of Pennsylvania. Elliot later resigned, and Dr. Alice Baldwin, dean of women at Duke University, took her place.[11] The Navy's initial move in consulting Dr. Gildersleeve turned out to be brilliant, for through her it was able to engage some of the most talented women in America.

One of the advisory council's earliest acts, and perhaps its most consequential, was to advise the Navy on the choice of the woman to head the WR. The candidate had to be of impeccable personal and professional reputation, a proven leader and administrator. Second, but nearly as important, she would have to command respect from Navy men and the women she would lead. Finally, she must be old enough to be considered mature, yet young enough to wear a Navy uniform with style and distinction. There was little time to ponder the choice, for the Navy wanted the matter settled before political pressures could be brought to bear on it. The council made its choice swiftly, recommending Mildred McAfee, president of Wellesley College, one of the most prestigious women's institutions in the country.[12]

Mildred McAfee: Leader of Women

Wellesley's seventh president came from a long line of clergymen and educators, descendants of people who had left Ireland to settle in Virginia and Kentucky in the mid-1700s. One of her grandfathers had founded Park College in Missouri, and her father, the Reverend Cleland Boyd McAfee, had held national offices in the Presbyterian Church. One of her two older sisters was married to the secretary of the American Bible Society, the other to the president of Hanover College in Indiana. High achievement was expected of Mildred McAfee, and by the time the Navy called her, at age forty-two, she had proved herself a worthy legatee.

At age twenty she was a Phi Beta Kappa graduate of Vassar, with a double major in economics and English. In addition, she had been a class president, a varsity debater, and a letter athlete. Over the next fourteen years she taught at secondary schools and at Tusculum College in Tennessee, earned a master's degree at the University of Chicago, became dean of women at Centre College in Kentucky, and served two years as the executive secretary of Vassar's alumnae association. In 1934 Oberlin College in Ohio, the first coeducational college in the United States, called her to become its dean of women, where she quickly made her mark with her characteristic blend of sagacity, verve, and humor. Two years later, when Wellesley's trustees invited her to become president, they specifically noted the last attribute. Her humor was irrepressible. In her farewell address to the Oberlin undergraduates McAfee said, "I am completely disillusioned about college presidents. A week ago, I believed that every college president could arise on any occasion and speak fully and fluently on any subject. But I find that I don't know any more than I knew last week and that I don't speak any better."[13]

Such gentle but pointed self-deprecation was a major asset for an administrator and educator who had, on any given day, to deal with faculty fiefdoms, with women undergraduates and their parents, and with alumnae. Her greatest asset was a wide-ranging vision that allowed her to welcome news and viewpoints from beyond campus walls. From this vision she drew confidence and courage. It took courage, for example, for a Vassar graduate and prospective Wellesley president to champion coeducation, which she did in the same speech at Oberlin.

The business of getting educated seems to me to be the lifetime problem and privilege of all mankind. We can never do much to make this an educated nation if the task is left wholly to occupants of academic halls. Every part of our perplexing social system needs men and women who are at home in a wide world. . . . I consider the person who can achieve a truly liberal education in a co-educational institution a more unusual but more fortunate person than one who achieves it in the relative artificiality of the segregated college.[14]

In her six years at Wellesley "Miss Mac" had won loyalty from students who admired her good looks and the style and grace of her bearing. Beyond campus walls she was known for her liberal views on the rights and responsibilities of women, especially educated women, and for the extraordinary energy she expended on numerous and diverse public, private, and professional agencies. For a small sampling, she was a trustee of the National Conference of Christians and Jews and of several schools, including Yencheng University in China, a member of the executive committee of the American Association of Colleges, and a member of the subcommittee on women in college and defense of the National Committee on Education and Defense. As a journalist for a Midwestern newspaper put it, "Her easy manner effectively conceals the fact that she is one of the busiest women in New England."[15] In sum, Mildred McAfee was just what the Women's Advisory Council was seeking: a successful college president who could make her way in the Navy.

When Gildersleeve brought the matter to her, McAfee was reluctant to leave her prestigious position, which she viewed as being at least as important to the nation as service in the Navy. But if Wellesley's board of trustees could be persuaded to release her, she might be willing to accept the Navy's offer. Accordingly, Gildersleeve traveled to Boston to put the matter before the Wellesley trustees. To her surprise, they talked

as if I were trying to sell them a third-rate railroad, the defects of which they pointed out freely. They emphasized the smallness of the proposed Reserve corps, the fact that the director would be only a lieutenant commander. . . . In the long run, however, Wellesley could not, of course, refuse such a request from the government in time of war.[16]

The Wellesley trustees also doubted whether Gildersleeve was in fact bearing an official request from the Navy. McAfee traveled to Washington and learned from Rear Admiral Jacobs that the Navy was indeed intent upon having her head its women's component. It was an offer she could not dismiss, because she held strong convictions about the obligations of educated women. She later told an interviewer, "If college women cannot take their place as contributing members of democratic society, particularly in days such as these, then there is something wrong with them or with the institutions which they attended."[17] She agreed to serve one year (actually, she served more than three), for which Wellesley's trustees gave her a leave of absence.

But none of the advisory council's good work, nor Wellesley's cooperation, nor the Navy's preparation would come to anything if the legislative logjam continued. In short, Senator Walsh had to be brought around, a task to which Elizabeth Reynard applied herself. By midsummer his views would change; but summer was not yet here.

On May 25 the Senate Naval Affairs Committee recommended to President Roosevelt that the legislation establishing a women's reserve for the Navy should parallel the WAAC legislation. The budget director concurred, and the president instructed Secretary Knox to reconsider the idea of service with rather than in the Navy. Knox remained firm.

This was another impasse, and once again women were instrumental in clearing it. Gildersleeve and Dean Elliot, at the time still a member of the council, each wrote immediately to the president's wife, Eleanor Roosevelt, explaining the Navy's views and using the same terms the Navy used—security and discipline—to argue that its women should not be in a separate corps like Army women. Eleanor Roosevelt showed Elliot's letter to her husband and passed Gildersleeve's letter on to Undersecretary of the Navy (and former naval aviator) James V. Forrestal. Five days later Forrestal replied, stating the Navy's position and noting that Secretary Knox had asked the president to reconsider. Perhaps it was that Mrs. Roosevelt (whose counsel the president highly respected) and his secretary of the Navy were speaking in concert, or perhaps it was those words that carry such added weight in wartime, *security* and *discipline*; but for whatever reason, the president changed his mind. On June 16 Secretary Knox informed Rear Admiral Jacobs that the president had given him carte blanche to proceed with organizing a women's reserve; Jacobs was urged to press for swift enactment of the appropriate legislation. Three days later Knox informed Senator Walsh of the president's decision, and on June 24 the Senate Naval Affairs Committee reported favorably on the bill. By July 21 it had been passed by both houses of Congress and sent to the president. He signed it into law on July 30, 1942.[18]

Provisions of the Women's Reserve Legislation

Public Law 689 established the Women's Reserve of the Navy. Consisting of sections 501 through 508, it was added as Title V to the Naval Reserve Act of 1938. The act constituted a Navy victory hammered out of the clash of personalities after months of conflict and maneuvering. It shaped the WR according to the Navy's wishes while also reflecting congressional pressures and concerns.

First, the law established the WR as a branch of the Naval Reserve to be "administered under the same provisions in all respects (except as may be necessary to adapt said provisions to the Women's Reserve, or as specifically provided herein) as those contained in this Act or which may hereafter be enacted. . . ." This was the sine qua non for which the Navy had fought. Navy women were clearly in the Naval Reserve, not just serving with it. Significantly, however, the parenthetical exception gave the Navy Department broad latitude to modify and interpret which provisions of the Naval Reserve Act would or would not apply to female reservists.

Next, women could be "commissioned or enlisted in such appropriate ranks and ratings, corresponding to those of the Regular Navy, as may be prescribed by the Secretary of the Navy. . . ." This was an important departure from the WAAC legislation. Giving women reservists the same ranks and ratings as the regular Navy emphasized their inclusion in the service and assured them equal pay for equal rank, something WAAC members did not have. This section also limited the number of positions open to women in given ranks. Thus no more than one woman could hold the rank of lieutenant commander, no more than thirty-five could be lieutenants, and no more than 35 percent of the rest of the women officers could be lieutenants (junior grade). Also, the military authority of women officers could be exercised only over other women reservists, and it was limited to administration.

The ranks established for women reflected the Navy's view that prestige must be offered in order to attract competent and experienced women. At that time, naval officers could usually achieve the rank of lieutenant commander only after seventeen to twenty years of commissioned service, much of it at sea. Many of the Navy's warships were under the command of lieutenant commanders. Thus, for the Navy to offer a woman with no naval training or experience this rank was to put great trust in her abilities. Even the limited number of lower ranks being offered was an expression of considerable trust. It was also, of course, an expression of the Navy's need for women officers.

Naval officers at that time had only limited professional experience with civilians in general, much less with business and professional women. The Navy had a very small shore establishment; its officers spent most of their time at sea. Consequently naval officers failed to see that what in their opinion was a generous offer would seem less so to many women in business and the professions. Limited numbers and ranks would prevent the enrollment of many well-qualified women who held civilian jobs with greater responsibilities and substantially higher salaries than those of Navy lieutenants, lieutenants (junior grade), and ensigns. Their junior status, moreover, would handicap women officers trying to advance their ideas within the naval hierarchy.

Women reservists had to be at least twenty years old, they would be restricted to "performance of shore duty ... within the continental United States," and they could not be assigned to Navy ships or combat aircraft. The House Naval Affairs Committee had insisted on these limitations, although Army women could enlist at eighteen and be sent almost anywhere in the world—differences that the committee never explained. In any event, that all its women were at least twenty was certainly one reason why the Navy experienced extremely few disciplinary problems with them.

Women reservists were not to be used to "replace civil-service personnel employed in the Naval Establishment." Rather, they were to be "trained and qualified ... to release male officers and enlisted men of the naval service for duty at sea." The swift pace of the Navy's expansion would soon make this provision more honored in the breach than in the observance. By 1943 women reservists would hold not only jobs previously held by Navy men but also hundreds of jobs never held by any Navy man, chiefly because warfare and weapons were now far more sophisticated, requiring new technical skills. Also, Navy women would eventually fill numerous jobs normally held by civil servants because there weren't enough of the latter to go around.

Women reservists would be entitled to National Service Life Insurance, the benefits of the Soldiers and Sailors Civil Relief Acts, and the same pay and allowances as male reservists. However, women killed or injured on active duty were not entitled to the same benefits granted to male reservists; rather, they would receive those prescribed by law for U.S. civil employees. Thus the women were excluded from a lump-sum death gratuity to beneficiaries, retirement pay, and compensation or hospital care from the Veterans Administration. In these distinctions Congress and the Navy implicitly treated women as female civil servants while placing them under full military control. Women would be in the Navy but not eligible for all of its benefits.

Finally, the law authorized the secretary of the Navy to appoint or enlist members of the WR "effective during the present war and six months thereafter" and to uniform and equip them.

Naming Women Reservists

The Navy's newest component was about to be launched. But first it had to be christened. Already the press had coined nicknames like goblettes and sailorettes. Elizabeth Reynard reported to Virginia Gildersleeve that when a New York paper used the latter in a headline, some Navy officials roared so loudly "you'd think they'd struck the Inchcape Rock." They ordered Reynard to come up immediately with something

> nautical, suitable, fool-proof and easy to pronounce. I realized that . . . two letters . . . had to be in it: *W* for women and *V* for volunteer, because the Navy wants to make it clear that this is a voluntary and not a drafted service. So I played with those two letters and the idea of the sea and finally came up with "Women Accepted for Volunteer Emergency Service"—W.A.V.E.S. I figure the word "Emergency" will comfort the older admirals, because it implies that we're only a temporary crisis and won't be around for keeps.[19]

Reynard had been with the Navy only a short time, but she had already discerned one of its deepest institutional anxieties.

Over a period of about nine months—from October 1941, when the WAAC legislation was introduced and the Navy suspected it too might soon have to accept women other than nurses, to the signing of Public Law 689—the Navy went through an extraordinary change of attitude regarding women in its ranks. It began by strenuously resisting the idea and ended up by offering to a small number of women the opportunity to become commissioned officers. It was a turnabout propelled solely by need and self-interest: As personnel shortages became ever more alarming, the Navy eventually saw that it would need women officers to lead and manage the thousands of women required to keep its shore establishment operating.

The Navy proceeded with characteristic caution. Before going ahead with legislative proposals it surveyed its needs and heeded recommendations that if women were to be accepted, they must be firmly included in its ranks or not at all. It sought distinguished help and invited an eminent woman to head its proposed corps. To these laudable efforts was added Congress's serendipitous decision to allow no woman younger than twenty to join the Navy. Time would prove this combination of caution, commitment, and good luck to be highly beneficial to the Navy.

3

—

The Navy's First Women Officers

*"*M*y first assignment was just getting enough women there to start doing something, and what they were to do was as vague to me as it was to all the rest of the Navy at that time."*

—MILDRED McAFEE HORTON

Having agreed to recruit and to accept a corps of women officers, the Navy had immediately to tackle a series of separate but linked challenges: where to find them, how and where to train them, and how to accomplish that training. As its needs grew, the Navy would be forced to employ women in fields for which it earlier had not even considered using them.

Almost without exception, the new women officers knew little or nothing about the Navy. To accept a commission was to leave a responsible position and leap into an unknown world. The greatest unknown was what they might be doing in that world. They had to discover for themselves how they fit into the Navy, for the Navy was not very clear on that point itself. The women officers sent out to recruit others of their kind had to persuade them to make the leap they themselves had just made.

Early Selections

The Navy was determined that if it was to have women in its ranks, they would be the best that could possibly be found. This was partly a matter of service pride, but even more a matter of practicality: Quality paid off in higher productivity and fewer problems, disciplinary or otherwise. Since women were needed, it was best to accommodate them in as handsome a manner as possible, for that would promote morale and enhance recruitment. ⟶ where they were selected

By June of 1942 the advisory council and Mildred McAfee were calling some of the nation's most accomplished women to become naval officers. They found many excellent candidates in women educators, for example, Deans Margaret Disert of Wilson College, Dorothy Stratton of Purdue, Elizabeth Crandall of Stanford, and Louise Wilde of Rockford College. Other professions also yielded successful candidates, among them Etta Belle Kitchen, a lawyer from Oregon, and Frances Rich, an engineering draftsman employed by Lockheed. Others were chosen from the business world. Mary Daily, an honors graduate of Northwestern University, was the personnel director for Continental Casualty Company's home office in Chicago, which had a staff of about 2,500. She frequently lectured at local colleges and universities on vocational counseling and job placement for women. Winifred Quick was another experienced personnel manager, employed by the Brunswick Drug Company in Los Angeles. The company thought highly enough of her to have paid for her postgraduate work at Radcliffe's management training program; she was one of the first five women chosen for this prestigious program. These women typified what the Navy was seeking. In every case, they had made their way up a steep ladder in a male world.

Selection procedures varied. Dean Gildersleeve called in candidates for interviews with her and two male naval officers in New York. In Chicago, Navy officials asked local universities and colleges to suggest names of likely candidates, whom they then invited for interviews at the Ninth Naval District Headquarters in Great Lakes.

Joy Bright Hancock was an exceptional case. She lacked a college degree but was nonetheless a well-educated woman. In 1920, after being mustered out of the Naval Reserve as a Yeoman (F), she married a naval aviator who was killed in a dirigible crash in 1921. In 1924 she married another naval aviator who in 1925 met the same fate. She then traveled extensively, studied art in Paris, and learned to fly, taking particular interest in maintenance and repair of aircraft engines. She also completed two years of study at the Crawford Foreign Service School in Washington, D.C. Since 1930 she had worked almost continuously in the Navy's Bureau of Aeronautics as an editor, writer, and researcher. Along with others, she had midwifed the birth of the WR. She brought to it invaluable knowledge of the Navy Department's workings, as well as innumerable friendships with naval aviators who often helped her clear bureaucratic and procedural hurdles.

As soon as the requisite legislation was signed by President Roosevelt, McAfee became the first woman ever commissioned in the Navy, as a lieutenant commander. About 150 other women were commissioned within the next sixty days. One group of sixteen came directly to work in the Bureau of Naval Personnel with Lieutenant Commander McAfee and Lieutenant Reynard, getting the program under way, while Lieutenant Hancock continued to work on plans for women in aviation. Another eleven were placed on duty immediately at various naval district headquarters around the country; their mission was to recruit officers and enlisted women. Finally, 120 were chosen to report in late August for the first training class for female officers; Lieutenant Crandall was ordered to report as regimental commander.

Experienced, well educated, and successful in their chosen fields, these women came because they were called, many of them directly by McAfee or a member of the advisory council. Few had any idea what they might be getting into, and the Navy could not tell them much, as its plans for them were still embryonic. Thus they had little assurance that signing on with the Navy would result in a greater contribution to the war effort than what they were already doing. Forty years later, speaking to a group of Navy women in Seattle, Mary Daily recalled how it had seemed to her in the summer of 1942:

> Many, myself included, would not have any chance for advancement, either in rank or income. I was told that if I was looking for glamour or position, this was not the place for me. . . . Many thousands of women volunteered from secure civilian status to unknown military experience—some taking substantial salary cuts; each one going into unknown assignments, unknown living conditions—there would be restrictions such as none had ever known. It was indeed an uncharted course of an unknown sea.[1]

It was primarily the prestige and distinction of McAfee and the council members that persuaded many of these women to accept the Navy's offer of a commission. Lacking these resources, the Navy would have had far more difficulty assembling in such a short time so able a group of women to become its first women officers, and much that followed would have turned out quite differently.

Early Difficulties

The first WAVE officers both in and outside of Washington faced many difficulties and challenges. Some arose from their unique circumstances of being, like WAAC officers, the first women in the United States to hold commissions in an armed service, while others arose from problems within the Navy itself. To a large extent, these women met the challenges with resourcefulness and good humor. In the heavy weather of their first six months as naval officers, they kept their small ship afloat and even made some headway.

Within Navy Department corridors in Washington, as well as in the dozen other American cities where they were serving, the first WAVE officers found themselves objects of curiosity. They also met with resentment, especially from men who were not anxious to be sent to sea. Many of the men with whom they worked did not know what to expect of them, while they (except for Hancock) knew little about how the Navy acted, worked, spoke, or thought. One of the women, Lt. Jean Palmer, later told an interviewer,

> Here was this stack of mail, and I began looking at it and I said, "Well, who's answering this?" ... Nobody knew. The letters had all been referred to the Women's Reserve because they were all questions about how do I get in and where do I go. I said, "I know the answers to these questions and I'm going to answer this mail." I had nothing else to do ... I had Navy stationery [and] ... I wasn't doing all this fancy Navy lingo, I just gave them the answers. ... About 50 people got told in one day what they wanted to know. I don't think that's happened before or since. ... I sent one [WAVE officer] down to Officer Personnel. ... She was very pretty, she was an Ensign, and she never came back. ... They just kept her down there. And that was fine, because we should have had a WAVE in Officer Personnel. ...[2]

They had to find their own way to meet male counterparts and discuss common problems. McAfee, for example, met the bureau's director of planning and control by accident at a dinner party two months after her arrival. She had believed that her role was to direct the WR, but the rest of the bureau behaved as if she were a figurehead; the major decisions were made in other offices, and she was to give "the women's point of view"—if and when asked.[3]

Navy officials overlooked the importance of remedying the women's ignorance of Navy ways. A male reserve officer assigned to assist McAfee and her small staff was helpful in many ways, but his own naval experience was hardly extensive. The assignment of a more experienced regular officer could have prevented many mistakes. For example, Lieutenant Palmer, working in Washington to establish a school for training enlisted WAVES, was asked whether the women would need "seabags." Because seabags were something like duffel bags, she deemed them unsuitable for packing women's clothes and said no. She did not know that the term included everything the Navy issued to its members, including blankets. Consequently, no blankets were sent to the school.

The important matter of women's uniforms was handled differently, partly because the Navy was willing to seek the best for its women. Mildred McAfee's good judgment and a bit of good luck helped too. Mrs. James Forrestal, wife of the undersecretary of the Navy, had prevailed upon a noted American designer, known as Mainbocher, to design a uniform for the WAVES. McAfee first learned of this nine days into her job when one of Rear Admiral Jacobs's aides told her that there was to be a showing of proposed uniforms at 5:00 P.M. that day. McAfee objected to a proposal for red, white, and blue stripes in place of the gold stripe worn by male officers. She was told that gold braid might be in short supply in wartime and therefore could not be considered for the women (no one said anything about possible shortages of gold braid for male reserve officers). Aware that the alleged shortage was only an excuse, but "not worth fighting about," McAfee agreed that pale blue stripes would be suitable. "All I cared about was that we *not* have red, white, and blue stripes."[4]

The Mainbocher design proved successful; in fact, dress uniforms worn by today's women naval officers closely resemble those worn by WAVE officers. The winter uniform was of navy-blue wool, worn with a white shirt and dark blue tie. The jacket was single-breasted and unbelted, with princess seaming. A six-gored skirt gave a smooth fit over the hips but was wide enough around the hemline to permit ease of movement. Black oxfords or plain black pumps with a medium heel, a brimmed hat, and black gloves completed the winter outfit. A novel and effective accessory was a hood, or havelock, that covered the hat and fitted closely around the face and neck; together with a navy-blue raincoat, it shielded the wearer from rain. (WAVES stationed in Washington, D.C., later called their newsletter the *Havelock—It Covers Everything.*) The summer dress uniform was identical but of lighter-weight, white material, and it was worn with white shoes. Some time elapsed before comfortable, practical, and reasonably attractive summer working uniforms were devised.

As with the Yeomen (F) uniforms, choice of a design was one thing, timely procurement another. Most of these early women officers served their first few weeks in civilian clothes. On at least one occasion, Filene's, a large department store in Boston, took on extra tailors and seamstresses so that women officers being trained in Northampton, Massachusetts, would be properly uniformed for a visit and inspection by Mrs. Franklin Roosevelt. Later on, Marshall Field's, the largest department store in

Chicago, went through a similar exercise to finish outfitting the large number of WAVES then serving in that city when they too were visited by the first lady.

Rear Admiral Jacobs did give McAfee direct access to his desk, signifying his intention to support the WR. But this blessing from on high, while important, could not transform overnight the way Navy officials were used to doing business, a way that did not include consulting with women even on decisions that affected them. Additionally, many high-ranking officers in the Navy Department viewed McAfee's direct access to Jacobs with suspicion and resentment. Before she was later included in overall planning conferences, she would take to him ideas that seemed sound to her, but these often conflicted with other areas of planning about which she knew nothing.[5]

Compounding the problem were the reorganization of the entire Navy Department in May 1942 and the fact that the Bureau of Naval Personnel was itself a new creation within the department. The resulting administrative turbulence made it difficult to incorporate women into the organization. An administrative order issued on September 16, 1942, improved matters somewhat in that it more clearly defined McAfee's position and mission, but lines of authority and channels of communication never became completely untangled, leading to jealousy and resentment. In this atmosphere, McAfee and her cohorts began addressing complex issues of policy and administration that had to be resolved as soon as possible.

Meanwhile, in naval district headquarters and without the benefit of any naval indoctrination, the first women officers set out to recruit WAVES. There was little to guide them other than their own good sense. Although McAfee and her assistants were hammering out policy as quickly as possible, occasionally in concert with other Navy Department planners, WAVES out in the field often had to make local policy on the spot. They too met with some resentment from Navy men, while from civilians they often encountered curiosity. In Seattle, Lt. Etta Belle Kitchen considered hanging around her neck a sign that read, "Yes, I'm a WAVE. Yes, I like it. I joined because. . . ." In some instances they received excellent support. In Philadelphia, for example, Lt. Margaret Disert spent her days and evenings going from one meeting to another finding women the Navy needed while male staff members at headquarters did the necessary paperwork. In Chicago, when she began her work at district headquarters, Lieutenant Daily found a backlog of mail, mostly inquiries from Midwestern women seeking to join the Navy; as she tackled it her male shipmates proved helpful and cooperative.[6] Of course, male naval officers out in the field had a different perspective from their fellow officers in Washington: Those at headquarters might promulgate, but those in the field had to get the job done. To many busy field commanders, the female officers sent to help them meet their recruiting quotas for women were like rescuing angels.

Compounding the difficulties of women officers both in the field and in the bureau was the inadequacy of the Navy's mobilization plans, which failed to take account of the sheer numbers of people that would be needed. In January 1941 the Navy was assuming that ten thousand naval reservists would meet its needs. Within months it quadrupled that estimate—and not for the last time.

Moreover, the Navy had not analyzed or even enumerated the many different kinds of skills needed to carry out its wartime commitments, although since World War I there had been marked progress in techniques of classifying and training personnel. A primary flaw in the mobilization plan for the Naval Reserve was its rigidity; each job to be filled was specified in detail, and a man applying for a reserve commission would be accepted only if he fit that job. Second, naval districts were charged to recruit reservists, but received little guidance. Finally, as late as July 1942 the office within the bureau that reviewed applications of those seeking reserve commissions was staffed by only one officer and three assistants. In short, the Navy had neither the plans nor the resources to do the job. Into this deeply flawed situation entered the women officers charged to build up the WR.

Establishing Women Officer Training

Commissioning a handful of women directly from civilian life and setting them to work immediately in the Navy Department and at naval district headquarters was a necessary step in launching the WR. However, the Navy deemed it crucial that subsequent women officers be given enough knowledge of service traditions and procedures to acquire naval habits of thought and behavior. In short, for the war's duration they were to be transformed into naval officers, replacing male officers in shore billets and allowing themselves and enlisted WAVES to be absorbed into the Navy with the least possible disruption. This is exactly what the pioneers in the Bureau of Aeronautics had been working toward. From its experience in training male reservists to serve in wartime alongside regular Navy men, the Navy now drew confidence that it could do the same for women. The first question to be decided was where training would take place.

College campuses had already been used for several years as training sites for male reserve officers. Why couldn't a women's college be used in similar fashion for female reserve officers? Not only would it offer facilities such as dormitories, classrooms, and playing fields, it would also give Navy training an aura of prestige, selectivity, and professionalism. Drawing on their intimate knowledge of women's campuses, the Women's Advisory Council looked for a college not only sufficiently large, attractive, and accessible, but also willing to commit its facilities for as long as the Navy might need them.

Vassar College was a likely choice in many ways, but its president was unwilling to make it available to the Navy for longer than four months.[7] The situation was different with Smith College in Northampton, Massachusetts. Elizabeth Reynard telephoned President Herbert A. Davis on June 7, 1942, to ask if Smith's facilities could be made available, and only five weeks later, on July 15, a contract was signed for the duration of the war. Soon thereafter Mount Holyoke College, eight miles southeast of Northampton, agreed to handle any overflow from the Smith campus. Smith turned over three entire dormitories, one whole classroom building, and part of a second, and agreed to share athletic facilities. The Northampton Hotel, just a short distance from the campus and capable of serving five hundred people at one sitting, agreed to devote its ample cooking and dining facilities to the exclusive use of the WAVES.[8]

The town, the college, and the Navy all incurred costs. Northampton residents and their guests gave up the use of the Northampton Hotel for the duration, Smith students returning in September had to double up in their dormitories, and many of their on-campus activities had to be staggered to accommodate the WAVES' schedule. The alumnae association surrendered part of its campus building. Because Smith's infirmary was deemed too small to handle the extra numbers of women that would be on campus, the Navy agreed to build a temporary wooden annex until a permanent additional wing—paid for by the Navy—would be ready for use. The service also furnished double-decker bunks, not only for its own women but also for displaced students.

But all parties benefited. For Northampton and Smith, the advantages were largely intangible, being chiefly pride in having made a significant contribution to the war effort, additional exposure and prestige in having been chosen by the Navy, and—perhaps most important—the fact of being fondly remembered by more than ten thousand women officers who were eventually trained there. As for the Navy, its spanking new WR could now boast one of the nation's most esteemed women's colleges as a training site, as well as an esteemed woman educator for its director. From the outset, these two facts gave to the WAVES an image of quality that became their hallmark and helped to promote recruiting, discipline, and morale.

Having launched the WAVES with such distinction, the Navy continued to emphasize quality by calling from retirement Capt. Herbert W. Underwood to assume command of the Northampton unit. Underwood had graduated from the Naval Academy in 1910, was a veteran of numerous naval battles, and had been awarded the Navy Cross, the second highest naval award for heroism. He had also been an instructor at the Naval Academy and at Naval Reserve Officer Training Corps (NROTC) units at the Universities of California and Texas. By all accounts he was an excellent choice: He believed in education and discipline; he understood the value of naval history and tradition; he appreciated the caliber of women placed under his command; he took his assignment seriously; and he was blessed with common sense. Not the least of his qualifications, as far as the town of Northampton was concerned, was that his wife was a close friend of town resident Grace Coolidge, widow of President Calvin Coolidge. Mrs. Coolidge loaned her home to the Underwoods for the duration of the war. She wanted them to live there rent-free, but Captain Underwood insisted on paying her the allowance the Navy gave him for housing.[9]

Underwood assumed command on August 13, 1942, just two weeks before the first class of women officers was to arrive. He admitted that he viewed their arrival "with far more nervousness than even a whacking good sea fight could inspire."[10] In October, Lt. Comdr. William Bullis became the unit's executive officer (second in command). Also a Naval Academy graduate, he had founded the well-regarded Bullis School in Washington, D.C., in 1930. Lt. Elizabeth Crandall was serving as regimental commander, and Lt. Eleanor Rigby (a Smith graduate, class of 1918) assumed duties as her assistant. The school's staff, including those serving at Mount Holyoke, eventually consisted of 112 officers (75 of them WAVES) and 37 enlisted personnel.

If the Navy had had its way, former Yeoman (F) Helen O'Neill would have been among them. For more than twenty years she had served in the Navy Department as private secretary to high-ranking officials, including three assistant secretaries of the Navy. When Secretary Frank Knox returned from inspecting the damage sustained by the Navy at Pearl Harbor on December 7, 1941, he entrusted his notes to O'Neill. She was still at work on these notes, which became the basis of Knox's secret report to the president, when she was identified as the person best qualified to instruct women officers in Navy Department correspondence and procedures. Because it was clear to her which assignment had higher priority, she declined the invitation to join the Navy staff at Northampton.

Strapped though it was for good men everywhere, the Navy Department nevertheless tried to send qualified male reserve officers to serve on the staff of the school, soon officially designated as the U.S. Naval Reserve Midshipmen's School (WR), Northampton. These men would be replaced by qualified women officers as soon as they were trained (except for Underwood—the law forbade women to serve as commanding officers); thus the men's tenure would be brief. Nevertheless, much depended on early impressions. If the caliber of Navy men assigned to the school was beneath that of the women being trained there, disillusionment and discontent might ensue. Officials combed Navy records and found two reserve officers just called to active duty and now in training at Cornell University, Lt. Edwin Smetheram and Ens. Timothy Neidhart. Both were married and mature, and both had taught at universities. They could be relied upon to behave decorously on an all-female campus, and they could hold their own with both the Smith faculty and the well-educated women they would be training. Smetheram knew he'd been accepted by the faculty when a history professor asked him to explain some eighteenth-century naval terms.[11]

At least one choice was unwise. A male lieutenant on the staff, a Naval Academy graduate, took out a WAVE student one evening and kept her out long after her curfew hour. He assured her he would be able to handle any disciplinary action that might be taken against her. Instead, when the matter was brought before Captain Underwood, the lieutenant found himself ordered off the staff within twenty-four hours.[12]

USS Northampton Gets Under Way

On August 28, 120 women officers, commissioned directly as ensigns or lieutenants (junior grade) depending on their age and experience, reported to the new school, soon dubbed "USS Northampton." Among them were specialists in engineering, radio, meteorology, and other technical fields as well as teachers, lawyers, and administrators.

The pace was fast, for these women were scheduled to become instructors and administrators themselves early in October. Within a month these women, most in their thirties and forties and many used to giving orders, had to become accustomed to taking orders, marching in squads, absorbing a large amount of unfamiliar material, and undergoing rigorous physical conditioning. Even more disconcerting were conditions in their sleeping quarters, furnished only with bunk beds and sheets. The women experienced considerable discomfort until the staff rounded up pillows and blankets from a local nursing home. Dr. Dorothy Stratton, erstwhile dean of women at Purdue University, confided to one of her colleagues that she thought she had made "the worst mistake of my life." Lieutenant Smetheram later recalled that he had never seen anyone "work as hard as those women did. They really pushed themselves, and they were determined to succeed."[13]

The curriculum was modeled on that of comparable units that indoctrinated male reservists. In addition to drill and physical education, the WAVES were instructed in naval organization, history, protocol, personnel administration, ships and aircraft, correspondence, communications, and law. The requisite training manuals failed to arrive on time, so Smetheram and his fellow instructors taught their earliest classes from their own knowledge and experience.

Learning how to drill was a particular challenge for mature women unaccustomed to rigorous physical activity. However, once conditioned, they took to it with verve, like the Yeomen (F) before them. Three times each day the approving citizens of Northampton watched them march down the street from the campus to the hotel for meals and back again. Lieutenants Crandall and Rigby, having themselves only two more weeks' practice in drill than their trainees, soon learned that efficient movement of troops requires giving the proper commands at the proper time, a skill no one acquires immediately. The first time that Crandall led her troops back to their classes after lunch, she discovered too late that she had headed them directly toward a parked car. In that instant, unable to recall a command that would remedy the situation, she called out, "Ladies, use your judgment!" Which is just what they did, swerving around the car.[14]

The Navy had bet that these were indeed ladies able to use their judgment. In their resourcefulness and their willingness, they validated the Navy's judgment and provided an example for all who would follow. On September 30, 1942, they completed their training; twenty-four were kept on at Northampton as instructors and staff members.

On October 6 the second class reported, consisting of 900 women. Of these, 124 arrived at Northampton, were commissioned after one month of training, and were sent out to join their predecessors. The Navy designated the remaining 776 as apprentice seamen. After completing one month of training, they were appointed as midshipmen and moved on to a month of advanced indoctrination. They were commissioned as ensigns and lieutenants (junior grade) only after successfully completing the entire eight-week course on December 16, 1942. All subsequent classes took the full two months of training. The training unit at Mount Holyoke opened in November 1942. From then until August 1943, both basic training and specialized communications training for selected women officers took place at both sites. Subsequently, the Mount Holyoke unit was dedicated solely to specialized training.[15]

By May 1943 the Northampton training program had taken on the shape it would maintain until it closed in January 1945, a shape much like the one the Navy employed to train regular and reserve male officers. No longer was a male reservist needed to serve as an executive officer; that billet was eliminated from the staff's structure and its duties were taken over by Lieutenant Crandall, who was redesignated as officer-in-charge of midshipmen. She was responsible for the entire regiment of trainees and reported directly to Captain Underwood. Directly under Crandall were the regimental commander, responsible for military performance, drills, and discipline, and the regimental adjutant, responsible for administration. Similarly, each of the regiment's battalions had a commander and adjutant. A parallel structure of student officers from the battalion and company levels downward gave each student hands-on experience in accepting specific responsibilities within a naval unit. Students learned to stand watches and be prepared for daily inspections of quarters, uniforms, and grooming.

Weekday schedules were rigorous. Reveille was at 6:30 A.M. and by 7:00 A.M. ranks were mustered for the march to breakfast. From 8:00 A.M. to noon, half the regiment had classes or study while the other half had athletics or drill. Following the march to lunch and return, the two halves traded places. Beginning at 5:00 P.M. students had their only free time of the day—forty-five minutes. Then they formed again for the march to dinner. From then until taps at 10:00 P.M., they studied or received special instruction. Captain's inspection took place each Saturday morning at 10:00 A.M., and at 1:15 P.M. all students except those assigned to watch duty were free until 7:30 Sunday evening.

On July 30, 1943, after the Northampton unit had been operating for nearly one year, Captain Underwood surveyed fourteen naval activities at which women officers trained under his command were serving, asking them to evaluate the women's performance. The responses offered some specific recommendations for the Northampton curriculum: more familiarization with official correspondence forms and terminology, more practical indoctrination in duties to be performed, more skill in touch-typing. Some responses spoke more to the criteria by which women had been selected than to their training at Northampton, noting that academic attainment had been overemphasized at the expense of demonstrated administrative ability. But in general the responses spoke highly of the women officers' performance, citing their adaptability, rapid assumption of responsibility, and ability to replace male officers. The Bureau of Ships responded thus: "The most cogent proof of their efficiencies, however, is the continuous demand for more WAVES, not only from individuals who already had some assigned to them, but also from divisions which previously did not consider them as potential replacements for male officers." The Navy was experiencing an internal struggle regarding the acceptance of women naval officers; clearly, the women's performance would be a major factor in determining how that struggle was decided.

Women Officers for the Coast Guard and Marine Corps

The law that established the Women's Reserve of the U.S. Coast Guard was passed on November 23, 1942. Several weeks earlier Rear Admiral Jacobs had asked Lieutenant Commander McAfee to suggest a woman to serve as that reserve's director. McAfee chose Lt. Dorothy Stratton, now helping to set up a school at the University of Wisconsin to train enlisted women as radio operators. When the enabling legislation was signed into law, she was brought to Washington and sworn in as the director of the SPARS, an acronym she created from the Coast Guard motto Semper Paratus ("always ready"). With McAfee's permission she went to Northampton to ask for volunteers from the December class. Twelve women midshipmen agreed to accept commissions as SPARS rather than WAVES. SPAR officer indoctrination continued at Northampton until June 1943, when the program was transferred to the Coast Guard Academy in New London, Connecticut.[16]

Similarly, when the Women's Reserve of the U.S. Marine Corps was established in February 1943, its director, Maj. Ruth Streeter, recruited nineteen of its nucleus of officers from Northampton midshipmen. At this point, her highly sensitive work for Secretary Knox concluded, Helen O'Neill once more donned uniform. She was commissioned directly from civilian life as a captain in the Marine Corps Reserve and appointed as Major Streeter's assistant, her encyclopedic knowledge of the Navy

Department proving invaluable. O'Neill's account of why she joined the
Marines instead of returning to the Navy credits one of her former bosses
with the decision. In 1935 she was working for a retired Marine colonel,
Acting Secretary of the Navy Henry Roosevelt. Admiral Claude Bloch,
the Navy's judge advocate general, asked Roosevelt to review proposed
legislation for a new Naval Reserve Act.

> After looking it over, the Secy [sic] said, "Claude, you don't have any
> women in this Act." Adm. Bloch replied, "No, Mr. Secy, we won't have
> any women in the Navy or Marine Corps in the next war." "You will
> so," said Col. Roosevelt, "and here's one sitting right here." (Me.) Later
> when the war came and the WAVES started up, I was asked to join
> them, but I felt I'd already been spoken for.[17]

In 1943 O'Neill was ordered to the headquarters of the Fleet Marine
Force in the Pacific. Released from active duty in 1946, she took an
opportunity not available to Yeomen (F) after World War I, that of
remaining in the reserves, and rose to the rank of lieutenant colonel
before retiring. Meanwhile, she resumed her career as a civil servant in
the Navy Department. At her retirement in 1959, she was the administrative officer for the Office of Naval Research.

Specialized Training

In December 1940 the Navy had on hand only twelve officers proficient
in written and spoken Japanese. To improve this situation, it established
an extremely demanding fourteen-month course in Japanese that soon
proved highly effective. However, finding enough qualified male applicants was difficult; approximately 95 percent of those applying failed to
meet the high standards, which included either previous training in
Japanese or membership in Phi Beta Kappa. Yet in October 1942, when
asked if women currently studying Japanese at the University of California in Berkeley might be needed in the WR, the chief of naval personnel
replied, "Not at present" (this despite the fact that the Navy had been
seeking women proficient in Russian, German, and Italian since February). Five months later, however, he viewed the situation differently.
Acknowledging the scarcity of male candidates, in April 1943 he recommended that the Navy's Japanese language course be opened to women
who could meet the same high qualifications as men. In June and July
1943, 600 women were interviewed and 88 selected. These women were

not required to meet the same physical standards as other women officers or to go through training at Northampton. Instead, they were sent directly to take the course, were commissioned after successfully completing its first three months, and reported for duty immediately afterward. Most of them served in communications units in Washington, D.C. They made some important discoveries, among them a description of an enemy aircraft previously unknown to U.S. intelligence agencies.

That episode typified the evolution of specialized training for women Navy officers. First the Navy encountered a shortage it had not foreseen; next it denied that women would be needed to fill it; then it accepted women when enough men could not be found; and finally it was gratified by the women's performance.

Navy planners had assumed from the start that their greatest need regarding women officers with specialized training would be to have them serve as communications watch officers. Some of this training was given at Northampton along with basic training, as a subcurriculum for designated students. As the demand for communications watch officers grew, the Mount Holyoke unit, from August 1943 to March 1944, was dedicated solely to filling it. By December of 1944 approximately 1,750 women had received communications training, 1,043 of them either at Northampton or Mount Holyoke.[18]

The Bureau of Aeronautics was prompt in seeking specialized training for women officers. On November 11, 1942, it requested that twenty-three women then in training at Northampton be selected for a nine-month meteorology course given at the Massachusetts Institute of Technology in Cambridge, Massachusetts, and on December 3 requested that an additional twenty-five be selected for a similar course given at the University of California in Los Angeles. In September 1943 another fifty began a nine-month course in aerological engineering at the University of Chicago. Eventually 113 women officers received such training and went on to take complete charge of aerological operations at various naval facilities.

As the Navy greatly expanded its training of aviators, a critical shortage of air navigation instructors developed. To meet this shortage, 121 women officers were trained at the Naval Aviation Training School in Hollywood, Florida. The curriculum included fifty flight hours; to comply with legislative restrictions on women's flying, officials had to state that the flights would be made in noncombatant aircraft.

Another substantial number of women officers, 121, were trained at the Naval Air Technical Training Command School in Corpus Christi, Texas, to become administrators of the rapidly expanding radio-radar program. The Naval Air Transport Service (NATS) in time came to have fifty-two women serving as air transport officers, completely responsible for planning and supervising fueling, loading of cargo, mail, passengers, and baggage, plus all the administrative details connected with each NATS flight. Other women officers received specialized training in air combat information, air combat communication procedures, photographic interpretation, aircraft recognition, and aviation gunnery instruction. Altogether, two thousand women officers were assigned to naval aviation activities; of these, six hundred were specially trained in aviation subjects.[19]

The Navy's Supply Corps, which provided everything from paychecks to parachutes to procurement policies, came to realize that women officers could well replace many of its male officers in shore billets. Beginning in January 1943, selected women who had completed their Northampton training were sent to Radcliffe College to join male officers being trained at Harvard University. By December 1944, 772 women officers were serving at Navy commissaries, supply depots, disbursing offices, and transportation centers. They managed inventories, shipping, salvage conservation, materiel catalogs, the assignment of stock numbers, and procurement and purchase contracts.[20]

Other Navy components followed suit, eagerly seeking the services of women officers and arranging for or endorsing the requisite special training. The Bureau of Ordnance, for example, which had stated in the fall of 1941 that it would not need the services of Navy women, saw things differently by early 1943. On September 25, 1943, ordnance schools already established for male officers were opened to women.[21]

By December 1944 over three thousand women officers had received specialized training in one of the areas already mentioned and in areas such as astronomy, radar operations and maintenance, ship design, navigation, aerology, and intelligence. In training so large a number in so many different technical fields in so short a time, the Navy gave an impressive performance.

The Navy took considerable pains—all the more notable in view of its many other wartime burdens—to find the right women to become officers in the WR, to find the right men to train them, and to find the right places to train them. The combination of prestigious college campuses, an admired woman leader, and a handsome uniform helped attract women of high caliber. Into their hands the Navy delegated much of the responsibility for building up and administering the WR. It trusted them to use their judgment wisely, and they did.

The women chosen to become officers left the comforts of responsible positions to become immersed, around-the-clock and for the war's duration, in an all-male institution about which they knew nothing except that it needed them. Yet most had enough confidence—arising from a combination of excellent education, superior ability, and for some, years of experience in competitive fields—to perform so successfully in that institution that they exceeded even the Navy's high expectations for them. Their spheres of activity were quite limited: They could serve only ashore, they could exercise authority only over other women, and at first nearly all worked in some administrative capacity. Their performance began to change the Navy's thinking (and even some of its attitudes) about what kinds of jobs were or were not suitable for women. The result was that hundreds of female officers ended up capably handling jobs that neither they nor the Navy had initially envisioned for them.

4

Recruitment and Training of Enlisted WAVES

"L ike every other part of the Women's Reserve, the training program just grew, like Topsy."
—*U.S. Naval Administration in World War II: The Women's Reserve*

Between 1941 and 1945 the Navy's enlisted force grew from almost a quarter million to nearly three million, an expansion for which the Navy was woefully unprepared. By 1942 it was stripping its shore establishment of the most experienced petty officers and sending them to sea along with any other able-bodied men it could find. To replace them the Navy had to recruit and then train a corps of enlisted women. It was not sure where to find or how to train them, but as the cadre of female officers grew the Navy increasingly turned over to them nearly every aspect of enlisted women's recruitment, training, and administration. The major challenge in dealing with enlisted women was recognizing how many would be needed and how many different kinds of jobs they could do.

For young women enlisting in the Navy the challenge was one of commitment: The Navy was asking for their services for the duration of the war, to live under military discipline according to policies that had yet to be developed and to be sent wherever it wished them to go. It was the same commitment required of men who joined the Navy. But unlike the men, the women did not have the draft at their backs. The first enlisted WAVES were volunteering for the unknown.

Recruitment

The Navy based its initial plans to recruit enlisted women on the assumption that most of the men they would replace would be clerks and communications technicians. Accordingly, recruiters were to require experience in these fields so that recruits could be assigned to their posts after only a short period of indoctrination. Other than these few specifics, plus the general requirements that a woman be at least twenty years old and in good health, male recruiters were not quite sure what they were looking for. One took quite literally the notion that the WAVES were to replace men, insisting that female recruits meet the height and weight requirements established for men. Only a few such women could be found, and according to McAfee they were "amazons, superb-looking women."[1] An equally narrow view, and a far more pervasive one, was that reflected in recruiting material that glamorized the WAVES. Lieutenant Commander McAfee and her cohorts had to keep reminding the recruiting officials responsible for this literature that women reservists were serious young *ladies* in uniform to do their *jobs,* and that the image portrayed on a recruiting poster determined the kind of young women the Navy would attract. Above all, McAfee insisted, the Navy needed women of quality.

It turned out that there was no need to worry about the quality of the women eager to enlist. To begin with, many women qualified to receive commissions could not do so because enabling legislation so severely restricted the number of women officers. Second, the Navy insisted that women officer candidates take the same qualifying test given to male candidates, a test that placed a premium on technical knowledge that few women, even college graduates, possessed. Many female college graduates, failing to qualify for a commission, enlisted instead. Finally, the mantle of prestige originally extended from McAfee and the Women's Advisory Council to women officers expanded to cover enlisted women. In general, the WAVES were perceived as a fine organization of which both daughters and their parents would approve, and so the Navy could be highly selective as to which women it accepted.

Not that the service attracted only privileged and educated women. As it did to some men, the call to military service offered to some women opportunities for adventure and advancement not available to them in civilian life. As one woman officer later put it, explaining why training as Navy cooks and bakers later proved popular with some enlisted women,

We didn't get all the snobbish, effete elite. We had some pretty plain youngsters . . . some from the country and some that saw no prospect of college. . . . We had every kind of girl, from debutantes to little peasants, some with extraordinary motivation, some partly self-interested. But if you did the job you got on in the Navy, you got a better rating and you got more pay.[2]

Training Recruits

The Navy's enlisted men all began with recruit training, or boot camp, at a large naval station where they received thorough indoctrination into the ways of the service. Only after they had received this firm foundation did a number of them go on to specialized schools. The Navy had been in the business of training male recruits for decades and knew it well. Navy officials were less certain about how and where to train enlisted women. Because it was believed that the tasks of most enlisted women would be largely clerical, officials saw no point in giving women as much basic training as men received. However, women would need some brief naval orientation before going to special schools that would prepare them for their specific Navy duties. One option was to conduct their training, like the men's, at naval stations, but these were already stretched to their limits to turn out ever-increasing numbers of male recruits.

Where, then, would the Navy train the enlisted women beginning to be recruited in the late summer of 1942? It so happened that there was an attractive option. During the 1930s the Navy had contracted with a number of civilian colleges to educate officers under the provisions of the NROTC program. The contract schools had increased their faculties and other resources to meet the Navy's needs. However, after the draft began in 1940 colleges and universities with all-male student bodies were threatened with dwindling enrollments and ensuing financial hardship. They brought their plight to the president and to the War Manpower Commission in 1941. One solution was that the Navy agreed to expand its use of college campuses.

The subsequent decision to use contract schools as orientation sites for enlisted WAVES had some merit. Because these sites were already available and staffed, the program could be launched promptly. Also, as the experience with women officers at Northampton suggested, the Navy could expect that the prospect of being trained on a college campus might prove enticing and thus promote recruitment. Moreover, such a plan was in keeping with the Navy's belief then that its women should be trained separately from men.

The Contract Training Schools

On September 11, 1942, the Navy Department accepted the first enlisted WAVES. All were between twenty and thirty-six years of age, high-school graduates, U.S. citizens of good character and in good health, and not married to Navy men. These women were ordered to report on October 9 to one of three different naval training units. Those to become yeomen reported to the unit at Oklahoma A&M College in Stillwater, prospective radiomen to the unit at the University of Wisconsin in Madison, and prospective storekeepers to the unit at Indiana University in Bloomington. Together, these three units could accommodate sixteen hundred women.

Each of these trail-blazing units had its share of difficulties. At Stillwater, for example, the Navy staff members delegated certain responsibilities to college officials. One appalling result was that the meals served to Navy women were unsavory. After an inspection, quantities of meat were condemned, and eventually the college repaid thousands of dollars to the Navy. Significant changes were made and the unit subsequently seemed to run well, although after it closed a large sum of money that should have been spent was found in the welfare fund.[3] Overall, the three units made such rapid progress that on November 11, barely a month after the first recruits had reported, the Navy announced that between February and June of the following year, 1943, almost ten thousand women trained as storekeepers, yeomen, and radiomen would be available to release enlisted men for duty at sea or overseas.

However, a major defect of the decision to provide basic training on different college campuses had become evident: Women recruits were not being trained in the naval atmosphere that characterized naval stations, nor were they receiving the same indoctrination. Some instructors in technical subjects were enlisted men, but others were civilians. Naval organization, naval regulations, and identification of naval ships and aircraft were in some cases taught by women officers whose own knowledge in these areas was minimal and new. Further, the three units, isolated from one another and from mainstream Navy facilities, could not provide cohesive indoctrination. Following an inspection trip to Stillwater, Madison, and Bloomington, Lt. Mary Jo Shelly recommended to

Lieutenant Commander McAfee that a single recruit training unit for women be established.

Despite shortcomings, the accomplishments of these three units constituted a breakthrough. For the first time in its history, the U.S. Navy was training large numbers of enlisted women. Speed and numbers were critical criteria imposed by the rapid expansion for which personnel planners had been ill prepared. Even as the three units were being established, Navy officials were beginning to realize that they needed far more women than nearly anyone had foreseen. They had originally anticipated being able to employ about ten thousand enlisted women (despite estimations by the Bureau of Aeronautics that it alone could employ twenty-six thousand). By early fall of 1942 the Navy had doubled its first estimate. This expansion, coinciding with Shelly's recommendation to establish a single basic training unit, caused a swift change in direction.

Cedar Falls: The Women's First Boot Camp

A second unit for women yeomen was about to be launched at Iowa State Teachers College at Cedar Falls. Now plans were rapidly switched and Cedar Falls was to become instead a basic training unit for enlisted women. Lieutenant Commander McAfee chose Lt. Margaret Disert, the former dean of Wilson College now on recruiting duty in Philadelphia, to become officer-in-charge of the Cedar Falls unit. A staff was gathered of about fifty male officers and petty officers and women officers fresh from Northampton. One of their first challenges was to ensure that adequate beds and mattresses were on hand, for the Navy's supply system had not yet caught up with the change in plans. On December 1 the unit's commanding officer, Capt. Randall Davis, arrived. Two weeks later the first class of 1,050 enlisted WAVES arrived to begin their five-week course.

The new recruits were met as they arrived by bus or train on December 15. Simply meeting the trains proved challenging for the staff members, for wartime demands often resulted in unannounced reroutings. Training modeled after men's boot camps began immediately. As one woman ensign on the staff explained to an audience of high-school girls, telling them what to expect if they were to become "one of us,"

after a long tiring train trip, the double-deck bunks you'll find in your billet will be most inviting, but don't think you can just flop down. You can't. Nor can you run out to the corner for a Coke. Somehow the Navy manages to budget time thoroughly and you as part of the Navy will be falling into line pronto. The Uniform Officers will undoubtedly have you standing for hours that first day, being fitted, and perhaps the Medical Department had agreed to give you the first of your shots the very minute you arrive and in addition, the Instruction Department will certainly decide to issue books right then and there. After about the tenth time up and down the ladder* another call comes to get your linen and immediately make up your bed. Be sure you make square corners. The Mess bell finally rings and although you don't care whether you eat or not by that time, the sight of the tin tray filled to the brim with the best food you ever saw changes your mind. After mess, you are really exhausted and a hot shower and that flannel nightie you brought were never more appealing—but this is the Navy now and one doesn't go to bed until taps.[4]

The daily routine was much like that of all Navy recruits: reveille at 5:30 A.M. or 6:00 A.M., breakfast at 6:30 A.M., classes and drill for four hours before lunch and four hours afterward. An hour of free time was allowed between 4:30 P.M. and 5:30 P.M. After dinner were two hours of study or instruction, followed by taps at 10:00 P.M. The captain's inspection took place every Saturday morning, after which recruits were at liberty from noon until 11:30 P.M. Reveille on Sunday was at 7:00 A.M. breakfast at 7:30 A.M. Church attendance was mandatory. Liberty began after church and ended at 7:30 P.M. when study hours began. Besides her six immunization shots—one against smallpox, two against tetanus, and three against typhoid—and fittings for uniforms ordered from local department stores, each recruit also took a series of aptitude tests and interviews to determine the job for which she might receive specialized training. As at Northampton, all organization, administration, and instruction were handled almost exclusively by naval personnel.

Cedar Falls recruits developed a special tradition, that of always singing the first and last verse of "The Star-Spangled Banner," which helped to develop pride. Pride was also inspired by Captain Davis. When he was transferred to other duties in May, the recruits honored him with a pledge, "Our pledge to you is this, in your own words: The WAVES will be the best, and the best of the WAVES will be the IOWAVES."[5]

Perhaps the best explanation for their enthusiasm was the quality of the recruits themselves, who seemed invigorated by the challenge of

*Navy term for stairway.

mastering Navy ways. One seaman assigned to duty as mate of the deck, unprepared when she saw Captain Davis approach one day, momentarily froze at the sight of his four gold stripes, but she recovered in time to salute him smartly and say, "Ahoy, sir!" The spirit was contagious. Another recruit who had been an indifferent high-school student evidently thrived under Navy training. She surprised one of her former teachers who visited her at Cedar Falls. The teacher asked, "How is it that now you're doing so cheerfully all those things you never liked to do, or wouldn't do, like getting to class on time, paying attention to details, being neat?" The recruit's answer revealed that the Navy's no-nonsense attitude toward recruits worked as well for women as for men: "Well, it isn't me, it's the *platoon*. We all do things together and we have to do them right, and you don't want to let anyone else in the platoon down. And besides, none of this is for my own good!"[6]

Even before the first class at Cedar Falls was to be graduated in January 1943, two changes took place, both a result of the Navy's increasing need for women and both testing their mettle. The first came when Lieutenant Commander McAfee called Lieutenant Disert to say that many women in the class would become metalsmiths, pigeon trainers, or aviation machinist-mates. The recruits had joined the Navy believing they would become yeomen, or storekeepers, or radiomen. Now, just before their Christmas leave, they learned they would be training for jobs most had never even heard of. But they took the news well, and Disert later "heard from the aviation men at Memphis that these women had done so well that they wanted nothing *but* women—they wanted 'wings manned by women.' "[7]

The larger change was in the overall program for training enlisted women, again rooted in the Navy's rapidly widening vision of how many more women it would need—in 1942, its estimate rose from ten thousand to seventy-five thousand—and in how many more kinds of jobs. The reassessment owed something to the excellent reports being received about the first group of WAVES. Also, many conservative notions of the kinds of work at which women could be successful were melting away in the crucible of need. Consequently, in December 1942 Rear Admiral Jacobs recommended to Secretary Knox that the Navy establish a boot camp capable of training up to five thousand women.

By spring of 1943 the Cedar Falls unit began to revert to its original mission as a school for yeomen. Henceforth enlisted women would receive basic training elsewhere.

Boot Camp Moves to Hunter College

The selection of Hunter College in the Bronx, the northernmost borough of the city of New York, as the site for the boot camp rested on several considerations. Of these, the most important was its size: The college had facilities to teach, train, and feed up to six thousand women at a time. As a member college of the City University of New York, it was under the local government's jurisdiction. New York's mayor, Fiorello La Guardia, and Hunter's president, George N. Shuster, were pleased with the prospect that thousands of Navy enlisted women would receive their initial training in one of the city's best-known schools. Dean Gildersleeve of Barnard College and Lt. Elizabeth Reynard knew Hunter well, and La Guardia was an old friend.

Still, there were numerous difficulties to be overcome and, like everything else in wartime, overcome quickly. The most urgent problem was to procure housing. Hunter itself had no dormitories, for its students were city residents who commuted to school. But a number of apartment buildings lay adjacent to the campus; they would have to be secured for use as barracks. Eventually seventeen apartment houses were commandeered for such use, much to the outrage and dismay of their residents, though they were provided adequate residence elsewhere. Also, the campus lacked an auditorium, gymnasium, and playing field large enough to accommodate the anticipated numbers of women. But the auditorium of an adjoining school and the nearby armory of the New York State National Guard could serve; they too would have to be procured. Numerous financial and other arrangements had to be made speedily.

In December 1942 Rear Admiral Jacobs and the school's prospective commanding officer, Capt. William Amsden, visited Hunter College to determine its suitability, accompanied by McAfee, Reynard, and a Navy financial officer. On January 5, 1943, Secretary Knox sent a letter of intent to Mayor La Guardia that was promptly confirmed. On February 1 a contract for the use of the college's facilities was signed by representatives of the Navy, the city, and the city's board of higher education. Eighty-five truckloads of furnishings that had been removed from two passenger liners, the SS *Manhattan* and SS *America,* were installed. On February 8, barely two months after the Navy had first inspected the site, the U.S. Naval Training School (WR), The Bronx, New York, was formally commissioned. The first recruits arrived nine days later.

From then until it was decommissioned in October 1945, every two weeks a new regiment of 1,680 women recruits arrived at Hunter for the six-week course. Thus there were on board at any one time 5,040 "boots" plus 1,000 staff members. The logistics of the operation were gargantuan. For every breakfast, ten thousand eggs were prepared. A meal of baked beans used half a ton of beans, and one and a half tons of salt were consumed each month. Every week twenty-five thousand items of clothing were laundered. The medical staff gave complete physical examinations to 260 recruits a day, an assembly-line routine aptly named the daisy chain. Six New York department stores—Loesser's, Abraham and Strauss, Saks Fifth Avenue, John Wanamaker and Sons, Bloomingdale's, and Macy's—formed the Retailers Uniform Agency to uniform recruits.[8]

In its haste to set up the school, the Navy had bypassed many normal procedures. Numerous difficulties resulted. For example, no arrangement had been made to provide a ship's store, a part of every naval unit, where personnel can purchase small personal items. Since recruits were not allowed to leave the school during the first weeks of training, they soon exhausted their supplies. In desperation, some had dropped notes out of their apartment-building barracks to civilian passersby asking them to buy wanted items, a practice the Navy strongly discouraged. Women officers on the staff tried to do the necessary shopping, but that too proved unsatisfactory. Without Navy Department authorization, a ship's store officer was informally appointed, and soon his self-service operation was doing business to the tune of $400 a day. Meanwhile a Supply Corps officer officially appointed to do the job opened his operation in February 1943. The first week's business amounted to $518, the second to $1,519. Neither officer knew of the other's business, and the situation was not resolved until May.[9]

Another initial difficulty was at the command level. Captain Amsden, deeply involved in setting up the Cedar Falls unit during November 1942, had plunged from that assignment immediately into the preparations for the opening of Hunter. He fell ill with pneumonia in February 1943 and did not recover fully until April. In addition, the executive officer was recovering from the experience of having two ships shot out from under him. Nevertheless, owing partly to Amsden's ability and leadership, and partly to the mutual trust and confidence between him and Lieutenant Reynard (now leading Hunter's training department), "USS Hunter" was launched with no significant mishaps. In April Lt. Eleanor Rigby, seasoned by her experience as regimental commander at Northampton, became the commandant of seamen at Hunter, and by May the administration and its command functions had been effectively streamlined and strengthened.[10]

As at Northampton, instructors at first were hampered by a lack of books and training aids. Reynard and Lt. Joy Hancock teamed up to furnish the trainees with numerous visual aids and equipment, including airplane and engine models, a Link flight simulator, parachutes, and a tail gun. Other Navy Department bureaus and offices provided charts, maps, and ship models.

These artifacts from the "real Navy" not only enhanced instruction, they also evoked for recruits the sights, sounds, and terminology of the service whose uniform they now wore. More specifically, such materials helped them to visualize something of the many kinds of jobs they might perform after graduating. Proper screening and selection to place each woman in the Navy job for which she was best suited would largely determine both her performance in that job and her morale, which, in turn, would profoundly affect the success of the entire WR. Hence every recruit was tested and interviewed to discover her aptitudes and preferences and to match them as closely as possible with a job that the Navy needed done.

The process was far from completely satisfactory. The Navy's own classification of jobs and the skills they required was proceeding hap-hazardly, driven more by the tempo of need than by the logic of analysis. Urgency sometimes overtook all other considerations. For example, all the graduates of three consecutive recruit classes were ordered immedi-ately after graduation for duty at the Navy's new and vastly expanded Communications Station Annex in Washington, D.C., overriding all the careful selection and screening undertaken during training. One result was underutilization of skills. Thanks to the Bureau of Aeronautics' acceptance of women and to Hancock's monitoring, enlisted WAVES in naval aviation suffered less from underutilization. Even so, mishaps occurred. For example, it had been readily assumed that women would be highly suitable as parachute riggers, perhaps because the job required using sewing machines. Subsequent testing revealed that nine out of ten female recruits did not know how to operate the machines.

For the recruits themselves, as for their male counterparts, the boot camp experience was in turn bewildering, exhausting, and finally exhila-rating. In March 1943 the first woman troop train to cross the country to Hunter was assembled. The cars were like those used to transport men, with bunks stacked three deep. Trains from the West joined up at Chicago, and all proceeded eastward together. On one of those trains, coming from Portland, Oregon, was Patricia G. Morgan, who arrived at New York's Grand Central Station four days after leaving the West Coast. As she recalled,

We had been told to bring no more luggage than we could carry, that we would have to carry it when we arrived and to have our orders with us, on our persons. As we staggered off the train (four days of train travel makes you feel the swaying of the train for days after you're actually on good old Terra Firma) a Red Cross worker grabbed our bags and took off with them. Many of us had stowed our orders in those bags expecting to have them in our hands. In due time we arrived by Navy bus at Hunter College. . . . What confusion as we scrambled in that pile of bags to find and claim the right one![11]

A few weeks later Marie Bennett traveled by train to Hunter from her home in Falfurrias, Texas. She found that boot camp consisted of the following:

Muster. Line up. Wait. Hurry up and wait. . . . We marched to break-fast. Marched to class. Marched to lunch. Marched for the nice sergeant. Marched to testing and lectures and marched to gym. Marched to see film on hygiene and marched to barracks. We marched to the head* and marched our sheep into the night as we slept.[12]

But among the marching and the waiting and the bewilderment was the excitement of meeting women from all over the country. In Bennett's class were a professional rodeo rider from Texas, a concert singer from New York City, a circus acrobat from Chicago, and a journalist from Minneapolis. Songfests for all hands and the promise of a brief liberty to explore the sights of New York prior to graduation also helped to keep up morale. In each class trained singers among recruits could audition for the month's "singing platoon," which was in great demand for public programs.

Despite the hurried planning, the initial confusion, and the lack of materials, by mid-1943 USS Hunter was running smoothly, "synchro-nized as if it were a delicate watch."[13] The Navy and Mayor La Guardia regarded it with great pride, and many U.S. and foreign dignitaries were invited to the twice-monthly graduation ceremonies during which nearly four thousand women marched past the reviewing stand. Marie Bennett thought about how she had arrived at Hunter, a "frightened country girl from Texas," and was now "a WAVE, bursting with knowledge about ships and craft, armaments. . . . I could tell sea stories of naval history, and our platoon could march with the best of them."[14]

A total of 85,885 WAVES, 1,914 SPARS, and 3,339 women Marines entered Hunter for basic training between February 18, 1943, and October 1, 1945. Of those, 80,936 WAVES, 1,844 SPARS, and 3,190 women Marines successfully completed the course, the remainder being

*Navy term for toilet.

discharged before completion for either medical or physical reasons, or for inability to adjust.[15]

Specialized Enlisted Training

Three different Navy bureaus handled the specialized training of enlisted women, and each did it differently. The Bureau of Naval Personnel followed its original bent by establishing separate facilities for women at civilian college campuses, while both the Bureau of Medicine and Surgery and the Bureau of Aeronautics folded the training of their enlisted women into that already established for men.

The Bureau of Naval Personnel added another school for radiomen at Miami University in Oxford, Ohio, and two more schools to train storekeepers, one at Georgia State College for Women in Milledgeville and the other at Burdett College in Boston. The units at Stillwater and Cedar Falls were devoted entirely to training yeomen. The sixteen-week radioman courses at Oxford and Madison included instruction in the organization of naval communications, operating procedures, touch-typing, and telegraphy. Every four weeks these two schools graduated 220 radiomen. The storekeeper courses at Bloomington, Boston, and Milledgeville lasted twelve weeks, six devoted to instruction in disbursing and six to instruction in the Navy's supply system. Every two weeks 1,120 storekeepers graduated. During the twelve-week yeoman courses at Stillwater and Cedar Falls, the students learned typing and shorthand, English usage and spelling, naval correspondence and organization, and the Navy's filing system. Every three weeks 735 yeomen graduated. At any given moment during the operation of these seven schools, 6,380 WAVES were under instruction.[16]

Other specialized training courses for enlisted women included a twelve-week course (later lengthened to sixteen weeks) for cooks and bakers at Hunter, established in August 1943; a six-week course for mail clerks, first established in Sampson, New York, and later moved to Hunter; and a four-week course at Hunter in dealing with personnel records.

The Bureau of Medicine and Surgery sponsored specialized training of the approximately thirteen thousand women who served in the Hospital Corps.[17] This bureau was well accustomed to teaching women, for it had been in the business of doing so since the establishment of the Navy Nurse Corps in 1908. It saw no need to spend time and money on establishing separate facilities. Until December 1943, as soon as they finished boot camp, women selected to serve in the Hospital Corps went for training to one of seventeen naval hospitals throughout the country. Thereafter they received instruction at either Bethesda, Maryland, or Great Lakes, Illinois. Most of these women were trained for general duties in naval hospitals, while others prepared for more specialized duties as occupational and physical therapists; as X-ray, laboratory, and dental technicians; and as pharmacist's mates. Hospital Corpsman Marie Bennett later recalled her days at the Hospital Corps School at the naval hospital in Long Beach, California:

> The male corpsmen looked at us with some misgivings when we ventured out through the hospital grounds. We were quartered in the first deck of a new square building, and corpsmen had to double up topside. Worse yet, a few were moved to neat rows of tents a few feet to the rear of the building. Maybe that is what the WAVE song means when sailors will "find ashore their man-sized chore was done by a Navy WAVE." And they did not like it a bit. First we took their jobs, which surely meant they would be "shipping out" soon, then we shoved them from their quarters. Things were pretty touchy for a few days, but after classes began and we were assigned our duty on the wards the situation eased considerably. . . . We sat through hours of lectures: anatomy, physiology, first aid, minor surgery, hygiene, sanitation, and ward duty, followed by detailed instructions on how to make tight square corners on hospital beds without disturbing the patients. . . . We received a big red-bound copy of *Handbook of the Hospital Corps,* U.S. Navy 1939, filled with over a thousand pages, everything from materia medica to embalming, and shore patrol duty to field sanitation procedures.[18]

In mid-1945, as the numbers of wounded returning to the United States swelled, the Bureau of Medicine and Surgery established a sixteen-week rehabilitation school for Hospital Corps WAVES at Hunter. On October 7, 1945, 132 students completed the course, for which they received sixteen college credits.

The Bureau of Aeronautics, like the Bureau of Medicine and Surgery, also trained its women in the same schools as men—partly to save time and money, but also because being trained alongside men enhanced women's credibility. Almost without exception, these schools were already established at Navy installations. Since most aviation duties were not considered "women's work," the Bureau of Aeronautics prudently sought guidance from naval aviation medical experts in establishing aptitude tests to select and screen candidates. WAVES were trained as aerographers and parachute riggers at Lakehurst, New Jersey; as aviation metalsmiths at Norman, Oklahoma, and Memphis, Tennessee; as control-tower operators and Link trainer instructors at Atlanta, Georgia; as celestial navigation instructors at Seattle, Washington, and Quonset Point, Rhode Island; as gunnery instructors at Pensacola, Florida, and at Great Lakes, Illinois; and as flight trainers at Glenview, Illinois. Approximately six thousand WAVES received such training.[19]

More significant than the numbers of women who entered these aviation specialties was the fact that women entered them at all. If credit can be ascribed to one person, that person is Lt. Joy Hancock, who had long believed that women could serve the Navy in far more roles than most Navy officials were prepared to offer them. As one observer put it, "Joy Hancock's role, backed by the interest on the part of [the Bureau of Aeronautics] was simply extraordinary.... We would have remained storekeepers, yeomen, radiomen, supply officers and so on, in the most modest of roles, if it hadn't been for Joy Hancock. She cracked it wide open."[20]

The enlisted women of naval aviation vindicated Hancock's faith in them, refuting old assumptions about women's poor mechanical abilities. One visitor to the training center near Memphis reported on the women preparing to become aviation machinist mates. She observed them

> bending over lathes, doping airplane wings, dissecting engines.... "How good are they?" I asked a head mechanic supervising machine-shop work. "Magnificent. Ducks to water." ... In the engine shop, former schoolteachers, shopgirls, and debutantes learn to tear down a giant airplane engine of about 3,000 parts and put it back together again. With engines roaring and props spinning, a harassed student may suddenly hear an offbeat, and it's up to her to find its ailment. Frequently it is a wad of chewing gum purposely stuck over a fuel vent by an instructor.[21]

Great credit is also due to McAfee, who realized early on that Hancock and her colleagues in the Bureau of Aeronautics had long held a clear vision of how to make the most effective use of women in naval aviation, and wisely gave her the freest hand possible in doing so. For her part, Hancock kept McAfee well advised of her activities.

Most significant of all was that the women kept pace with, and sometimes surpassed, their fellow male students. Hancock recalled one particular ceremony for several hundred men and women graduates at the Naval Air Station in Norman, Oklahoma, commanded by an old friend of hers, Capt. Virgil Griffin.

He wasn't at first in favor of the women's program, but no one could have done more than he did once he knew he was to train them. At graduations he always presented what looked like a Naval Academy heavy gold ring to the number one student. . . . At this particular graduation, he got up and made his usual nice speech and said he was now presenting the ring to the honor graduate. And then a 5'2" WAVE walked forward. He had put the ring on a ribbon and he hung it around her neck . . . this big man's ring. . . . That whole class stood up and cheered.[22]

Constant revision and expansion became the Navy's norm for training its enlisted WAVES. In 1942 its estimates of how many women it would need rose rapidly, suggesting the depth of its initial reluctance to use women at all, a reluctance overcome only by the imperatives of war. The Navy also discovered that it would have to put all its enlisted women recruits through a single basic boot camp, just as it did men. Once the need for a single site capable of training large numbers of women became obvious, the speed with which it was established was a tribute to the Navy, the City of New York, and the staff, especially the new women graduates from Northampton.

The different approaches to specialized training all achieved the desired goal. The Bureau of Personnel's training of women in all-female units located at college campuses worked well for yeomen, radiomen, and storekeepers. The Bureau of Medicine, accustomed to training at hospitals, decided to train women alongside men. The Bureau of Aeronautics also concluded that separate schools were not needed and received a bonus for its decision: Men were more willing to accept women in nontraditional roles after they had trained together.

The first enlisted WAVES had a rough passage through training school, but their successors' experience proved smoother. The women quickly acquired new skills, developed confidence and spirit, and earned the respect of the men with whom they worked. From the beginning, the Navy expected a great deal from them and got it.

5

—

A Maturing Relationship

*"*C *an't imagine why anyone would want women [in the Navy], but my women are marvelous."*

—MALE CHIEF PETTY OFFICER TO CAPT. MILDRED McAFEE

The Navy had launched the WR with verve and distinction. By mid-1943 WR training programs were proceeding smoothly, and large numbers of qualified women were being recruited. Nearly four thousand women were already serving as officers and more than twenty-one thousand enlisted women had completed initial training. Their morale was high, they were performing well, and the general public viewed them favorably. Now they and the Navy had to pull together for the war's duration, which might be years.

For the Navy, the challenge was to keep on adjusting to new ideas about women's capabilities and to assign them to a far wider range of jobs than it had originally envisioned. As the number of women grew the Navy also struggled to use them as efficiently as possible and to maintain their initial enthusiasm. Sometimes this meant developing formal policies for their administration, sometimes it meant ad hoc accommodation to their needs. The difficulty lay in determining when to treat them the same as men and when not to. Finally, the Navy had to broaden its vision of what the WR could be and do: Contrary to original expectations, it could serve overseas and it could include black women.

The few dozen senior women officers who advised the chief of naval personnel in Washington and commanding officers in the field led these efforts. Their challenge was to discover how to integrate themselves into Navy systems and make them work for women. For the rest of the women, the challenge was simply to do whatever the Navy asked of them, and to keep on doing it until the war was won.

WAVES at Work

In 1943 Ens. Elizabeth Ender and Betty St. Clair wrote a song that could be sung in harmony with "Anchor's Aweigh." Its lyrics captured the challenge for wartime WAVES:

> WAVES of the Navy, there's a ship sailing down the bay,
> And she won't come into port until that vict'ry day.
> Carry on for that gallant ship and for every hero brave,
> Who will find ashore his man-sized chore was done by a Navy WAVE.

The enthusiasm with which the WAVES responded to all that the Navy asked of them and their abundant success have to some degree obscured the difficulties they faced in carrying on with their "man-sized chores."

Underlying all other difficulties were the differing, often contradictory attitudes from men with and for whom the WAVES worked. Many Navy men at all levels put aside their initial doubts and private reservations, enthusiastically welcomed women's contributions, and treated them fairly. Other Navy men were downright hostile, like the one who greeted the woman officer about to work for him with "You know we don't want you, don't you?" She answered, "Yes, sir." He then told her that the first twenty enlisted women assigned to the command would report the following Monday (this was Friday). When she asked where they were to be quartered, he told her, "That's your problem." Some men were resentful because being replaced by women meant they would be sent to fight at sea. As one woman officer observed, going out and getting killed "wasn't very popular." To compound this attitude, in at least one naval district the senior woman officer reported that "the replacement problem is a little difficult because one WAVE has replaced two men in our office." In some instances, Navy men tried to be supportive by dealing too leniently with the women who worked for them. They had to be reminded that if women weren't treated as firmly as their male counterparts, then they weren't part of the team.[1]

Frequently the problems stemmed from the jobs themselves. Despite efforts to keep publicity about the WAVES serious and responsible and to assign them to jobs that would make the best use of their abilities, some women nevertheless worked in jobs that were duller or more difficult than they had expected, or for which they were ill suited. As McAfee later reflected,

The military organization went to great lengths to place qualified people in appropriate positions, but efficiency in the use of personnel is not a major concern of a nation in wartime. The job has to be done by anybody within reach. That makes fearful and wonderful claims on military men and women. It is discouraging to those who are not asked to use their full abilities and terrifying to those required to stretch themselves.[2]

Confronted with assignments beyond their physical capability, women often used ingenuity to replace brawn. McAfee learned of a case where two husky enlisted men reasoned that if the women sent to replace them could not do their jobs, then the men could keep those jobs and avoid being sent to sea. They told the women, "Get those truck tires stowed properly in the loft," and then went serenely off to lunch, sure the women could barely lift the tires. But they returned to find the tires stowed properly: The women had rigged a pulley. In some assignments, more was asked of the women than even their enthusiasm and ingenuity could master. Ironically, the Bureau of Medicine and Surgery was the outstanding offender; some women serving in dispensaries and hospitals worked as many as seventy hours a week and broke under the strain.[3]

Another group enduring harsh working conditions were those decoding messages in Washington, D.C. By 1945 WAVES constituted 80 percent of all personnel in the Washington Communications Office, and in the code rooms they did all encoding and decoding. When Veronica Mackey enlisted in 1943 she had no idea she would become part of that effort. After boot camp, she had been sent to the National Cash Register Company's assembly lines in Dayton, Ohio, where for three months, together with some other WAVES selected for their mechanical aptitude, she wired rotors. They were never told what they were doing or why, but that didn't matter to her. "We'd signed up for the duration of the war, and we did what we were told." She then reported to the Naval Communication Station in Washington, D.C., and lived for the next twenty-nine months in a barracks across the street that housed nearly three thousand WAVES. She worked in a room that held twelve large machines, each about 6 feet tall, 10 feet wide, and 3 feet deep. The front of each machine was covered with dials and several dozen familiar objects, rotors like those she had wired back in Dayton. The machines were codebreakers, and their effectiveness rested on the Japanese and German governments' ignorance of their existence. Because of the need for absolute secrecy, decoding was broken up into a series of small, separate, tedious tasks;

each WAVE worked on only one task, repeating it eight hours a day, day after day. Mackey recalled her job as

> dull, and anyone could have done it. We were given a graph, which told us to set the dials and rotors on certain numbers. Then we punched a switch and the machine would print out a piece of paper. We took the paper to a room down the hall and knocked. The door would open, someone would take the paper from us, and then we'd return to reset the dials and rotors from yet another graph.[4]

The sole duty of certain other women at the same facility was to stare at TV-like screens, reporting to a supervisor whenever a blip appeared. The monotony was deadly and became more bearable only when astute women officers explained to the enlisted women how their individual tasks contributed to the larger process.

In some cases women were not assigned to jobs for which they had been trained. Hancock found, for instance, that at one station women who had been carefully trained to become machinist's mates were being used instead as clerks—not only a waste of resources but also a source of resentment for the women. The cause of the situation seemed trivial but had significant consequences.

> There were no toilet facilities for the women in the hangars, so they weren't assigning the women there. . . . I talked to the leading chief and he said he didn't particularly want the women aviation machinist's mates to come in. However, he'd never worked with them. His was a part of that feeling, . . . particularly on the part of the old-time chiefs, that women couldn't do the jobs properly . . . one chief . . . said to me, "Well, I guess we're going to have to have them. And here's what I'd do. Put a peg outside the door of the head, and when a man goes in he hangs his hat on the peg and no women go in. When a WAVE goes in let her hang her hat on the peg and the men will stay out." And that's how we solved the problem. But it was something they couldn't face up to without a push. (Later they installed additional plumbing as a courtesy for the women.) If we had waited for this new plumbing, we would have lost all that work from the women. Instead, being able to put your hat on a peg did the trick. And those same chiefs . . . once they had the women working there were delighted.[5]

In other cases women were accepted and employed properly only after sheer need compelled commanding officers to set aside their prejudices. When they found that they had women on board who could do those jobs for which no men were available, be it engineering or administration, they actually began to request WAVES. One captain had a personal change of attitude. Early in the war he had called the Bureau of Naval Personnel to complain that he had been sent a woman yeoman: "They're no good!" He was told that no male yeomen were available, and if he wanted a yeoman at all he would have to take a woman. Toward the end of the war when he had become an admiral he called once again, this time to complain that he had just been sent a male yeoman: "They're no good!"[6]

When all was said and done, men and women were in the same Navy fighting the same war: Loyalty to one's shipmates was fundamental. McAfee concluded that "what saved the life and reputation of the women in the Navy in the earliest days was the tradition that, if he's on my ship, he's all right. And we got women on so many 'ships' (i.e., stations and units) the Navy loved us dearly!"[7]

Policy Development

The challenge the Navy faced regarding its policy for women had two aspects. The first and more immediate challenge was in the routine details of personnel administration. How should established policies be applied to women? What worked and what didn't? The second and more difficult challenge was to expand earlier concepts of what the WR could accomplish, then to develop the means—by policy, regulation, or legislation—to implement expansions.

Administrative Struggles

Compounding the confusion early on was a lack of clear-cut directives on policy for WAVES. Often McAfee, Hancock, or others from Washington would visit naval activities and work things out on the spot. Matters improved when a pamphlet compiled by Hancock and containing all relevant policies and directives appeared in March 1943. At the same time Lt. Tova Peterson Wiley, brought to Washington from San Francisco to serve as McAfee's assistant, began the huge task of redrafting Navy regulations to include women. Beginning that year, WAVE district directors met each September in Washington to thrash out numerous common problems. The resulting reports helped to make policy development and dissemination more uniform.

The women in the Bureau of Naval Personnel never completely solved the problem of coordination and liaison with the bureau's many offices. Lt. Jean Palmer later said that her greatest service as the WAVE representative in the Enlisted Personnel Office was "finding out what the policies were for men and getting them adapted for women." Along with other women she also learned, as Hancock had long known, that getting chief petty officers on one's side was the way to accomplish things. In one case involving policy for female parachute riggers, Palmer and a male chief parachute rigger thrashed a problem out to their own satisfaction, face to face, and then watched their recommendation rise up the chain of command. At the top of that particular chain, the cognizant admiral asked for the WAVE representative's comment. As Palmer recalled, "I got to endorse my own idea, and then the admiral says yes, that's what I think, too."[8]

Discipline and Discharges

WAVES presented very few disciplinary problems, which helped boost their popularity among supervisors. When a commanding officer had to discipline a woman he usually restricted her to her quarters; confining her to a Navy brig was considered unsuitable. The rare woman who could not or would not work and live peaceably within the Navy community was discharged rather than being subjected to repeated punishment.

Few women had to be discharged. As of June 1943 only 469, or less than 3 percent of enlisted women, had been separated from the service. Reasons for discharge included inaptitude, physical disability, undesirableness, and unsuitability. The disciplinary record of the ten thousand women appointed as officers during the war was likewise exemplary: only four were discharged for disciplinary reasons, whereas the comparable number of male officers was four out of one thousand, or ten times greater.[9]

By no means were all enlisted women in the categories listed above disciplinary cases, for these numbers included women who had married while in indoctrination and who presumably knew that such action would lead to discharge. They also included women who became pregnant. At first, a woman who "is or has been" pregnant would be given an honorable discharge "for the convenience of the government." Later the "has been" was dropped. Thus, if a woman was no longer pregnant by the time she came to receive her physical examination for discharge, she could choose to stay in service.

The Navy did its best to avoid the quagmire implicit in such questions as whether a pregnant woman was married and why a woman was no longer pregnant. If "legal evidence" was found for an induced abortion, the woman could be discharged as unsuitable. In point of fact, medical authorities advised, such evidence was hard to obtain. If a woman became pregnant a second time she was automatically separated from the service. But not until 1945 did the Navy authorize any maternity or postnatal care.

Transfers

Some women, like some men, had trouble adjusting to the Navy. The Bureau of Ships, for instance, reported that in general

> young women just out of college and without any business experience, and older women who have spent years in a routine type of work, found it most difficult to fit into their assigned Navy niches. Women coming from progressive industrial companies or from provocative professional fields carved their own places. . . .[10]

As we have seen, other women were placed in inappropriate jobs, and others were stationed too far from home to be able to return during leave. Many who encountered difficulties gritted their teeth and carried on, but not all could endure. The possibility of transfer from one duty station to another could have ameliorated many such situations, but appropriate provisions had not been made for women. As late as November 1943 women were discouraged from applying for transfers, the Navy's stated policy being that they would be allowed to transfer "only for the good of the service."

The Bureau of Naval Personnel at first responded by trying to make more suitable initial assignments. Its efforts had negligible results and did nothing for women already misassigned, although their situation improved somewhat when more liberal leaves of absence were permitted. After 1944 transfers were considered and permitted for enlisted women who had been hospitalized if medical authorities certified that their jobs had contributed to their poor health and if they had served at least eighteen months in their current duty station. A woman could also request transfer on the grounds that her placement resulted in hardship to her family.

Promotions

As noted in chapter 2, the legislation that established the WR (Public Law 689) limited the number of women officers: Only one woman could hold the rank of lieutenant commander, only thirty-five could be lieutenants, and of the rest only 35 percent could be lieutenants (junior grade). The quota for lieutenants was quickly filled by the women assigned to the senior billets in Washington, at the training schools, and at the twelve naval districts in the continental United States. Thus, practically speaking, out of every hundred women eligible to be appointed as commissioned officers, sixty-five would be ensigns. In general, as with male reservists, age and experience determined which women were appointed to the higher rank. With time, inconsistencies appeared, as women coming in later would be appointed ensigns, even though their age and experience were comparable to or greater than those of lieutenants (junior grade) who had entered earlier.

The limitations on rank carried several penalties. First, with the higher ranks virtually closed, promotion for junior officers was stifled. It did not enhance a woman officer's morale to see her male contemporaries receiving promotions for which she had not a chance. Further, some highly qualified women who may have wanted to join the Navy did not because the pay of junior officers was far less than they were receiving as civilians, and family obligations made them unable to afford the cut.

Many women qualified to become officers, on finding that commissioned ranks were filled, instead chose to enter as enlisted women. In March 1943, recognizing excellent officer candidates among its enlisted WAVES, the Navy allowed qualified enlisted women to apply for training at Northampton and receive commissions. A candidate had to have served six months and be recommended by her commanding officer. Educational requirements could be waived if the commanding officer attested to the candidate's superior qualifications or if she had special skills that met the needs of the service.

However, until the number of women officers could be increased, recruitment of more women officers, whether directly from civilian life or from enlisted ranks, and promotion for those already on board would be sluggish. On November 8, 1943, recognizing that the WR would include much larger numbers than originally planned, Public Law 183 was signed; it allowed one woman to be appointed captain and removed restrictions in the lower ranks. The secretary of the Navy promoted McAfee to captain, her senior assistant, Tova Peterson Wiley, to commander, and thirty-five women lieutenants to the rank of lieutenant commander. Congress rationalized these numbers by arguing that more promotions to higher rank for women would be unfair to men who had earned such ranks only after years of service (it overlooked the fact that male reservists with no more Navy experience than women faced no such limitations).

Congress had set no limits on rates for enlisted women. Thus they were promoted up the enlisted ladder in roughly the same way as enlisted men, with two exceptions. First, an enlisted man was advanced only if he had an appropriate amount of sea duty; this requirement was waived for a woman. The second exception was that the promotion of women to chief petty officer, at that time the highest rung on the enlisted promotion ladder, was severely restricted. The right to wear a chief's distinctive insignia was guarded jealously and gained only after years at sea and ashore in highly responsible positions. Navy chiefs were believed able to cope with anything, but the Navy was cautious about asking them to cope with the specter of female chiefs. Hence for women the Navy created the rating of specialist, whose duties were primarily the supervision and discipline of enlisted women. Even so, by the war's end in 1945 more than a hundred WAVES had qualified as chief petty officers. The question of advancement for enlisted women remained uncertain; as late as September 1944 district directors were still urging that advancement procedures be outlined.

WAVES/Wives

Policies concerning women who were married, or wished to marry, changed rapidly and significantly during the WAVES' first year. There were two main issues: first, whether the husband was in the service, and in which branch; and second, when the marriage took place.

Originally, no wife of any man serving in any armed force could enter the WR. Nor could a WAVE marry during indoctrination. After indoctrination she could marry anyone except a man in the Navy, Coast Guard, Merchant Marine, or Marine Corps. Within three months of the WAVES' launching, the policies were changed so that a woman could be married to a man in any branch of the service except the Navy. However, women who entered prior to October 20, 1942, could apply for special rulings, an accommodation that owed its existence mostly to the example of Lt. Tova Peterson. One of the first women commissioned and sent directly to work on a naval district staff, she was engaged to a naval officer when she was appointed and had no intention of either breaking her engagement or postponing her marriage. When McAfee advised Admiral Jacobs that the prohibition would force Peterson to resign, he said, "Oh, we don't want to lose her; she's too good."[11]

By March 1943 the Navy abandoned all attempts to make its women choose between continued service or marriage to a Navy man. After indoctrination a woman could marry anyone she chose without jeopardizing her naval status. A final change occurred in November 1943: A woman already married to a Navy man below the rank of ensign could now be accepted in the WR, but not a woman already married to a commissioned officer in the Navy, Marine Corps, or Coast Guard. The concern was that such a woman might carry undue influence because of her husband's rank. Thus, WAVES could become Navy wives, but some Navy wives couldn't become WAVES.

Benefits

Legislation provided that female reservists could receive allowances for their dependents, just as male reservists could. Nevertheless, on February 26, 1943, the U.S. comptroller general ruled that female reservists were not part of the legislative intent of the general provisions for dependents' allowances. This ruling damaged the WR; it hindered the recruitment of women who had parents or siblings to support, and even forced some WAVES who could not support their dependents without the allowance to resign. Months later, Congress amended the matter. Public Law 183, the same law that relaxed rank limitations, provided unequivocally that women reservists with dependents were entitled to allowances for them. This apparent triumph for the principle of equity was flawed by a further stipulation. Having reexamined the matter, Congress declared that no allowance could be authorized for a woman's husband, even if he did in fact depend on her for his support. Thus Congress would not visit upon a husband with no means of support other than his wife's Navy pay the "indignity" of being termed a dependent.

WAVES Pioneer for the Navy

By September 1943, more than thirty-six thousand women other than nurses were in Navy uniform, and that number would more than double by the war's end. Their growing presence impelled the Navy to cross certain frontiers. Two were basic, having to do with housing and food.

The third, the integration of black women into the WR, had genuine historic significance.

Housing. One of the first changes made to accommodate women was in housing standards. Ashore, male enlisted sailors were traditionally housed in barracks with rows of double-decker bunks lined up in large, unpartitioned rooms. But McAfee and many other women officers knew that women's morale would benefit from a modicum of privacy. Hence they persisted in requiring that barracks being built or modified to house women have cubicles that two or four women could share and decorate with curtains and bedspreads. Showers were to be partitioned, and doors hung on toilet stalls. The Bureau of Medicine and Surgery supported these standards; it had previously recommended cubicles for all barracks to contain the spread of communicable diseases. The Navy had done nothing about these recommendations for its men, but it saw them in a different light when setting up women's housing. Experience would prove that epidemics did in fact run faster through unpartitioned male barracks than through women's cubicles. The marked improvement that cubicle arrangements and other concessions toward privacy made in barracks' general habitability did not escape the Navy's attention; in the late 1950s such features came to be standard.

Male sailors were accustomed to spending many of their leisure hours off base. But women were accustomed to relaxing and entertaining visitors in their homes and to doing their own laundry. Thus the Navy saw the wisdom of providing lounges and laundry facilities for women's barracks, as well as more and better recreational facilities on base. This also benefited the men, who now found life on a base with WAVES a little more like home. Everyone from chaplains to chief masters-at-arms noted the men's improved behavior: fewer disciplinary problems, better grooming, and cleaner language. Because many women attended chapel regularly, the men's attendance increased. In one naval district, chapel facilities had to be tripled after the WAVES arrived.

Food. Like most institutional food, the Navy variety—although of good quality—was high in calories. For an all-male population, many of them in their late teens, such a diet was suitable. The WAVES, however, were all past their teens, and they had little appetite for food like beans for breakfast. Women subsisting on a steady Navy diet gained excessive weight. Lt. Comdr. Mary Daily, advisor to the commandant of the Thirteenth Naval District in Seattle, reported in 1943 that the 200 women assigned there had gained an average of about 10 pounds each since their arrival for a total weight gain of one ton—a provocative statistic. Local commanders promptly ordered salads and other lower-calorie items to be introduced into their mess halls, a move soon followed at many Navy bases. Not only did women find the new offerings more appealing, so did many men.

Black Women Admitted to the WR

The WR crossed another frontier for the Navy: It reminded the Navy that units could be racially integrated.

Black women were excluded from the WAVES for more than two years, despite efforts by many people both in and out of the Navy to include them. Black leaders and others in prewar America, concerned about color barriers in the nation's armed forces, had already applied political pressure to break them down. In May 1942 they put their views before the Senate Naval Affairs Committee as it considered proposed legislation for the WR, asking for a clause forbidding "distinction in selection, appointment, training or classification . . . on the ground of race or color." They got nowhere, although nothing in the language of the legislation actually barred black women. Soon after the legislation passed several dozen black women applied to enlist, but none was accepted, which provoked some public criticism.[12]

From the Navy's point of view, the question of accepting black women was complex. Racial discrimination was rampant throughout the country, in some areas undergirded by strict laws. Navy policies regarding blacks reflected this state of affairs. There were no black naval officers, and only a handful of black petty officers. Although black men had served honorably in the U.S. Navy in earlier times, for the past twenty years they had been allowed to enlist only as messmen and stewards, that is, cooks and waiters. In 1942, in response to public pressure, the Navy permitted black men to serve in construction battalions (as Seabees) and for general shore duty. But in the Navy's view, these changes did not justify admitting black women to the WR. As the chief of naval personnel wrote to the Young Women's Christian Association (YWCA) on December 30, 1942, "At this time the Navy does not have any substantial body of Negro men available for general service at sea, [and] it has no occasion to replace Negro enlisted men with Negro enlisted women."[13] Navy officials still grappling with the notion that white women were capable of replacing white men could scarcely imagine that black women could replace white men.

More concretely, the Navy was already struggling with the challenge of providing separate housing and training for men and women. How could it deal with yet another separate system for black women? Would it be possible to run counter to social mores by housing and training black and white women together? The most immediate impediment to the admission of black women was Secretary Knox. He was violently opposed to the idea, although he stated publicly that the matter was "under review."[14]

Soon after reporting for duty, McAfee received inquiries from officials of the Urban League and the National Association for the Advancement of Colored People (NAACP), the two most prominent and active black organizations. She also talked with the highly esteemed black educator Mary McLeod Bethune, whom she had known for many years. McAfee arranged for black women leaders to discuss the situation with high-ranking naval officers.

At first McAfee assumed that black women would be accepted fairly soon but on a segregated basis. She discussed with black women leaders where and how this separate training might take place and posed these questions:

Would it be better to have a training school for Negro women at a State university where they would be the only military units, so that it would be military but not conspicuously racial? Or would it be better to put them in a big coeducational university where there were already many Negro students? Or should we take a place like Greensboro College down in North Carolina and have a training school corresponding to what Smith was up here?[15]

In July 1943 she reported that she was "prepared to recommend admission without discrimination," although she was "well aware of the practical difficulty involved." The Navy Department was already under pressure to accept black women on a fully integrated basis, and on August 6, 1943, the Women's Advisory Council recommended full integration. However, in September 1943 the WAVE district directors, responsible for implementing whatever decisions might be made, recommended deferring the admission of black women for as long as possible.[16]

Throughout 1943 and 1944 McAfee continued to explore ideas and possibilities with black leaders. Over time she noted a change in their attitude. At first they were patient and understanding about the difficulties. But by 1944 black men had been fighting and dying for more than two years, and they now vigorously opposed any arrangement under which the Navy might accept black women but treat them differently from white women.

Two developments combined to open Navy doors to black women. The first was the death of Frank Knox in April of 1944. He was succeeded as secretary of the Navy by his undersecretary, James Forrestal, who was as much in favor of black women entering the Navy as Knox had been opposed. On July 28 Forrestal recommended to President Roosevelt that the Navy admit and treat black women exactly as it did white women. Politics now took a hand in the matter. Campaigning for an unprecedented fourth term as president, Roosevelt wished to refute his opponent's accusation that he was indifferent to racial discrimination in the armed forces. On October 19, less than a month before election day, the Navy announced that the president had approved plans to commission especially qualified black women, and the first black women to be enlisted would report for training no later than the first day of 1945.[17]

This sudden move put the Navy on the spot, for the last class of officer candidates at Northampton was due to begin training in mid-November 1944 and graduate on December 21. Harriet Ida Pickens and Frances Wills, two black women from New York City, one of them a summa cum laude graduate in history, were sworn in and rushed up to Northampton, arriving a week after the class convened. At graduation Pickens stood third among her classmates, all of whom were commissioned on December 22. The degree of racial prejudice existing at the time is suggested by the fact that three women naval officers of a foreign country, France, had received training at Northampton before this pair of black American women was granted the same opportunity.[18]

Despite the publicity given to the Navy's acceptance of black women on a nondiscriminatory basis, the response was slight. In the first six months in which the program was open to them, only seventy-two black enlisted women reported to Hunter for basic training. Their arrival caused little fuss. The commanding officer, Captain William Amsden, reported that all went smoothly on the day the first black recruits arrived. As the new WAVES assembled, a white woman told one of her superiors, "I think there must be some mistake. . . . My roommate is . . . a Negro girl." The reply was, "Well, we're in the Navy now, and we're all citizens," whereupon the woman returned to her room and helped her roommate make up her bunk.[19]

The field activities to which black women would be assigned had nearly three months in which to prepare for their arrival. Field commanders and recruiters had been advised of the change in policy on October 31, 1944, but the first black enlisted WAVES were not ready for assignment until early February 1945. The Bureau of Naval Personnel assigned several of them to duty in its own offices, on the same terms of nondiscriminatory treatment outlined to the field activities. That the black women were so few in number may have eased their entry, but it may also have engendered feelings of isolation.

From a larger historical perspective, the relatively uneventful entry of black women into the Navy set a precedent for the later integration of black men.

WAVES in Hawaii

By 1944 the great naval installation at Pearl Harbor had largely recovered from the damage inflicted by the Japanese attack in December 1941. As headquarters for Adm. Chester Nimitz, commander in chief, Pacific, it was now the nerve center of an immense military and naval complex. Ships, planes, and men passed through it on their way to and from the front lines. So did women, including Army nurses and WACs headed for duty in the southwest Pacific. Many Navy nurses were already stationed at Pearl Harbor. But as of mid-1944 no WAVES were there. Navy surveys, together with requests from field commanders, revealed that WAVES could be used at several overseas sites. The legislation of 1942, however, specifically prohibited them from serving outside the contiguous United States. Navy officials chafed under this restriction. A board including retired and active-duty admirals, plus the commissioner of the U.S. Civil Service, the president of Penn Mutual Life Insurance, and a senior official of Lockheed Aircraft had just conducted the first survey of naval manpower. It reported that "lack of sufficient women service personnel is preventing the transfer of able-bodied males from billets which could be filled by women to duties in the combat areas" and recommended that the Navy be allowed to order women to Puerto Rico, Alaska, and Hawaii.[20] Accordingly, the Navy petitioned Congress to remove the prohibition and in anticipation began to make carefully detailed plans for sending WAVES overseas. After twice rebuffing the Navy's requests, Congress passed Public Law 441 (signed on September 27, 1944), allowing women to volunteer for assignment to Hawaii, Alaska, the Caribbean, and Panama.

The need for WAVES seemed most urgent in Hawaii, the Fourteenth Naval District. Navy planners there had identified more than six thousand billets that women could fill and enough suitable places to house them. Within three weeks of the passage of Public Law 441, Hancock and Palmer were in Hawaii, together with senior women officers from the

Marine Corps and the Coast Guard. They were met by Admiral Nimitz himself, who had moved far beyond his earlier opposition to women in the Navy.[21]

Upon their return, Palmer submitted an extensively detailed report emphasizing that the women assigned to overseas duty must be carefully selected: They would have to volunteer for overseas duty; they must have served satisfactorily for at least six months; their commanding officer was to attest to their maturity, responsibility, and adaptability; and they must have no dependents who might require their presence in the United States. They were to be assigned overseas for at least eighteen months, possibly longer. During this time they would not be granted any leaves in the United States. Furthermore, the women were to expect little glamour: All enlisted personnel in Hawaii had curfew at 6:00 P.M., officers and civilians at 10:00 P.M. However, because of these restrictions many excellent recreational facilities were provided on local bases, including a beach house exclusively for the use of WAVES.

In December 1944, 203 enlisted women and 10 women officers, with Lt. Winifred Love in charge, were gathered near San Francisco and assigned space in a troop transport ship, the SS *Matsonia*. The first leg of the journey—up to Seattle to take on additional passengers—was a rough passage, and about 90 percent of the women experienced some degree of seasickness. Once outbound from Seattle they recovered sufficiently to volunteer to help male crew members with their work. They arrived in Honolulu on January 6, 1945, to a tumultuous welcome.[22]

Under the leadership of Lt. Comdr. Eleanor Rigby and Lt. Winifred Quick the women proved helpful, and Admiral Nimitz was glad to have a woman officer on hand when members of the Senate Armed Services Committee arrived in Hawaii. He gave Rigby a special assignment, to escort Senator Margaret Chase Smith when the committee went aboard the USS *Saratoga* to view flight operations.[23]

Within five weeks the Fourteenth Naval District was tartly urging the Bureau of Naval Personnel to speed up the flow of women that it had promised:

> It is requested that WAVE officers be ordered via air according to the priority listings (enclosed). These officers are urgently needed. . . . Present rate of receipt of officers . . . does not permit adequate replacement rate now required. . . . WAVE enlisted personnel have been requested for 6,657 billets.[24]

And a few days later after an inspection trip to Pearl Harbor, Lt. Louise Wilde reported to McAfee,

Commanding officers where WAVES are already at work have the highest praise for the work which the girls are doing. As the tempo in the Pacific increases and the pressure on these naval activities continues they feel that ComFourteen* should have every priority on getting WAVES speedily and in large numbers. The internal Navy problems of volunteers for overseas duty and of replacements for these WAVES do not impress them as much as the urgency of the work to be done in the Fourteenth Naval District.[25]

The "problem of volunteers for overseas duty" was simply that there weren't enough of them. To encourage WAVE volunteers, it was recommended that their minimum period for overseas duty be reduced to twelve months, and other blandishments were contemplated.

But suddenly the war was over. On August 6, 1945, the first atomic bomb was dropped on Hiroshima, on August 8 the Soviet Union declared war on Japan, and on August 9 the second atomic bomb was dropped, on Nagasaki. The speed of Japan's surrender on August 14 took most people, including Navy planners, by surprise.

WAVES' Contributions

In the summer of 1945 the Navy had approximately 317,000 officers, of whom nearly 8,400 were women, and 3 million enlisted members, of whom more than 73,000 were women.[26] That is, women constituted roughly 2 percent of the Navy. But that statistic is misleading, for in certain critical areas of naval activity WAVES constituted majorities. Some of them were large indeed, according to a Navy Department press release dated July 21, 1945:

1. At the Navy Department in Washington, 55 percent of uniformed personnel were WAVES.
2. WAVES did about 80 percent of the administrative and supervisory work of the Navy's mail service for the fleet and for Navy activities outside the United States.
3. WAVES filled 75 percent of the jobs in Radio Washington, the nerve center of the Navy's communications system.
4. Of those working in the Bureau of Naval Personnel, 70 percent were WAVES.

*Commander, Fourteenth Naval District.

5. At air training stations, a vital area of instruction was handled almost exclusively by the one thousand WAVE Link trainer instructors who gave lessons in instrument flying to four thousand men a day.
6. At the Indian Head rocket-powder plant, which did about 70 percent of the testing for all U.S. rocket propellant, WAVES performed approximately half of the ballistic calculations, "manned" one of the two firing bays, and completely operated the plant's laboratory.[27]

Also, in June 1945 the Navy designated eighty women officers as naval air navigators, proudly noting that these were the "first women to perform duties as part of a United States military air crew." Two women officers had even been ordered to teach at the all-male U.S. Naval Academy.

The WAVES' contribution could be measured in other ways. In 1944 Captain McAfee found that the number of WAVES on duty that year equaled the number of men it would have taken in peacetime to man ten battleships, ten aircraft carriers, twenty-eight cruisers, and fifty destroyers. The many different kinds of work that WAVES performed, from packing parachutes to teaching antiaircraft gunnery to manning guns on merchant ships, undergirded the work of innumerable naval activities. Furthermore, WAVES had contributed not only to U.S. efforts but also to the Allied cause. Three WAVES, for instance, had been awarded the French Cross of Lorraine for their services in training French pilots.[28]

Demobilization

Early in 1945, with Germany's defeat imminent and Japan's a certainty, the Navy assigned three male officers and Comdr. Mary Jo Shelly to produce a demobilization plan. The inclusion of a woman officer on the planning team suggests that Navy officials understood the importance of demobilizing women as carefully as it had recruited and trained them. Public opinion of the WAVES was highly favorable, as was the WAVES' own opinion of the Navy. A smooth demobilization could help to protect these valuable assets. Nor could it be overlooked that the WAVES, unlike the Yeomen (F) released at the end of World War I, were voters as well as veterans.

Several considerations governed the demobilization plans for WAVES. First, since they were an integral part of the Navy rather than a separate component, their demobilization should proceed like the men's, with one important modification. The order in which Navy men were to be released was to be based on a system of points accumulated for age, length of service, time spent overseas and in combat, and number of dependents. But the women's point quotas were to be lower than the men's, even though the women, in general, were older; none had been able to serve in the Navy until the latter half of 1942, and none had served overseas until January of 1945; none had seen combat, and few had dependents. Had the women's point quotas not been lower than the men's, almost all the male reservists would have been out of uniform before most of the women. The women might have resented that since they had not been subject to the draft but had nonetheless answered the call to colors; it would not have been fair to hold them longer than the men. Retaining women against their will could also have offended a public that easily sympathized with the Navy's wartime manpower needs but hardly comprehended those of peacetime.

Second, it was to be assumed for planning purposes that all WAVES should be demobilized within six months of the end of the "shooting war." Third, since many of the jobs WAVES were doing would still need to be done after they were released, the question of who would do them had to be considered.

On May 1, 1945, the Navy announced that enlisted men or women more than forty-two years old could be discharged by their commanding officers so long as it did not impair the readiness of their respective units. Some WAVES grew restless at this point, especially those whose husbands were returning home. Thus, on June 20 the Navy authorized extended leave and/or transfers closer to home for the wives of returning veterans. The wives of disabled veterans could be discharged upon request.

Peacetime Needs

When the war ended, the Navy faced the task of releasing about 265,000 officers and 2.5 million enlisted personnel—roughly 85 percent of its members—as quickly as possible. Public belief that demobilization would be quick was reinforced by newspaper headlines like the one that appeared on the front page of the *New York Times* on August 28, 1945: "Navy Will Speed Demobilization." Although the government could retain reservists for the duration of the war plus six months, and the date on which the war officially ended was to be determined by the president and Congress, the overriding fact to millions of Americans in uniform was that the shooting was done, their enemies had surrendered, and it was time to go home.

But several sobering realities caused the government to proceed cautiously. On September 6, 1945, President Truman warned that "certain wartime statutes . . . continue to be effective until a formal state of peace had been restored." Not until July 25, 1947, did Congress declare that "the present war shall be deemed terminated as of this date." One sobering reality was that vast numbers of American servicemen and women, together with huge amounts of equipment and supplies, had been dispersed around the globe; they now must be brought home. The Navy's so-called Magic Carpet, including battleships, cruisers, and aircraft carriers, brought back men and women of all the armed services. Also, for the first time in history substantial numbers of American soldiers would be occupying the territories of two defeated enemies. They would need a continuing stream of supplies to maintain their garrisons. Thus the Navy would be sustaining a two-way transoceanic flow of people and materiel. In addition, the atomic bomb tests carried out during 1946 in remote Pacific waters required many ships and thousands of men. These obligations, combined with rapid demobilization, left the Navy shorthanded. The secretary of the Navy reported to Congress that by June 30, 1946, many ships of the active fleet were "immobilized by lack of crews to operate them. Others were operating on a reduced scale, and the shore establishment as a whole was undermanned." Personnel shortages led several Navy bureaus and offices, when surveyed in January 1946, to request that they be allowed to keep their WAVES; the combined total of these requests was for approximately 1,300 women officers and 9,500 enlisted women.[29]

The Navy also faced a task of heroic proportions in caring for and rehabilitating large numbers of wounded sailors and Marines. Even before the war ended, the Bureau of Medicine and Surgery had asked that an additional thousand enlisted women be recruited each month to serve in the Hospital Corps. Further, the women officers training unit (moved to Washington, D.C., at the end of 1944) was now dedicated solely to training physical or occupational therapists.

Finally, the process of demobilization itself required a substantial amount of manpower. Navy plans called for separation centers through which nearly three million men and women would pass on their return to civilian life. The process of separation would require vast amounts of paperwork, innumerable physical examinations, and the preparation and assembly of medical records, bunks, and meals for the three days each person being demobilized would spend at a separation center.

Large numbers of yeomen, hospital corpsmen, cooks, and storekeepers would be required to operate the centers. Since most of these personnel within the continental United States were WAVES, their loss could slow the demobilization process to a crawl.

The WAVES Go Home

Navy officials had set up five separation centers solely for WAVES and Navy nurses at Washington, D.C., Memphis, San Francisco, Chicago, and New York and had planned a trial run at an interim facility. Because of public pressure for speedy demobilization, the trial run was canceled, and on October 1, 1945, the first WAVES began to pass through the separation centers. Within thirty days nearly nine thousand WAVES and nurses were separated, and by year's end almost twenty-one thousand more had been released to civilian life. Because WAVES came from forty-eight states and were stationed at more than nine hundred naval installations throughout the country and in Hawaii, it soon became apparent that more separation sites were needed. Ten auxiliary centers were quickly set up.[30]

The demobilization plans had been soundly made and were carried off well despite the hasty implementation. Most women were released without incident two or three days after arriving at a separation center, having received physical exams, some orientation regarding their rights as veterans, a final settling of their pay accounts, and the price of a train ticket home. The settling of pay accounts brought a pleasant surprise to some. When Yeoman First Class Mary Gore and other WAVES went through the separation center in Washington, D.C., the women were asked if they had spent any time overseas. Of course most said they had not. Then one of the center staff members said, "When you yeomen left Hunter to go to yeoman school in Oklahoma, wasn't your train routed through Canada? That entitles you to an extra $100."[31] For Hospital Corpsman Marie Bennett, demobilization at the separation center in Memphis provided moments of déjà vu:

> It took three days to get through the regular routine of being discharged: lectures and movies on the conversion of our G.I. insurance, the G.I. Bill of Rights, and such. Then the grand finale . . . the daisy chain, just like at Boot Camp, X-rays, dental clinic, blood tests, E.E.N.T., psychologist, and a dozen more. . . .
>
> Finally I went to the Administration Building for my mustering out pay of $45 for travel expenses from Memphis to Falfurrias and $165

cash. It was the most I have had since the $100 bill . . . that the finance officer gave me at Boot Camp and took away immediately for uniform allowance.

I received a paper saying, "The bearer Marie (N.M.I.)° Bennett is entitled to purchase the American Theater Ribbon," and was issued a Naval Air Technical Training Center coupon book to buy my last bit of necessities before facing civilian prices.

I pinned the "Order of the Ruptured Duck," a little yellow honorable discharge pin from the Naval Reserve, on my lapel and went to a short and concise ceremony, where twenty of us received literature on how to become a civilian. We were no longer expendable government property.[32]

In August 1946, the last contingent of WAVES remaining in Hawaii returned to the United States, and by September demobilization of the WR was largely completed. It had gone well. Even the nation's newspapers, which criticized severely both the Army's and the Navy's demobilization of men, treated it kindly. This chapter in Navy history, it seemed, was closing on the same graceful note on which it had opened.

Both the Navy and the women in it benefited greatly from the wartime experience of the WR. The Navy learned that it could recruit and train large numbers of women rapidly, and employ them in many more fields than originally expected. Moreover, it could manage and lead them as it did its men, when necessary developing appropriate modifications. Women's presence impelled the Navy to improve the quality of life on naval bases, which resulted in unexpected benefits for men and women alike. Finally, the Navy learned that black women could train, live, and serve alongside white women, and that women could serve overseas as well as in the continental United States.

The WAVES' experience instilled in them high self-esteem, especially in retrospect as the Navy publicly acknowledged their many contributions. It expanded horizons by training them for unfamiliar jobs; by compelling them to live and work with women from many different backgrounds; and by enforcing strong discipline and rewarding them with additional responsibilities when they performed well. Most of the women consequently developed, like the Yeomen (F) before them, a strong affection for and loyalty to the Navy—although, as the urgent need for their services abated, most also were more than happy to return home.

°No middle initial.

In 1946 Mildred McAfee Horton (now married to Douglas Horton, a Presbyterian minister) analyzed the women's Navy experience for readers of the *American Journal of Sociology*:

Throw hundreds of young women into a recruit school. Put them into identical clothing; assign identical tasks; provide them with identical stowage space, with instructions as to identical methods of stowage; march them together into a messhall, where they eat what is provided for everyone; submit them to the same tests. Nothing could be more conducive to the emergence of the individual girl, for the first time separated from the setting with which she is normally identified. Wealth, social position, ancestry, professional experience—all vanished upon entrance into the service; and everyone started again to become identified as a person in this new relationship. . . . This loss of civilian reputation gave opportunity for release from limitations to many women. . . . Many discovered new skills and learned new techniques. . . .

Women did not join the military in order to carve out careers for themselves. They knew they were meeting a war need, and they took great satisfaction in doing that. They liked belonging to a great branch of the service. . . . But they are not militarists. They do not like war, with its waste, its worry, its woe. . . . They emerge from the war as more experienced and interesting people.[33]

In the midst of wartime's turbulence and uncertainty, the WAVES created an invaluable legacy for all the Navy women who followed them: spirit, hard work, competence, and dignity. The magnitude of their contributions helped to secure for women a place in the peacetime Navy. However, so successful was the WR that the assumptions on which it was based—some of them quite limiting, such as the unacceptability of women commanding men—dominated the Navy's thinking about its women for the next thirty years. Not until the mid-1960s would these assumptions even be questioned.

6

—

Setting a New Course

"The maintenance of women in the peacetime Naval service is important in the interest of national security."
— REAR ADM. LOUIS DENFELD

As we have seen, during the twenty months following the surrender of America's World War II enemies, the Navy learned that demobilizing would require more women and for a longer period than it had expected. To the extent that Navy planners thought about retaining WAVES at all, it was at first only in the context of short-term needs. By 1946, however, various bureaus and offices were coming to realize how useful women could be in peacetime, and by 1947 the Navy was asking Congress for authority to maintain a small force of women for the regular Navy.

As for the women, most decided to return home, just as most male reservists did. Many resumed the civilian careers they had interrupted to serve the nation's wartime needs. Fortunately for the Navy, a few of its most capable women decided to remain on board. If and when Congress allowed them to do so they were ready to pursue Navy careers, albeit careers limited by traditional assumptions about women's proper roles.

Too Valuable to Release, 1945–48

Secretary of the Navy Forrestal sounded the first alarm about peacetime personnel shortages on August 1, 1945, one week before the first atomic bomb exploded over Hiroshima: "Due to the large number of war casualties remaining in naval hospitals it is necessary to retain all male naval Hospital Corpsmen who have completed less than 18 months' service." Female hospital corpsmen, although not involuntarily retained, were urged to "voluntarily postpone demobilization for any period be-

97

tween 1 September 1946 and 1 July 1947." Two weeks later Navy officials invited all reservists who wished to remain on active duty to apply for extension and repeated the invitation a few days later. But most reservists were ready to go home. Because the oldest and most experienced left earliest, soon "gaping holes began to appear in the naval organization."[1]

On September 9, 1945, the Navy authorized commanding officers to retain those "otherwise eligible for separation . . . for reasons of military necessity" for up to 120 days past their eligibility date until civilians could be employed to finish demobilization. To retain enough officers, in October commanding officers were authorized to recommend for a "spot promotion" any officer above the rank of lieutenant commander who agreed to remain for 180 days past his eligibility date, and in December the Bureau of Naval Personnel reminded them that women officers were eligible for such promotions.

By the end of the year it was clear that civilians were not hurrying to fill the rapidly emptying billets. Thus on January 5, 1946, the Navy inaugurated what became known as gravy train advancement. Commanding officers were notified that since "qualified civilian replacements" were lacking, enlisted women in essential billets were to "be encouraged to voluntarily extend . . . until 1 September 1946," and those volunteering could be advanced one pay grade. Twelve days later, however, lest anyone mistake its intentions about WAVES, the Navy advised commanding officers that "retention of women beyond 1 September is not contemplated."[2]

Perhaps retention beyond that date was not contemplated by some in the Navy Department, but by others it certainly was. Early in February 1946, Capt. Jean Palmer took over as director of the WR from Captain McAfee Horton, who returned full time to her duties at Wellesley. A few days before becoming director Palmer wrote to Lt. Comdr. Winifred Quick in Hawaii that Admiral Denfeld (now chief of naval personnel) "announced in very explosive language to six Admirals and me that the Navy has decided to keep women on active duty in peacetime and we are jolly well to get on our horses and make plans for their administration." On February 19 Palmer sent a more formal message to district directors telling them that plans were now being made for the "incorporation of women into the peacetime structure," even though there was "no assurance that WAVE legislation currently under discussion will be adopted."[3] From "not contemplated" to "legislation currently under discussion" was a major policy change. Regardless of who was or was not contemplating what, and when, the plain fact was that the Navy needed to retain the women. From virtually every corner of the Navy Department clear messages were coming that the numbers of women needed, and the value placed upon their performance, made it no longer wise or feasible to rely on temporary, stopgap extensions.

The Bureau of Aeronautics had employed more women to better advantage than any other component of the Navy, with the possible exception of the Bureau of Medicine and Surgery. WAVES had played a significant role in training Navy aviators and in maintaining their aircraft; these women were too valuable an asset to lose. On July 18, 1945, weeks before the war came to its swift close, it reported that it wanted to keep on active duty five thousand enlisted WAVES and five hundred women officers. These numbers were based on "extensive studies within the aeronautic organization and are based primarily on the fact that experience in the present war has shown that in certain specialized lines of naval aviation work, the capabilities and performances of the women have been superior to those of men."[4]

The Navy's chief of communications also viewed the loss of WAVES with apprehension, citing a need for hundreds of women officers and enlisted women for cryptographic and cryptoanalytic work, for handling highly classified communications, and for radio and wire telegraphy. In addition, WAVES were requested for communications duties overseas for which civilians were not suitable. By February 1946 other bureaus and offices were acknowledging similar needs. The Bureau of Medicine and Surgery (having already involuntarily retained male hospital corpsmen for eighteen months) said it needed large numbers of women officers and enlisted women, as did the Bureau of Supplies and Accounts. The Bureau of Ships and the Bureau of Yards and Docks first said they needed no women, then later changed their minds. The Office of Public Information asked for women officers, saying they were "particularly valuable where contact with feminine activities is required, as with women's magazines and special organizations." In sum, bureaus and offices were calling for a total of about 1,100 women officers and 9,100 enlisted WAVES to serve in the peacetime Navy.[5]

But the Navy's legal authority to keep women in its ranks would expire six months after the war's end. Further legislation would be needed if women were to be retained in peacetime. Until that legislation appeared, the key to retaining women lay in the extension policy already applied to male reservists. In March 1946 the Navy activated the postwar Naval Reserve, and male reservists could be extended on active duty until June 30, 1947. Sauce for the gander could be sauce for the goose, and the Navy promptly asked women officers to volunteer to serve in their present ranks until July 1, 1947, expressing the hope that "a determination of the

**Projected Demand by Navy Bureaus for WAVES
in Peacetime, 1945**

Navy Office	Officers	Enlisted
Bureau of Aeronautics	500	5,000
Communications: United States	378	870
Communications: Overseas	35	173
Bureau of Medicine	150	3,000
Bureaus of S&A and Y&D*	2	32
Public Information	17	0
Totals	1,082	9,075

*The Bureau of Supplies and Accounts and the Bureau of Yards and Docks

place of women in the peacetime Navy can be made" prior to that date.
Of the approximately 3,600 female officers still on active duty, 952,
or about 25 percent, applied. Because of budget limits no more than 500
could be accepted, and a board was convened to select those best
qualified. An additional 300 were approved for retention only until
January 1, 1947, pending their replacement by men. Of that additional
300 one-third were in Supply Corps billets, which were critical because
so many involved the disposition of surplus equipment and the termination of wartime contracts, and because male replacements were unavail-
able. Eight months later, in November 1946, Navy planners asked reserve
officers still on active duty for an even longer commitment, until July 1,
1948.[6]

Why some women officers chose to extend and others did not can be
inferred from the recollections of a few. Like their male counterparts,
most wanted to return to the work they had left for the sake of wartime
service. Mildred McAfee Horton, Mary Josephine Shelly, and Dorothy
Stratton, for example, returned to well-established academic careers,
while Jean Palmer moved on to become dean of admissions at Barnard.
Women of equally high caliber chose to remain in Navy uniform—Louise
Wilde, for instance, who had had a successful academic career before the
war. Joy Hancock, of course, continued the Navy career begun so many
years earlier as a Yeoman (F). Winifred Quick, having made a brilliant
start in the business world before the war, found in the Navy many
opportunities for continued leadership and administrative acumen. So
did Rita Lenihan, a lighting engineer with a classical education who had
spent the war engaged in acquisition, inventory, and planning for some
five hundred of the Navy's shore facilities; one of her jobs was to justify to

Congress the Navy's expenditure on certain facilities. Etta Belle Kitchen left active duty in January 1946, before the postwar reserve was activated, to return to practice law in Oregon. As soon as legislation permitted, she was one of the first women to return to the Navy. These and others like them who stayed or came back provided an extremely competent and loyal cadre of leadership for Navy women in the years to come.

Dr. Grace Murray Hopper wanted to stay on active duty, but the Navy rejected her because she was over the age limit, turning away the most brilliant woman ever to have worn its uniform and one who loved the Navy deeply. Born in 1906, Grace Murray was a Phi Beta Kappa graduate of Vassar with a major in mathematics and physics. In 1930 she married Vincent Hopper, a Phi Beta Kappa graduate of Princeton who later earned his Ph.D. from Columbia. By 1934 she'd earned her Ph.D. in mathematics from Yale, a rare accomplishment for anyone in those days and particularly for a woman. Teaching stints at Vassar and Barnard College followed. When war came she wanted to join the Navy but faced several obstacles. First, the government had determined that mathematicians could best serve as civilians. Also she had to be granted a leave of absence from the Vassar faculty. Finally, she was considered underweight and had to seek a waiver.

One by one she cleared the obstacles and was sworn into the Navy in December 1943. At the Midshipmen's School at Northampton she trained alongside some of her former students. Graduating first in her class, she was commissioned a lieutenant (junior grade) in June 1944. She later told a biographer that when she was commissioned, she took flowers to the grave of her great-grandfather, Rear Adm. Alexander Wilson Russell, and told him it was "all right for females to be Navy officers." The Navy sent her straight to Harvard, where she worked on a computation project. Her arrival coincided with that of the automatic sequence-controlled calculator, also known as the Mark 1 computer. Throughout the war she was part of a team of four other officers and four enlisted men that operated Mark 1 around the clock to perform complex calculations needed to aim the Navy's new guns, acoustic and magnetic mines, self-propelled rockets, and eventually the atomic bomb. When the Navy declined to keep her on active duty after the war, she joined the inactive reserve. Thus did the fortunes of war launch an extraordinary woman on twin paths in computer science and in the Navy. One day those paths would reunite into a career that was as extraordinary as Hopper herself.[7]

At the same time (March 1946) that the Navy was asking women officers to stay on, it was inviting enlisted women to extend until July 1, 1947. The deadline for application was May 1, but by that date only 959, or less than 1 percent, of the 11,500 remaining enlisted women had responded. The Navy extended the deadline to July 1, then once more to July 31. It also invited former WAVES to reenlist, which may have suggested to those still on active duty that perhaps the Navy did have serious long-term intentions for them. In any event, by July 31 about 1,800 more had volunteered to extend, and by December the Navy had reenlisted enough former WAVES to close the invitation. At this time it evidently occurred to someone that the Navy would be well advised to collect the names and addresses of women being released; the Bureau of Navy Personnel urgently requested field activities to forward such information. The following April, women being released were offered the option of enrolling in the inactive reserve or volunteering for the volunteer reserve. As inducements, the Navy offered to allow those enrolling or volunteering to retain their present ratings and seniority, and it held out the possibility of annual two-week periods of active duty. Not mentioned was the obvious advantage to the Navy—that it would have the names and addresses of already-trained women to whom reenlistment might be offered at some future time. Spot checks of some separation centers revealed that as many as 90 percent of the women returning to civilian life were willing to continue some formal association with the Navy.[8]

The Case for Women in the Peacetime Navy

The Navy's determination to acquire permanent status for its women owed something to the WAVES' highly applauded contributions during World War II, but little to a desire to grant them a more equitable footing with Navy men. Rather, it reflected general apprehension that the recent war had not necessarily resulted in a world made safe for democracy. Even before the shooting stopped in August 1945, the United States found itself at ever-increasing odds with the Soviet Union, its erstwhile ally. So long as that confrontation stayed relatively manageable at the diplomatic level American armed power might be allowed to shrink back closer to prewar levels—but only if the means for rapid expansion were readily at hand. It was on this view of a smaller but rapidly expansible force that the Navy predicated its case for seeking permanent status for its women.

Two and a half years of struggle would elapse before Congress granted the desired authority. The struggle was made all the harder by the fact that the Navy itself was a house divided; not everyone in it believed that women should serve in peacetime.

The Flawed Strategy of 1946

In February 1946 Comdr. Joy Bright Hancock was transferred to the Bureau of Naval Personnel expressly to begin the process of drafting proposals to Congress for the needed legislation. She based her work on two major premises: that, insofar as practical, women should fit into existing Navy structures and that they should serve not only in the regular Navy on a career basis but also in the active and inactive Naval Reserve. She met considerable resistance.

> I recall frustrations of mind because of the apathy on the part of a large number of persons with whom I must deal. At times this apathy appeared to me to be lack of cooperation and it finally brought me to the point where I began conferences by saying, "I have been instructed by the Chief of Naval Personnel to prepare these plans concerning the possible use of the services of women in the Navy on a permanent basis. If you care to work from an absolutely negative recommendation, I will be glad to append your views to my report to the Chief." Such an approach was a measure of my desperation.[9]

But she made sufficient headway that in March Representative Carl Vinson introduced to the second session of the Seventy-Ninth Congress a bill to amend the 1942 legislation, and hearings before the House Committee on Naval Affairs were scheduled for May.

Navy officials took the view that since the legislation concerned Navy women, they should be the ones to testify before the committee. This strategy proved fatal to the proposed bill for two reasons. First, committee members, faced mainly with Navy women, were not convinced that the bill represented the Navy's own views: Why weren't more Navy leaders front and foremost in testifying for it? Second, the senior Navy woman, Capt. Jean Palmer, was herself planning to return to civilian life the following month. In testifying for the bill she was only carrying out orders, for she did not believe in a career for women in the Navy and frankly said so.

Further, the wartime leaders of women in all the services had, like Capt. Mildred McAfee Horton, returned to civilian life. Their views opposing the service of women in peacetime were known and weighed heavily against the bill. These women were concerned about the welfare of a relatively small number of women expected to adjust to a rigid male environment. Also, they suspected that male acceptance of the women thus far had been only tentative, based chiefly on wartime urgency. In peacetime, acceptance would likely be even less, to the detriment of the women's morale and well-being. These views did not necessarily reflect those of many younger women who hoped for a continuing career in uniform, who might have agreed with their leaders' observations but could have drawn different conclusions. Since many civilian professions were hardly notable for the extent to which they accepted women, lack of full acceptance in the Navy was therefore no conclusive reason to leave a way of life and service they had come to like. All things considered, they were willing, even eager, to take their chances with the Navy. But Congress never heard their views.

The bill died in committee, and the Seventy-Ninth Congress adjourned in the summer of 1946 before further action could be taken.

Navy Pulls Together: The Second Attempt

In June 1946 Hancock, now a captain and succeeding Jean Palmer as director of the WR, pondered the lessons of defeat and began to mount a second campaign. Her accession to the top post introduced something new: For the first time women of the Navy were led by one whose whole life had been a preparation for the job she now held. Joy Bright was born in 1898 to William Henry and Priscilla Buck Bright, in Wildwood, New Jersey. The third of six children, she grew up learning many skills, including carpentry and mechanical repairs. The summer that she was fourteen, her parents left her in charge of their business office for two weeks while they attended a political convention in Chicago. Years later, when her father was New Jersey's lieutenant governor and president of its Senate, he installed Joy's sister, Eloise, as the senate's executive secretary, the first woman to hold that post. In the Bright family, position depended more on ability than on gender. From the time she put on the uniform of a Yeoman (F), Hancock's whole life was taken up with the Navy. If ever anyone was born to a position, Joy Bright Hancock was born to become director of the Navy's WR.

Her first step as director was to gather a strong team of women officers. Comdr. Bess Dunn and Lt. Comdr. Winifred Quick were transferred from their respective posts in Corpus Christi and Hawaii to join her. They both had significant experience as senior women officers in field activities where large numbers of WAVES had served, and in addition Quick had an extensive background in personnel planning, in both civilian life and the Navy. Dunn served as assistant director, handling day-to-day details, freeing Hancock and the others to concentrate on preparations for the next legislative proposal. Also assigned was Comdr. Louise Wilde, who had been instrumental in getting favorable publicity for the wartime WAVES.

The next step was to develop a more unified approach to Congress. Hancock argued that any legislative proposal must be seen as a Navy bill, not just a women's bill. Accordingly, Navy men must carry the ball the next time around, just as they did for all other naval legislation. She asked permission to get help and advice from all divisions in the Bureau of Naval Personnel and from field activities. Her final request was that a senior male officer be assigned to help her prepare material needed for the next round of congressional hearings.[10]

Hancock was able to report some highly favorable responses to the prospect of women in the peacetime Navy:

> The proposed legislation to include women both in the Regular Navy and the Naval Reserve during peacetime was discussed with commanding officers and department heads at each activity. Each officer interviewed on this subject favored such legislation not only because the WAVES have proved their usefulness in the Naval establishment, but also because it is important to maintain a nucleus of trained personnel for planning purposes in case of any future national emergency. Vice Admiral George Murray, Commandant of the 9th Naval District, was particularly enthusiastic about the continuation of the WAVE program [in view of] the work record, morale and good disciplinary record of WAVES who have served under his command. [However, some officers felt that if appropriations were to be cut way back, women should be let go before men.][11]

Meanwhile, Quick was working out details of a personnel plan for women in the regular Navy. In what billets would they be needed, with what skills, and for how long? A central issue was the rotation of women, like men, from one assignment to another to increase their professional experience and give them the opportunity to plot a Navy career. Also, age limitations for women officers would have to be more elastic than for male officers in the same ranks, at least initially, because the original legislation had limited all but a few women to the most junior ranks regardless of age. Quick went from one Navy office to another seeking advice and endorsement of her evolving plans. Neither was gained easily; for many Navy men, the notion of women pursuing careers in the Navy was too alien to grasp. Realizing that the men's arguments were based more on opposition to the whole concept of women in the regular Navy than on the merit of her proposals, Quick developed a simple but devastating tactic to gain endorsement. She said to them,

> Look, I'm not fighting the battle of whether or not women should be in the Regular Navy. That's a Congressional battle. All I'm doing is trying to set up plans so that we have something to go on if and when the legislation passes. If you oppose my suggestions, please write down the reason for your opposition so that the chief of naval personnel may review your reasoning.

Without exception, opponents declined to commit themselves in writing.[12]

Assigned to counsel Hancock in preparing material was Capt. Fred R. Stickney, neither in full accord with the provisions nor convinced that the Navy needed women in peacetime. But he set aside his personal opinions and proved a shrewd, loyal, and thoroughly professional guide. Franklin Schuyler, a longtime civilian legislative aide in the bureau, also provided invaluable support by scrutinizing material that Hancock gathered.[13]

Before a proposal could be offered to Congress it had to pass muster with the Navy's own lawyers, the staff of the judge advocate general (JAG) of the Navy. Here again Hancock met with frustration when some JAG staff members opposed the proposed legislation. But like Stickney they accepted their marching orders. As they worked together Hancock found herself playing "that old game of 'Well, what do *you* think?' and 'What's *your* idea?' " With her knowledge of what women had done in naval aviation during the war, supplemented by enthusiastic testimony regarding women's abilities from aircraft company executives, she was able to swing Navy lawyers around to her way of thinking. This was a critical turn, for

> they were not about to draft anything [legislation] they couldn't defend before Congress, so they'd actually develop the arguments! Well, as the JAG men got more and more involved with this legislation, and worked on how to present it to Congress, soon they started thinking of it as *their* legislation. So of course the Navy Department had to get behind [it]. . . .[14]

The efforts of Capt. Ira Nunn of JAG's legislative division were particularly useful in redrafting the proposed bill so that it not only met the Navy's needs but also was acceptable to Congress.

In 1947 Congress passed the National Security Act, under which the three armed services retained their separate identities but were federated under the Department of Defense. This development meant that Hancock and her cohorts had to work with their counterparts in the other services to present mutually supportive testimony to Congress. In contrast to the men's debates on unification issues, the women's interservice conferences were characterized by a spirit of amiable cooperation.[15]

Once More unto Congress

Hearings on a combined Army-Navy bill before the Senate Armed Services Committee began on July 2, 1947. In what the *New York Times* described on July 3 as "an all-out legislative effort" on the part of the Army and the Navy, the two best-known and most widely admired wartime leaders came forth to endorse the request for permanent status for servicewomen. Gen. Dwight D. Eisenhower and Adm. Chester W. Nimitz both gracefully conceded that they were converts to the cause. Eisenhower emphasized the urgent need for women so that men could be released to serve in the infantry. Furthermore, he said, "We cannot ask those women to remain on duty, nor can we ask qualified personnel to volunteer, if we cannot offer them permanent status and prestige." Nimitz spoke in a similar vein and echoed a point Eisenhower had made that disciplinary problems with women were "practically non-existent." A parade of Navy admirals followed. Vice Adm. Donald B. Duncan, deputy CNO for air, made a case in favor of WAVES

> on the basis of an essential preparation for possible future war. . . . After the enemy blow falls there is not the time to create the needed facilities without great loss of life and money. . . . After the Women's Reserve program got underway, no pilot went into combat without having received somewhere in his training instruction from WAVE specialists.

Rear Adm. W. A. Buck of the Supply Corps stated that in many billets "women are at least as capable as men. In many of the detailed tasks required to assure the necessary flow [of supplies] they are more adept." Rear Adm. Clifford Swanson, the Navy's surgeon general, said, "There exists at this time an urgent need for 2,000 WAVES," while Rear Adm. E. E. Stone, the chief of naval communications, testified that military personnel were needed for communications duties—civil servants were "not as satisfactory."[16]

These witnesses, each from the perspective of his own branch, were outlining for Congress the case that Rear Adm. Louis Denfeld, of the Bureau of Naval Personnel, had summed up for the secretary of the Navy earlier in the year.

Under the terms of the wartime legislation currently in effect, the service of women has been of inestimable value to the Navy. In certain specialized fields women have proved themselves to be superior in the performance of the work. The duty performed by WAVES has become so vital to shore activities that the termination of authority to utilize their services in the Navy would be a serious loss to the efficiency of the shore establishment and to the trained resources upon which the Navy needs to draw in time of emergency. This is particularly true in communications, aviation, supply and in the Hospital Corps. . . . It is inconceivable that in any future emergency the services of the women will not again be needed. The opposite is true and there will be a need for overwhelmingly larger numbers. Therefore the maintenance of women in the peacetime Naval service is important in the interest of national security.

Lessons of World War II should not be disregarded. Seven months elapsed after December 7, 1941 before the Congress enacted the basic legislation permitting women to serve in the Naval Reserve. It took over six months more before the first groups of women were recruited, trained, and reported to their duty stations.

The training was to a large extent trial and error. We were handicapped by having no [women] petty officers for many months and there were no commissioned [women] officers with previous Naval experience. In a few short years the women trained for service in this war will not be available for recall to active duty. It is therefore important that a trained nucleus be kept on active duty should a rapid expansion be necessary.

With constant developments in the technological, scientific and medical fields we must keep our nucleus of women activated in order to keep abreast of these developments.[17]

The Senate Committee reported favorably on the bill two weeks later, but not before it had heard one piece of surprising testimony. Committee members had questioned the possibility of women being incapacitated during menopause. An admiral testified that since 1942 only eighteen WAVES had been given discharges for ailments related to menopause,

and the Army's surgeon general testified that the discomforts of menopause could be satisfactorily treated. Hancock sensed that the testimony
had not completely assured the committee, so she asked the Navy's
surgeon general to provide a stronger statement. One can only guess with
what emotions the men on the committee received these words from
Rear Admiral Swanson:

> The commonly held idea that women are invalided in their middle
> years by the onset of the menopause is largely a popular fallacy. It is
> well known that men pass through the same physiological change with
> symptomatology closely resembling that of women.
>
> Experience with our Navy nurses has shown that the question of the
> climacteric or menopause has never been a problem. The average
> professional woman is well balanced mentally and physically, and this
> normal physiological change occurring in late middle life is usu-
> ally passed with little or no serious disability or residual effects. . . .
> Since 1931, 440 nurses have been physically retired from the naval
> service, and of these only one was retired with the diagnosis of meno-
> pause. . . . Finally, in comparing the possible extra hazard in the fe-
> male officer . . . I repeat, a similar involutional period occurs in the
> male.[18]

Hearings before the House Armed Services Committee began on
March 23, 1948. The eight-month interim was necessary because now
two more groups of servicewomen were to be included in proposed
legislation: women in the Marine Corps, which had reversed its position
that women should serve only in the reserve, and women in the Air Force.
More significant, however, was that subcommittees of the House committee could not agree on whether women should serve only in peacetime
reserves or in regular components as well. As the subcommittees delib-
erated, women leaders in the services told Senator Margaret Chase Smith
of Maine, their champion, that they would sacrifice the provision for
regular status if it seemed that insisting on it might kill the bill. Senator
Smith would have none of this. To her the issue was straightforward:
Either the services needed women permanently or they did not. If the
need was permanent, then women should be granted regular status.
Smith was not prepared to vote for reserve status only.[19]

While all the services used the interim to prepare the strongest affirm-
ative testimony, various opponents were conveying their views to the
House committee members. Some of these opinions were transmitted
furtively to the committee, and their proponents were never publicly
identified. The Fleet Reserve Association (at that time an organization of

retired Navy enlisted men) was believed to be among the covert opponents.[20]

Among the issues addressed in open committee was the sensitive question of whether servicemen might ever have to take orders from servicewomen. The bill's wording was amended to give service secretaries discretion to prescribe both the duties and the authority that women would have in their respective services. The House committee, like its Senate counterpart, wanted to ensure that women would not be employed as combatants. For the Navy, this issue was resolved by the provision that they would not be assigned to combat ships and aircraft.

Another sensitive issue was aired when Representative Dewey Short of Missouri said to Hancock, "Tell me how many pregnancies you've had with these women in the Navy." Hancock responded that she did not have that information, that pregnancy was a medical question. Short asked, "Isn't there any discipline connected with it when a woman had a baby?" Hancock said no, no more than there was for the man who fathered the child. She explained that eligibility to serve was the issue, not discipline; Navy policy was that women with children were not eligible for naval service. Then she asked Short, "Are you under the impression that these women who became pregnant weren't married?" He did not answer. After a moment Representative James E. Van Zandt of Pennsylvania, who had served in the Navy during both world wars and retired as a rear admiral in the Naval Reserve in 1946, leaped to his feet and admonished his colleague, "I think the Captain should have an apology for that implication, if that's what you're implying!"[21] No further questions arose on the issue.

Most of the questions asked by the House committee related to overall policy and the program's implementation. They were answered by Vice Adm. Thomas L. Sprague, chief of naval personnel, and Captain Stickney. That the largest burden of testimony was presented by senior male officers gave weight to the Navy's position.

The House committee voted to pass only that portion of the legislation authorizing women in reserve status. Now it remained for a joint committee of the House and the Senate to determine whether the Senate version of the bill recommending their full integration into regular status was to be adopted. Senator Smith, angered that the House committee appeared to have acted on pressures applied by unidentified informants and otherwise used underhanded parliamentary maneuvering, wrote a sharp letter to James V. Forrestal, former secretary of the Navy and now the nation's first secretary of defense. She noted that while civilian and military heads of the armed services had unanimously urged regular status for women, legislative and liaison officers of the same services had opposed it covertly.[22]

> The basic question is whether we are to accept official "on the record" statements of the executive and military heads of the Armed Services or the "behind closed doors" statements of your legislative representatives to individual members of the Committee. . . . I believe that immediate action and reply on your part is imperative.[23]

Forrestal promptly stated to the various committee members that the Department of Defense believed it was imperative that permanent regular status be granted to women. In addition to this unequivocal statement from the respected Forrestal, the House committee also began to receive telegrams and letters from influential individuals and organizations throughout the country, including business and professional associations for women such as the American Association of University Women, urging acceptance of the Senate version. Once again Eisenhower and Nimitz, as well as the Commandant of the Marine Corps, Gen. Alexander A. Vandergrift, testified to the value of women's services and the importance of their integration into the regular forces. Faced with this barrage, the House committee gave up all opposition.

On June 12, 1948, Congress passed the Women's Armed Services Integration Act (Public Law 625). President Truman signed it on July 30, exactly six years after President Roosevelt had signed the bill that allowed women to enter the Naval Reserve. Both the Navy and its women had come a long way in those years.

Public Law 625

The primary purpose of the Women's Armed Services Integration Act was to provide an ongoing means by which to call upon large numbers of women in the event of another national emergency. Experience gained from a peacetime nucleus would help to identify and catalog the service billets most suitable for women and to determine the types of training needed. The act's provisions reflected service objectives as well as apprehensions regarding women. Specifically, the act

1. Gave permanent status to women in the regular and reserve components of all the armed forces
2. Authorized the enlistment of women and the appointment of commissioned and warrant officers in the regular and reserve components
3. Limited the number of women on duty in the regular component to no more than 2 percent of each service
4. Allowed only one woman in each service to hold the rank of captain (colonel in the Army, Air Force, and Marine Corps) and only temporarily, with the Navy woman captain to be known as an assistant to the chief of naval personnel, responsible for plans and policy for women, or ACNP(W)
5. Allowed only 10 percent of remaining women officers to hold the rank of commander (lieutenant colonel in the other services), and, in the Navy, only 20 percent could hold the rank of lieutenant commander
6. Separated women officers' promotion lists from those for male officers, except in the Air Force
7. Set the minimum enlistment age at eighteen, with parental consent required for any woman under age twenty-one who wished to enlist
8. Authorized service secretaries to prescribe the authority women might exercise and prohibited women from duty in aircraft "while such aircraft are engaged in combat missions," nor could they be assigned to duty on any Navy vessels except hospital ships and naval transports
9. Allowed women to claim husbands and/or children as dependents only if they could prove that these family members were in fact dependent on them for "chief support"
10. Gave the service secretaries blanket authority to terminate the regular commission or enlistment of any woman "under circumstances and in accordance with regulations prescribed by the President"

The limitations on ranks and percentages of women allowed in any given service were in keeping with the nucleus concept. Allowing women to reach no permanent rank higher than commander (or lieutenant colonel) severely restricted not only individual advancement but also their impact on any but women's programs. Even the most senior woman in a service, as only a temporary captain or colonel, had neither entree to nor influence on that service's highest decision-making councils. The provisions concerning authority and types of duty ensured that women would not serve in combat or exercise military authority over men. The separate promotion list meant that women would be competing for promotion only with women, not with men. The requirement for parental consent for women under the age of twenty-one to enlist reflected society's view that women needed parental guidance longer than men did, while the provision regarding husbands and children reflected its view that, unless proven otherwise, husbands rather than wives were breadwinners. Finally, the service secretaries' blanket authority to discharge any woman, officer or enlisted, facilitated the discharge of pregnant women or women who married men with dependent children.

The period from 1945 to 1948 was critical in the history of women in the Navy. When it began, most Navy planners saw only immediate postwar needs; many assumed that once these needs were met the Navy could return to being a small, all-male professional force. But the cold war precluded this, and by 1947 the Navy realized the need for a cadre of women members in case another shooting war required full mobilization. The Navy joined the Army and the Air Force in seeking legislation to include women in the peacetime armed forces. The wartime assumptions that restricted the use of women carried over into the provisions of the Women's Armed Services Integration Act of 1948, casting them in legal concrete that would last for a quarter of a century.

From today's vantage point, the Integration Act might more accurately have been named the Incorporation Act. Prohibited from duty in any unit designated as having a combat mission, women were effectively not integrated into the heart of the military and naval professions; that is, they were merely incorporated in service organizations. Still, the act remains a landmark in the history of women in the armed forces, and subsequent legislation has amended some of its more discriminatory provisions. Its passage implied that the armed forces could not allow themselves the luxury of depending solely on *man*power.

The most obvious aspect of the act remained almost totally unacknowledged for many years: Although the WAVES no longer existed, the obsolete acronym continued in popular and official usage by both men and women until the early 1970s. The senior Navy woman on active duty continued to be referred to far more often as the director of the WAVES than as ACNP (W). Although the acronym was apt and former WAVES remaining in the Navy were much attached to it, this and other anachronisms symbolized the Navy's ambivalence toward its women. So long as they were referred to comfortably as WAVES, it could be inferred that they were somehow not members of the real Navy.

Nonetheless, the act represented a remarkable advancement for Navy women. Now they could capitalize on what the WAVES had won: a career in the peacetime Navy. For them, well aware that until six years earlier nurses had been the only women allowed to serve in peacetime, the act's very passage far outshone its restrictions. As Joy Hancock later wrote, "The victory was sweet."[24]

PART THREE

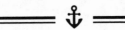

Women in the Regular Navy

7

—

A Nucleus Is Launched and Tested

"Y ou were . . . only staff, advisory. The only way you got anything done was by diplomacy and persuasion."
—CAPT. WINIFRED QUICK COLLINS, ACNP (W)

On July 7, 1948, six enlisted women inaugurated a new era in the history of women in the U.S. Navy. On that day Kay Langdon, Wilma Marchal, Edna Young, Frances Devaney, Doris Robertson, and Ruth Flora were sworn into the regular Navy. They joined those branches of the Navy where WAVES had served in the greatest numbers and made the most significant contributions: Langdon, attached to the Naval Air Transport Command, represented the thousands who had performed so many varied and nontraditional jobs in aviation; Marchal and Young represented the vast number of clerical workers; Devaney, the large number of storekeepers and disbursing clerks; Robertson, the many who had shouldered much of the Navy's vital communications burden; and finally Flora, the thousands of hospital corpsmen on whom the Navy had depended so heavily.[1] Like Loretta Perfectus Walsh, the first woman to be enlisted in the Naval Reserve back in 1917, these six women, the first ever to be enlisted in the regular Navy, were a new phenomenon.

From the women officers who had remained on active duty, nearly three hundred were selected to be commissioned in the regular Navy. The first eight of these—Joy Hancock, Winifred Quick, Ann King, Frances Willoughby, Ellen Ford, Doris Cranmore, Doris Defenderfer, and Betty Rae Tennant—were sworn in on October 15, 1948. Like the six enlisted women this group also represented major areas of the WAVES' contribution. Hancock, for example, had served in aviation, Quick in personnel, Ford in the Supply Corps, and Cranmore in the medical field.

There would now be a nucleus of women that could quickly be expanded in case of war. It was to be small, approximately five hundred officers and six thousand enlisted personnel, and versatile, including clerks and storekeepers; medical, aviation, and communications specialists; and administrators, recruiters, instructors, and leaders. It offered the Navy the opportunity to discover, in peacetime, what other tasks they could or should be trained to do. Before this opportunity could be explored, however, the Navy was once more in a shooting war, and its most immediate concern regarding women was to expand their numbers as quickly as possible. Korea forced the Navy to test the nucleus concept.

The Nucleus Gets Under Way

Of whom was this nucleus to consist? First were the 1,926 WAVES who remained on active duty from the end of the war in 1945 to July 1948. Second were former WAVES who had returned to civilian life. Like those who had stayed on active duty, they were invited to apply for acceptance into the regular Navy. This group, not in need of initial training, could provide a cadre of experienced petty officers and commissioned officers. Finally, the Navy would seek new blood. Recruiting for women with no Navy experience started on September 15, 1948. Although the new legislation authorized the enlistment of eighteen-year-olds, and the other armed services did in fact accept them, Navy planners decided as a matter of administrative policy to keep a minimum age of twenty years for enlisted women and twenty-one years for women officers.

In many ways the nucleus concept was validated immediately. The basic machinery with which to recruit, train, and classify Navy women was in place. Qualifications had already been determined and tested between 1942 and 1945. What had been learned at the training sites during World War II—Northampton, Hunter, and Cedar Falls—could be applied at the first women's regular Navy boot camp, the Naval Training Station at Great Lakes, Illinois. On October 5, 1948, only three weeks after recruiting began, the first class of 320 women recruits reported for training. The officer-in-charge was Lt. Kathryn Dougherty, assisted by eleven other women officers and fourteen women petty officers. No need now to call upon men to train the recruits; Navy women veterans could do the job.

Other dividends from the WAVES' experience immediately became apparent. Jobs to which women could be assigned had already been identified, and women had already proven themselves capable of handling them. More significantly, the idea of women serving in the armed forces was no longer novel; Navy men as well as the general public were accustomed to it, although whether some welcomed it was something else again.

One small question that arose was soon answered happily. The WAVES' uniform had been dark blue with stripes of light blue (known as reserve blue), whereas male naval officers and Navy nurses wore midnight blue with gold stripes. But now shouldn't women's uniforms reflect their new status? Here was a delicate issue. Relations between WAVE officers and Navy nurses had sometimes been touchy. Some believed the nurses resented the fact that a few WAVE officers had been granted relatively high rank immediately after the WR was created. Also, public attention had focused on the WAVES as a new phenomenon, to the exclusion of women nurses who had been serving in the Navy since 1908 (and, for that matter, of the Yeomen [F] who had preceded the WAVES by a quarter of a century). Would adoption of midnight-blue uniforms with gold stripes by women officers who were not nurses exacerbate the resentment? On the other hand, former WAVES did not want to adopt the nurses' uniform, which was far less attractive. With her usual tact Capt. Joy Hancock discussed the matter with the director of the Navy Nurse Corps, Capt. Nellie Jane DeWitt. There quickly appeared the makings of an amicable deal. Captain DeWitt conceded that the nurses would appreciate being able to adopt the more attractive WAVE uniform. In return, they would take no umbrage at midnight-blue uniforms with gold stripes being worn by other women naval officers. Following a survey of preferences regarding the proposal, the new uniform was authorized on May 1, 1950.[2]

Training for Enlisted Women

By the end of its first year of operation the recruit training unit at Great Lakes had graduated 1,257 women. All were high-school graduates (or had passed a high-school equivalency test), some had additional informal training or college experience, and a few held college degrees. Their work experience prior to joining the Navy reflected these educational levels. Most had been in clerical jobs, while a few had been teachers; among the rest numerous occupations were represented, for example, photographer, laboratory assistant, radio operator. They came from all over the country, from small and large cities and towns and from rural areas as well. Their motives for joining the Navy varied: travel, or a career, or a challenge, or independence from their families. In other words they were much like the Yeomen (F) and the WAVES before them, with one exception. Their predecessors had joined the Navy during wartime, chiefly to serve their country. Women recruits of the peacetime era did not necessarily lack patriotism, but it was not their primary reason for enlisting. Their enthusiasm was equally marked (they were, after all, volunteers), but it was sparked more by their own desires and interests than by their country's.

The task facing women veterans who trained these recruits was the same one that faced all who "pushed boots": to turn a heterogeneous group of young people into sailors. Indeed, for the women recruits the training staff had the following objectives, which were much like those for men recruits:

- Develop observance of naval customs and traditions, appreciation of naval history, and obedience to naval discipline
- Teach naval subjects and develop physical fitness thoroughly enough to enable recruits to be immediately useful to their assigned units
- Promote high standards of responsibility, conduct, manners, and morals
- Inculcate an understanding and appreciation of the fundamental workings of democracy, and of the Navy's role in American society
- Develop each recruit's understanding of her place within the Navy and her importance to it, and develop pride in herself and in the Navy[3]

The staff had ten weeks to accomplish these aims. Recruits followed a regime that would have caused instant déjà vu in any veteran of Cedar Falls or Hunter, with the exception of two new wrinkles. Greatly improved was the classification process by which Navy and recruit sized each other up. Before a recruit took her classification interviews, she was taught far more than her predecessors about jobs open to women, for far more was now known about such jobs. She was also taught much more about Navy jobs open only to men, because, according to the Bureau of Naval Personnel,

the Navy is still going to be made up of men—98 percent of it or more. If women recruits are to be able to fit into their own small niches, assuming their proper positions as working members of a very large outfit where there are many jobs which are beyond them physically, then it is necessary for them to recognize the ratings held by men only and to understand something of the basic responsibilities of those ratings.[4]

In other words, the new women recruits needed a more comprehensive understanding of the Navy's enlisted rating structure because, unlike the Yeomen (F) and WAVES, some of them might serve for an entire career. Phrases like "their own small niches" and "proper position" reveal the Navy's fundamental view of women—as well as women's own view about their place in the Navy. Acceptance and propriety were expected of Navy women in 1948 and for nearly twenty years more.

The second wrinkle was Great Lakes itself. Here was a large naval station where the Navy had been training recruits for decades. It was a far cry from the civilian college campus at Hunter for which Lts. Elizabeth Reynard and Joy Hancock had scrounged a handful of artifacts to create a Navy atmosphere for WAVE recruits. And women recruits at Great Lakes were not as landlocked as WAVE recruits had been, for they could be taken for brief trips on small Navy vessels berthed at piers on Lake Michigan. As for the recruits, they viewed their training positively but not uncritically. One told an observer, "It's interesting and educational, but very hard at times. Military training should be compulsory for all girls for a year or two."[5]

Following recruit training, more than half the women were assigned to specialized training schools. The airman school was the most popular, followed by the radioman, hospitalman, and yeoman schools. In smaller numbers women reported to schools for training as telemen, dental and electronic technicians, storekeepers, disbursing clerks, personnelmen, printers, lithographers, and journalists. Those who went directly to duty assignments were scattered among the Navy's major shore installations: San Diego, San Francisco, and Seattle on the West Coast; Boston, Philadelphia, Norfolk, and Charleston on the East Coast; and Chicago in the Midwest. The Naval Air Training Command (centered at Pensacola, Florida) and the Potomac River Naval Command in Washington, D.C., claimed the largest numbers of graduated recruits.

Training for Women Officers

In May 1949 twenty-nine female ensigns graduated from a five-month training course at Newport, Rhode Island, the first to enter the Navy since the last class had graduated from Northampton early in 1945. The officer-in-charge of the newly established indoctrination unit (later known as the Women Officers School) was Lt. Comdr. Sybil A. Grant, who had formerly been attached to the training division of the Bureau of Naval Personnel. She was assisted by a male lieutenant commander and three female lieutenants.

As it did for their enlisted shipmates, the training for new officers built strongly on WAVE experience—veterans of Northampton probably could have walked through the Newport program in their sleep. The trainees studied naval tradition, history, customs, organization, administration, and correspondence, and they learned to recognize different kinds of Navy aircraft and ships. Those who could not type were taught to do so. They learned to drill, and daily swimming classes were mandatory. They also stood watch and took turns as platoon leaders and company commanders. The most significant carryover from the WAVE years was the unremitting emphasis on ladylike behavior. Trainees were issued a handbook that closed with these words: "Remember always that you are a lady, a woman whose habits, manners, and sentiments are characteristic of the highest degree of refinement."[6] Like the enlisted recruits, they came from varied backgrounds, and their reasons for joining the Navy had more to do with a desire for new opportunities, for travel and adventure, than with patriotism. All were between twenty-one and twenty-five years of age, and all were college graduates.

Also like the enlisted recruits, these new women officers had a longer training period than their WAVE predecessors (five months instead of four), and their training took place on a naval station rather than on a college campus. The naval station at Newport was home to numerous naval activities, notably the Naval War College and several squadrons of destroyers. Further up Narragansett Bay was the Naval Air Station at Quonset Point, and not far away was the Navy's premier submarine complex at New London, Connecticut. Day-long visits to these installations would give the women a glimpse into Navy operations not available to WAVE officers trained at Northampton.

Also at Newport was the Officer Candidate School (OCS) where the Navy indoctrinated male college graduates and then commissioned and sent them to active duty. The women trained at Newport had credentials similar to those of the OCS students. Besides possessing a bachelor's degree, they had passed a physical examination, they were within the prescribed age limits, and they wanted to join the Navy. These men and women had more in common than not. Logically, a single training unit could have prepared both for their duties, its curriculum diverging toward the end to emphasize fleet billets for men and shore billets for women. But that was not acceptable in 1949. Twenty years would pass before training for future officers of both sexes would even begin to be integrated.

A significant difference from the WAVE experience was that much attention had been given to the question of the women's career patterns. For more than a year, the Bureau of Naval Personnel had been developing guidelines for the proper assignment, rotation, and distribution of women officers. These guidelines, stated in the Navy's *Training Bulletin*, had two aims. The first was to develop each officer's individual skills so as "to produce the most useful women career officers, capable of assuming the maximum amount of responsibility in the shore establishment." The second was to develop within the women's corps the ability to absorb, train, and deploy vastly expanded numbers of women if necessary. Personnel studies had also considered how to round out the experience of former WAVE officers now commissioned in the regular Navy. Many of those officers had served in only one or two billets during their six years of duty. They needed to be rotated through various duty assignments so that they could "provide the necessary leadership in the many fields where large numbers of women would be utilized in the event of a national emergency."

Both experienced women officers and those now coming on board, like their male counterparts, were expected to continue training and education while on active duty. They were encouraged to apply for correspondence courses, special schools, and postgraduate schools. These included courses in public information and educational services, naval justice, aerological engineering, foreign languages, personnel administration and training, and naval intelligence.

Shaping the Nucleus

As the first six enlisted women were being sworn into the regular Navy, a group of planners was studying the Navy's enlisted job structure to determine where women could and should serve. They identified twenty-eight ratings as "highly desirable," three as "desirable," six as "acceptable," and the remaining twenty-four as "not suited." Almost all those listed in the fourth category were jobs performed chiefly on ships. Thus, of sixty-one ratings held by enlisted Navy men the planners determined that almost half were highly desirable for women; if the nine in the desirable and acceptable categories were added, then a total of thirty-seven, or more than half, could be held by women.[7]

Yet in 1950 a proposal to restrict women to only eighteen of these ratings gained attention as it worked its way through the Navy's policy-making levels (see table). Most aviation ratings and nearly all technical ratings were to be closed to women.

This proposal was rejected, partly because the bureau's director of research considered it counter to both the nucleus concept and Congress's wishes. He wrote,

> In the event of mobilization there will be an urgent need for trained personnel in these ratings. Training in these ratings in peacetime will

Ratings Held by Navy Enlisted Women in 1948, Grouped by Bureau of Naval Personnel Criteria

Highly Desirable

Aviation Electronicsman	Instrumentman	Opticalman
Aviation Electronic Technician	Commissaryman	Lithographer
Aviation Electrician's Mate	Ships Serviceman	Printer
Aviation Structural Mechanic	Disbursing Clerk*	Yeoman*
Aviation Storekeeper*	Air Controlman*	Radioman*
Communication Technician*	Parachute Rigger*	Draftsman*
Training Deviceman*	Dental Technician*	Journalist*
Photographer's Mate*	Personnelman*	Storekeeper*
Aerographer's Mate*	Hospital Corpsman*	Teleman*
Machine Accountant*		

Desirable

Fire Control Technician	Aviation Machinist's Mate	Electronics Technician

Acceptable

Aviation Ordnanceman	Patternmaker	Musician
Machinery Repairman	Radarman	Sonarman

*Ratings to which women were to be restricted according to a 1950 proposal by Navy analysts. Sources: Bureau of Personnel memos Pers-153-rb of July 6, 1948, and Pers-B2f-NCF of July 7, 1950, file 106, "Utilization (1948–66)," box 17, series I, ACNP(W), Navy Operational Archives.

provide a nucleus of qualified women immediately available for assignment to duty as petty officers and as leaders. . . . Congress was assured that enlisted women would be utilized not only in clerical ratings but also in various technical and other ratings. This was to avoid possible repercussions from the Civil Service Commission.[8]

Nevertheless, and despite women's proven capabilities in many aviation and technical ratings, the thrust of the rejected proposal soon prevailed. While it was under discussion, in fact, three aviation ratings were closed to women. As a result, 104 well-trained, experienced women in those ratings were involuntarily transferred into others deemed more suitable.[9] During the next decade the number of ratings open to women would continue to decline.

The single strongest impetus for limiting women to traditional ratings lay in the fact that the Navy perceived no great need for them in its technical fields. The basis for limiting women to *fewer* ratings was that there were so few women: They constituted no more than about 1 percent of the Navy's total active-duty force. By far the largest numbers were in administrative, clerical, and medical ratings; in any given technical rating women numbered only in the dozens. Except at very large facilities women were few and far between, yet Navy policy was to have all enlisted women live in barracks on the facility, and the Navy had strict standards for women's living quarters. Why spend money and effort to provide suitable quarters at smaller facilities where only a handful of women might be serving? A quick way to reduce the scope of the problem was to reduce the number of technical ratings for women.

Sometimes the wide dispersal affected performance adversely. Where only one or perhaps two women were assigned to a unit, they might not be given—or they might avoid—the heavier or messier tasks associated with their jobs. Instead of working on aircraft, for example, a woman aviation structural mechanic might spend her days doing errands and making coffee. Absent were the urgency and patriotic fervor that had enveloped the WAVES during wartime, and now there was more male muscle on hand. As a result, some women's professional performances were not respected either by themselves or by their shipmates, and they did not gain practical experience. Not surprisingly, when opportunities arose for promotion or advanced training they went to the men. Some female officers suggested concentrating women in such ratings at one location, rather than dispersing them, but that suggestion ran counter to the prevailing philosophy that Navy women were to be integrated as fully as possible with their male counterparts.

New Opportunities

Nonetheless, while the variety of Navy jobs for women was shrinking from
wartime levels, other opportunities were opening up. For example, in
April 1949 the first woman naval officer to serve in Europe reported to
U.S. Navy headquarters in London. Two months later the director of
naval intelligence requested nine enlisted women for duty at naval
attaché offices in London, Paris, and Rome. Between October and
December 1949, small numbers of U.S. Navy women began to report to
assignments in Guam, Alaska, Egypt, and Germany, and the Navy announced that women would once again be stationed in Hawaii. By 1952
approximately four hundred Navy women were serving outside the
contiguous United States. Also, February 1950 saw the first woman
reserve officer to serve on a board convened to select reserve officers for
promotion.[10]

That such opportunities were opening up owed much to the alertness,
tenacity, and negotiating skills of women in the Bureau of Naval Personnel. More often than not, when they sought to assign a woman to a job
traditionally held by a man they met resistance. The resistance might be
founded on a fear of innovation, or on a desire to preserve the limited
number of career-enhancing, prestigious, or otherwise desirable billets
for men, or on doubts as to whether women could perform certain jobs.
Most threatened were former enlisted men who had been promoted to
commissioned rank during the war. Unlike women officers they had little
or no college-level education; their promotions to the officer corps were
based on technical expertise alone. Diplomatic negotiations and barter-
ing sometimes won the job in question for a woman. The strongest
weapon women held in such struggles was the sturdy record of performance already compiled by Navy women and their qualifications (sometimes superior to those of men being proposed for the same jobs).

Ultimately, it was the senior women officers in the Bureau of Naval
Personnel who had to decide how strongly to push for expanded opportunities. They spent much time and effort on basic policies of recruiting,
training, assigning, advancing, and housing, but they also wasted no
opportunity to gain new ground. The Integration Act of 1948 had established a significant beachhead; the job now was to secure and—judi-
ciously—expand it.

As the second anniversary of the Integration Act approached, the Navy
could be well satisfied with USS Nucleus. Navy women had opportunities
for travel, training, and experience not available to most civilian women.
There was now in place a well-marked path along which the ambitious,

talented, enterprising, and industrious could move to higher positions and retire with a pension. Those considering only a "hitch" with the Navy could expect some interesting, valuable training and experience before they settled down to become wives and mothers.

No one knew that very soon USS Nucleus would be put to the test.

The Korean Conflict

To their astonishment and dismay, in the last week of June 1950 Americans were once more in a shooting war or, as it was officially referred to, a police action. As a result of postwar developments the Soviets had come to dominate that half of Korea north of the 38th parallel. Although they had provided the North Koreans with a powerful arsenal, no one believed it would be used. Then on June 25, 1950, the North Koreans staged a powerful attack the length of the 38th parallel and advanced steadily southward. Their hope was to capture South Korea so swiftly that there would be no time or opportunity for intervention. They would present the world with a fait accompli—a united Korea firmly dominated by the Soviets.

Within days, U.S. forces were ordered to repel the North Koreans. Almost simultaneously the United Nations resolved to muster forces from member nations to join U.S. and South Korean troops. Eventually fifteen nations joined the United States in providing combat forces to repel the communist aggression, while five others provided medical assistance. But it was the United States, as the most powerful nation of the free world, that shouldered most of the burden of support.

At first the American public supported the UN police action, for the North Korean invasion clearly constituted aggression. But as the fighting dragged on Americans grew weary and resentful of the mounting casualties in a land where they could see no threat to vital U.S. interests. There seemed nothing to be gained, other than the nebulous goal of repelling aggression, and too much blood to be spilled. Public approval of American involvement dropped from 75 percent in August 1950 to 50 percent by the end of the year.[11] At the same time, fears that the police action might escalate to a full-scale war with the Soviet Union stayed President Truman from committing larger forces to the conflict. Americans—except for those fighting and dying in Korea and their families—lost interest.

The U.S. Navy's Role

The police action was largely a land war fought by soldiers and Marines, yet the U.S. Navy played a significant role. Korea lay 7,000 miles across the Pacific, over which the Navy transported the men and materiel to wage battle. The Navy also provided a vital link in the necessary communications networks across the Pacific and among services. Navy pilots based on aircraft carriers off the Korean coast joined Air Force fighters and bombers to support ground troops, while Navy minesweepers cleared coastal waters for amphibious operations. Finally, Navy medical units played a crucial role throughout the hostilities. By October 1950 three Navy hospital ships—the *Consolation, Repose,* and *Haven*—lay off the Korean coast, providing 2,500 beds for wounded American troops. By 1951 the one hundred–bed Navy dispensary in Yokosuka, Japan, had added seven hundred more beds to care for the battle casualties.[12]

On July 7, 1950, the CNO, Adm. Forrest Sherman, ordered the reactivation of numerous ships that had been "mothballed" since the Japanese surrender in 1945. By July 10 the number of Navy ships carrying cargo across the Pacific had risen from twenty-five to seventy, plus another fifty sent from Japan. These transport ships had been scheduled to carry 66,000 tons in July; they ended up carrying 312,000 tons. On July 25, 1950, there were nearly 11,000 Navy personnel in the western Pacific; within the next five weeks the number nearly tripled. This huge wave of men and supplies was gathered from units stationed throughout the Pacific and on the U.S. West Coast.[13] Women were part of this immense effort.

Building Up

To replenish drained units and increase their numbers, the U.S. armed forces began a four-pronged campaign:

- Both inactive and active reservists were sought to volunteer for extended active duty.
- Selected reservists were involuntarily recalled.
- Divisions of the National Guard were called up.
- The draft was activated for the first time since February 1949.

The Navy's nucleus of women was affected by these mobilization plans in several ways. First, the discharge policy for married women was changed. From late in 1944, when married women were allowed to leave the Navy to join their wounded or discharged veteran husbands, until this time, any woman who married after entering the service was allowed to leave upon request. Now, with the need to expand the women's nucleus, this policy was changed: Like it or not, the Navy woman who married would not be allowed to leave for that reason alone. Second, enlisted women reservists in critical ratings (chiefly hospital corpsmen and supply clerks) were involuntarily recalled beginning in September 1950. Discrepancies in the administration of the reserve program soon became apparent. Some women reservists had had children since leaving active duty but had not informed their reserve units. They could not go on active duty and thus were discharged from the reserve forces. Also, of those women who had entered the Naval Reserve since 1948 many had received little or no training—a circumstance so serious that by April 1950 the chief of naval personnel ordered corrective measures. These discrepancies (and many others that plagued the entire reserve program) could all be traced to lack of money, the inevitable result of slender peacetime budgets.[14]

Finally, the Navy sought to enlist a large number of women, expecting that they would respond to recruiting calls as they had in the two world wars. In August 1950 it raised its quota every six weeks for women recruits from 100 to 160. By the following March the quota had more than tripled, to 528 every six weeks, and there were plans to raise it to 716. The Navy announced its intention to have 10,000 enlisted women on active duty, even though it had failed to reach its peacetime goal of 6,000. Anticipating these increases, the Navy in 1951 moved women's recruit training from Great Lakes—now receiving swelling numbers of male recruits—to Bainbridge, Maryland, where larger facilities were available.[15]

Pressure to meet the rising quotas impelled the Navy to lower its minimum age for women to eighteen. The Army and Air Force had been enlisting eighteen- and nineteen-year-old women right along, but senior Navy women much preferred to keep the minimum age at twenty. They believed the added maturity helped to maintain a high-caliber enlisted corps. But by May 1951 their resistance was overcome, and younger women were invited to apply to Navy recruiting stations so that (or so it was announced) the Navy's qualifications would "conform with Army and Air Force qualifications."[16]

Overall the younger recruits were less mature and disciplined than the older. This led to a need for more experienced petty officers, but the near-tripling of Navy women between 1950 and 1953 resulted in a shortage of rated women. In 1950, 40 percent of enlisted Navy women were experienced petty officers; by 1952 that had plummeted to 17 percent. The petty officers were most needed in recruiting billets and as recruit instructors. Furthermore, only rated women were eligible for the sought-after billets in Europe.[17] Hence female petty officers serving in the continental United States were spread thin. For a larger and younger force, there were fewer veteran leaders and role models.

Birth of DACOWITS

The Navy was rudely awakened by its experience recruiting women for the Korean buildup. This tripling of women personnel between 1950 and 1953 fell decidedly short of what the Navy had expected, unlike the situation in 1917 and again in 1942 when women had thronged to enroll. The other services were likewise alarmed. In 1951, spurred by inquiries from Senator Margaret Chase Smith, and at the suggestion of his assistant for manpower, Anna Rosenberg, Secretary of Defense George Marshall convened a group of fifty distinguished civilian women (later cut to twenty-five) to consider what might be done. The group was named the Defense Advisory Committee on Women in the Service (DACOWITS), and it exists to this day. Led by Mrs. Oswald Lord, who had chaired a similar Army committee, the first DACOWITS also included Sarah Blanding, president of Vassar College, Beatrice Gould, editor of *Ladies Home Journal,* and Dr. Lillian Gilbreth, industrial engineer and former member of the Women's Advisory Council during World War II. Other members were prominent in business, public affairs, law, and medicine. Each was appointed for a three-year term and received no salary or compensation. They were independent, free of suspicion of partisanship or self-interest.

One of the first DACOWITS recommendations, in the fall of 1951, was that the Department of Defense sponsor a heavily publicized nationwide campaign to recruit women. President Truman launched the campaign on November 11, 1951. DACOWITS was given credit for having raised the recruiting rate for women in all services from an average of 850 a month in 1951 to 1,850 a month in 1952, but results were nevertheless disappointing, with the Army and Air Force women's programs falling far short of their goals. The Navy had been more conservative in its projections and fared somewhat better; its goal was to have 11,000 women on active duty, and by June 1952 it had 8,000.[18]

Even before the Korean emergency various commands had requested more women officers than Lt. Dorothy Council, their detailer, could provide. Now as the tide of requests swelled she began sifting through the files of a great many women reserve officers, searching for and telephoning those with the right background to fill needed slots. Because so many volunteered to return to active duty (172 by December 1950), there was no need to recall women officers involuntarily. To speed the entry of new women officers, the Navy shortened the training course at Newport from five months to sixteen weeks starting in March 1951. Also, beginning in September 1952, women were commissioned in the Naval Reserve rather than directly into the regular Navy, with the understanding that they could subsequently apply for regular status. Reserve commissions took less time than regular commissions, which Congress had to approve individually. Commissions were offered to selected enlisted women between the ages of twenty-one and twenty-seven with bachelor's degrees and no dependents younger than eighteen.[19]

In 1950 another path to commissions opened up for women, the Reserve Officer Candidate Program (also open to men). To qualified college juniors the program offered eight weeks of training during the summer after their junior year, another eight weeks following graduation, then commissioning and active duty as reserve officers. Although launched with considerable optimism and fanfare, the program died in 1953. The fighting in Korea undoubtedly contributed to its demise. As selected college juniors had to enlist in the reserves, failure to graduate or to complete their training could subject them to involuntary enlisted active duty.

Meeting the Test

The number of Navy women on active duty in July 1950 nearly doubled by July 1951, from 3,240 to 6,300. A year later it had increased again by a third, to 8,340. By the time a cease-fire agreement had been reached in Korea, on July 25, 1953, nearly 9,000 Navy women were serving on active duty.[20] These figures do not reflect the unknown numbers of married women who took the opportunity to leave the Navy after the "freeze" prompted by the Korean emergency was lifted, nor of the involuntarily recalled reservists who left after completing their obligated service of twenty-one months (limited because Congress had not officially declared war). It can reasonably be inferred that some of the approximately 3,200 women on active duty when the Korean conflict erupted in June 1950 left service before the cease-fire three years later. Thus, for the number of Navy women on active duty to have reached nearly 9,000 by July 1953, somewhat more than 5,800 women must have begun or resumed active duty.

The vast majority of women performed the duties WAVES had during World War II, in medical care, communications, clerical and supply, and aviation. In the medical field the total number of hospital corpsmen, male and female, doubled between June 1950 and June 1951 from 15,660 to 31,080. To support the embattled First Marine Division, 1,400 hospital corpsmen were assigned to the Pacific Fleet Marine Force as a pool committed solely to replace as needed corpsmen serving alongside Marines in combat.[21] As it had before, the Navy now relied on women hospital corpsmen to replace men taken from stateside duties to serve overseas, to expand stateside services, and to care for the active-duty Navy force, which approximately doubled between 1950 and 1952. Women were also invaluable in communications. Without women in the clerical and administrative jobs the Navy might well have drowned in its own paperwork.

For Katherine Keating the war provided an opportunity to break new ground. Keating had enlisted during World War II and been trained as a radioman. Immediately after the war she went to the pharmacy school at the University of Colorado. When she signed up for the regular Navy, she tried to enter the Hospital Corps but was sent back to communications. In 1950 she finally managed a switch to the Hospital Corps, then applied to the Navy's newly established Medical Service Corps. In August 1950 she became the first woman commissioned in that corps, which was so new that there were no sleeve devices for women; she had to embroider her own insignia. In early 1953 enlisted Hospital Corps women were beginning to go to sea on transports, so Keating began to petition to be sent to a hospital ship. She finally received orders to the USS *Haven,* which, lacking a full complement of nurses, had an extra berth. As the *Haven*'s pharmacist she became the first woman officer to relieve* a man at sea. While on board, Keating stood watches with the men and had several collateral duties including officer training and cryptography. Conferences to exchange prisoners of war were held on the *Haven,* which was neutral ground. Finally, on the way home, the ship was diverted to Saigon to evacuate the French Foreign Legion survivors from Dien Bien

*Navy term for replacing and assuming one's duties

Phu, joining other Navy ships carrying refugees from Vietnam long before most Americans had ever heard of that country. Keating went on to have a long and successful career, eventually retiring as a captain in July 1972.[22]

Its peacetime nucleus of women brought immediate benefits to the Navy. This small permanent force, only two thousand to three thousand women in the first years of its existence, was able to administer itself with little help from Navy men. Yet planners paid little attention to them. For its own convenience in assigning and housing them the Navy allowed women into only a handful of ratings, far fewer than the number of ratings in which women had proven they could excel.

Although the original members of this nucleus force all had several years of Navy experience, their new status as careerists presented them with fresh challenges. One was to optimize the training of women for service in the peacetime Navy. Another was to plot career paths, which required them to plan rotations from one duty station to another and to qualify for promotions by means of additional education and increasingly responsible positions.

Bringing women into the Navy on a permanent basis involved trade-offs on both sides. The Navy accepted women's continuing presence but was prepared to make few accommodations for them. Women gained the opportunity for career advancement but were excluded from many jobs for which they were well qualified. Hardly had the female nucleus been launched when the Korean police action required it to demonstrate the primary justification for its existence: expanding when needed. It did so smoothly and rapidly by tripling in three years, an impressive achievement in view of the deepening shortage of experienced female petty officers.

But overall the services failed to reach their recruiting goals for women in the Korean emergency. This brought about two lasting changes. Under pressure to expand, the Navy altered two long-standing policies regarding women: Married women would no longer be allowed to leave the service upon request, and the minimum age for enlistment was dropped from twenty to eighteen. These changes would affect both quality and morale.

The nucleus had proved its worth, but the challenge of recruiting and retaining women belonged to the larger organization of the Navy. Korea was proof that it had much to learn about bringing women into the fold.

8

1953–63: Surviving the Peace

"That the women's programs survived the Cold War . . . was due more to bureaucratic inertia and political expediency than to any conviction on the part of military leaders that women were necessary to the national defense."

—MAJ. GEN. JEANNE HOLM, USAF (RET.)

Beginning in 1953 with the cease-fire in Korea, the U.S. armed forces entered a period marked by public apathy during which few men and women showed interest in joining a military service. The nation's economy was expanding and young people entering the civilian work force met with a wide range of opportunity. Even with the draft, recruiters could hardly sign up enough high-quality men, and now the services found it almost as difficult to retain men and women as to recruit them.

For Navy women, the period from 1953 to 1963 was bleak in many ways. Promotions were slow, opportunities to enter technical fields were far fewer than in World War II, and discriminatory policies discouraged married women from continuing on active duty while all but prohibiting mothers from serving. Whereas disciplinary cases among women had been almost nonexistent, now they began to appear. This development stemmed largely from the combined effect of the 1951 decision to enlist eighteen-year-olds and the shortage of female petty officers.

Nonetheless, women managed to maintain some headway. Legislation in 1955 somewhat improved women's chances for promotion, and starting in 1959 the Women Officers School included newly commissioned Navy nurses. Like their male shipmates, enlisted women seized any opportunities the Navy offered. Wherever the chance arose—to audit a class, to fill a billet, to gain a qualification—a bright, tenacious, and hardworking woman was apt to seize it.

A New Era

On June 25, 1953, the cease-fire agreement was signed in Korea and the United States was once more at peace. With the end of hostilities came another ending, that of the career of Capt. Joy Bright Hancock. Upon her retirement she was awarded the Legion of Merit, the Navy's highest award for noncombat service. In 1954 she married Vice Adm. Ralph Ofstie, a naval aviator. When he became commander of the Sixth Fleet in the Mediterranean, she accompanied him on many of his official visits and took the opportunity to visit Navy women stationed in Europe. In 1972 the Naval Institute Press published her memoir, *Lady in the Navy*. She died in 1986, confident as ever that American women would always be ready to serve their country.

Comdr. Louise K. Wilde was promoted to captain and succeeded Hancock on June 30, 1953. No one knew better than she the difficulties Navy women were facing in this new era. Like many of the first women naval officers commissioned in the early war years, she had a strong academic background. She had graduated from Mount Holyoke College in 1931, then spent several years working as a journalist. After earning a master's degree in public administration from Columbia University she became a dean at Rockford College. Throughout World War II she had directed public relations for the WR, and as a result she fully appreciated the importance of public opinion to its success. In trying to convince senior recruiting officers that WAVES should be presented to the public as serious young ladies doing a serious job, she discovered that few naval professionals had any appreciation of public relations. It was in large part because of her persistence and skill that public opinion generally favored the WAVES. In 1945 she was ordered to Hawaii as district director for the four thousand WAVES on duty there.

At the war's end those who knew her well were not surprised that she elected to stay on duty for as long as possible. In 1946 she returned to Washington and for the next six years served as Capt. Jean Palmer's and then as Hancock's chief assistant. From 1952 to 1953 she served on the staff of the commander of the Western Sea Frontier, headquartered in San Francisco.[1]

Now forty-three years old, quick-witted and decisive, Wilde was eminently qualified to succeed Hancock. To her new post she brought a wide acquaintance with the news media and with leaders in women's education, as well as the experience of eleven years of naval service in varied and consequential billets. One of her major contributions as ACNP(W) was initiating a series of memoranda that eventually became known to Navy women as the "Pers-K newsletter" (Pers-K being her office's code name within the Bureau of Naval Personnel). The first such memorandum, which appeared in July 1954, contained a "brief review of the current program for women" that was to be disseminated "in lieu of the traditional anniversary greeting to all WAVES." For the next nineteen years the memoranda appeared several times each year and regularly carried news of promotions, transfers, changes in policies, and regulations. It gave the women, few and dispersed as they were, not only information but also a sense of community and camaraderie within a large organization that often underrated their abilities and ignored their needs.

The Effects of a Younger Force

When in 1951 the Navy lowered its enlistment age for women to eighteen years, it was with unfortunate results. Many of the younger recruits made less suitable decisions about which ratings to enter; screening and testing procedures did not work as well for them as for older women. The growing number of unsuitably placed women exhibited less judgment, lower morale, and less desire to serve, and fewer and fewer Navy enlisted women completed their first enlistments.[2]

As we have seen, there were too few women petty officers to train and lead this younger force. Inevitably, disciplinary cases among women began to rise. As they rose, male petty officers, lacking women counterparts to whom they could go for advice on "how to handle women," began to take a dimmer view of female abilities. Lower standards of women's performance and behavior sometimes resulted, which in turn heightened Navy men's resentment of women. Charges of favoritism toward women were heard; letters to the editor of *Navy Times* between August and October 1959 publicly raised the question that had previously only been murmured: Why have women in the Navy at all? Such grumbling did nothing to improve the morale of the still-large majority of Navy women who behaved responsibly and did their jobs well; it is reasonable to suppose that some women who might otherwise have reenlisted decided to return to civilian life.

Marriage versus the Navy

Throughout the decade following Korea most Navy women, both officers and enlisted, were single, since the majority of those who married left.

But little by little, the number of Navy women who married and remained in service grew in the 1950s and early 1960s. This was partly the result of a policy shift in 1957: Any woman who had completed a Navy training school beyond the boot-camp level must serve at least eighteen more months or complete her enlistment, regardless of whether she was married. With a weather eye toward public opinion, the Navy had previously been reluctant to hold any woman in service involuntarily, especially a married woman. Captain Wilde saw that a stiffer policy might "deter poorly motivated or indecisive students from beginning a school course."[3]

The growing force of married women caused the Navy to reexamine its policies regarding civilian husbands of Navy women: Should they be granted the same privileges as civilian wives of Navy men? Those wives had long been granted dependent status, reflecting the societal norm that a married man supported his wife financially. Even those Navy wives who worked outside their homes and whose income might equal or even exceed that of their husbands were considered dependents. Benefits of this status included free medical care at military facilities, shopping at military exchanges and commissaries where prices were lower than in civilian shops, and access to recreational facilities on the base (usually also lower in price and sometimes, in remote areas, of higher quality than those "outside the gate"). Married Navy men were also eligible to occupy government-owned housing with their families where it was available. Where it was not, both single and married Navy men received a housing allowance, that of married men being somewhat larger.

The married Navy woman and her civilian husband received none of these benefits. The issue was tested when a young woman Army officer asked to have her husband declared a dependent because he was a full-time college student and her salary was the couple's sole income. When denied, she appealed the case to the highest possible level, the government's General Accounting Office, which ruled that her husband could be granted dependent status only if he was unable to work. In unofficial, more subjective judgments, Navy women heard from their male colleagues that civilian husbands were "freeloaders" who ought not to be allowed on the base.[4]

The Navy woman who married a civilian faced another problem: When she was transferred, would he be willing or able to relocate with her? In the climate of the times, for a man to consider relocation purely on the basis of his wife's Navy orders was nearly unthinkable. As for housing allowances, the idea that a married Navy woman should receive one when her husband was expected to provide her with a home was strongly opposed.

A Navy woman marrying a serviceman had the additional concern of orders that might separate them. The armed services had no collocation policy, that is, he got his orders, she got hers, and one could only hope that the twain might meet. To arrange matters more auspiciously required extensive negotiations with the couple's respective detailers; collocation might result, but there were no promises. For example, in 1957 when Chief Yeoman Lois Berman married an Army sergeant stationed in New York, she persuaded the Navy to transfer her there. She knew she was lucky. Not only did she have an excellent service record, but both she and her husband had high-ranking bosses. Otherwise "they would probably have requested that I retire or get out. . . . The billet structure often wasn't available for you to be placed with your husband, so it was a long-distance marriage or get out." Eleven years later, when Lt. (jg) Kathleen Donaho married Lt. Kelly Byerly, the Navy hadn't changed: "There was no guidance, no directives about how you got orders to the same place. Nor were there any role models to tell us how you did it; all the senior women were single."[5]

The growing number of Navy couples also posed challenges to policy regarding housing allowances: Should they be paid to both members? That would discriminate against Navy members married to civilians, for those couples received only one housing allowance. If the allowance was paid to only one member of the couple, then the other member could claim discrimination. Modification has followed upon modification, but to this day the issue continues to vex Navy planners.

The cost in personal sacrifice can never be known, but for any individual Navy woman it may have been enormous. Should she marry and give up a career that she loved and in which she was doing well? If she married, should she try to maintain the career and thereby risk prolonged separation? Many a woman facing such decisions may have felt that there was altogether too much truth in a variation of an old Navy saying, "If the Navy wanted you to have a husband, it would have issued you one." Or, more bluntly, marry at your own risk. It is a wry tribute to the appeal of a Navy career that so many of the Navy's brightest, most ambitious women either postponed marriage until they retired or did not marry at all. Of those who married before retirement, one can only imagine the anguish many felt as they faced the next choice, between motherhood and continuing service.

Motherhood versus the Navy

Since 1942 the Navy's policy on motherhood for its members had been unequivocal: No woman with a child under the age of eighteen could serve in the Navy. Now, however, questions about this policy began to arise. What about the woman who married a widower with minor children or the woman with younger siblings who came into her custody when her parents died? Were their careers also at risk?

In a word, yes. But Navy policy did bend slightly during this time, to the extent that a woman could now be the parent of a minor child if that child resided with her no more than thirty days out of the year. This loophole allowed, for example, a couple to have their child live 335 days out of the year with its grandparents. Or a divorced man whose former wife had custody of their children could have his children live with him and his Navy wife for thirty days out of the year. Or the thirty-day rule might be met by putting a child in boarding school for nine months and in summer camp for two. (At what cost, one wonders, to both child and parents?) At least two cases are known in which Navy women married widowers with minor children yet stayed on active duty while the children resided year-round with them. Both cases occurred in the early 1960s, and in both it was common knowledge that the couple was flouting policy. Why no official action was taken to terminate the women's service is unknown. One likelihood is that they were performing their duties well, and those in authority had no desire to oust them. Another is that the policy was seen as essentially unfair and not worthy of being invoked.[6] In any event, these cases made a significant point: Combining motherhood and a Navy career *was* possible.

Unequal Opportunity

Officers. As we have seen, the Women's Armed Services Integration Act of 1948 strictly limited the upper ranks of women officers. Under the act women lieutenants who had served thirteen years were involuntarily separated from the Navy if they were not promoted to lieutenant commander. The 20 percent cap allowed only a few to be selected. Increased promotion of lieutenant commanders to commander would have eased this choke point. Male officers achieved the rank of commander only after fifteen to seventeen years of commissioned service. None of the women eligible for promotion had served that long, because none had been

Yeoman (F) First Class Joy Bright in 1918. As Joy Bright Hancock, she served again in the Navy in World War II, retiring in 1953 as a captain and assistant chief of naval personnel for women.
U.S. Navy

Yeoman (F) in dress uniform undergoing inspection on the Washington Monument grounds in 1918. *U.S. Navy*

Lt. Comdr. Mildred McAfee, director of the WAVES in World War II, presents her staff to Rear Adm. Randall Jacobs, chief of naval personnel; 1942. From left: Lt. Elizabeth Reynard, Lt. Jean Palmer, Lt. (jg) Virginia Carlin, Lt. (jg) Marian Enright, and Ens. Dorothy Foster. *U.S. Navy*

WAVES pass in review at Hunter College in New York City. The Navy trained more than 85,000 enlisted women at "USS Hunter" during World War II. *U.S. Navy*

A WAVE aerographer's mate adjusts weather collection instruments at the Naval Air Training Center, Corpus Christi, Texas; 1943.
U.S. Navy

A WAVE Link trainer instructor and student pilot at the Naval Air Training Center, Corpus Christi, Texas; 1943.
U.S. Navy

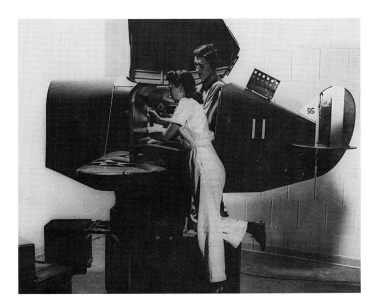

Aviation Machinist's Mate Violet Falkum at the Naval Air Station, Jacksonville, Florida; 1943. More than 25,000 WAVES served in naval aviation in World War II. *U.S. Navy*

WAVE gunnery instructors head to the target range at the Naval Air Gunners School, Hollywood, Florida; 1944. *U.S. Navy*

The first African-American women officers, Frances Wills and Harriet Ida Pickens, are sworn into the Women's Reserve in New York in 1944. *U.S. Navy*

Chief Aviation Machinist's Mate Ellen E. Duncan and Aviation Machinist's Mate 3rd Class Audree J. Kelly pulling the chocks off a trainer at Corry Field, Pensacola, Florida; 1949. *U.S. Navy*

Capt. Joy Bright Hancock modeling new evening dress uniform first authorized in 1950. *U.S. Navy*

Chief Yeoman Lois Berman in 1954, one of the first career enlisted women, showing off the gold hash marks signifying twelve years of exemplary service. *U.S. Navy*

Lt. Elizabeth Wylie upon hearing in 1967 that she is the first Navy woman line officer to be assigned to Vietnam.
U.S. Navy/PHC R. Lister

Adm. Elmo Zumwalt, Comdr. Robin Quigley, Capt. Rita Lenihan, and Secretary of the Navy John Chafee in 1971. Under Zumwalt's leadership, Quigley succeeded Lenihan as assistant chief of naval personnel for women, and Navy women entered a new era.
U.S. Navy

Equipment Operator Constructionman Camella J. Jones, the first woman to qualify as a heavy equipment operator, assigned to one of the U.S. Navy Construction Battalions—the Seabees; 1972.
U.S. Navy/P. Mansfield

Seaman Nancy K. Garner in 1973—the first woman to graduate from the Navy Diving School. *U.S. Navy*

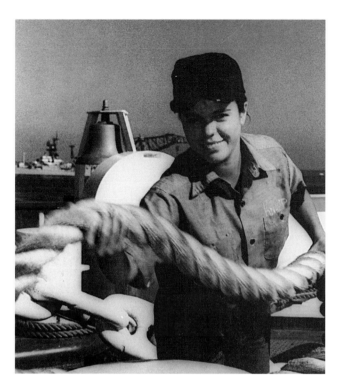

Seaman Annaliese Knapp unravels line aboard the hospital ship USS *Sanctuary* at Mayport, Florida; 1974. At the time, it was the only ship in commission on which federal statute permitted women to serve.
U.S. Navy/L. Anderson

Lt. Comdr. Kathleen Byerly (later Bruyere) in 1976, one of *Time*'s "Women of the Year" for 1975. She later joined five other women in a suit that successfully challenged the aforementioned statute's constitutionality and led to new legislation permitting women to serve on noncombatant ships.
U.S. Navy/PH1 C. Begy

Rear Adm. Fran McKee, director of naval educational development and the first woman line admiral, in 1976 at the Guantanamo Bay Naval Air Station in Cuba.
U.S. Navy/JO2 A. Riccio

In July 1976, the U.S. Naval Academy included women for the first time. Elizabeth Belzer, the first to graduate, stands at far right.
U.S. Navy

Midshipman Cindy Mason (left) and Lt. Mary Jorgenson prior to taking off in a TA-4 Skyhawk at the Miramar Naval Air Station, California; 1980.
U.S. Navy/T. Mitchell

Rear Adm. Grace Hopper, computer pioneer, receives a salute and a bouquet of roses from the commanding officer of the USS *Constitution* upon her retirement in 1986. The Navy retained "Amazing Grace" long past the normal age of retirement. *U.S. Navy*

Comdr. Deborah Gernes, selected in 1990 to be the first woman to command a Navy ship, shown here in 1986 as executive officer of the destroyer tender USS *Cape Cod.* Lt. Comdr. Darlene Iskra actually took command before Gernes. *U.S. Navy/R. Bayles*

Seabee Lt. Susan Globokar supervised the building of a fleet hospital in Saudi Arabia during the Persian Gulf War. *U.S. Navy/ J. Gawlowicz*

Lt. Comdr. Darlene Iskra, the first woman to command a Navy ship, on the bridge of the USS *Opportune*; 1991.
U.S. Navy/M. O'Shaughnessy

Comdr. Rosemary Mariner, the first woman to command an operational unit of the U.S. Navy, at the Lemoore Naval Air Station, California; 1991. *U.S. Navy*

Lt. Paula Coughlin recounting how she was assaulted by fellow naval aviators at the Tailhook convention in September 1991. The Navy's ineffectual response derailed the careers of several admirals and led the secretary of the Navy to resign. *Navy Times/ Kate Patterson*

Aviation Mechanic Kimberley Warnock conducting a pre-flight check of an SH-2 helicopter at the North Island Naval Air Station, San Diego, California. *U.S. Navy/PH3 R. Weissleder*

Engineman Ann Marie Daub participating in a person-overboard drill. *U.S. Navy/PHC D. Fraker*

Seaman Robin P. Robinson performing lookout duties aboard the USS *Lexington* during the Gulf War. *U.S. Navy*

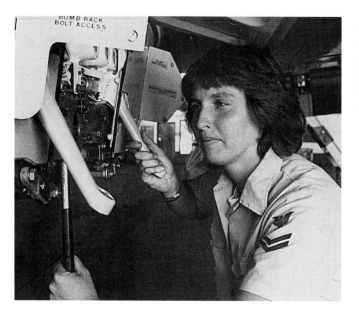

Aviation Ordnanceman 2d Class Jency A. Jordan works on a bomb rack of a P3-C Orion aircraft. *U.S. Navy/PH2 D. De Angelis*

Ens. Matice Wright, a naval flight officer in a strategic communications squadron, one of about 58,000 women proudly serving in the Navy today. *U.S. Navy*

commissioned earlier than 1942. To promote women who had less service than the men would have seemed unfair; thus, although the law would have allowed about thirty women commanders, there was not even one-third that many.[7] Women officers were in a double bind: Women lieutenant commanders faced high odds against promotion, yet if not promoted they were forced out by age fifty.

Some improvement came about in June 1956 when President Eisenhower signed Public Law 585-84, which removed the 20 percent limitation on the number of women lieutenant commanders and allowed greater flexibility in distribution of women officers in the grades of commander and lieutenant commander. These and other provisions somewhat ameliorated the "lieutenant logjam" for women, but the remedial effects were to prove temporary.

The only long-lasting answer was to increase the number of women officers; consequently, their recruitment began to receive more attention. But the problem persisted. In 1961 the chief of naval personnel approved a promotion plan for women officers that would attempt to provide a promotion opportunity of 75 percent to lieutenants and of 45 percent to lieutenant commanders. It was notably unsuccessful: throughout the 1950s and the 1960s promotion opportunities for female officers were far fewer than for males. For example, in October 1961, 2,500 male lieutenant commanders were competing for 800 vacancies in the rank of commander, for a promotion opportunity of about 33 percent; at the same time 41 women lieutenant commanders were competing for 2 vacancies, an opportunity of 5 percent. Again, from 1964 to 1968, 80 percent of the male lieutenants eligible for promotion to lieutenant commander were selected, while only 13 percent of the women were.[8]

Enlisted Women. Inequality for enlisted women lay elsewhere than in mandated ceilings and stifled promotions. Rather, it was in the ratings open to them. In 1952, thirty-six, or roughly 60 percent, of the Navy's ratings were open to women; by 1956 only twenty-five were open, and by 1962 only twenty-one. Furthermore, women did not actually work in all the ratings that were open to them; two occupational groups—administrative and clerical, and medical and dental—claimed approximately 90 percent of enlisted women.[9] The chief cause was that the draft (or the threat of it) provided enough young men to keep technical billets filled. Also, many Navy planners believed that keeping women, who needed special arrangements in housing, discipline, and administration, congregated in traditional work at traditional locations was the most cost-effective way to use them. This misperception died hard.

The effect on recruiting and retention was obvious: In the absence of a national emergency, why should women join the Navy to do work hardly different from civilian work? Or for those eighteen- or nineteen-year-old women who joined the Navy in order to live and work away from home, why stay on after reaching an age at which such independence could be as easily claimed in civilian life?

"One Sharp WAVE"

Kathleen Amick was one of the talented and ambitious women who found a Navy career far more attractive than civilian life. Her parents had farmed and run a grocery store in South Carolina, and her father repaired automobiles. After high school she worked at her uncle's small store in North Carolina, but "it wasn't very exciting. I was looking for something more."[10] As soon as she turned twenty in 1943, Amick enlisted and was among the first WAVES to receive training at Hunter. There the Navy discovered her mechanical ability and trained her to overhaul and repair gyro-operated aircraft instruments. Subsequently she was rated as an aviation machinist's mate. At her first duty station in Norfolk she worked with her father, now employed by the Navy Department to assemble and repair aircraft instruments. She was one of the first WAVES to serve at the Barber's Point Naval Air Station near Honolulu. By the war's end she had advanced to petty officer second class.

In December 1945 she was discharged in San Francisco and went to work in Los Angeles. "But I missed the Navy and by September 1946 I was back in." The Navy sent her to the Naval Air Station at Corpus Christi, Texas, where she learned more about the repair and calibration of electrically operated aircraft instruments. Within two years she had advanced to first class. Soon thereafter the rating of aviation machinist's mate was phased out of the Navy, and "they changed me to an aviation electrician's mate. But then the Navy sent a lot of us to Pensacola for the infamous 'women mechanics' program, and had us working out on the flight line."

Not too pleased with this state of affairs—work on the flight line seemed a waste of a person experienced in repairing delicate instruments—Amick's patience ended when she received a very low grade on her quarterly evaluation marks. Knowing that the marks were unmerited, she investigated and found that many of the women mechanics had received low marks. "It was as if someone wanted us to look bad. I think some people thought it wasn't appropriate for women to be in the mechanics ratings—although Captain Hancock would have fought that.

She was very protective of her mechs." Amick insisted that the grade be changed to reflect her performance more accurately.

Her career as an aviation electrician hardly had time to blossom before she heard scuttlebutt to the effect that "there wasn't much future for women AEs, so I decided to go for aviation storekeeper." When reviewing her records to prepare for the change, Amick discovered that the correction of her evaluation marks had not been recorded. "I made them change it right then and there." Now an aviation storekeeper first class, she was delighted to return to Barber's Point in 1953 and was there advanced to chief petty officer.

Over the next few years, her leadership skills were tested in tours where she was responsible for a women's barracks and for the supply departments at naval air stations in Atlantic City and Lakehurst, New Jersey. In neither capacity did she encounter real disciplinary problems: Chief Amick demanded and got respect and cooperation from all hands. It was inevitable that she would be ordered to the recruit training staff at Bainbridge following her graduation from instructor school at Norfolk. "I didn't have a choice—they said go! I didn't want to, I was happy doing my work with aviation instruments. But I wouldn't have missed that experience for the world—I wouldn't want to repeat it, either."

At Bainbridge Amick became the chief company commander, a leader among leaders.

It was a hard life—responsibility for 40 people, be with them a good portion of the day, teach them everything—how to fold their clothes, iron their shirts, shine their shoes. These kids didn't know a thing! Wasn't like that at Hunter. We knew how to do all that, these kids didn't.

Taking in the 18-year-olds wasn't too good of an idea. We got some good ones, but some weren't dry behind the ears, and there weren't too many of us petty officers. What they were looking for when they came to Bainbridge was discipline. You can read their critiques, which they didn't have to sign, and see that's what they valued. Duty at Bainbridge did enhance your career. When it came to promotion, it certainly helped.

When the Navy added the rates of senior chief and master chief to its ladder of enlisted rates in the late 1950s, Amick was among the first women to achieve them, for some time the first and only woman in an aviation rating to do so. She was also one of the first women to complete the Navy's Maintenance Analysis School in Memphis, Tennessee. "It was the hardest thing I ever did in my life. They put us through a college course in math. I could show others how to do the problems, but I couldn't

do them on the exam. I had to take a two-week setback to get out of there."
As one of the Navy's few master chiefs, male or female, qualified as a
maintenance analyst, Amick was able to persuade her detailer in late 1966
that she should be sent to the Naval Air Station at Rota, Spain. A staff
position called for someone with her qualifications, but no Navy enlisted
woman had ever been ordered there. Other obstacles arose, but she
persisted and arrived in January to a cool welcome. "They wouldn't let
me stay on the base even one night, said they had no enlisted quarters
for women. They could have given me a room at the BOQ [bachelor
officers' quarters]—that's been done many, many times. They already
had women officers living there. So I had to stay in a hotel until I found
a place to live."

Despite this start, Amick's Rota tour turned out to be one of the best
of her career. Several months before her departure for Spain in January
of 1967, she had met Sidney Temple, a retired master chief petty officer
also in the aviation maintenanceman rating and a widower with grown
children. In September 1967 she came back to the United States on leave
to marry him. Together they returned to Rota, where they lived comfortably off base and traveled through Europe as often as her duties would
allow. Temple recalls that he "took a lot of kidding as Kathy's husband. I
was even asked to join the Navy Wives Club. As a retired master chief I
could have worked somewhere on the base—I had a couple of jobs
offered me. But I didn't want to tie myself down, I said, I was having too
much fun traveling with Kathy." They returned to Norfolk in 1971 and
Amick retired in 1974.

Amick personified the Navy women in whom Hancock had placed so
much faith: She excelled at technical work, adapted easily to new situations, seized new opportunities, and thrived within the system. Small,
trim, attractive, well-spoken, impeccably uniformed, she was, as Navy
slang of the time put it, "one sharp WAVE."

Maintaining Headway

In August 1957 Comdr. Winifred Quick succeeded Captain Wilde as
ACNP(W) and was promoted to captain. Quick had been among the first
group of women officers to be trained at Northampton. Following graduation she remained on the staff and developed classification procedures
for trainees. Late in 1944 she followed Lieutenant Commanders Hancock
and Palmer to Hawaii to plan for the administration of the four thousand

WAVES who began arriving there in January 1945. Following the war she went to Washington and helped to ready plans for the time when women would be integrated into the regular Navy. Then, until 1951, she served as the detailer for women officers. Among the first Navy women officers to be sent to graduate school, she completed a master's degree at Stanford University in 1952 and then reported to the commandant of the Twelfth Naval District in San Francisco as assistant personnel director.* She was serving as a staff officer in London when the call came to succeed Wilde.

Quick approached her new job as ACNP(W) with verve, calling first upon Adm. Arleigh Burke, the CNO, and then Secretary of the Navy Thomas S. Gates. When the latter asked her to list the problems she faced, she said, "I have only ten fingers, and there's a problem for every finger, and I have more problems than that!" Gates promptly offered support by inviting her and a number of admirals to an informal lunch in his office. Admirals who had previously shown little interest in helping her now became more responsive.[11]

Quick's most highly symbolic victory was that of persuading the Navy to name a woman as a commanding officer. The woman was Comdr. Etta Belle Kitchen, a lawyer who had served during World War II. In 1946 Kitchen returned to practice law in Oregon, then resumed her naval career after the Integration Act of 1948. She was serving as officer-in-charge of recruit training for women at Bainbridge, Maryland, when the billet was redesignated as commanding officer in September 1962. Quick had retired by that time, but the chief of naval personnel, Vice Adm. Charles Duncan, knew to whom the credit belonged. He phoned her to say, "Winnie, I'm very sorry this didn't happen on your watch. It took me only five minutes, but you now have a woman commanding officer at Bainbridge."[12]

Less dramatic but more far-reaching was the way Quick changed career plans for both enlisted and commissioned women. She identified three kinds of jobs in which it was essential that top-quality women be placed. These were recruiters, who formed public opinion about Navy women; women's representatives, who advised commanding officers on the administration of women in their command and also served as role models

---

*When her immediate superior retired she was nominated to take his place, an idea that so appalled the commandant that he called the chief of naval personnel in Washington to protest. Upon reviewing her record, the chief told the commandant that if he did not accept Quick for the billet, it would remain unfilled. "So the Commandant swallowed, and took me. Let's say I was not the most beloved person on his staff."

and counselors; and instructors at Bainbridge and Newport. None of these jobs was particularly popular and women avoided them. Quick changed that by charting career paths and making duty in one or more of these jobs necessary for promotion. Soon top-quality Navy women began to compete for these jobs they had previously shunned.

Yet recruiting and retaining women of high caliber remained a challenge. In 1958 enlisted women were offered three-year reenlistments in addition to four- and six-year reenlistments. The difficulty of attracting qualified women to become officers was reflected in the declining numbers of students at the Women Officers School at Newport. From classes of seventy or more in 1952 and 1953 the number dropped, at one point in 1956, to ten. Quick and others feared the school might be closed. Since it required a staff of at least ten, the student-instructor ratio of one to one might strike Pentagon budgeters as an expensive luxury, and it could only offer ammunition to those who would just as soon rid the Navy of all uniformed women except nurses. Quick began to consider a course that had been proposed earlier but was never taken—including newly appointed Navy nurses in the four-month school. At this time Navy nursing recruits received a five-week indoctrination at the U.S. Naval Hospital in St. Albans, New York. Why not merge the two sets of students? Capt. Ruth Houghton, director of the Navy Nurse Corps, received the idea enthusiastically. Accordingly, in January 1959 a group of new Navy nurses was assigned to an eight-week pilot course at the school. In April three Nurse Corps officers joined the school's staff, and thenceforth all Navy nurses were trained there for eight weeks before reporting to their first duty stations.

This development involved some strain because the nurses were all commissioned while the women of the line were not. In June 1954, in an effort to align the training of women officers more closely with that of men at the OCS, the curriculum had been restructured: Line women now reported to Newport as officer candidate seamen apprentices, and after the first half of the sixteen-week course, they were commissioned. Although all women students were housed together and took many of the same classes, the nurses outranked (and received higher pay than) those line women still in their first eight weeks, which caused resentment.[13] Nonetheless, nurses and line women now had a shared experience at the very start of their Navy careers and at least an opportunity for mutual understanding that might serve them well as they moved up the ranks.

The future of the Women Officers School was now secure. By 1963 entering classes numbered about 150, most of them nurses. From June 1958 to March 1962 only 302 line women entered the school, of whom

238 graduated. Of those only about half were augmented into the regular Navy. Of the remainder, about 6 percent agreed to extend their active duty beyond the obligated two-year service; the rest left when their two years were up.[14]

Welcome Changes

In 1953 a Spanish-speaking Navy woman named Ileana Ramirez, studying to enter the yeoman rating, received an unusual assignment: to attend the Navy's air-conditioning and refrigeration school in Norfolk. Three Venezuelan sailors who spoke no English were attending the school, and Ramirez was to serve as their interpreter. She also enrolled and completed the course. Thus she was an early pioneer of a method of gaining Navy training not officially open to women, that of infiltrating. During the 1950s and much of the 1960s women attempting to enroll officially in the Industrial College of the Armed Forces, the Armed Forces Staff College, and the Naval War College were rebuffed time after time on the grounds that the courses offered were of no value to women's careers. But women served on the staffs of these schools, and many were sufficiently enterprising to attend such classes as they could and to study while off duty.[15]

Openings

In July 1955 Captain Wilde laid the groundwork for an important opening for women officers. After reviewing the curriculum for the Navy's General Line School (a nine-month professional course for junior and midgrade officers), she advised the chief of naval personnel that many of the school's courses, especially those in administration, would be "especially important to the development of the professional knowledge of career women officers." She recommended a modified five-month course for women, which was accepted. The first fourteen women officers completed their course the following July and reported favorably on their experience. Over the following eighteen months Wilde and her assistants, pointing to these positive results, tried but failed to keep the ball rolling by suggesting that women now be allowed official attendance at other advanced service schools. The truth was that the General Line School did not enjoy the same prestige as other schools. Still, a valuable precedent had been set, and in 1958 postgraduate education for women officers was expanded. For example, at the Navy's Postgraduate School in Monterey women could now study advanced aeronautical engineering and naval management. At the Department of Defense Intelligence School in Washington, D.C., they could study naval intelligence. They could be sent to Harvard to study business administration or to George Washington University to study comptrollership. By the early 1960s, in fact, a member of the postgraduate selection board noted that the Navy was choosing a higher percentage of women than of men for postgraduate education, chiefly because the women were better educated.[16]

Elsewhere on the education front, beginning in 1953 aspiring enlisted women who had at least two years of college or the equivalent were invited to seek a Navy commission, as were similarly qualified men. In 1955 this opportunity was formalized in the "seaman-to-admiral" program. In 1958 the Navy opened its so-called five-term program whereby men and women officers able to complete a bachelor's degree in five semesters were allowed to go to school full time. Among the first women to take advantage of these opportunities were Yeoman Joan Mackey and Radioman Lucille Kuhn. When selected (in 1953 and 1954, respectively), they went first to the Women Officers School and received commissions. In 1958 Lieutenant (jg) Kuhn was the first woman selected for the five-term program, soon followed by Lieutenant (jg) Mackey. Both had distinguished Navy careers and eventually were promoted to captain.

In 1955 women hospital corpsmen were offered a chance to win commissions as nurses. The qualifying standards were high, but so were the rewards. Applicants had to have served at least one year on active duty, with six months of duty in a hospital ward; have graduated in the top half of their class in Hospital Corps school; and be able to satisfy college entrance requirements. Those chosen were enrolled at civilian collegiate schools of nursing selected by the Bureau of Medicine and Surgery, with all expenses of their three years of schooling paid by the Navy. Graduates were commissioned as ensigns in the Nurse Corps and were obligated to serve for six years.

In 1958 the Navy initiated another program in which highly qualified enlisted personnel, both men and women, could gain commissions. Known as the naval enlisted scientific education program (NESEP), it paid full tuition costs at any one of twenty-two civilian colleges for selected enlisted members whose full-time active duty would then consist of completing degrees in various scientific and technical majors. Graduates were then commissioned in the regular Navy. The first woman to earn a degree under this program was Jean Syzmanski, who enlisted in 1958 and was selected for NESEP in 1960. In February 1965 Cornell University granted her a B.S. in electrical engineering, and she was commissioned after completing the sixteen-week course at the Women Officers School. Three other women soon followed her. One studied chemistry at Marquette University, another meteorology at the University of Utah, and another mathematics at the University of Missouri. A total of twenty-eight women had completed the program when it ended in 1976.[17]

A Winner from Dixie

Lucille Kuhn's career illustrates the rewards reaped by both the Navy and its women as the result of these educational opportunities. Although she was doing well in her job for an insurance company in her hometown of Richmond, Virginia, Kuhn leaped at the chance to wear her country's uniform when the Integration Act of 1948 was passed. She began recruit training in January 1949 at Great Lakes, where "the chief thing we learned was to take orders. It never occurred to us to give anyone any backtalk. We were all 20 or 21, we'd all worked, some had a year or two of college, and we all wanted to succeed. Everybody graduated, not because the standards were low—oh, no!—but because we wanted to do it right." By the end of boot camp she had acquired the nickname Dixie and chosen to become a radioman. "I liked working with my hands, and it seemed more like part of the operational Navy." At the twenty-four-week radioman school she saw that the men who had been to sea had some advantages over the women, but that was no reason for her to come in second to anyone. She graduated at the head of her class.[18]

At her first duty station at Fifth Naval District headquarters in Norfolk, Kuhn's drive and competence advanced her to radioman second class. In January 1953 she was transferred to a coveted billet in London and that spring advanced to radioman first class.

Meanwhile she was learning how to get along in a man's world, helped by

the Women's Representatives [WRs] in the barracks I lived in. Regular barracks meetings helped us keep up high standards of performance and behavior. We felt the WRs were concerned about our development as *women* enlisted persons in the Navy. They helped us to get a firm foundation, to remember that we were women in a man's world, but also ladies. They did more to help us do that than has been acknowledged or remembered.

Many male chiefs also helped.

They were willing to give women a chance, if the women were willing to work. Some women weren't. Those who wanted to be treated as ladies were—but also as shipmates. We didn't ask for special favors, and the men didn't like the women who didn't act professionally. There were so few women that if you shone, you really shone, and the smart Navy men like to be associated with winners.

Her supervisor in London told her about the seaman-to-admiral program and she applied in 1954. "The exam took an entire day, was the worst one I ever took—it covered *everything*." Of the more than 2,000 people who applied at the same time, 227 were chosen, Kuhn being the only woman among them. After graduating from the Women Officers School, she came to the Bureau of Naval Personnel as a placement officer. Her job involved talking to the commanding officers of destroyers, some of whom balked at doing business with a woman. Her boss told them, "If you don't talk to her, then you don't talk to anybody here."

Realizing that lack of a college degree would be a handicap to her career, Kuhn began taking college courses at night. "It was a great opportunity. They had tuition aid, and buses ran right from the Pentagon— I'd have been crazy not to take advantage of it." Her initiative paid off. When the five-term program came along she had completed enough courses to be eligible. She graduated from George Washington University in 1960 with a degree in psychology.

After a tour of duty with a security group in Newport that involved stocking ships with classified documents and cryptographic machines, she spent nearly three years recruiting women officers in the district that included Washington, D.C.

To pay me for a job that was such fun, I almost felt bad about taking the money. I love to talk, I love the Navy. Also, I was going to an area where hardly anybody'd been recruited for the Navy for a long time, because people outside the metropolitan D.C. area didn't know anything about the Navy, especially that there were women in it, so I had a lot of interesting information to give them. I got a new convertible and drove around towns and cities with the top down—they ate it up! I lived out of my suitcase for seven or eight weeks at a time; I had no recruiting money, few materials, only one little booklet that dealt mostly with men. I talked more women out of coming into the Navy than I ever did talking them into it—just talking to them, you'd know they weren't right.

During these years, student protesters on college campuses began to make trouble for recruiters. Kuhn met protests during her visits to the University of Maryland and American University, for instance. "Nothing violent, but it's not nice to hear your service, your country maligned and not be able to react. That's hard. I always made my recruiting goals, and about 15 years later 75 percent of those I recruited were still in service. Not many stayed that long in those days." Kuhn's talent, perspicacity, and hard work would take her to high positions in the Navy by the time she retired in 1984.

Sea Duty

Prior to 1953, except in rare cases, nurses were the only Navy women serving in ships. But in September of that year the first of sixty-three women hospital corpsmen slated to serve aboard transport ships reported for sea duty. One of them, Hospital Corpsman Third Class JoAnne Sylvester, completed five transatlantic roundtrips by July 1956. Nurses, hospital corpsmen, and Medical Service Corps officers all had a common profession: health care. The armed forces and the public accepted the idea of women serving on ships or close to battlefields so long as they were in the business of health care, and nothing else. In 1956 a single assignment presaged the advent of women in nonmedical specialties aboard Navy ships. That April, when the Navy's attack transport USS *Telfair* returned to San Diego from Hawaii, Journalist Third Class Liz Salas was among her crew.[19]

Possibly because none of the ships to which these women were assigned met any disaster (sinking, fire, mutiny), the path was clear to the next milestone, the assignment of Lt. Charlene Suneson, a line officer, to the transport USS *Mann* in July 1961. Although Suneson had an excellent record and was well qualified, the assignment was far from a success. Her immediate senior officer aboard ship later recalled, "She came on the ship with a footlocker full of seagoing pubs such as Knight's *Modern Seamanship*, Bowditch tables, nautical almanac, etc. I presume she thought she was going to be assigned real seagoing type duties." Indeed, prior to reporting she had asked the commanding officer if she could be assigned watch duty while the ship was under way. Such expectations from a woman were far too advanced for the time; she was assigned instead to assist the transportation officer, her duties restricted to those of a seagoing purser, a job she had not expected and did not want. She was capable and diligent, but complaints from the passengers with whom she dealt resulted in her receiving poor fitness reports. She submitted a long response to the Bureau of Naval Personnel—a right granted every officer who receives such a report—but it only made matters worse. Not promoted, she resigned after thirteen years of service, and the Navy lost a capable member because it was not yet ready to allow any woman line officer the responsibilities it routinely required of men.[20] Suneson's detailer later said, "She was born twenty years too soon."[21] Only after another eleven years marked by great social changes would the Navy order women to ships.

Uniforms

The women wore a summer uniform, a gray-and-white seersucker dress, that had never been popular. It was unflattering, uncomfortable, and hard to care for; they called it the mattress cover and were delighted when they were able to replace it in 1959. Few of them knew to what extent Captain Quick was responsible for the change. She had designed the replacement, a two-piece outfit made up in a blue-and-white pinstriped cotton cord, then set out to convince the Uniform Board to authorize the change.

> I picked out a pretty girl to model the new design and a not-so-pretty girl to model the mattress cover. At the last minute the pretty girl got sick, and I thought I was a goner. The Chief of the Board said he thought the gray was very nice but I told him the women, including the Navy nurses, despised it. One of my Supply Corps friends was at the meeting and he spoke up quickly. "Admiral, we face a problem with this gray uniform. Most of the gray material we have in storage is rotting. Also, it's not a practical material from our testing standpoint." So we won that one.[22]

The smarter appearance, easier care, and greater comfort of the new uniform improved morale.

In 1962 women officers were able to add to their array of uniforms a white, long-skirted uniform suitable for formal wear. A similar dark-blue uniform had been approved for winter formal wear back in 1948. Although the new formal uniforms were worn infrequently and only by officers, they too improved morale. Their introduction subtly testified to the fact that women members were now eligible for full naval careers. They had earned a place at even the most formal Navy social functions.

Individual Achievements

Throughout the decade of the 1950s Navy women could take pride in the achievements and distinctions of individuals. A few examples will suffice. Prudence Rhoades was chief aerologist at the Patuxent River Naval Air Test Center in 1956, one of five women weather forecasters in the Navy and a graduate of Mount Holyoke College. When she completed her aerographer program at Lakehurst, New Jersey, she earned one of the highest general-classification test grades recorded in the Navy. Similarly, in 1952 Julie Chernik was the first Navy woman to be the honor graduate of the Navy's dental technician school at Bainbridge. She earned a final grade of 95.607, beating out thirty-four men and four other women. In 1961 Comdr. Frances Biadasz earned her Ph.D. in international relations from George Washington University (she wrote her dissertation in her spare time while serving on the staff of NATO in Paris) and subsequently taught that subject at the Navy's Postgraduate School in Monterey. In sports, a few Navy women gained prominence as expert rifle and pistol shots, swimmers, weightlifters, softball players, and bowlers. In 1961 one Navy woman was noted for jogging up the Washington Monument three times each weekend.[23]

As the new decade began, one event seemed to set a seal on Navy women's single biggest achievement to date, that of having survived the peace. In April 1962 Chief Storekeeper Barbara Metras became the first Navy woman to be retired to the Fleet Reserve, with retirement pay, having completed nineteen years and six months on active duty. (Retirement to the Fleet Reserve, technically upon completion of twenty years of active duty, was normally allowed six months earlier as a sort of bonus for long and faithful service.) She was one of ten enlisted women who had served continuously since entering as WAVES. Two more of those were expected to follow her soon, while the remaining six elected to remain on active duty.[24]

In 1960 Captain Quick married Rear Adm. Howard Collins, and in 1962 she retired. The Navy chose Comdr. Viola Sanders to become the next woman captain and lead Navy women into their third consecutive decade of service.

*   *   *

In the decade following Korea, women in the Navy might have disappeared altogether; instead, they survived. In the wake of this single, critical achievement came several developments. First, they learned how to plan a career; how to transfer comfortably from one job to another, one duty station to another, one career field to another; and how to create a network of friends and contacts that spanned continents and oceans. Second, in certain fields where they were clustered—administration and communication, for example—they developed expertise well beyond that of many men in the same fields. Finally, as the 1950s edged into the 1960s Navy men could no longer view their female counterparts as a novelty, a momentary aberration; some women had been in service longer than some Navy men had been alive.

Navy women survived because their contributions were essential to the Navy, yet they posed no threat to Navy men. The fields in which they excelled were seen as peripheral to the Navy's chief reason for being, which was readiness for war at sea. Thus circumstance at least offered them the protection of a low profile. Most were so busy making headway with their careers—chiefly by seizing every opportunity available—that they saw no point in rocking the boat.

When the benefits and opportunities offered Navy men at that time are compared with those offered Navy women, it becomes evident that women were considered second-class citizens. While a few outstanding people like Kathleen Amick and Lucille Kuhn might achieve all that their male peers did, most women had a harder time. Whatever they achieved professionally came at the expense of marriage and family. Yet the women concentrated far more on what the Navy offered than on what it denied them. These were prefeminist times, and many a Navy woman remembered not only World War II but also the Great Depression that preceded it. They appreciated full-time, peacetime membership in a formerly all-male organization and saw the benefits as outweighing the disadvantages.

By the time the decade ended, the first Navy women to have completed full careers were retiring from active duty. They were realizations of what the Integration Act of 1948 had promised.

9

—

Upheaval: Vietnam and Its Legacy

"For many Navy traditionalists, it is even harder to give up the notion that their beloved service should be all male than to give up the notion that it should be all white."

—ADM. ELMO R. ZUMWALT

The armed forces' doldrums ended during the 1960s as the United States was drawn into the unpopular war in Vietnam. Nearly all Navy women played their usual role: They took over the jobs of Navy men in the United States, releasing them to fight the war in Southeast Asia. A handful, nine women line officers, served in Vietnam. Manpower shortages during the war led the Department of Defense to reexamine its policies on women. One result of this reexamination was the passage of Public Law 90-130, which improved women's career opportunities.

Among the casualties of Vietnam was the draft. Its demise in 1973, together with the upheavals engendered by the civil rights and feminist movements, changed dramatically the roles military women would play thereafter. The sometimes conflicting views of two Navy leaders, CNO Adm. Elmo Zumwalt and senior woman line officer Capt. Robin Quigley, significantly shaped those changes.

Into the Quagmire

The United States was again at war far across the Pacific. In 1954 it had sent a handful of military advisors to assist in training South Vietnamese forces. By 1963 the number of American service personnel had risen to fifteen thousand. In August 1964, following alleged skirmishes between U.S. and North Vietnamese naval units in the Tonkin Gulf, Congress passed a resolution that allowed U.S. military activities in Southeast Asia to escalate. By 1968, more than half a million members of the U.S. armed forces were serving there.

As the Navy began to carry out wartime tasks, its personnel prospects were not bright. Civilian jobs were plentiful and better paid than military jobs. To avoid the draft enough recruits joined the Navy, but most of these shed their uniforms once they had completed their minimum obligated service. In 1966 the Department of Defense initiated a project whereby 100,000 men formerly deemed physically or mentally unfit for service would henceforth be accepted. The Navy made no effort to increase its number of women, even though their entry qualifications were already higher than men's. Between June 1964 and June 1968 the number of enlisted Navy women grew by only 493, or slightly less than 10 percent, while male enlisted strength grew by nearly 48,000, or almost 17 percent. At the same time, the number of women line officers actually declined, from approximately 560 in 1964 to about 450 in 1966, returning to about 530 in 1968. In contrast, male officer strength increased by more than 9,000, or approximately 12 percent.[1]

Navy Women in Vietnam

Most Navy women served during the war in the fields traditionally assigned to them—administration, communications, and medical services. Many volunteered to serve in Vietnam, noting that Army and Air Force women served there. One Navy woman sent to Capt. Rita Lenihan, ACNP(W) from 1966 to 1971, a newspaper clipping about WACS assigned to Vietnam. Across it she wrote: "Why not the WAVES? As a petty officer I think it is our responsibility as well as the men's." These requests were all denied until April 1967, when Captain Lenihan announced that Lt. Elizabeth G. Wylie would become the first Navy woman who was not a nurse to serve in Vietnam. Nevertheless, Lenihan emphasized, Navy women were not to expect that any significant number of such assignments might be forthcoming, although they might submit requests that would be kept on record. The number of women who volunteered is not known, but at least twenty-six formally requested that their desire to serve in Vietnam appear in their records.[2]

Wylie's father, an admiral and author of a book on naval strategy, and her mother were "nonplussed" that their twenty-eight-year-old daughter wanted to volunteer for service in Vietnam. But when she assured them that she really wanted to go, they supported her completely. The Navy was less supportive. Beginning in 1966 Wylie had written three letters to the Bureau of Naval Personnel, requesting assignment to Vietnam. The bureau had answered only one, denying her request on the grounds that the assignment would be inappropriate. Wylie found the response illogical, for she knew that hundreds of women nurses of the Navy, Army, and Air Force were serving in Vietnam. In her opinion, either it *was* appropriate for women to serve there and all properly qualified volunteers should be accepted, or it was *not* appropriate, in which case the nurses ought to be recalled immediately. Several months later her request was granted. Wylie completed a modified version of the Navy's survival, evasion, resistance, and escape course at the amphibious base in Little Creek, Virginia, then reported to the staff of the commander of naval forces, Vietnam, in Saigon in June 1967.[3]

Originally Wylie had been assigned to work with computers in Saigon, but the equipment did not arrive there until after her departure. Consequently, she worked in the Command Information Center, which prepared various kinds of reports including briefings to visiting journalists and politicians. To keep briefings current she spent three to six days each month in the field gathering information and taking pictures. "I'd go back if I had the chance," she later told a newspaper reporter. "The opportunity to see the heart of the Navy at work is unique and rewarding." Well aware of her pioneering role, she did not want "to glorify what I did in Vietnam. I never was under hostile fire or anything like that." Speaking of the women with whom she shared quarters in Saigon, she said, "The only difficulties encountered were the same as the men. We were all away from home, families, and not in a particularly pleasant situation." Upon returning from Vietnam in July 1968, she was ordered to the staff of the Women Officers School.[4]

The second of the nine women officers to serve in Vietnam was Lt. Susan F. Hamilton, who in 1968 was assigned, as Wylie had been, to the staff of the commander of naval forces, Vietnam, in Saigon. Lt. Comdr. Barbara Bole and Lt. Sally Bostwick later joined her. Lts. Mary Anderson (first recipient of the Arleigh Burke Honor Award, given upon her graduation from the Women Officers School in October 1969) and Ann Moriarty reported to the naval support activity in Cam Ranh Bay in 1971. In 1972 Lt. (jg) Kathleen Dugan reported to Saigon; Comdrs. Carol Adsit and Elizabeth Barrett also served there. No enlisted Navy women served in Vietnam.[5]

Barrett was the highest-ranking woman naval line officer to serve in Vietnam and the first to hold a command in a combat zone. She arrived in Saigon in January 1972 and in November became commanding officer of the 450 enlisted men in the naval advisory group, a position she held until she left Vietnam in March 1973. A graduate of Mount Holyoke College with a degree in chemistry, she was forty years old, had nineteen years of naval service behind her, and was well aware that some of the men in her command were "not too pleased" to have a female commanding officer. "It gave them something to talk about," she said. During her fifteen months in Vietnam she had three days off: "February 2, 1972, when I went sailing at Cat Lo, March 29 when I went swimming at Vung Tau and December 19 when I wrote Christmas cards."[6]

Additional Navy women might have served in Vietnam had Captain Lenihan been more receptive to the idea. Lenihan, who had been commissioned in 1943, had conservative ideas about what was appropriate for Navy women; acceptance and propriety weighed more heavily with her than innovation. She was concerned that living and working conditions in Vietnam would not be appropriate for women. Exactly what led her to permit a few women to serve in Vietnam is not clear. She may have known that Liz Carpenter of the White House staff had asked Sanders, on behalf of President Lyndon Johnson, what kinds of jobs Navy women could fill in Vietnam. Perhaps Lenihan expected to receive inquiries from the commander in chief. Also, DACOWITS had discussed Vietnam assignments for women, and the Army and Air Force had already sent women. As she considered how to advise the chief of naval personnel about Wylie's request, she realized that if assigning some Navy women to Vietnam was inevitable, Wylie's personal and professional background made her an ideal choice to be the first. Lenihan was probably reassured when Wylie wrote her from Vietnam: "I can assure you that military women here act and dress discreetly and with propriety. Given the adequate living facilities and outstanding working atmosphere, I strongly believe that the Navy women who desire to serve here should have this opportunity."[7] By late 1967, owing partly to the excellent impression that Wylie made on her bosses in Saigon, a policy was worked out whereby a woman officer could be sent *if* a Navy commanding officer asked for her by name and stated that she was particularly qualified for a certain job. Thus were the nine women officers allowed service in Vietnam. With this stringent policy in place, the wonder is that any Navy women officers served in the war zone at all.

The Navy was more reluctant than the Army, Air Force, and Marine Corps to send women (except nurses) to Vietnam. The Army eventually sent five hundred women other than nurses to the war zone, the Air Force between five hundred and six hundred. Both these services had larger numbers of troops ashore than the Navy, but even the Marine Corps, which has no nurses, sent thirty-six women. Of the nearly six thousand military women who served in Vietnam, only 20 percent were neither nurses nor medical specialists.[8]

Far more military women volunteered to serve in Vietnam than were sent. Their services' reluctance to send them struck these volunteers as patronizing, a devaluation of their abilities and patriotism. Maj. Gen. Jeanne Holm, director of women in the Air Force, recalled:

> In early 1966 a plainspoken master sergeant, a veteran of World War II, demanded to know why she had just been told by a "fresh-faced" lieutenant in the base personnel office that he would not accept her request for duty in Southeast Asia. "He wouldn't know one end of an M-16 from the other," she exclaimed in exasperation, pointing to her triple rows of ribbons. "I served in North Africa and Italy—I can sure as hell serve in Vietnam."[9]

The women knew that if they were not allowed to carry a share of the burden, then the men would have to carry more. They also knew that their lack of Vietnam service would eventually result in decreased competitiveness for career-enhancing jobs and hence for promotion.

Turbulence at Home

As the war dragged on, American confidence in the certainty of victory began to wane. Casualties rose, and the war in Vietnam became the first in history to enter homes night after night via television newscasts. A strong antiwar movement arose. Evading the draft either legally by prolonging one's education or illegally by fleeing the country became more common. At the same time, the civil rights movement focused attention on discriminatory policies and practices throughout society; the armed services received a full share of that attention. The perception that poor black youths were more likely than white youths to be sent to Vietnam linked racial inequality at home with the conduct of war abroad. That made the draft a political liability, and long before it actually ended in 1973 military leaders began to realize that one day their forces might well be composed of nothing but volunteers.

Meanwhile a third powerful force was contributing to the domestic turmoil: the feminist movement. By the mid-1960s more and more women began to question why they were excluded from opportunities that men had long taken for granted. Why, they asked, were well-educated women actively discouraged from seeking careers and relegated primarily to domestic and volunteer work? Unsatisfactory answers to such questions awakened interest in the Equal Rights Amendment (ERA), which had first been introduced to Congress in 1923. It had been defeated at that time and every time it was reintroduced since then. Ironically, over the years its opponents included a number of prominent women such as Eleanor Roosevelt who were active in promoting women's causes. They believed that an ERA would jeopardize existing state and federal legislation that protected women.

In 1970, encouraged by the recent passage of civil rights legislation and backed by numerous women's organizations, Congresswoman Martha Griffiths of Michigan was able to move the ERA onto the floor of Congress. The House of Representatives passed it in October 1971 by a vote of 354 to 23, the Senate in March 1972 by a vote of 84 to 8. It would become part of the Constitution if three-quarters (thirty-eight) of the states ratified it within the next ten years. Within three months, twenty states had ratified it, and within a year ten more. It appeared that the ERA's time had come.

Leaders of the armed forces watched intently as the ERA marched toward ratification, for when it became part of the Constitution, as seemed likely, many service policies and practices regarding women would be subject to legal challenge. Clearly, it would be preferable to get their respective houses in order before Congress and the courts did it for them. Although some saw the ERA as a threat, others saw it as an opportunity to review women's policies and programs that had changed little since 1948, bringing them more in line with current social and political expectations.

Public Law 90-130

Even before the draft ended, the manpower demands of the war in Vietnam put pressure on the Department of Defense to reexamine its utilization of women. The vexing issue of career parity for women had been surfacing repeatedly in DACOWITS reports throughout the 1960s. The pressures of Vietnam finally brought it to the fore. One woman who had watched this development was Capt. Viola Sanders, who relieved Capt. Winifred Quick Collins as ACNP(W) in 1962. As we have seen, Sanders, a Mississippi native whose Navy career began in 1943, had helped pioneer the peacetime training of women recruits at Great Lakes and Bainbridge. She had served in Japan for two years, been Collins's deputy in the late 1950s, and then served eighteen months as director of naval personnel in the Fifth Naval District in Norfolk, Virginia. By the time she relieved Collins, she had seen from many perspectives the problems an inequitable promotion system caused women. In her view,

> the catalyst for the legislation came in the late fifties or early sixties when the decision was made at high levels to revise the codes covering military promotions for all the services to make them more uniform; to incorporate the different categories of officer personnel that had evolved since WWII; and to include revisions and the like into the Code. And here the ladies got a break. Instead of arriving to where we are in bits and pieces over a long period of time, it came nicely packaged. . . . I do believe there was a growing realization that women were contributing, but mainly, that their contributions could and would be increased and diversified and that promotional opportunities had to be enhanced to attain their goals—quality procurement of personnel would be a tangible, added factor.
>
> It certainly was understandable that restrictions had been imposed in the original Women's Armed Forces Integration Act. We had not the necessary experience or length of service to qualify for higher rank. But by this time, we had and we did and we got it.[10]

In 1966 the Department of Defense established an interservice working group to study women's programs. In response to the findings of the study, intense lobbying by DACOWITS, and rising political sensitivity about discriminatory laws and policies, in 1967 Congress passed Public Law 90-130, which significantly improved military women's career opportunities. Its major provisions were to remove percentage restrictions on women's ranks and numbers, allow women to hold permanent rank as captains in the Navy and as colonels in the other services, and allow them to become admirals or generals. Yet, as Major General Holm later wrote, "while it constituted an important step forward, the new law was a sign of its time and in no way signalled a major break with the conservative traditions of the military. . . . The essentially masculine character of the military profession and the unequal status of women within it were never challenged."[11]

The Navy promptly promoted six women commanders to the rank of captain: Marie Kelleher, Dorothy Council, Winifred Love, Alma Ellis, Mary Kate Bonds, and Beatrice Truitt. The seventh was ACNP(W) Rita Lenihan; her temporary rank of captain was made permanent. The following year, Comdrs. Frances Biadasz, Anne Ducey, Elizabeth Harrison, Muriel Lewis, Mary Gore, Fran McKee, Mary Donnelly, and Celia Barteau were promoted. Being selected was one thing; actual employment as a captain turned out to be another, as Captain Kelleher later reported.

> When the legislation . . . was introduced, the Navy was very supportive—or, at least more supportive than I expected. Then came reality—they really hadn't planned for our utilization as I rapidly found out. We were removed from the Woman Officer Detailer and turned over to the Captain (non-aviation) Detailer. Since I was in a CDR [commander] billet and coming up for rotation in the not-too-distant future, I made an appointment to meet with him. I had two sub- specialty designators—Personnel Management and Computer Systems Management, so I thought there should be some shore job in those areas I could fill. Guess what he said? "You'll have to find someone who will take you." For once, I held my Irish temper and went on my way. Subsequently I heard the Director of the DOD [Department of Defense] Computer Institute had put in for retirement. Since I also had a Master's Degree in Education from Stanford, I thought I was reasonably qualified. BuPers was the DOD manager of that command, and the folks in training were immediately supportive and my name went forward. The incumbent immediately withdrew his retirement papers—*he* wasn't going to be replaced by a *woman!*[12]

At least a few women had been promoted to captain promptly; the first promotions to rear admiral (lowest of the Navy's "flag ranks") took much longer.

A New Hand on the Navy's Tiller

In June 1970 Admiral Zumwalt became CNO. Younger and more junior than all other candidates for the position, Zumwalt was philosophically and intellectually in accord with the changes that the Navy would have to make if the ERA was ratified and temperamentally prepared to make them boldly. Bushy eyebrows and an aquiline nose gave him a dashing appearance, which he often heightened during his visits to the fleet by wearing a flight jacket emblazoned with a large Z across the back. The news media found him fascinating. Together with Secretary of the Navy John Chafee, who was of like mind, he set out to clear the decks.

High among Zumwalt's priorities were more enlightened personnel policies and practices. Such reforms were urgent if the Navy's alarmingly low retention rates were to be raised, and if, in view of the approaching end of the draft, the Navy would be able to recruit enough young men and women to serve even one hitch. Within two weeks of becoming CNO he set up the first of several retention study groups, each composed of approximately a dozen junior members of a particular Navy community, such as aviation officers or submarine enlisted men. Group participants were brought to Washington to confer for several days and come up with recommendations addressing the Navy practices and policies that most adversely affected recruitment and retention. The groups presented their findings to Zumwalt in person. In 1974 thirteen such groups were convened. The result was a volley of messages (promptly dubbed Z-grams) from the CNO to the entire Navy promulgating policy and/or guidelines.

The two groups for women met in 1971. Upon hearing the results of their deliberations, Zumwalt was "sadly enlightened" to learn that for various reasons the Navy had wasted much of its women's talent. Subsequently, in August 1972, a Z-gram designated Z-116 announced changes in policies that would make better use of that talent and thus improve the retention of women, who would be sorely needed once the all-volunteer force became a reality. Z-116 also obliquely acknowledged the pressure for change emanating from the apparently imminent passage of the ERA: "In the very near future we may have authority to utilize officer and enlisted women on board ships."[13]

Accordingly, Z-116 informed all hands that all laws, regulations, and policies would be examined to "eliminate any disadvantages to women resulting from either legal or attitudinal restrictions." Then the following actions were being taken:

1. Enlisted women were authorized limited entry to all ratings.
2. Under a pilot program, a limited number of officer and enlisted women were assigned to the crew of the USS *Sanctuary*, a noncombatant.
3. Women would be assigned as commanding officers of units ashore.
4. The NROTC program would be opened to women in fiscal year 1974.

5. Qualified women would be considered for promotion to the rank of rear admiral.
6. Women could be selected to study at the joint-service colleges, that is, the National War College and the Industrial College of the Armed Forces.

It is hard to say which of these initiatives was the most enticing to women. Taken together, they promised Navy women wider horizons than ever before—but not necessarily smoother sailing.

The Corner into Tomorrow

Capt. Robin Quigley succeeded Captain Lenihan as ACNP(W) in January 1971. Her service record was exemplary. Twice she had served in the office of the CNO and then spent two and a half years as senior aide to a high-level admiral in Paris. Two other tours of duty had been more pedestrian: In the late 1950s she was a field recruiter in San Francisco, and in the late 1960s she worked in the Bureau of Naval Personnel, responsible for officers recruiting programs. After being promoted to commander relatively early, she served as a special assistant on the staff of the Submarine School in Groton, Connecticut. Only nine months after becoming a commander she was selected to succeed Lenihan and consequently promoted to captain.

She had begun her Navy career in 1954; all the other women captains had seen service in World War II. Her youthfulness was accentuated by good looks and a forthright manner. These attributes led those with authority to advance Quigley to believe that she represented a new, postwar breed of female naval officer. They thought, she later told an interviewer, that she would be "jazzy and right in the line with [Admiral Zumwalt's] philosophies. As it turned out, unfortunately, they didn't get what they thought they were going to get."[14]

Actually, Robin Quigley's appearance and demeanor belied her conservative views. One of two daughters of an Air Force colonel, she grew up with confidence in her own abilities, a mind skilled at logical analysis, and an interest in ethical and moral issues. In 1951 she graduated from Dominican College in San Rafael, California, with a bachelor's degree in music and some knowledge of radio broadcasting. Unable to find work in radio, she worked temporarily in public schools but at that time "had no desire for a career. . . . I wanted to marry and have a home." Her parents urged her to join the Air Force, but she was not particularly interested. When her father was ordered to London she went along with the family. Now on the European side of the Atlantic she began to appreciate the value of her father's service and to consider service for herself. After exploring Air Force and Navy programs for women, she chose the latter. "I just had a feel for the Navy and I can't tell you why. . . . I had found out that the Navy had been his [her father's] first love. . . . With great delight, both of my parents received my announcement."[15]

In one significant area Quigley was in agreement with Zumwalt: Morale in the enlisted ranks was low, which called for drastic measures. The retention statistics for enlisted women were appalling, she discovered. During the preceding eight to ten years, 88 to 96 percent of the women who enlisted in the Navy had failed to complete their first enlistment. As she traveled to more than 140 commands to meet with enlisted women, Quigley discerned a self-defeating attitude on the part of women that originated in semantics but extended far beyond.[16]

On February 23, 1972, she issued a jolting memorandum to all Navy women. She reminded her readers that for quite a few years there had been no such organization as the WAVES. They had not joined the WAVES, they had joined the Navy, and continued use of an outmoded acronym implied that they were a ladies auxiliary of the Navy. As Navy personnel, women could use professional labels such as radioman or officer. To modify these labels with the adjective WAVE was to modify one's status as well. Quit doing this to yourselves, she warned, or you "will continue too frequently to wind up running the ditto machine and the coffee mess. . . ."[17]

Quigley was soundly denounced for this stand. The acronym WAVES had been much loved from the moment Elizabeth Reynard coined it. To give it up seemed wrong to many, almost a denial of their heritage. They might have taken less offense if they had known, as Quigley did, that Joy Hancock herself had made a similar suggestion back in 1952: She had written to the officer-in-charge of the Women Officers School, saying that she wished the school staff would stop using the acronym WAVES in their literature because they and the women they were training were naval officers, not WAVE officers.* In this respect at least, Quigley was riding the tide of history; despite complaints the term *WAVE* soon lost

*Author Ebbert, who was in training at the Women Officers School in 1952, seldom if ever heard herself referred to as a WAVE officer while there, but she often heard it afterward.

currency, and sentimentally inspired suggestions to revive it in 1982 received little support.

Quigley saw something else in her visits to those 140 commands: a double standard the women were applying to themselves. In numerous instances they wanted to be fully integrated into the Navy, yet they also wanted special consideration as women. In her view they could not have it both ways. This problem was fostered by a system of administration that employed in every command a women's representative or assistant for women. The commanding officer or officer-in-charge would designate as representative a senior woman officer (or in small units, a senior woman petty officer) to advise him on matters concerning women. In theory and often in practice this system worked well. Certainly it had been needed earlier when women were a relatively new phenomenon in the Navy, and it had been helpful in later years. By decreeing that a women's representative would always be on hand to advise the commanding officer, the Navy was protecting him from errors in judgment as well as the women in his charge from exploitation. However, what had been seen earlier as protection now seemed more like paternalism. At worst, everyone suffered: the commanding officer because he was not learning how to lead a mixed-gender unit; the representatives because they had responsibility out of proportion to their authority; the women because they in effect had two chains of command; and finally the men in the command, because they perceived the women as being favored with a special advocate.

This system reflected the relationship between the ACNP(W) and the chief of naval personnel. At best, although she lacked authority, the ACNP(W) could and did offer useful counsel to her superior, with excellent results for the Navy and its women. At worst, men could ignore women's concerns, assuring themselves that she would handle them. No matter how skilled, resourceful, or energetic she might be, the ACNP(W) still often found herself in the role Captain McAfee had described herself as playing back in the early days of the WAVES, of dangling link on the chain of command.

Quigley's sense of logic told her that this entire situation must change. Hence her memo of February 23, 1972, lobbed another bombshell at her readers: The women's representative system was to be suspended, and women would use the channels of communication and action already established for men. She acknowledged that these channels were not perfect; they might not always respond to women or give them what they wanted. However, if you want full status as respected professionals then you must use and respect what the profession has to offer. If you want to be the ladies auxiliary then you must accept the more comfortable but subordinate status that has to offer. But you must commit yourselves one way or the other, because you cannot have the best of both the worlds.

She concluded by acknowledging that some might agree in principle with this move while arguing that now was not the time to take it. She believed, to the contrary, that

> we are ready . . . to stand on our own as real professionals. . . . Admiral Zumwalt has brought us into the "NOW Navy." The corner into tomorrow is there waiting to be turned. . . . If we women fail . . . to turn that corner with the rest of the Navy, then we will be relegated—and rightly so—to the perimeters of this profession tomorrow and forever.[18]

As she further pondered the function of her office, Quigley determined that it was largely superfluous. Most of the papers that crossed her desk, she thought, belonged elsewhere and landed in her office only because they concerned women. Accordingly, she began to route all such matters to offices where in her opinion they more properly belonged and thereby systematically dismantled her own office.

The effect was stunning. Although she had hoped to accomplish her objective gradually, Navy women found her action precipitous: "One day Pers-K was there and the next day it wasn't." Particularly missed were the Pers-K newsletters that had listed women's promotions and orders.[19] Without an ACNP(W), important changes for women that were imminent or already under way were inadequately monitored. Obviously, some central oversight of policies affecting women was still needed. In the next few years the Navy convened various panels to provide that oversight, with varying degrees of effectiveness.

Quigley was able to retire the WAVE name and disperse the functions of her office because these were logical, necessary changes for which the Navy was ready (although not everyone thought so at the time). Both in the vision that fostered them and the manner in which they were made they seemed consonant with the changes generated by Z-grams, which had also been denounced by some as precipitous and accepted unwillingly. Zumwalt and Quigley, it appeared, were in full harmony.

In fact, they were not. The first dissonant note sounded when Quigley had been ACNP(W) for only two months. Zumwalt convened a WAVE retention study group in March 1971 and designated Quigley its sponsor. She disagreed with many of the group's recommendations but could do nothing to change them, since Zumwalt had insisted that sponsors were not to offer input, only to facilitate. In July 1972 he created a committee to draft what would become Z-116. Quigley declined an invitation to attend its meetings, sending her deputy instead, because she believed the intent was to get around her known opposition to one of Z-116's recommendations, to send women to sea. (She had also recommended that women not be admitted to the Naval Academy or allowed into flight training.) Once Z-116 was promulgated, in August 1972, there was little to be gained and possibly much cause for embarrassment if she stayed on. Her dismantling of Pers-K provided a plausible pretext for her departure from Washington. In April 1973 she became the first woman to be given a major command, that of the service schools in San Diego, California. She retired in November 1974.

Captain Quigley served Navy women well by propelling them toward some important, necessary steps. Yet her skepticism about some of the bold initiatives for women seemed limiting to many Navy women. For example, she thought that allowing women into aviation would prove nothing more than a "glamorous carrot" because their careers as pilots would eventually be stymied. Nor could she justify women at the Naval Academy. Her reason was chiefly fiscal, as the Women Officers School, which cost the Navy much less, was supplying plenty of women officers of high quality. As for the pilot program for women at sea, she seemed to see it as tokenism, describing it as "shallow" and "superficial."[20]

Quigley's views in these matters did not prevail; what she saw as reasons not to advance others saw as challenges to be met while advancing. Ironically, it was not she but rather the women who would take their places on ships, in aircraft, and at the Naval Academy who would turn the corner into tomorrow.

Once again the upheavals and exigencies of war extended the horizons for military women. The extreme unpopularity of the Vietnam War sounded the death knell for the draft, compounding the services' difficulties in meeting manpower needs. These difficulties, combined with changes that might ensue from the proposed ERA, forced the Navy to reexamine its women's programs. Increased and better utilization of women began to look more attractive, especially as the feminist movement was challenging society's traditional assumptions about and restrictions on women. The passage of Public Law 90-130 removed some barriers.

Yet it took a bold hand to make happen what the law now permitted. It took Admiral Zumwalt's initiatives, especially Z-116, to set Navy women on the path to the new opportunities. At the same time, in what turned out to be a complementary initiative, Captain Quigley challenged Navy women to jettison outworn attitudes and assume higher standards of professionalism. When she dismantled her own billet on the grounds that its functions should be integrated within other existing Navy offices, she impelled women to become more integrated with the established Navy structure, albeit at the price of less cohesion among themselves.

The nine Navy women line officers who served in Vietnam had a significance far beyond their number. Like hundreds of women in the Army and Air Force and dozens in the Marine Corps, they made it impossible to deny that women other than nurses could serve in a combat zone—a presage of the later issue of women in combat. More generally, their competence, industry, and patriotism demonstrated that Navy women were both ready and able to stride through the doors that were now opening to them.

PART FOUR

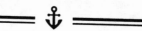

Modern Navy Women

10

—

Sustaining a Volunteer Force

"Whether this nation can sustain its armed forces solely by voluntary means could well depend on how effectively the female labor source is employed."
— MARTIN J. BINKIN AND SHIRLEY J. BACH, *Women and the Military*

The end of the draft led to a rapid and steady increase in the Navy's proportion of women members. This highlighted the need to reestablish a central office to oversee policies and practices regarding women. It also compelled the Navy to develop policy on issues relating to their private lives—on the status of spouses, pregnancy, the custody of minor children, and lesbianism. Such matters had previously been dealt with quietly, often covertly, on an individual basis. Two other issues now began to claim more attention: fraternization and sexual harassment. Fraternization had long been proscribed within military organizations. Now fraternization cases were sometimes complicated by questions of gender. Sexual harassment gained greater prominence not only because more women were in the Navy but also because they were now entering precincts formerly all male.

The Navy would deal with these new realities only reluctantly.

The Oncoming Tide

On June 30, 1972, Navy women numbered only a few more than 9,400 out of a total force of just over 588,000. Of nearly 73,200 officers, approximately 1,000 were women other than nurses. The numbers began to increase, slowly at first, then more quickly. Just over ten years later the total number of Navy members remained virtually unchanged, but the number of women was now 43,164. In one decade, women rose from 1.3 to 4.6 percent of the Navy's officers and from 1.1 to 7.7 percent of the enlisted ranks. In the next decade the rate of increase slackened somewhat, although the numbers kept rising. In 1990, out of more than 74,000 officers, almost 5,700 were women, about 7 percent. Of a total enlisted strength of slightly more than 524,000, about 10 percent were women.[1]

The increase began as a response to the expected passage of the ERA and, after its failure, continued because of two other powerful forces. First was the end of the draft in early 1973. Second was the end of the so-called baby boom. The pool of males aged seventeen to twenty-five years was beginning to shrink, with the end of diminishing numbers nowhere in sight. To "man" the fleet and its shore establishment, the Navy would need to recruit and retain more women than at any time since World War II.

OP-01(W)

When Capt. Robin Quigley abolished the position of ACNP(W) in 1972, her logic was sound, and time has validated her vision. Precisely because ACNP(W) disappeared abruptly, old assumptions were jostled and the task of integrating women into the Navy moved more swiftly—although often as a matter more of resolute obedience than of preference.

Sound logic notwithstanding, the reality is that Navy women are a minority with needs different from those of the male majority, partly because society views them differently and partly because special laws apply to their naval service. For the rest of the 1970s the Navy employed various panels, none of them fully successful, to oversee the development and execution of policies for women. In 1979 it created a billet designated special assistant for women's policy (OP-01[W]), a newer version of ACNP(W), charged to advise the chief of naval personnel on matters concerning women and to oversee and monitor policies applied to them. Once more a single office was maintaining focus on women's treatment. This new office suffered at first because it was a collateral duty rather than a full-time job; a Navy study reported in 1987 that incumbents were "hardpressed to devote adequate time to it." Consequently, in 1988 Capt. Kathleen D. Bruyere (formerly Byerly) was assigned to it full time. However, OP-01(W) remained only an advocacy agent. More was needed, and in 1990 she was also made responsible for another office, the Women's Policy Branch (OP-13W), which formulates and implements policy for women. Today the reach of these two offices far exceeds that of their predecessors, largely because they are concerned with approximately 10 percent of the Navy's total force instead of about 1 percent. Their far greater role in initiating, developing, carrying out, and monitoring policy is considerably enhanced by the fact that other senior women officers now hold numerous key billets throughout the Navy Department.[2]

Women's Families

The armed services have long accepted the need to make certain specialized provisions for their members' families. Before World War II, in an all-male force, family meant wife and children. Until the late 1960s nearly all women in military or naval service chose to remain single, and those who married were able to leave service, almost at will, solely because of marriage. Thereafter the armed forces increasingly had to accept that women members were also likely to have families. Policies that discriminated against women with families might impair recruitment and be subject to legal challenge. On some family issues the Navy was able simply, quietly to modify its policies, on others it changed only after protracted internal struggle, and on yet others it changed only in response to court orders.

Collocation

By the early 1970s married Navy women were no longer rarities, and the Navy had to accommodate them or risk losing valuable members. In 1980 it had about 6,500 couples consisting of two Navy members. About 95 percent of those were assigned to jobs in the same general area, indicating that Navy detailers were already managing to accommodate them. In 1982 the Navy made collocation its official policy.

It is not an easy policy to uphold. The Navy's ability to locate couples together hangs on whether it can match its needs with theirs without disregarding someone else's requirements and preferences for assignments. Easiest to place are very junior members with few special qualifications who can be placed in areas with large Navy populations. Each pair of assignments represents a chain of complex decisions. To make them for hundreds of Navy couples each time one or both members are due for reassignment suggests how far the Navy is willing to go to keep qualified people on board. When the couple has children with special medical or schooling needs, the challenge increases exponentially.

Sometimes the Navy cannot offer assignments consistent with its own needs and both his and her best interests. Whose career is put on hold while the other's is advanced? Anecdotes abound about how detailers and couples themselves have assumed that the woman's career was the one to be sacrificed.[3] Undoubtedly this attitude once prevailed and probably it has weakened, but no evidence exists to verify and plot its decline.

Dependent Husbands

For nearly thirty years, the Navy granted dependent privileges to only a few husbands, those who could prove financial dependence on their wives. DACOWITS tried and failed to alter this policy.

Air Force Lt. Sharron Frontiero changed all that in 1970. Her husband was financially dependent on her, and she did not want to leave the service. She filed a class-action suit in federal court, claiming that the Air Force discriminated against women by denying their families equal access to benefits enjoyed by men's families; her case eventually reached the Supreme Court, which upheld her claims. The resulting servicewide change finally entitled servicewomen's families to the same privileges long enjoyed by those of servicemen.[4] The major privileges included medical benefits (potentially the most valuable), housing allowances computed at the higher rate allowed for couples (previously the allowance for married servicewomen had been computed at the lower rate for single persons), and access to military shopping facilities. Most significant was the fact of entitlement itself, which acknowledged that these privileges derived from the woman's own service, not from her spouse's need. Furthermore, she and he were spared the indignity of having to prove need.

Although the armed services lost the Frontiero case, the Supreme Court's decision actually saved them. They were forced to jettison old practices that would have kept them from attracting and retaining the number of women they needed.

↜ Motherhood

Until 1972 the Navy resolutely considered the naval service incompatible with motherhood (although never with fatherhood). First, it viewed motherhood as a full-time job, overlooking how many mothers did in fact work outside their homes, either through choice or necessity. Second, naval personnel had to be ready to leave home on short notice for extended periods of time. The Navy was ready to separate a father from his family suddenly and with little or no warning—that was part and parcel of his contract with the Navy and did not offend public sensibility. But it would not put itself in a position where it had to separate a mother from her children. Only persistent hearsay suggests that it had, case by case and with the utmost discretion, allowed a very few Navy women with children to remain on active duty. By the early 1970s the feminist movement had made it more acceptable philosophically for mothers to work outside their homes, while the rising cost of living had made it more necessary. Now there was less justification for the inequity that forced Navy women out of active duty when they had children, and the Navy could ill afford to dismiss women solely because they became mothers.

On September 28, 1970, Capt. Tommie Sue Smith, an Air Force lawyer with sole custody of her eight-year-old son, filed suit in federal court claiming that the Air Force was forcing her to choose between staying in service and having her son live with her. The Air Force was already considering amending its policy regarding women with children under the age of eighteen, and on September 29 announced that it would do so. The Army had also faced court action as the result of a similar case.[5]

Events that led to the Navy's change of policy began in September 1969, when Senior Chief Personnelman Winifred Hamerlinck realized she might be pregnant. She had been married for more than ten years; as she wrote to the chief of naval personnel, "It is obvious that this is not planned parenthood." She had served with distinction for nearly eighteen years, yet if she left prior to May 1971 she would receive no retirement benefits. Furthermore, the Navy would lose a valuable member with an outstanding record: She had become a petty officer first class after only four years and four months of service, a chief petty officer at about ten years, and senior chief at fourteen years, and she was slated to advance to master chief, the Navy's highest enlisted rank. Someone in the command unofficially alerted Capt. Marie Kelleher to the situation. One of the first eight women to be promoted to captain after the legislation of 1967, Kelleher knew that a recent policy change permitted pregnant enlisted women within a few months of retirement to stay on active duty until their eligibility date. At her suggestion Hamerlinck requested a waiver, asking to be allowed to remain on active duty until she was eligible for retirement. Her mother and mother-in-law would care for the baby, and she would request neither a monetary allowance nor any other special consideration because of the child. Her commanding officer forwarded her request and strongly recommended approval, describing her dedication and competence in glowing terms and stating that her "continued assignment to this command would be desirable." The request was granted, and Hamerlinck thus became the first Navy enlisted woman officially allowed to remain on active duty after having a baby.[6] The Navy's willingness to retain Hamerlinck reflected some sensitivity to the shifts in public opinion impelled by the feminist movement. Also, the Navy was aware that the other services were reviewing their policies on pregnancy.

Another episode, this one drawing some publicity, occurred a few months later, in the spring of 1970. Seaman Anna Flores, stationed at Pensacola, Florida, became pregnant while engaged to a Navy enlisted man. Although she miscarried before the wedding date and the pregnancy policy therefore no longer applied, her commanding officer moved to discharge her on the grounds that not to do so would be seen as condoning unwed pregnancy. By viewing Flores's pregnancy in moral rather than medical terms he laid the Navy open to charges of hypocrisy and discrimination, for there was no move to discharge her fiancé. With the help of the American Civil Liberties Union Flores filed suit, claiming it was unconstitutional to force pregnant women out of service but not the Navy men responsible for their pregnancies. The Navy backed down, and Flores remained.[7]

At the same time, Lt. Comdr. Jordine Von Wantoch, also pregnant, was making her case to remain on active duty. Having served thirteen years, she would not be eligible for retirement for seven more. Lieutenant commanders were customarily retained on active duty until eligible for retirement, that is, for twenty years of service, and their vested interest in retirement could be denied them only by disciplinary action. If it forced Von Wantoch out of service before she became eligible to retire, the Navy would highlight the discriminatory nature of its pregnancy policy. In June 1970, after considerable research on precedents—she knew of Hamerlinck's case and of a Supply Corps officer with eighteen years' service who had had a baby and remained on active duty until retirement—Von Wantoch requested a waiver from the chief of naval personnel. Her request, like Hamerlinck's, noted that she had made arrangements for child care that would allow her to continue in all her duties, which were chiefly managerial, not physically demanding, and did not necessitate being in uniform since she worked mostly with civilians. She referred to the Navy's "emphasis on retention of career motivated, highly qualified personnel" and listed her own qualifications, which included the Joint Service Commendation Medal and a master of arts degree. She noted shifts in society's ideas about women, legislation that had upheld women's rights in the workplace, and the U.S. Civil Service policy of allowing sick leave for maternity absence. Finally, she pointed out that she would have sufficient earned leave to cover the time needed to give birth and recover. Her commanding officer heartily endorsed her request: "To lose her permanently would be a severe loss to the United States Navy." His commanding officer in turn concurred: "Her departure from the Navy during this [sic], the most productive years of her career, would be an unfortunate loss."[8]

On July 16, 1970, the secretary of the Navy approved Von Wantoch's request but noted that the approval was "not to be construed as a revision of existing policy." Revision, no; serious challenge, yes. The Navy was not just allowing a valued member to stay for a few months until retirement, it was allowing her to combine motherhood and active duty over a period of several years. The Bureau of Naval Personnel then told her to take five months' leave immediately, returning to duty no earlier than December 31, well after her baby's birth. She was to "submit an irrevocable request for voluntary retirement to be effective" as soon as she was eligible. In other words, she could not stay on active duty beyond twenty years, which effectively precluded her from being considered for promotion. Von Wantoch accepted these conditions in order to stay on active duty but added a few of her own. She requested the retirement "provided that I give birth to a living child, that prior to the retirement date my status as a parent is not changed, and that no change in policy has been established which would make less stringent the requirement for women to leave the service because of parenthood." If a door opened in the future, she wanted to make sure she could walk through it.[9]

That same year Col. Jeanette Sustad, the director of women Marines, said publicly what many others were already saying privately, namely, that pregnant women need not leave active duty. This view sharply challenged that held by Capt. Rita Lenihan, ACNP(W), and exposed the Navy's existing policy to further pressure. That policy was suspended in February 1971 following Lenihan's retirement. Until a new policy was announced, the case of every Navy woman to be discharged for pregnancy or dependency of minor children was to be reviewed by the chief of naval personnel.

Capt. Robin Quigley, Lenihan's successor, viewed the former policy as unfair, too subject to varying interpretations. She thus strove "to set out a policy . . . that allowed, by exception, women to remain in the Naval service with dependents." The new policy appeared in November 1971. Despite careful verbiage honoring the traditional view that the demands of motherhood and naval service were incompatible, the door cracked open: Case by case, exceptions would be granted. Von Wantoch later cited this change as "sufficiently less stringent than before to render my request from retirement not binding." She was subsequently promoted to commander, then to captain. When she retired in 1986 she was commanding officer of the personnel support activity in San Diego and her sixteen-year-old daughter, Lian, was a senior in high school preparing to enter Johns Hopkins University.[10]

Within a few months the Navy announced that it would consider allowing pregnant women to stay on active duty if they would use twelve weeks of their earned leave to cover the period of delivery and recovery. In addition, for the first time since World War I, custody of minors would not bar a woman from entering the Navy. Over the next few years more and more pregnant women in all the services sought waivers that allowed them to stay on active duty. The Department of Defense could see which way the courts and public opinion were heading; in June 1974 it dictated that hereafter separation of women for pregnancy and parenthood was to be strictly voluntary, and by May 1975 all services were to develop such policies. The advice was timely, for in 1976, in a case involving a woman Marine (Crawford vs. Cushman), the Second Circuit Court ruled that involuntary separation of a servicewoman solely on the grounds of pregnancy violated due process guaranteed by the Fifth Amendment. In the same year about two thousand Navy women became pregnant, of whom about half decided to stay on active duty. In 1977 the Navy issued a uniform for pregnant women, the first armed service to do so.

By 1982 pregnant women were not only allowed to stay on active duty, they might be *required* to stay if they belonged to certain groups—women, for example, who had received educational benefits (Naval Academy, NROTC, or nursing school) and those who had incurred obligated service for flight training or medical residency. Finally, those with critical skills could be retained. In 1989 the Navy went even further and said that pregnancy would normally not be accepted as a reason to release a woman from service.

The policy that allows or requires pregnant women and mothers to stay on active duty has its critics, those who claim that the time a woman is absent from her job during pregnancy and childbirth compromises the Navy's readiness for action. Others have gathered evidence to show that readiness is far more compromised by higher male rates of absenteeism for brawling, intoxication, and resultant incarceration. To separate fact from fiction, the Navy has studied the issue in recent years.

In one study, the naval hospital in San Diego found that of nearly nine hundred junior enlisted women on active duty who reported for prenatal care from August 1986 to May 1987, 41 percent were unmarried and half of those were twenty-one years old or younger. Nearly 30 percent of the women chose to leave the service. During the second half of 1987 the percentage of pregnant unmarried women dropped 7 percent, perhaps in response to the hospital's aggressive counseling and education efforts. Comdr. Judy Glenn, a Navy nurse who had conducted the survey and initiated the counseling and education programs, concluded that the Navy still had much to learn about the problems it faces with young, single, pregnant sailors. A major report on women in the Navy, released at about the same time (1987), echoed that point. Its major conclusion regarding pregnancy was that data on the subject were incomplete and did not "measure the significance of lost time or sudden losses." This, from the Navy's perspective, is the heart of the problem. A 1990 update of the 1987 report reached the same conclusion as Commander Glenn:

> It is the pregnant, junior enlisted woman who is more likely to experience significant difficulty and occasion more challenge to her work center and command, particularly if she is unmarried and without a support system. [Her] difficulties . . . are not only a function of relative inexperience but also of limited financial assets.[11]

The Navy's major study of the impact of pregnancy and single parenthood on its mission was a three-year effort completed in 1991. Undertaken by the Navy Personnel Research and Development Center in San Diego, the study determined that women and men lost the same amount of time from jobs each month for reasons of illness, discipline, or pregnancy. Nonetheless, beliefs about the impact of pregnancy on readiness still vary widely.[12]

Child Care

As it turned out, the difficulty lay not so much with pregnancy as with parenthood. The Navy's challenges on this issue have less to do with pregnant women than with mothers and fathers.

Navy personnel must be mobile, able to work long and/or irregular hours, and deployable. This trio of requirements complicates their efforts to obtain long-term, adequate care for their children. First, they are away from family members who might lend a hand. Second, transfers interfere with even favorable child-care situations. Third, long and often irregular hours demand more flexibility than many child-care givers are willing to allow. Finally, deployment complicates everything. For married couples, it shifts the total burden to the parent remaining at home, and for the single parent it means finding someone willing to be a surrogate parent for a period of months.

These difficulties barely existed back when ninety-nine out of every hundred Navy hands were male, when most married Navy men had wives who stayed home, when divorced Navy men seldom had custody of their children, and when Navy women were childless. By the 1970s and 1980s few married mothers stayed home, and divorced fathers with custody became more numerous, as did unwed mothers. Only those Navy personnel able to support or hire a live-in surrogate have been able to consider their child-care needs solved. For all the rest, keeping a steady, affordable source of adequate care for their children is a continuing anxiety.

From about the 1950s on, most Navy bases offered some sort of nursery or child-care facility. But beginning in the late 1970s many on-base facilities could not keep up with the increasing demand. Unable to expand rapidly because funds to do so had to come from Congress, they became overcrowded and long waiting lists developed. Off-base private facilities proliferated, some of questionable quality, others too expensive for many Navy parents. Few facilities, whether on or off base, could offer extended hours or around-the-clock care.

The implications for the Navy's readiness became increasingly visible. By 1982 the situation had caught the attention of those at high levels; a deputy to an assistant secretary of the Navy told DACOWITS, "The Navy ... is making plans to insure more bases have adequate child-care facilities." Its efforts in this direction lagged behind those of other services, for funds to construct such facilities had been omitted from the Navy's budget. By 1989 it proposed to spend $17.5 million over two years to build twelve more child-care centers, and at least sixteen more between 1990 and 1994. In 1989 Congress agreed to fund a "major expansion" of all military child-care facilities. With the funding came scrutiny of management, resulting in better standards and reduced fees. This persuaded more military families to switch to base facilities from private child-care providers, further lengthening waiting lists. However, in 1990, with the drawdown of military forces, hiring was frozen. By the summer of 1991 the effect on military child-care programs was devastating. On August 9, 1991, a special hiring authority took effect, enabling the services to increase child-care staffs by 12 percent worldwide. This move demonstrates the priority now given to such matters.[13]

The child-care issue is complicated by parental leave policy. As Representative Patricia Schroeder noted, military women are required to be back on duty five weeks after they give birth, but many on-base child-care facilities do not accept children before they are six months old. In 1989 the Navy extended parental leave, but only from thirty to forty-two days and only if complications result from delivery.[14]

The challenge of child care has become a major issue for the Navy. It cannot allow parents to use lack of child care as an excuse to shirk their duties, nor can it be indifferent to the children's welfare. In 1985 it announced that all parents must file a certificate designating custodians who would assume responsibility for their children when they deployed or when they were temporarily assigned to another duty station or a base lacking child-care facilities. However, this requirement has been inconsistently enforced.

It is single parents about whom the Navy is most concerned. In 1988 the vice chief of naval operations made those concerns explicit. Warning against "supporting and encouraging a lifestyle of parenthood outside of marriage," he went on, "I don't believe most single parents in this category, and regrettably, that includes some who are there because of broken marriages, can meet [both] their deployment responsibilities and parental responsibilities. . . ." A few weeks later the master chief petty officer of the Navy said much the same thing. Some disagree with these views, citing single parents they have commanded who have met both responsibilities well.[15]

Are single parents adversely affecting the Navy's readiness? No one knows the answer, partly because no one knows exactly how many single parents the Navy has; estimates range from fourteen thousand to twenty-four thousand. Much depends on how the term single parent is defined. Is it the divorced petty officer whose widowed mother lives with him and stays at home with his two sons? Or does it include the widowed commander whose son and daughter are both away at college? Congress has ordered the services to study the subject. If they can show that single parents impair readiness, lawmakers could use the studies to ban them from service. At present, the services do not discharge single parents but will not commission or enlist them. One result is that some single parents, seeing military service as a guarantee of a steady paycheck and medical benefits, "give" custody of their children to others before entering, then later "readopt" them.[16]

Even though more Navy men than women are single parents, because they outnumber Navy women ten to one or some of them pay child support, a considerably larger ratio of the women are single, custodial parents. Of these, commanders and shipmates see as most troubled and troubling the very junior enlisted women, those who lack the maturity, skills, and money to obtain adequate care for their children. Navy women fear that so much negative attention on so few of their number affects the acceptance of all.

Fraternization

In a profession whose members can be ordered into danger, charges of favoritism carry notable gravity. Even the appearance of favoritism can damage morale. This is the unchanging basis of the armed forces' aversion to fraternization, the word they use to describe personal relationships between officers and enlisted personnel, or between senior and junior members of each group, that are unduly familiar. Until recently the Navy had no explicit regulation against fraternization. Whenever fraternization was charged, the legal basis for disciplinary action consisted of two articles in the Uniform Code of Military Justice. Under article 133 an officer may be charged with "conduct unbecoming an officer," and article 134 prohibits "all disorders and neglects to the prejudice of good order and discipline . . . [and] all conduct of a nature to bring discredit upon the armed force." These articles backed by the weight of custom sufficed to control fraternization.

The situation began to change in the early 1970s when social and sexual behavior was becoming more casual and informal and when many military customs were being questioned. In this atmosphere, the increased number of women in the Navy complicated fraternization cases with questions of gender and sex. Was the Navy's stand against fraternization still valid where romance was concerned?

In 1983 the senior officers of U.S. Navy forces in Europe found inconsistent treatment of cases and tried to write a statement of policy to clarify the situation. The statement was sunk summarily by higher authority in Washington, who regarded it as unnecessary. But events of the next few years indicated that the European commanders had judged the situation more clearly than their seniors.[17]

Three examples of cases occurring between 1985 and 1988 reveal the difficulties. In the first, the commanding officer of an aviation squadron deployed overseas lived in his government-provided quarters with a junior woman officer in his squadron. He was officially separated from his wife but not divorced; the woman officer's previous marriage had been annulled. Another officer in the squadron filed a complaint against the commanding officer after receiving a poor fitness report from him. The commanding officer was found guilty, under article 134, of fraternizing and then lying about it. After paying a fine of $2,500 he was allowed to remain in service, but with virtually no possibility for promotion. One fellow officer called this punishment a "limp-wrist slap." The second case concerned another commanding officer, this one of a shore-based unit in the United States. He was found guilty of four counts of fraternization with enlisted women and one count of adultery. He was fined $10,000 and ordered to forfeit another $30,000 in future pay. The court also recommended that he receive a general discharge under honorable conditions, inferior to an honorable discharge. A third case involved a reserve flag officer who had dated an enlisted woman in his command for two years—apparently discreetly—and was then "administratively removed" from his command.[18]

These three cases drew public attention, partly because they involved senior commissioned officers. But virtually identical situations arise just as often for senior petty officers and junior commissioned officers. These are more likely to be handled within a command and never reach the public eye. The question for all cases is whether they are being treated consistently. Representative Rod Chandler of Washington State began to ask this question after Marine officials accused one of his constituents, a Navy dentist who had dated and married a Marine lance corporal of another command, of fraternization. After Chandler met with the commandant of the Marine Corps and other senior officials the case was dropped, but it caused him and Representative Beverly Bryon of Maryland to urge the Department of Defense to reexamine fraternization policy. Chandler said, "Either we need to say we do not tolerate fraternization under any circumstances, or we need to find a way to accommodate legitimate dating where there are no chain-of-command problems."[19]

A few months later, in January 1989, the Coast Guard issued its first written policy guidelines on fraternization. The Navy's guidelines appeared in February. The two documents are similar in intent and tone, leaning on custom, experience, and familiar words. The Navy defines fraternization as any personal relationship between an officer and an enlisted member, or within either group, that is "unduly familiar and does not respect differences in rank and grade where a senior-junior supervisory relationship exists." Further, married service personnel are assigned to different chains of command whenever possible; seniors are to be "especially attentive to their personal associations" and are primarily responsible for avoiding inappropriate behavior; leadership and example are the first courses of action for preventing such behavior, counseling the second, then "administrative remedies" such as reassignment.[20]

The effect of the written policy is yet to be determined. Its principal author, Vice Adm. Michael Boorda, chief of naval personnel, was optimistic: The Navy could only "profit from articulating the policy in a way that every single person can read and understand, and we've done that. And it wasn't easy." The expectation is reasonable—the trouble is, men and women often are not. Two years after the written policy appeared, a well-known naval aviator, commanding officer of a naval air station, was relieved of his command, officially reprimanded, and fined $3,000 for fraternizing with a woman officer on his staff. Both were married to others; he has two children. According to the *Los Angeles Times*, her husband reported the relationship to officials.[21]

Sexual Harassment

As with fraternization, a major difficulty in dealing with the issue of sexual harassment lies in defining it: It means different things to different people. Not until 1980 did the Navy declare a formal policy against sexual harassment, and not until 1990 did it become an offense formalized in article 1166 of Navy Regulations. The Navy defines sexual harassment as

> sexual advances, requests for sexual favors, and other verbal or physical conduct of a sexual nature when (1) submission to such conduct is made either explicitly or implicitly a term or condition of a person's job, pay, or career; (2) submission to or rejection of such conduct by a person is used as a basis for career or employment decisions affecting this person; or (3) such conduct has the purpose or effect of interfering with an individual's performance or creating an intimidating, hostile, or offensive environment.[22]

There is no record of the question of sexual harassment ever arising in the brief span of the Yeomen (F)'s active duty. From those early years and until the late 1960s, ladylike demeanor and the common sense to stay away from potentially difficult situations constituted much of a Navy woman's defense against sexual harassment, while social standards of acceptable behavior and normal naval discipline did the rest.

As standards of social and sexual behavior relaxed, nearly everyone felt at least some confusion as to what was permissible, acceptable, or desirable. At the same time, the effects of the feminist movement made women less willing than before to accept or overlook unpleasantries. Sexual harassment began to assume more serious proportions. In 1980 high-ranking women officers, including Rear Adm. Fran McKee, testified to the House Armed Services Committee that military women were subjected to sexual harassment "probably at every military installation," and other women testified that they were afraid to report such behavior because they believed they would be ignored or cast as troublemakers. In 1982 deputy assistant secretary of the Navy E. C. Grayson told assembled DACOWITS members,

> Sexual harassment is an extremely serious problem which many of you women have been dealing with for years. Only recently has it begun to be assessed and addressed by the services. . . . The Department of the Navy recognizes that sexual harassment is unacceptable behavior and has promulgated clear guidance prohibiting it.[23]

The news that sexual harassment was prohibited appeared not to have reached certain quarters. One of them was the Naval Academy, where women midshipmen were subjected to everything from insulting remarks to physical abuse. Another was the ranks of flag officers. In 1985 a married rear admiral was charged with sexually harassing an enlisted woman. He received a "nonpunitive letter" and was immediately retired from active duty. At the time, Navy officials said that twenty-four sexual harassment cases had been brought up for hearings in the preceding fiscal year; nine were dismissed when the charges could not be substantiated, but some punishment had resulted in the remaining fifteen. A Navy spokesman admitted the obvious: "Punishment for sexual harassment is still a relatively new concept in the Navy."[24] Navy women could be forgiven for considerable skepticism on the subject. How, they asked, had the Navy expected to prohibit sexual harassment if it wasn't prepared to punish offenders?

In the summer of 1987 the issue erupted publicly. The commanding officer of the USS *Safeguard* made crude public statements, supposedly facetious, about enlisted women in his crew. The women reported the episode to DACOWITS during one of its fact-finding tours. When DACOWITS members toured Navy bases in the Philippines they found sexually oriented entertainment prevalent throughout service clubs, condoned and supported by the Navy, which offended many Navy women and made them feel unwelcome. DACOWITS concluded that in such an atmosphere sexual harassment "should not be considered surprising," and that Navy and Marine leaders condoned "overt and blatant sexual harassment" of women in the services.[25]

Out of the embarrassment came one good result, a top-level, wide-ranging report on women in the Navy. The report's major conclusion was damning: Sexual harassment ranging from verbal abuse (most prevalent) to molestation (rare) pervaded the Navy, and many commanding officers were unaware of the extent to which it existed in their own commands. The report recommended that from the CNO down the Navy must commit itself to rooting out harassment. It called for better training, more effective reporting of violations, and formal inquiries by the Navy's inspector general. In short, the Navy must back its words with action.[26]

In the fall of 1990, findings by the inspector general drew attention to how the Navy was handling rape cases at the Recruit Training Command in Orlando. Almost simultaneously, the public learned of some incidents at the Naval Academy (discussed in chapter 11) and that the commanding officer of a U.S. Navy unit in Great Britain had been found guilty of sexually harassing five women in his command. It began to ask if the Navy was capable of or interested in keeping its house in order. Senator Sam Nunn of the Senate Armed Services Committee called for an investigation: "That such (sexually abusive) behavior is not dealt with more seriously than documented in the Navy Inspector General's report suggests that there may be institutional problems in the Navy and its treatment of women." One result of the uproar was that the Navy accelerated its planned update of the 1987 report, bringing it out in 1990 instead of 1991. Vice Admiral Boorda announced that training policies instituted in the wake of the 1987 report were beginning to show positive results. Of the women surveyed for the 1990 report, 76 percent believed the Navy was taking steps to correct the problem. That, he said, is a "vote of confidence."[27]

Lesbianism

The U.S. armed forces have long prohibited homosexuals from service on the grounds that they threaten both security and discipline. Any man or woman who, during enlistment or induction proceedings, lied about pre-service behavior or feelings could be charged with fraudulent enlistment. The question of security, arising from their alleged vulnerability to blackmail, has lost some strength since the changing social and political climate has allowed more homosexuals to become more open about their sexual preference.

The issue of discipline for homosexuals remains as potent as ever, especially in the Navy. Naval service requires large numbers of young people to live and work closely together for extended periods of time, often without access to companionship of the opposite sex. Some are still developing their sexual identity; some are away from home for the first time; many are lonely and naive. The Navy's experience has led it to believe that homosexual activity foments division and threatens order and discipline, and that no good can come of it. Its primary policy toward homosexuals has been to discharge them; its methods of identifying and discharging them have often been questioned.

Until the early 1970s the Navy dealt with lesbians quietly, chiefly to protect its women's ladylike image. The question didn't arise with the Yeomen (F), as only a few lived in Navy facilities. The early ranks of WAVE officers included many women educators accustomed to supervising women's dormitories and sorority houses; they probably understood the potential for lesbianism and recognized the Navy's continuing emphasis on order and discipline as a tool to contain it. In the late 1940s and early 1950s the U.S. government became increasingly agitated over aberrant sexual behavior among its members and employees, a corollary of that era's witchhunt for subversive persons. Between 1947 and 1950 more than four thousand persons were expelled from the armed forces because of homosexuality. The Navy warned women recruits about lesbians in highly charged terms, labeling them, according to one source, as "sexual vampires." Navy women directly engaged with the issue of lesbianism were women's representatives and ranking women petty officers who served as chief masters-at-arms of women's barracks. Where these leaders were diligent and conscientious, lesbians caused no problems. Where the leaders were not, aggressive lesbians could make barracks life miserable for their women shipmates, the overwhelming majority of whom were firmly heterosexual.[28] In some situations command apathy nurtured lesbian activity. For example, when Lt. Sarah Watlington was assigned as the women's representative for a large, geographically remote command in the mid-1960s, she found women's recreational needs neglected. Their playing field and picnic ground had been closed because some senior Navy women, in the belief that female athletic teams fostered lesbianism, wanted to deemphasize sports. None of the women could live off base and few had cars; so the only recreational facility readily available to them was the base enlisted club. Alternatives to the women's barracks where lesbian activity was occurring were few, impelling some occupants to flee to the men's barracks. Some were seeking adventure; most were looking for a safe place to sleep. It turned out to be less safe than they supposed—an unusually high proportion became pregnant. When the commanding officer was finally persuaded that healthful recreation, morale, and discipline were as important for women as for men, the situation improved.[29]

Since the early 1970s homosexuals have become more open about their sexual preferences and far more restive about restraints on their civil liberties. A series of legal challenges to armed service policy plus the Navy's growing number of women have publicized its struggles with lesbianism.

According to the 1990 update report on women in the Navy, most service personnel, both men and women, agree that homosexual behavior and naval service are incompatible. Where homosexuality is known to exist within a command, it is viewed as a problem. Lesbianism seems to attract more attention and be more disruptive than male homosexual behavior; junior enlisted women, however, believe that supervisors are more willing to tolerate lesbians than male homosexuals. Hence, some are intimidated by lesbian activity, and fear of retaliation keeps them from reporting it to authorities. One chronic challenge in prosecuting charges of lesbianism has been the difficulty of substantiating allegations. False accusations have been made by males whose advances were rejected as well as by apprehended lesbians determined to implicate others.[30]

Women are more likely than men to be discharged from the military for homosexuality. Between October 1, 1984, and September 30, 1987, such discharges averaged 0.13 percent of the male and 0.27 percent of the female enlisted forces. During the same period the average for both male and female officers was 0.02 percent. Of all the services, the Navy had the highest overall rate of discharge for homosexuality for both men and women, probably because, Pentagon officials said, such activity is more easily detected aboard ships. In 1987, 16 percent of the sailors discharged for homosexuality were women, although women were only 9 percent of the total Navy force.[31]

If these reports are accurate, it appears that the Navy treats lesbians differently from male homosexuals. Lesbians seem more tolerated until the weight of evidence gives commanding officers a case strong enough to result in involuntary discharge. Perhaps supervisors fear charges of sexism if they act against lesbians. Perhaps the situation just reflects the Navy's longer experience in dealing with male homosexuals. Perhaps more of the men gain clemency because they have families to support. The vast majority of Navy women are not lesbians and are uneasy about the higher rate of involuntary discharges for female homosexuals, suspecting it is a pretext to question the value to the Navy of all its women.

*   *   *

In the early 1970s the Navy was ill prepared to deal with the growing number of women on whom it now depended to fill its ranks. Integrating them proved complex, for they differed from their predecessors significantly: They expected from the Navy the same choices regarding family and personal life that men had.

To give its women choices, the Navy, like other services, had to change the assumptions that it had held since 1942. Changes came only when the courts upheld women's entitlements to benefits for their husbands and women's right to bear and raise children while working. Had the judiciary not made clearcut decisions, each service might have been even slower to overturn old attitudes and assumptions, and the ensuing piecemeal solutions could well have been less satisfactory than they were. With no other option, the Navy complied: Its women no longer had to choose between a family and a Navy career.

Other issues remain. The Navy has barely begun to comprehend the extent and complexities of fraternization, sexual harassment, and lesbianism. It has attempted to deal with all three, but little that it has done has met with much approval. These issues will remain lively challenges for years to come.

11

—

Professional Advances: A Matter of Equity

"A lmost every assignment [I have] had since 1972 . . . would have been impossible prior to Z-gram 116."

—CAPT. GEORGIA CLARK SADLER, *Naval Review, 1983*

In the 1970s three pressures affected how the Navy utilized its women. One pressure came from initiatives set forth in Z-116 that opened to women numerous ratings, programs, and assignments from which they had previously been excluded. Another came from Congress, which in 1967 had opened the path for women to become admirals and in 1976 mandated that women enter the Naval Academy. The third came from the Navy's own pursuit of efficiency and convenience, which impelled it to integrate women's recruit training with men's and the Women Officers School with the OCS. As a result of all three developments, women gained more equitable treatment and greater responsibility within the profession.

While these changes opened to women many areas of naval service that had previously been all male, other changes occurring in the Navy left the vast majority of women officers in a community almost exclusively female.

Changes for Enlisted Women

From the end of World War II on, what set enlisted Navy women apart from their civilian counterparts was not their work but their lifestyle: They were subject to rotation from one duty station to another, to the naval promotion system, and to naval discipline. Their work, however, for the most part closely resembled that of civilian women. This began to change in 1972 after Z-116, when they took on jobs previously done only by men and did those jobs in units previously filled only by men. The modern woman's introduction to the integrated Navy begins in boot camp.

Initial Training

During the spring of 1972 the Navy closed the enlisted women's recruit training unit at Bainbridge, Maryland, and began training women recruits at Orlando, Florida, one of the Navy's three huge boot camps (the others are at San Diego and Great Lakes). Capt. Mary Gore, then commanding the Bainbridge unit, moved with most of her staff of sixty-one women to Orlando, while Comdr. Sarah Watlington, her executive officer, graduated the final class at Bainbridge. The first class of about one hundred women recruits reported to Orlando in midsummer to begin the ten-week course, and by fall a full complement of approximately five hundred women was experiencing traditionally rigorous introduction to Navy life.

Originally the women at Orlando were to be trained separately from the men, but when it became apparent that such a scheme would unnecessarily duplicate staffs and facilities, the two commands were combined into one, Captain Gore becoming chief of staff to its commanding officer. The integration gave some male instructors a new view of Navy women. For example, Chief Signalman Lloyd Murray reported, "I've got more respect for servicewomen. There's no doubt in my mind they can do any job, or endure any arduous sea duty. They're not as frail as we seem to think." In 1979 Capt. Lucille Kuhn, who had already directed the now-integrated OCS in Newport, became the first woman to command the unit at Orlando. In that year, as in most years since, about 20,000 men and 9,500 women made the transition at Orlando from civilian to Navy life.[1]

Even after two decades of integrated recruit training, the Navy struggled to optimize policies and procedures, trying to adapt to changing social standards while remaining faithful to its own tested methods of turning civilians into sailors. For example, there was the question of how much the experiences of men and women should differ during boot camp. They undertake the same curriculum, attend class together, and meet common standards. Yet recruits were grouped into all-male or all-female companies of about eighty each, the company being the basic training unit. Male and female companies lived in the same barracks, but each company had its own floor. Since drill was conducted at the company level, they drilled separately. Advocates of separate drill pointed out that men and women generally tend to master the intricate movements at differing tempos, and when separated each group experiences less frustration. An alternative view was that the sooner all recruits learn to tolerate, appreciate, and adjust to one another's varying abilities, the better.

In 1992 the Navy began a pilot program of more fully integrated training that attracted considerable attention. Men and women were now in the same companies. The 433 men and women who completed training on April 3 did not understand the publicity. One recruit summed it up when he said, "If we are going to work together in the future, we may as well work together starting now." Navy officials said the overall performance of four of the five integrated companies matched or exceeded that of former companies. Indeed, two of the "coed" companies were given the "Hall of Fame" designation, a rare honor.[2]

Moving into Nontraditional Ratings

When Z-116 opened all ratings to enlisted women, the intent was to encourage them to enter nontraditional ratings. This would not only give the women more opportunities but also give Navy detailers more flexibility in assigning them. The next step planned was selectively to close those ratings in which most billets were on board combatant ships. At the time women were not serving in any ships, although some shipboard duty was being planned for them. Even if and when some women did serve in ships, initially too few billets would be available for them to have viable careers in the so-called sea-intensive ratings. The thrust therefore was to get women into those ratings that were not sea intensive, but from which they had been excluded chiefly as a matter of policy. Women already on active duty would be given the opportunity to retrain for these ratings, while women recruits would be steered toward them. After a good start that owed much to the interest of Rear Adm. James Watkins and detailers in the Bureau of Naval Personnel, the plan faltered as a result of three major factors: Watkins's successor took less interest in the scheme; no ACNP(W) existed to monitor and encourage it; and women themselves showed strong preference for the traditionally female fields.

By 1983, more than a decade after Z-116 appeared, enlisted women were still found mainly in twenty-two, or roughly a third, of the Navy's ratings, most of them in the administrative, medical, and dental fields.

This concentration led to warnings that women would be barred from reenlisting in these ratings. They were encouraged to switch to less crowded ones, both to improve their own chances of advancement and for the good of the Navy. The fact that encouragement was needed was clear evidence that the intent of Z-116 was still far from being met.

It might appear that Navy women are by simple virtue of being in uniform working in nontraditional fields, and in fact, in 1986 investigators concluded that 35 percent of all servicewomen held nontraditional jobs, compared with only 3 percent of working civilian women. But the services need more technical workers because the percentage of technical jobs in the military is about twice that in the civilian world. Thus, although the number of Navy women was approaching fifty-four thousand, the service needed women for technical fields in which they had traditionally been sparse or nonexistent. A recruiting advertisement of the time showed the Navy's intent: An enlisted woman is at the wheel of a boat or a ship, her shirtsleeve bearing the three chevrons of a petty officer first class, her gaze steady on a distant horizon. The caption reads: "I joined for a job no one else could give me. Now I've got experience no one can take away." The advertisement shrewdly gauged the Navy's singular appeal to women attracted by the chance to learn and advance in unusual jobs. Yet while the expansion represented significant opportunity for some women, more could have seized it than did. The Navy was wooing reluctant maidens.

Some of the reluctance was easy to understand. Many ratings opening to women demanded heavy physical labor, and few women found sweat and callouses appealing. But if advances into nontraditional fields were to continue, women had to be found who would take on such jobs. As Adm. Roberta Hazard told a group of Navy women in 1987, "Equality means a much more physical orientation to our daily efforts, especially for enlisted personnel, and we must be ready to accommodate that fact as we push for new opportunities."[3]

Joy Hancock might have predicted that such women were indeed to be found; the Navy just had to look harder for them. In 1988, to attract women with technical skills or aptitude, Navy recruiters guaranteed them initial technical training after boot camp, which in turn ensured they would be competitive for advancement. Women recruits were also encouraged to enter the job-oriented basic skills (JOBS) program, a course focused on remedial mechanical skills. Women recruits had always been eligible to enter the program but never been pushed. Now they were. It seems to have worked: By 1990 the Navy reported more than forty-two thousand women in nontraditional ratings, or more than 60 percent of all rated women (petty officer third class or above).[4] The surge of women into nontraditional ratings has had its costs. As is so often the case, the few who do poorly or become pregnant to escape disagreeable duty reflect badly on the rest. Attempting to give women experience ashore that approximates that gained by men at sea, the Navy also set aside shore billets in some ratings exclusively for them. On occasion, qualified men encountered hardship or inconvenience as a result, which aggravated or engendered resentment.

Overall, women are filling nontraditional billets successfully, chiefly because their needs and the Navy's converge: They want that "job no one else can give," and the Navy needs their skills. Both adapt as necessary. At the Naval Air Station in Adak, Alaska, for example, where from 1984 to 1986 women went from none to 76 percent of the firefighters, the combination of lighter-weight equipment, five instead of four firefighters per engine company, and greater emphasis on physical conditioning has enabled women to hold all positions from firefighter to driver operator and truck captain. Also, in some cases a woman's smaller size is helpful. For example, Damage Controlman First Class Connie Weichsler, stationed aboard a submarine tender, told a *Navy Times* reporter, "Women were built to repair submarines. I fit in the bilges real well. . . . I'm real easy to hold upside down."[5]

Becoming an Officer

During this period, two Navy programs to help qualified enlisted men to become officers opened to enlisted women. The broadened opportunities for officer selection and training (BOOST) program, conducted in San Diego, allows candidates a year of intense academic preparation to compete—usually successfully—for scholarships in NROTC or appointments to the Naval Academy. In 1989 and 1990, a total of 217 enlisted men and 26 enlisted women completed the BOOST program. Enlisted women also take advantage of the Naval Academy Preparatory School in Newport, Rhode Island. Between 1989 and 1991, 6 completed the program, while approximately 150 enlisted men did. From time to time the Navy activates two other paths to commissions that are also open to women. One is the limited duty officer (LDO) program, which women first entered in 1981. LDOs are chosen from among the Navy's most proficient senior petty officers; as the name suggests, they are limited to duty in their technical fields. In 1988 one out of approximately every hundred women naval officers was an LDO. Competition is keen; of the nearly 3,500 enlisted men and women who applied that year to become LDOs, only 255 were selected.[6] Another path is the Aviation Officer Candidate (AOC) School, open to enlisted personnel with two years of college and a strong desire to fly.

Opportunities for Women Officers

After 1948 there was only one route for civilian women seeking Navy commissions, the Women Officers School at Newport, while there were three such paths for men. In the 1970s these paths would also open to women.

Officer Candidate School

In 1967 the Women Officers School received its first male students by virtue of two developments: Navy nurses now attended the school, and Navy nurses now included men. Some difficulties attended the integration such as having men reside in the formerly all-female barracks. One woman officer on the staff at that time later concluded that "we had every experience in integrating men that the Naval Academy had a decade later in integrating women." The difficulties were resolved, which raised the question of merging the women's school with the OCS less than half a mile away. Between 1967 and 1972 the Navy began to align the women's curriculum more closely with the men's, and by October 1972 the time seemed ripe for consolidation. The Navy announced that integrated training "would provide a more realistic working environment for both groups and a broader recognition among junior male line officers of the capabilities and contributions of the women line officers of the Navy. . . ." The first fully integrated class graduated in November 1973.[7]

The merging effectively eliminated one of the few major leadership positions available to women. Now the question arose, Why shouldn't a woman become director of the integrated OCS? When Comdr. Dixie Kuhn asked that question, the answer she got, that the job required experience at sea, struck her as illogical: "You don't need to have been to sea; it's a leadership job. You can get people who've been to sea to work for you." Opposition to her appointment weakened in the face of her persistence and collapsed after she was selected for captain one year ahead of schedule. On July 1, 1975, she became the first woman in its twenty-four-year history to direct the OCS, and the first woman in any of the U.S. armed forces to head an integrated basic officer training school.[8]

Naval Reserve Officers Training Corps

For years the Navy had trained male students at civilian colleges by means of the NROTC program. Under the scholarship program, the Navy selects qualified high-school seniors to receive, at government expense and for a maximum of four years at a participating college, tuition, textbooks, uniforms, and a small monthly allowance. During the academic year they study naval science taught by Navy personnel assigned to the college's NROTC unit; they must also complete three summer training sessions. Graduates are commissioned in the regular Navy or Marine Corps and must serve a minimum of four years on active duty. Under the contract program, qualified students may be accepted by the college's NROTC unit to take naval science courses and complete one summer training session. They receive uniforms and naval science textbooks when they join the unit but incur no obligation to the Navy until they enter their junior year. During their final two years the Navy gives them an allowance. When the students graduate they are commissioned in either the Naval or Marine Corps Reserve and are obligated to serve at least three years on active duty.

The Navy had never offered women these opportunities, although the possibility of doing so was raised on at least two occasions; in both instances, the Navy saw no reason to subsidize women's college education via NROTC when it had an adequate supply of women officer candidates educated at their own expense. Now the question of whether NROTC might be opened to women hinged not only on the Navy's needs but also on equity—an issue to which the service was becoming increasingly sensitive.

On February 8, 1972, Secretary of the Navy John Warner authorized a pilot program providing Navy scholarships for seventeen women enrolled at four institutions: the University of Washington, Jacksonville University, Purdue University, and Southern A&M. The women made the same commitment to the Navy that their male counterparts did: In return for scholarship aid they were to serve four years on active duty following graduation. These seventeen scholarships were only a token, for the Navy was authorized to offer scholarships to as many as sixty women, or 1 percent of the six thousand men for whom scholarships were authorized. Later that year, Secretary Warner approved plans to admit women to both the scholarship and contract programs beginning in the fall of 1973. Women students have made good use of NROTC. For the classes of 1987 through 1991 a total of 339 were accepted into the scholarship program, with 221—approximately two-thirds—graduating and becoming commissioned officers, compared with slightly more than one half of the men (4,627 out of the 8,703 admitted).[9]

Initially, the training for women differed in one significant way from men's. Every summer male NROTC midshipmen, like their counterparts at the Naval Academy, are sent to sea or to an operating marine or aviation unit. In 1976 women NROTC midshipmen arriving at their summer stations were turned away, because the law's combat-exclusion clause (section 6015) was strictly interpreted. They were finally allowed on board if they first took leave and could therefore be considered "guests" of the units, wearing civilian clothes. No such restrictions applied to civilian women who worked with the Navy, or even to women members of other armed services. The restrictions eased as section 6015 was amended (see chapter 12) and as berthing spaces for women aboard fleet units—including combatants—became available. Today, as a matter of policy, women NROTC midshipmen have opportunities for summer training cruises similar to those of male NROTC midshipmen. However, if a ship is to receive only one woman midshipman, then a woman officer must be part of that ship's crew; to ships lacking female officers, no fewer than two women midshipmen may be assigned.[10]

Omnes Vir No More*

President Gerald Ford signed Public Law 94-106 on October 7, 1975, and the following July the service academies accepted their first women. It was less a case of acceptance than of submission to congressional mandate. In 1972 Senator Jacob Javits of New York and Representative Jack MacDonald of Michigan nominated women to the Naval Academy, which rejected them. Javits also cosponsored a Senate resolution saying that women should not be denied admission solely on the basis of gender. The resolution passed the Senate handily, but in the House of Representatives it died in committee. In 1973 a bill to admit women to the academies was introduced in the House, and two more of its members nominated women to the Naval Academy and its Air Force equivalent.

*The U.S. Naval Academy Class of 1979 was the last all-male class. It adopted *Omnes Vir* (all male) as its class motto.

Late that year the Senate affirmed its support for admitting women, and then the House Armed Services Committee agreed to hold hearings.[11]

Representatives of all three services joined other opponents of the proposed legislation in testifying against the admission of women. Their arguments ranged from the financial (again, the services did not need to offer college education when they could already attract sufficient numbers of well-qualified women educated at their own expense) to the professional (the academies existed to train combat-eligible officers, and existing laws precluded women from combat) to the social (women students would lower the academies' high standards, thereby eroding their unique spirit).

Proponents raised different issues. They pointed out that to deny the benefits of academy training to women was discriminatory, for the academies not only offered young men a college education, they also enhanced graduates' subsequent service careers. Proponents tackled the combat issue by noting that only a small proportion of academy graduates eventually saw combat; by questioning whether combat training was in fact the academies' mission; and by pointing out that if keeping women out of combat was the goal, then the services should have only male nurses. In the end, Congress agreed with the proponents: The issue was equal access to career education, and the mission of the academies was to train officers for military careers rather than for combat. Subsequently, the academies omitted all reference to combat in their official mission statements. The Naval Academy's mission statement now reads "to prepare midshipmen morally, mentally, and physically to be professional officers in the naval service."[12]

The Naval Academy prepared for women's arrival with studied coolness, its superintendent, Rear Adm. Kinnard McKee, commenting, "The whole business is the nonevent of the year," but a news reporter described the academy's preparations as "one of the most carefully planned naval operations since the Battle of Midway." The academy's approach was to minimize the differences between men and women. Like men, women would be called midshipmen, and their uniforms were to be nearly identical. They would compete for admission under the same standards, and those admitted would take the same academic and professional courses, be subject to the same discipline, and comply with the same restraints and demands. Some physical requirements were adjusted for women, an acknowledgment that their physiology differed from men's and that fewer athletic programs were available to them in their high-school years. Simultaneously, the academy began to instruct staff officers and selected midshipmen who would be in the first (senior) class when women arrived on what to expect from their presence. No one thought to explain to the incoming women what to expect from the men.[13]

On July 6, 1976, 81 women were sworn in as midshipmen along with 1,212 men. Over the next four years, 26 of the women (32 percent) and 322 of the men (27 percent) dropped out.[14] The male attrition rate differed little from those of preceding years; no one could yet say what attrition rates would be for the women. Service academies take attrition rates seriously because they accept no transfers.

Beginning in 1984, the U.S. Naval Institute interviewed several women graduates of the class of 1980 for its oral history program.[15] Transcripts of five of these interviews have become available to researchers. What happened to these pioneering women foreshadowed much that happened to their successors. From the moment they reported to the academy, the women of the class of 1980 were deluged by the media, a circumstance that caused or heightened resentment in their male peers. It soon became apparent that many of the male officers, civilian faculty, and alumni also resented their presence. Only a few women officers were present who could serve as any kind of role model, and none had ever been a midshipman. Yet, when one female officer and one female midshipman tried to gather the women together for mutual support, the attempt was interpreted as having mutinous overtones, and no further attempts were made. Thus this beleaguered minority lost any comfort they might have gained from bonding with each other, and they certainly were not bonding with their male peers.

As plebe year ended, the women expected that things might get better; instead they got worse. Academy policy limits how much any plebe, male or female, might be harassed by upperclassmen in the name of indoctrination. Once the women left their plebe year behind that minimal protection ended, and expressions of resentment grew uglier and more overt. The women were subjected to a steady barrage of insulting remarks. Male midshipmen openly accused them of being pampered. Some had food thrown into their rooms at night, and rumors of uglier incidents, such as molestation, could be heard.

Yet there were a few bright spots for the pioneers. One was the commandant, Capt. James Winnefeld, whom the women correctly perceived as a strong supporter. Some male midshipmen strove to be fair, as did some male officers. The latter admitted that they didn't necessarily agree with the decision to admit women to the academy but did their best to implement it. Some of the female athletic teams had outstanding seasons, which reflected well on all the women.

While their male classmates were spending the second summer of their academy years on larger Navy ships, the women, precluded at that time from such duty, were assigned to local yard patrol (YP) vessels. At least they were afloat; they performed well and enjoyed the experience. By the summer of 1979 the women of the class of 1980 were first-class midshipmen. Some were squad leaders for incoming plebes, and for plebe summer Midshipman First Class Elizabeth Belzer became the first woman to wear the five stripes designating her as deputy brigade commander, the second highest rank in the student body. Their commandant gave them high marks in typically understated Navy fashion, saying they "aren't doing any better or worse than the men. They do average, and average at the U.S. Naval Academy is very, very good."[16]

In December 1986, the Naval Academy convened the Women Midshipmen Study Group "to review the progress toward integrating women into the Brigade and to develop recommendations for improving their assimilation." The attrition statistics reported by the study group carried a mixed message:

> The overall attrition rate of women midshipmen in the first eight classes . . . has been 35.1 percent, well below the average of all colleges and universities in the United States, and even below the attrition rate for women at the other two service academies (42.0% at USMA, 42.9% at USAFA). The . . . attrition rate for women midshipmen has, however, been significantly higher than that of their male counterparts, which averaged less than 23 percent for the classes of 1980 to 1987. This difference between male and female attrition rates has also been higher for the Naval Academy than for either West Point or the Air Force Academy. Percentages of involuntary separations . . . have been comparable for male and female midshipmen (about 11% each). But the percentage of voluntary attrition for women (24%) is double the voluntary attrition rate for men (12%). Essentially all voluntary attrition occurs during fourth class (freshman) and third class (sophomore) years.[17]

That is, twice as many women as men were deciding, within two years, to leave the Naval Academy. Evidently the academy's assimilation of women left something to be desired.

The report confirmed that women were still not being accepted by male midshipmen, which was the overriding reason why so many women dropped out and why the academy environment was so difficult for those who remained. There were several reasons for the resistance to women.

First, they constituted no more than 8.2 percent of the brigade, although women in recent years have made up about 10 percent of the Navy's officers. Accordingly, the study group recommended that the academy work toward a goal of 10 percent. Second, male midshipmen believed that their female counterparts were shown favoritism. To what extent this may be true is difficult to show, but the perception is what counts. Certainly women midshipmen received far more media attention than their peers. Third, as a group women entrants were less prepared—physically, academically, culturally—for the academy program than their male peers, although every woman admitted had to meet the same high admission requirements. Fourth, many male midshipmen believed that women should not be at the academy at all. To the extent that they saw themselves as combat eligible and the women as not, they suspected (with some justification) that the women's presence owed more to political considerations about equal opportunity than to the Navy's needs. Most midshipmen knew little about the contributions that women officers historically made to the Navy, and many graduated with this ignorance intact. Thus the study group recommended that midshipmen be better informed about women's roles in the Navy and that more "well-qualified women officers" be put on the academy staff "in positions to lead, evaluate, and grade midshipmen."[18]

Yet three clear facts reflected well on both women midshipmen and the academy. First, female midshipmen had already compiled enviable records. As athletes, students, and leaders, most had performed well at the academy, and several had distinguished themselves. Two notable examples were Elizabeth Belzer, class of 1980, the first woman to be named a Trident Scholar (one of a very few first-class midshipmen of sufficient academic distinction to be allowed to undertake a program of independent research and study), and Kristin Holderied, who graduated first in her class in 1984. Second, academy leaders took seriously the challenges posed by the entry of women. For example, by 1983 a number of women were aboard fleet ships for their first-class summer cruise, and by 1988 some were being sent to ships for both third- and first-class cruises, with the same considerations governing their assignment as those for women NROTC midshipmen.

The academy also tried to treat fairly the difficulties inherent in sexual issues. The policy on pregnancy, for example, was directed toward both men and women: Being either pregnant or responsible for a pregnancy was grounds for dismissal. The age-old trouble, of course, is that it is far easier to determine the former condition than the latter.

In general, academy life for women midshipmen today is better than it was, although far from what it could and should be. Even a skeptical reading of the study group report makes clear that the improvement owes much to the academy's own continuing self-scrutiny. Particularly significant is that some of the women applying are the younger sisters of women midshipmen: Evidently the older sisters' testimonies were more positive than not. For example, Hope Katcharian graduated with the class of 1988 and is an engineer with a Seabee battalion. Her sisters, Anne Marie and Heather, graduated in 1990 and 1992, respectively, both becoming supply officers. Their father said he has seen "subtle changes in the Academy's treatment of women. . . . I think there's more acceptance." In addition, enlisted women continue to seek admission; in 1991, for example, six of them became midshipmen.[19]

In 1990, accounts of a disagreeable incident that had taken place in December 1989 appeared in newspapers from coast to coast and on national television. In the week preceding the annual Army-Navy game, traditionally a period for pranks, a female third-class midshipman was chained to a urinal by two male midshipmen and photographed while other midshipmen watched. She told her parents three days later, and in April she resigned from the academy. The two men were punished but not expelled. The academy and its superintendent were severely criticized, first for allowing such a thing to happen, then for an insensitive and insufficient response. The public and some academy alumni and Navy personnel were outraged by the episode. Something was wrong at the academy, they argued, if any midshipman treated any person, man or woman, that way. Others rose to the academy's defense, asserting that the men had believed the woman knew it was all in fun. The woman had previously asked that her transcript be sent to another college, and some saw this as evidence that she was anxious to leave the academy anyway. The superintendent insisted that he was as outraged as anyone and that the punishments handed out were more severe than the public understood.[20]

One result was that the study group, already scheduled to update its 1987 report in 1991, returned to work sooner. In addition, a blue-ribbon panel, including members of Congress and the academy's Board of Visitors, conferred at length with academy and other Navy authorities. They found that the academy was improving but slowly. Steps taken in the wake of the 1987 report helped—for example, more women officers, including academy graduates, were being assigned to faculty and staff—but much still needed to be done. Male midshipmen were still ignorant about women's contribution to the Navy, and far too much offensive behavior had been overlooked or condoned under the label of high jinks. A General Accounting Office report published in May 1992 came to many of the same conclusions, which indicates that despite all the progress to date, a significant percentage of male midshipmen still believe that women do not belong at the academy.[21]

In the spring of 1991 the academy appointed Midshipman Juliane Gallina as brigade commander, the first woman to be named to that position. While few doubted her qualifications, some observers interpreted her selection as an attempt by the academy to offset unfavorable publicity. Others saw her selection as a signal to the entire academy community that it was time for them to take women's leadership seriously. Gallina put such thoughts behind her, confident that judgment of her leadership would rest on her performance.[22]

Staff Corps and Restricted Line

When women first entered the regular Navy in 1948, they were intended as a nucleus of generalists. Except for a few in the supply and medical fields, they were commissioned in what the Navy calls the unrestricted line (URL). Male officers, on the other hand, had become increasingly specialized; many with technical skills were designated as restricted line officers. Female reserve officers were more readily allowed into the restricted line, especially if they had particular technical skills, because they were envisioned as coming on active duty only in wartime, that is, during emergency conditions.

Z-116 directed that qualified women could apply for regular commissions in the staff corps or the restricted line, a new course that reflected two emergent realities. First, the feminist movement had encouraged women to enter graduate and professional schools as well as more technical specialties; female lawyers, engineers, systems analysts, and physicians were no longer rarities. Second, civilian men in such professions were paid well, making it harder for the Navy to recruit as many as it needed. To maintain numbers *and* quality, it needed women. Quickly it found them, and by mid-1973 the last two staff corps to receive women had been integrated. Lt. (jg) Jeri Rigoulot became the first woman since World War II to enter the Civil Engineer Corps, and Lt. (jg) Florence Pohlman, a Presbyterian minister, became the first woman to enter the Chaplain Corps.[23]

The staff corps and the restricted line have offered certain advantages to women officers, in that at-sea experience plays a smaller role in the competition for advancement. Yet, in the Navy, at-sea experience is always significant, and now that such experience is at least possible for women, restricted line and staff corps women are increasingly frustrated by the limited amount of sea duty available to them.

The General Unrestricted Line

In 1972 the Navy regrouped its URL officers. Remaining in the URL were officers in the three warfare communities: surface, aviation, submarine. Into a fourth community were grouped all women line officers and the few remaining male line officers not in one of the warfare communities. In 1981 this community was formally named the general unrestricted line (GURL). That this acronym would be pronounced *girl* seems to have been a genuine oversight. It was corrected in 1988, and the accepted acronym is now Gen URL.

In some ways women have benefited from the development of the Gen URL. First, it is a community they dominate: In 1990 it consisted of about 2,550 women and 440 men. Second, between 1984 and 1987 Gen URL detailing was weaned from that of the surface-warfare community and devoted exclusively to management of its members' careers. It has evolved into a community with a genuine specialty, administration, and is developing a career pattern that leads to command for the best qualified. Over the years, Gen URL officers' chances of achieving command have been slightly higher than those of aviators, identical to those of surface-warfare officers, and generally lower than those of submariners. On the other hand, this community has its drawbacks, the most significant being that the warfare specialists are the heart of the profession, and administrative specialists are perceived as peripheral. Also, for some years any male line officer not qualified as a warfare specialist was automatically designated as Gen URL, creating an "image . . . associated with failure." In October 1989 Gen URL managers won the right to screen those coming into it, which has improved that image.

The hardest struggle of all for this primarily female community has been to win its fair share of desirable shore billets. Until the 1970s those billets were reserved for warfare specialists, who competed for them avidly. Women were hardly even considered. Partly as a result of Z-116 women now began to compete more vigorously for the desirable jobs. As their rising numbers put pressure on detailers at least to consider them, male resistance rose. A few farsighted men worked hard to ensure that women were considered and given a chance. One such man was Comdr. Kelsey Stewart, assigned in 1978 to provide officers for the staffs of all educational activities except for the three programs that trained aviators, submariners, and surface warfare officers. Stewart recalled that

> all these activities of course wanted only the best officers and only top quality males. They would take a woman every now and then to keep us happy but they did not like it. . . . We did, however, begin to make offers that most commands, including the major training commands (read that as USNA, Naval War College, etc.), could not refuse. "This is the officer proposed (read as woman), she is qualified, if you don't want her someone else will, and that billet will rot before *anyone* is placed against it". . . . *Almost without exception,* and usually by the crusty male diehards, they would say "send me more like *'woman's name.'* She is great." My assistant and I did this for a few reasons—it was the right thing to do, most of the women were of very high quality and wanted to go to that location. The detailers needed to place them and it solved our problem of filling billets.[24]

At a few other places at Navy headquarters, similar encounters took place, allowing more and more women officers to enter key positions, quietly and with a little push from above.

Women Officers' Professional Association

In the 1970s as Navy women crossed so many frontiers, they had much to learn from and share with one another. What they needed was something like the defunct WAVE network that had centered in the office of ACNP(W). In 1978 Comdr. Rebecca Vinson and Lt. Kay Roberts, both stationed in Washington, D.C., led efforts to establish an informal organization they named the Women Officers' Professional Network. After compiling a roster of all women naval officers in the Washington area, the group began to host a series of luncheons to which it invited prominent speakers such as the CNO. The group was a success—perhaps a little too much so, for its members heard that some male officers viewed warily the idea of a women's network.

Attendance at the luncheon meetings grew, and in 1984 members incorporated as the Women Officers' Professional Association (WOPA). To ensure that membership would bring no backlash, DACOWITS asked service leaders to affirm their support for such organizations. Navy officials assured the committee they had supported WOPA's recent formation and noted that the chief of naval personnel had been its first speaker.

WOPA's membership grew to over three hundred by 1991 and included officers on active duty in all services, retired and former officers, midshipmen, and civilians. Activities now include a monthly newsletter, frequent workshops and symposia on career opportunities, and traditional, formal military dinners known as dining in. Recently WOPA officers began to assemble an archive, now located in the OP-01(W) office.

The most telling evidence of the association's vitality is its expansion outside Washington, D.C. Six chapters now exist across the country, from Norfolk to San Diego, some of them with hundreds of members. In five other areas female officers have volunteered to serve as "points of contact" for WOPA.

Women in Command

As we have seen, not until 1962 was a woman officer, the person in charge of women's recruit training at Bainbridge, designated a commanding officer. For another decade no other command was held by a woman, despite the passage of Public Law 90-130 in 1967, which removed legal barriers. By 1970 the Navy was beginning to question whether it could continue to deny its most prestigious positions to senior women officers. Would they continue to accept exclusion? Would junior officers remain? Would top-notch women continue to join?

Competition for commands was strenuous. A command given to a woman was one less available for a man, and some men charged to assign commands resisted assigning them to women. By April 1974, almost two years after Z-116 appeared, only five women had been named commanding officers. Capt. Robin Quigley commanded the Service School Command in San Diego, an activity with a staff of over a thousand that each year trained thirty thousand sailors, most of them men. Capt. Ruth Tomsuden of the Supply Corps took command of the Navy Food Service System Office, responsible for the financial control and technical direction of a thousand dining facilities and the training of more than twenty-three thousand personnel. Capt. Sarah Koestline headed the vast Personnel Accounting Machine Installation in Norfolk. Capt. Fran McKee was named commanding officer of the naval security group activity at Fort Meade, Maryland, with a staff of about a thousand, responsible for managing extremely sensitive and highly classified material. Capt. Mary Gore became the first woman to command a navy recruiting area. She was responsible for recruiting throughout the entire northeast.[25]

The number of commands held by women grew slowly—by 1977 it was only ten. The major impediment was the long-established preference given to warfare specialists. Under pressure from senior women officers and DACOWITS, Navy planners began to question the assumptions underlying this preference and to identify commands for which they were not valid. As the detailing of women was initially done by the surface-ship community, the percentage of women allowed to succeed to command in any given year was tied to that of surface-warfare officers. Women's command opportunities could not be perceived to exceed those of men, a tacit acknowledgment of male sensitivity on the issue. By 1984 about thirty women other than nurses held commands ranging from small (navy recruiting district or naval reserve center) to very large. Most significantly, in 1985 Capt. Elizabeth Wylie took charge of the Atlantic Military Sealift Command (MSC), the largest of four similar units. Her command had critical strategic missions. Within it were twenty-eight Navy ships and on average twenty merchant ships chartered by MSC; she managed an annual budget of close to $750 million. For the first time a woman's command involved operational control of ships.[26]

In some cases, official guidance to detailers must be changed before they can select Gen URL officers for certain billets, a process that can contain pitfalls and consume much time. For example, while one reference to warfare qualification has been removed from the language governing selection of commanding officers for NROTC units, another remains, with the result that until 1987 no Gen URL captains were selected for these positions, and since then only two have been.[27]

Women's chances for major command remain worse than men's. As late as 1987, no woman had commanded or been executive officer of a naval air station or a fleet training center. Some women had been executive officers of naval stations and fleet operations and control centers, but these placements often came about circuitously. For example, Capt. Kelsey Stewart, then commanding officer of the Naval Station at Norfolk, Virginia, wanted as an executive officer either a man who had already served in that position at sea or a "quality woman," for he knew that even the best women officers would consider it a plum. His first two executive officers were men who saw the job as less desirable than one at sea. When the job next opened up, in 1986, Stewart insisted on a "hot shot woman Commander. Nothing else is acceptable."

Comdr. Ronne Froman was assigned the job. A 1972 graduate of the Women Officers School, she had begun service as an education officer and then became a recruiter. After a series of billets stretching from the East Coast to Hawaii, she was serving with the Joint Chiefs of Staff at the Pentagon when the orders came to report to Norfolk. She dove into the new assignment. It was challenging, for the very size of the base and the huge number of ships homeported there meant constant and hectic activity. Stewart's assessment was, "Results FANTASTIC! Did a super job . . . NEVER ONCE DID I REGRET bringing her on board." Stewart later reported that Froman and every woman at the naval station performed superbly. "I believe there is no limit to their capabilities and as soon as we can get over this gender hang-up, we can get on with manning a class Navy." Froman next was ordered to become the commanding officer of the personnel support activity at Pearl Harbor (where she had formerly served as executive officer). "After Norfolk," she said, "the C.O. job in Hawaii was a breeze."[28]

Women Flag Officers

Public Law 90-130 placed no limit on the number of women who might be selected for flag rank, but neither did it require that any woman be selected. The Army named its first two women generals in 1970, the Air Force in 1971, but not until mid-1972 did the Navy promote Capt. Alene B. Duerk, chief of the Navy Nurse Corps, to the rank of rear admiral. Four more years would pass before a woman line officer would attain that rank, partly because a legislative anomaly allowed the Navy to promote a woman captain only if she were actually serving in a billet that called for a flag officer. Vice Adm. James Watkins, chief of naval personnel, monitored the situation carefully, looking for the ripe moment for the right woman. He later recalled, "Each year the question would arise—is this the year to select a woman flag officer? We had to make sure the woman selected was fully qualified. When it comes to flag officer selection, eight or ten women captains is not a big base from which to choose."[29] Nonetheless, the strong impression is that, had it not been for the pressures arising from the Army and the Air Force promotions, the impetus of Z-116, intense scrutiny from DACOWITS, and Admiral Watkins's strong personal interest, the Navy might have delayed even longer.

In 1976 Capt. Fran McKee was chosen to become the first woman line rear admiral. At the time she was commanding the naval security group activity at Fort Meade, Maryland, capping a career that included two overseas tours, postgraduate education, recruiting and staff billets, and assignment as the officer-in-charge of the Women Officers School in Newport. After graduating from the University of Alabama, she had joined the Navy in 1951, planning to remain for only one tour and then go to medical school. Now just short of her fiftieth birthday, her dignity, intelligence, energy, and wit made her the epitome of the Navy's finest woman officers. She was devoted to the Navy and realistic about her place in it: "I was a volunteer, and I could accept the Navy's parameters or go home. I understood its limitations on women were for good reasons, if not always the wisest, and I appreciated that because I wanted to belong to a first-class outfit."[30]

Finally, McKee was a graduate of the Navy's most prestigious school, the Naval Warfare course at the Naval War College in Newport. For years, women had unofficially audited lectures and completed course work at the Navy's top-level professional schools; in August 1969 McKee became the first official female student. She was ordered to the junior section of the naval warfare course, but as the most senior in that section, according to custom, she would become its president. As she later learned, "The college staff decided that the men students wouldn't put up with a woman being president, so the simplest solution was to put me in the senior section." The prejudice that placed her in the senior section only enhanced her already sterling credentials to become a rear admiral.[31]

By 1992 only six Navy women other than nurses had attained flag rank. After McKee retired in 1981, Capt. Pauline Hartington was the second woman line officer to be promoted to rear admiral (in 1982), followed by Capts. Grace Hopper (1984), Roberta Hazard (1984), Louise Wilmot (1988), and Marsha Evans (1992). Until Wilmot's promotion, only one woman line rear admiral of the regular Navy was on active duty at any given time; with Evans's promotion, now there were three. Rear Admiral Hopper, the computer pioneer, was a Naval Reserve officer. Well past the normal retirement age of sixty-two when she was selected for two-star rank, she had been retained on active duty under a procedure that allowed for yearly extensions; these continued until she retired in 1986.[32] As more women serve at sea and in command, the share of women holding credentials comparable to those of their male contemporaries will increase, and the number of women flag officers on active duty may grow. For the present, to have raised their flag and kept it flying is a solid achievement for Navy women.

It is also deeply gratifying for their predecessors. In 1982 one of this book's authors attended a reunion in Seattle of more than a thousand former Yeomen (F), WAVES, and other Navy women. As Admiral Hartington hove into view, flanked by Capts. Elizabeth Wylie and Sarah Watlington, a spontaneous roar of cheers and sobs greeted them. At that moment, every woman there who had ever worn the Navy uniform knew that Hartington's stars were hers too.

So extensive were the changes promulgated in Z-116 and so radical those mandated by Congress that it has taken the Navy two decades to implement them fully. Different reasons account for the long period between promise and fulfillment. For enlisted women entering nontraditional ratings, the pace was slow because so many dovetailing procedures of training and assignment had to be modified. In addition, and perhaps more important, fewer women wanted to enter those ratings than the Navy needed; the Navy had to work hard to get them. As for women officers, male traditionalists resisted their progress toward high rank, command, and the most desirable billets. For women midshipmen at the Naval Academy, a number of unsettling episodes revealed that despite their impressive overall performance, they had yet fully to be accepted. Regardless of such difficulties, the Navy had to keep the promise of Z-116, not only for its own overall benefit but also because Navy women would accept no less. They could and would be patient, but they would not be denied.

By contrast, women seeking commissions as restricted line and limited duty officers and in staff corps where women had never served before were able to take their new places quickly and quietly. Further, the women in Gen URL advanced naval administration into a recognized specialty.

The integration of women and men in recruit and officer-candidate training was a fundamental break with the past. Now, unlike their predecessors trained in segregated units, Navy women from the outset train, learn, work, and compete with men.

12

—

Women at Sea

"I don't know of any job that can't be done by a woman, including mine."

—CAPT. A. E. WALTHER, COMMANDING OFFICER OF THE USS *McKee*

As the era of the all-volunteer force began in the early 1970s, Navy leaders knew that by the end of the decade they would have trouble finding enough qualified men to put aboard ships. Navy women could make up the impending shortage, but the legislation of 1948 allowed the Navy to put women only in transports and hospital ships, of which there were few. At the same time, a growing number of Navy women were beginning to realize how severely the legal prohibition against serving in ships was restricting their careers; in 1976 six of them filed a suit claiming it was unconstitutional. Both the Navy and its women stood to benefit from changing the law.

In what turned out to be one of its most far-reaching provisions, Z-116 had already opened the way for a solution. In 1972 a thirty-month pilot program began in which women outside the medical field would make up a portion of the crew of the USS *Sanctuary*, a hospital ship scheduled to be decommissioned in 1975. The success of that program assured the Navy that women were capable of serving in ships, and a few Navy leaders began to plan for a change in the law. The decision of a federal court in 1978 that the 1948 statute was unconstitutional strengthened their hand and helped to persuade Congress to grant their request for amendment. Thus the gangways were opened, and a remarkable new era was at hand for both the Navy and its women.

This new era required the Navy to change three things: the ships themselves, to accommodate women; women's training; and women's career paths. In addition, Navy leaders would have to make every effort to gain men's acceptance of the new reality, and they would have to decide how to deal with pregnant sailors aboard ships. Women also faced change.

215

The opportunity to serve in ships would allow them to expand their range of professional skills and, in the case of female officers aspiring to a seagoing career, prepare themselves for the Navy's sternest professional challenge, command of a ship. They would also have to accept radical changes in their personal lives, for now they would face what Navy men had always endured—long periods of duty at sea that separated them from family and friends.

The USS *Sanctuary*[1]

On September 8, 1972, Personnelman Third Class Peggy Sue Griffith reported aboard the USS *Sanctuary* at Hunter's Point, California, the first of a group of thirty-two enlisted women and two female officers setting off on uncharted seas. The Navy assigned the enlisted women to work in the ship's deck, supply, and operations departments as well as in administration. (In addition, twenty-one enlisted women were assigned to the ship's hospital.) These women were now embarked as the U.S. Navy's first real female *sailors*, expected to perform the same duties as their male shipmates. One officer, Lt. (jg) Ann Kerr, served primarily as an administrative assistant, with additional watchstanding duties both in port and at sea. The other, Ens. Rosemary Nelson of the Supply Corps, was responsible for the officers' wardroom mess (dining room) and also stood watches in port.

Ever since the WAVES had been established in 1942, governing legislation had allowed the Navy to assign women to transports and hospital ships. That it had rarely assigned any women except for Hospital Corps personnel and nurses was a matter of policy, not law. By assigning Griffith and the nonmedical women to the *Sanctuary*, the Navy could test the waters against the day when it might need to assign larger numbers of women to ships without committing itself to a radical change. What the Navy might learn from this pilot program was therefore of the greatest interest. The *Sanctuary* experience had built-in limitations. The ship was to be decommissioned in March 1975, hence she would have a mixed crew for only thirty months. Much might be learned in this time, yet if some lessons turned out to be particularly hard, the experience would be short-lived. The Navy might be experimenting, but it was doing so with its classic prudence.

The experience proved to be fairly painless. The women performed their duties competently, often exceptionally so. They presented no special disciplinary problems; during the first year, 17 percent of the enlisted women were formally disciplined, compared with 19.8 percent of the enlisted men. Of the fourteen women brought up for discipline only two appeared more than once, while twenty-four of the eighty-six enlisted men brought up were repeat offenders. The women proved themselves as adaptable to shipboard life as their male shipmates. Few modifications had to be made to the ship to accommodate them, nor did their presence adversely affect the performance of their male shipmates. The *Sanctuary*'s commanding officer concluded after a year's experience with his mixed crew that "women are capable and may serve on board the *Sanctuary*, under the present administrative conditions, in perpetuity."

There were difficulties, however. First, the women had not been carefully screened. Among the enlisted were four whose rowdy behavior disrupted the women's berthing spaces until firm command action restored order. The commanding officer might have acted sooner had he known of the problem. Apparently the well-behaved majority hesitated to report the trouble, perhaps fearing that complaints about some of their number might reflect badly on all. A fight that erupted days before the ship's first deployment revealed the situation. Second, some other women manipulated inexperienced male petty officers. Men supervising women had to learn that failure to uphold the same standards of performance for both sexes was, pure and simple, a leadership failure that lowered morale and achievement.

Third, while personal relationships were a sensitive area, common sense and firm leaderships could keep them from hindering performance. Public displays of affection were prohibited; personal relationships were to be kept private. The commanding officer reported that most of his crew "constantly exhibited high moral standards," and "a few, through their good fortune . . . found true affection and have gotten married." Regardless, it soon became clear that a married couple should not be in the same ship's crew, and the secretary of the Navy ruled to that effect.

The spouses of many crewmembers required special consideration. Many of the wives felt threatened, partly because the press focused on problems that might arise from having women in the crew. The command conducted a series of informative meetings with the wives prior to the ship's sailing, which convinced most that their fears were unfounded.

Fifth, there were losses to the crew resulting from pregnancy—a novel situation for a Navy ship's commanding officer to confront. Seven enlisted women left the service for that reason. While a small percentage of the total crew, they were a large percentage of the women on board, and their number compared unfavorably with the discharge rate of enlisted men in the crew.

An additional problem stemmed from the Navy's failure to supply adequate uniforms to its women. The women of the *Sanctuary* found that many basic items of their normal complement of uniforms, from caps to shoes, were nearly useless at sea: too heavy, too light, too cumbersome, too hard to keep clean, or too bulky for storage. The women adapted by purchasing foul-weather gear, dungarees, and chambray shirts, or borrowing them from male shipmates. These adaptations met the needs of the moment but cost the women something in terms of comfort and appearance, and hence in morale. A year after the *Sanctuary* was decommissioned, the Navy still supplied no functional working uniform for women serving in ships, even though by that time women had begun regularly serving in small craft.

The major lesson came from the time the *Sanctuary* actually spent at sea. During the first thirteen months with a mixed crew, she was under way for a total of forty-two days. In the next two months she sailed down the Pacific coast to Buenaventura, Colombia, then through the Panama Canal to Port-au-Prince, Haiti, and finally to her new homeport of Mayport, Florida. During the remaining sixteen months until decommissioning she got under way for brief training periods. Compared with the operating schedules of many Navy ships, this was little time at sea, yet some women line officers assigned to the ship earned their qualifications as officers of the deck under way. They demonstrated that not only could the ship handle women, but that women could handle the ship.

During the *Sanctuary*'s final months at Mayport, benefits from many of the lessons began to appear. Male petty officers had gained experience in supervising women, and a cadre of women petty officers now had shipboard experience. During this period no women were reassigned or discharged for pregnancy while aboard ship, and the number of disciplinary actions for women, relative to those for men, decreased.

Women in Small Craft

Far less fanfare and planning accompanied the early assignment of women to small Navy craft. As early as the fall of 1972, only weeks after Z-116 was issued, eleven enlisted women reported straight out of boot camp to the Annapolis Naval Station for duty aboard the station's yard patrol craft used to train Naval Academy midshipmen. A total of forty women were expected to report to the station eventually to relieve the men stationed there for sea duty. Early in 1975 twenty-three enlisted women were assigned to tugboats at the San Diego Naval Station. There it soon became evident that the Navy had not heeded some important lessons taught by the *Sanctuary* experience.

First, neither the women nor their shipmates-to-be received specific preparatory training for being in a mixed crew. The men saw the introduction of women into their close-knit groups as a threat to their prestige and morale, while the tugboat craftmasters, unsure about how to lead women, responded inconsistently and thus ineffectively to both men and women. The women at first were enthusiastic about their assignment—although none had volunteered—but their enthusiasm diminished as they met open rejection from male shipmates and indecision from supervisors. Second, the women stood no night watches because of fears for their safety in waterfront areas at night, and they were kept from less desirable jobs because they were assumed to be unprepared and physically incapable of handling them. Such double standards inevitably lowered morale and affected discipline, resulting in a decline in productivity. The situation improved only when the Navy called in a management consulting team and began to apply the lessons of the *Sanctuary* experience. One significant result was that the Navy now began to train *all* recruits in the same seamanship skills; it also opened special apprentice training to women.

By 1976, more than three hundred enlisted women were serving in small craft at several other locations, including Norfolk, Treasure Island and Point Mugu in California, and Newport. They handled and spliced lines, scraped paint, cleaned bilges, maintained damage control and training equipment, and sometimes, as coxswains, took the helm. Also in 1976 the Navy assigned a woman officer to duty with small craft: That year Lt. Bonnie Latsch, who had previously served in the *Sanctuary*, began a tour as officer-in-charge of the four yard patrol craft at the Naval Education Training Center at Newport. These craft provided at-sea training for officer candidates and students at the Navy's Surface Warfare Officers School. (In January 1979 Latsch became the first woman to graduate from that school's course for department heads.)

These assignments provided a modicum of professional experience afloat to a handful of women—not the breadth and depth many of them needed to advance in their ratings. Only duty aboard larger ships, from which they were excluded, could provide that.

Women Bring Suit

On November 10, 1976, four enlisted women filed suit in U.S. District Court in Washington, D.C., asking that the federal statute prohibiting them from serving aboard almost all major Navy ships (section 6015 of Title 10 U.S. Code) be ruled unconstitutional.[2]

The Navy itself created the situation that paved the way for this critical legal challenge. In 1974 the USNS (U.S. naval ship) *Michaelson,* a survey ship, needed an interior communications electrician (IC). No eligible male IC was available for sea duty, but IC Second Class Yona Owens was. In fact, she had already inquired about a sea-duty assignment and been recommended for it:

> I got the orders and my detailers told me to go down to the ship . . . meet the CO and the crew, talk to them and see if I really can do the job. And I did, for two days. I had a marvelous time. The men couldn't quite figure out what I was doing there, but they were totally receptive . . . enthusiastic. I then told my detailers that I could do it but two weeks later they called me and said the orders were canceled.[3]

The cancellation resulted from a ruling by the Navy's judge advocate general that such an assignment would violate the law, even though naval survey ships frequently carried female civilian scientists and thus had berthing facilities for women. Other inconsistencies pervaded Navy policy regarding women and ships: Civilian women trained to repair complex electronic equipment on Navy ships could and did board them, while Navy women could not; Army and Air Force women could be and sometimes were transported on Navy ships, but Navy women could not be; Navy women helicopter pilots were not allowed to let their aircraft hover over an aircraft carrier.[4]

Disappointed by the cancellation, Owens began what turned into months of extensive research on the general question of military women's rights. She then wrote to *Navy Times,* offering to send the information she had compiled to anyone needing help. "I found out very suddenly the horrible facts of life. . . . I got 312 responses from that letter." During this time, she met Yeoman Suzanne Holtman, then working in a newly established office charged to coordinate information for enlisted women. Together with Photographer's Mate Natoka Peden and Seaman Valerie Sites, they decided to bring a class-action suit against the Navy Department and the Department of Defense. They requested help from several women's organizations, all of which showed interest but could offer no funds. Finally the American Civil Liberties Union and the League of Women Voters Educational Fund offered support, and the suit was filed in November 1976. The plaintiffs claimed that the Navy discriminated against them and 21,870 other Navy women who could not serve in any major Navy ships except hospital ships and transports. At that time, no ships of either type were in commission.[5]

Meanwhile, the Navy's policies were being questioned by a group of young male and female officers in San Diego. These included Lt. JoEllen Drag, an aviator, Lt. Suzanne Rhiddlehoover, and Lt. Kathleen Byerly, who in May 1975 had become the first woman to serve as the flag secretary to an admiral commanding an operational staff.

Drag, one of the first eight women chosen to become naval aviators and at that time one of the Navy's three female helicopter pilots, had long been frustrated by interpretations of the law that kept her from gaining the skills and proficiency that her male peers could obtain at sea. For more than three years she had "exhausted every administrative remedy available" to acquire that experience.[6]

Byerly, the daughter of an Army officer, had joined the Navy in 1966 after graduating from Chestnut Hill College in Pennsylvania. She was attracted by the opportunity for travel, for significant responsibility, and for pay equal to that of men. At the Women Officers School she trained under two people destined to become admirals: Lt. Comdr. Fran McKee and Lt. Roberta Hazard. In 1972 Byerly began a tour of duty at the Bureau of Naval Personnel, where she met

> a lot of senior women officers and [began] to realize all the things they and I couldn't do. . . . When Z-116 opened up so much, I began to realize how closed it had all been. . . . Then I went back to San Diego, to an air staff, and that was my enlightenment. There I met the women aviators . . . also, by that time we could see how things were changing in the civilian world. Some of the junior women wanted to go to sea and were asking "Why is this law still here?"[7]

Lt. Suzanne Rhiddlehoover, who was attending law school at San Diego University at night, had a professor who thought the law's constitutionality could be challenged. In the fall of 1975 the group hired him to begin research. Soon thereafter they learned of the Owens suit. After they made sure the ACLU would not engage in high-profile or sensational tactics, Byerly, Drag, and Rhiddlehoover agreed to join the original plaintiffs and thereby strengthen the suit's contention that the law discriminated against all Navy women, enlisted and officers alike. The plaintiffs could not now be dismissed as disgruntled feminists; clearly they were serious professionals raising questions that had occurred to many men and women both in and out of the Navy who wished it well and deplored a law that tied its hands. The officers' entry underscored how much was at stake, for they had invested more time in education and in their Navy careers than the enlisted women.

Then in an independent development Byerly was chosen by *Time* as one of its twelve Women of the Year (1976), whose photographs appeared on the magazine's cover in January. This burst of publicity stunned the group, especially Byerly, who was

> as astounded as anyone else. I hadn't known anything about it until a Navy Public Affairs Officer told me that *Time* was perhaps going to choose some women to be "Man of the Year" and they wanted to interview me. *Time* knew nothing of the suit—only my immediate family, my boss, and the San Diego group knew about that. Now, how would the *Time* story look? But we had to keep going, and later that month we announced that we were joining the suit—actually, the Navy Department decided it and we would issue simultaneous press releases.

Reactions within the Navy were mixed. Many of her friends told Byerly her Navy career was over—she would never be promoted. She learned that someone had tried to rescind orders she had received to the Naval War College. Among the supporters were her boss, Rear Adm. Alan Hill, who said the plaintiffs had every right to press on, and Vice Adm. James Watkins, chief of naval personnel, who protected her orders to the war college. Other senior officers also known to support the suit wanted to have the issue clarified.[8]

On July 27, 1978, District Judge John J. Sirica ruled that the statute in question was indeed unconstitutional. It kept women from "gaining access to a wide range of opportunities for the development of job skills and areas of technical expertise." Although Sirica stopped short of ordering the Navy to send women to sea, the decision was an important victory for Navy women. Any statute ruled unconstitutional was vulnerable to legal challenge.

Return to the Fleet

The court decision was only one reality putting pressure on the Navy's policies. Of longer standing was the fact that the Navy was having difficulty recruiting a sufficient number of qualified men while at the same time it was turning away women with excellent credentials. Meanwhile, the drive to ratify the ERA continued, which caused many national agencies and institutions to reconsider inequities in their policies.

It seemed to Vice Admiral Watkins that it was time for the Navy to seize the initiative; if it didn't take charge, someone else would. With strong support from CNO Adm. James Holloway and Secretary of the Navy Graham Claytor, Navy officials drafted a proposal to amend the statute and, led by Watkins, testified before Congress. They proposed that the Navy be allowed to assign women not only to transports and hospital ships but also to ships that normally do not perform combat missions. Women could also be assigned temporarily to *any* ship for a period of no longer than six months if the ship was not expected to be assigned a combat mission during that period. In the fall of 1978 Congress accepted the proposal and amended the law accordingly. In a letter to all flag officers and commanding officers, the CNO emphasized that the Navy had asked for this legislation as a "sensible, pragmatic move . . . to provide adequate resources to carry out our commitments" and reminded them that while civilians might stress the social aspects of such change, the Navy must stress its professional aspects. He expected the Navy to implement the legislation smoothly and well.[9]

The CNO's hardly subtle letter testified to the fact that not everyone in the Navy was pleased that women might march up the gangways. By 1977 the issue of women going to sea was already being hotly debated, with numerous articles and letters appearing in *Sea Power* (the magazine of the Navy League), *Navy Times*, and daily newspapers throughout the nation. Opinions ranged widely.

Opponents of women going to sea raised several prospects: promiscuity aboard ships, with pregnant sailors and demoralized Navy wives the result; women's inability to handle shipboard tasks and their failure to be accepted by male shipmates; an insufficient number of women willing or able to accept the rigors of sea duty. One opponent was retired Capt. Robin Quigley, former ACNP(W), who insisted that whether women should be allowed to serve at sea was a misphrasing of the question; more properly, she said, it was whether they should be *required*. She thought not enough women would volunteer to join the Navy if they knew they might be required to undergo "the incommodious, spartan, unrelieved, and physically demanding life of months aboard a destroyer or fleet oiler." Another woman officer argued that women were not "psychologically prepared to accept the confinement, deprivation and stress of shipboard life." Thus the presence of women aboard ship, she said, would give rise to a host of problems that would adversely affect the Navy's ability to carry out its mission.[10]

Many disagreed. Often citing firsthand experiences that validated women's abilities, proponents rejected these arguments as biased or outdated. Vice Adm. Samuel Gravely, who is black, likened the arguments about women to previous arguments about blacks and urged that the Navy get on with it: "Frankly, I don't have any heartburn with females on Navy ships. I think they are ready and the political climate demands it." Perhaps the most balanced view of the question came from Rear Adm. Fran McKee. Addressing approximately 1,400 active-duty, retired, and former Navy women attending a convention in San Francisco in August 1977, McKee said that if the law was in fact amended as the Navy proposed, then Navy women would have both the opportunity and the obligation to go to sea. As for the difficulties of shipboard duty, she pointed out that men as well as women may not want to go to sea, yet everyone in the Navy has volunteered to serve the country according to the service's needs. "Whatever view is taken, we can't have it both ways—we can't demand equality when it suits us and fall back on the being-a-woman syndrome when the going gets rough. . . . From a practical point of view in an all-volunteer force we cannot afford to discriminate on the basis of sex." Sounding the same note that the CNO would emphasize in his letter to the Navy's senior officers, she said that if and when the statute was changed, those who served must say "aye-aye, and get on with it."[11]

Getting Under Way

To those in the Navy charged with actually assigning women to sea duty, questions about whether they should serve in ships took second place to the question of how best to bring it about. The basic challenges were several and intertwined.

First, to what ships should women first be assigned? At the time, forty-nine Navy ships could have included women in their crews under the law's provisions. Five were initially selected: USS *Norton Sound*, a test and development ship for guided missiles; USS *L. Y. Spear*, a submarine tender; USS *Samuel Gompers*, a destroyer tender; USS *Vulcan*, a repair ship; and USS *Compass Island*, an auxiliary. Later USS *Point Loma*, a deep-submergence support ship, was substituted for the *Compass Island*. These ships were chosen because they represented the various types of ships approved for women by the amendment; they needed few modifications to their berthing spaces to accommodate women, incurring minimum cost; and they were homeported on both coasts.

Second, how many women should be assigned, and which ones? The numbers question was particularly difficult. The evolution began slowly, with 16 women officers and 375 enlisted women assigned variously to the crews of the *Vulcan, Spear, Norton Sound,* and *Gompers,* with females constituting approximately 10 percent of each ship's crew. The level planned for was 25 percent, but that could not be reached until more enlisted women gained skills in ratings not previously open to them, until more female senior petty officers were available, and until more women officers acquired enough sea experience to qualify for senior leadership positions on board.[12]

The Navy began at once to recruit, train, and assign women so as to produce in due time the numbers needed. It had already asked for women volunteers for sea duty and announced that if more were needed they would be chosen on an involuntary basis. To allow for that eventuality, it then reworded enlistment contracts to say that women might be required to go to sea. In July 1978, even as Judge Sirica was handing down his decision, the Navy started five female ensigns down the path trod by men aspiring to be surface warfare officers, sending them to the basic course at the Surface Warfare Officers School in Newport. All five—Mary Carroll, Elizabeth Bres, JoAnne Carlton, Lisa Crocket, and Linda Day— graduated in November. That year too the Navy opened five sea-going ratings to enlisted women.[13]

As to which women would be assigned, the first were those who had volunteered. Later assignments would be made just as men's were: When a woman's reassignment came up, she was subject to shipboard duty if that's where the Navy needed her.

Ens. Mary Carroll reported to the repair ship *Vulcan* in November 1978, the first woman to report to a ship under the amended law. Only three and a half years had elapsed since the *Sanctuary* had been decommissioned, yet the press treated the *Vulcan* and her crew as a great novelty. When the *Vulcan* made her first two-day trip (from Norfolk to the Naval Weapons Station at Colt's Neck, New Jersey) in March 1979, and then a five-month deployment to the Mediterranean beginning in September 1979, no one seemed to recall that the *Sanctuary*, with two women officers and fifty-three enlisted women, had completed a two-month voyage from California to Florida only six years earlier. When crewmembers from the commanding officer on down commented that *Vulcan* women had performed their duties well and been generally accepted by male shipmates, and that Navy wives had not complained much, these reports were taken as a revelation, with no acknowledgment that they echoed earlier reports emerging from the *Sanctuary*. What was new was that the *Vulcan* was neither a hospital ship nor a transport; nonetheless, she was perceived as the first Navy ship to have a mixed crew.

By the first months of 1979, one other woman officer and 55 enlisted women had joined Ensign Carroll in the *Vulcan*; by year's end an additional 341 enlisted women were serving in 4 more ships, and 54 women officers were serving in another 13. They found what generations of male sailors had found before them: that to live and work in a cramped ship requires adjustment; that the work is hard, the hours are long, and sailing through a storm packing 60-knot winds and 35-foot seas is frightening; that foreign port calls are adventures requiring survival skills; and that leaving loved ones behind is painful. Yet the women remained enthusiastic, their commanding officers reported favorably on their performance and behavior, and male crewmembers accepted them. One episode revealed that women were not immune to the occasional grim reality of shipboard life: On September 27, 1979, only 9 weeks after reporting aboard the *Norton Sound* with 58 other women, 22-year-old Fireman Muriel McBride was swept overboard and lost at sea approximately 230 miles southwest of Vancouver Island.[14]

Steady Expansion

In the latest version of an old story, the Navy needed more technically educable sailors than it could find among men alone to crew its growing number of ships. By the end of the 1970s, as one senior officer later testified to Congress, "some of our ships were not able to get underway [not for] lack of fuel, lack of ammunition, or lack of equipment. The problem was a lack of people. We simply did not have the right kind of people to man our ships and aircraft properly." The shortage was particularly acute in more technical ratings. As the Navy had once needed WAVES to free men to go to sea, it now needed to put women in its noncombatant ships to free men to serve in the combatants. The extent of its need is suggested by the steady rise in the number of enlisted women actually put in ships: Between 1981 and 1990 it quadrupled, from about two thousand to nearly eight thousand.[15]

To achieve this expansion, which is still continuing, two streams of activity have had to be coordinated. One consists of the ships themselves.

Each year the Navy identifies those ships that already have, or could be modified to have, adequate berthing spaces to accommodate more women. The required modifications then become part of each affected ship's schedule for alterations. This stream of activity absorbs large amounts of time and money, both expended incrementally.

The other stream, personnel management, is more complex. Vice Admiral Watkins, chief of naval personnel when the expansion began, later recalled the following:

> We figured about 15 percent [of the crew] would be the bare minimum to permit a positive change in the crew's attitude to allow it to work. We didn't say 15 percent was optimum—we knew that about 50-50 was probably optimum. But we did say, if you can't fill enough billets at the outset, and if you can't match the correct grade structure (that is, we can't have all 15 percent be female seamen), then don't raise expectations only to dash women's hopes in actual execution of the plan. You almost have to phase in to even the 15-percent level. . . . We really had to encourage people to come in at different pay-grade levels, to make sure we had enough strength in there, so that within that command you didn't jeopardize command readiness. It's very hard to start up something like this and get to the desired end point except in evolutionary fashion. That interim period is very dicey, very hard to manage.[16]

Enlisted Women at Sea

Crucial to this expansion was a steady increase in the number of enlisted females in sea-intensive ratings. The Navy opened to women those ratings not clustered chiefly in combatant ships, but sometimes not enough women could be recruited to fill the seats set aside for them in basic training courses. Consequently, the Navy intensified efforts to recruit and train women for them.

The harvest reaped was an eightfold increase in the number of women in sea-intensive ratings, from approximately 2,500 in 1981 to about 16,850 in 1990. From this group and with a growing number of women in senior pay grades, the Navy could begin to rotate them from sea to shore duty in roughly the same manner that it did men. Until this number was reached, male and female sea-shore rotation patterns and policies necessarily differed, with neither group fully persuaded of the fairness of the system. With these numbers, the Navy could also place women in such remote and unpopular overseas locations as Diego Garcia, a small island in the Indian Ocean rapidly built up in the 1980s to become a major forward base for the fleet. The Navy planned to send 192 enlisted women there; the first ones arrived in 1981.[17]

Women in more traditional ratings also had challenges to meet. As more ships became available, some senior women petty officers found themselves in ships for the first time in their careers. They lacked experience in the shipboard aspects of their ratings and had never received applicable training, and yet they were expected to display the same level of leadership afloat as ashore.

The commitment of commanding officers to integration of women into ships' crews played a critical role in its success. A woman doctor serving aboard the USS *Samuel Gompers* concluded:

> The incorporation of women aboard ship was not easy. Months of preparation took place before the first female ever crossed the brow. . . . In retrospect, two major factors allowed the integration of women at sea to progress so successfully. First, a strong chain of command existed as did many mature, compassionate, open-minded individuals who paid meticulous attention to details. . . . The absolute fairness, firmness and amount of concern exhibited by the commanding officer—no more, no less than for men—was crucial. . . . On the other hand, [there was] universal concern to [sic] the problems women faced. . . . The Executive Officer kept himself acutely aware at all times of any problems concerning women at sea and often counseled women with personal problems.[18]

Where command attention to detail was absent or inadequate, results were correspondingly poor. After a visit in mid-1984 to the USS *Hunley*, a submarine tender homeported in Holy Loch, Scotland, DACOWITS members reported to Navy officials a lack of both planning and communication up and down the chain of command. Women crewmembers had received no orientation with reference to the ship's spaces and no training with, for example, the M-16 rifles they were expected to use in emergencies. Nor did they receive support when local landlords refused to rent to them or when local women harassed and intimidated them.[19]

For the hundreds and then thousands of women who took their places as crewmembers during this first decade, the challenge was to adapt to shipboard life. This included cramped quarters, little or no privacy, and their share of the many collateral duties—like damage control, compartment cleaning, and quarterdeck watches—that keep a ship safe, clean, and in working order. In 1985 Electronics Technician Second Class Leith

Regan, who had a bachelor's degree in psychology from Syracuse University, reported to the USS *Jason* one week before deploying for seven months to the western Pacific and experienced "cultural shock." She told a Navy journalist,

> I'm not sure how much [Navy] schools can teach you about being on a deployment for seven months—sleeping in a rack in the same compartment with 140 other women, having to share showers and being considerate. . . . We chipped and painted the outside bulkheads of women's berthing. . . . I've done everything right along with the men. . . . Shipboard duty *is* the Navy.[20]

One factor that helped their adjustment to shipboard life and work was that the Navy made some moderate but important changes to women's uniforms, at least partly in response to the *Sanctuary* experience. A wider range of working uniforms and some modified designs, more in line with men's uniforms, became available. Gone, for instance, was the two-piece blue seersucker uniform for summer introduced in the late 1950s; it was replaced by two shirt-and-skirt or shirt-and-pants outfits, one white and one khaki, and a much greater inventory of women's dungarees. Also, with certain working uniforms women could now wear the convenient and comfortable "ball cap" already much favored by men, especially aboard ship.

The Navy had to cross a significant threshold when it sent women to sea. It had to acknowledge, and require its women to acknowledge, that being a full-fledged sailor meant going to sea when ordered, even if that meant leaving families on the pier. Commanding officers had to accept the separation of a mother from her children as dispassionately as the separation of a father from his. Capt. Raymond Sharpe, a former commanding officer of the USS *Shenandoah,* explained how he rigidly enforced a Navy-wide policy that applied to both men and women: "Within 60 days of reporting, you sign a statement saying that your child will be cared for and you are available to deploy worldwide. If you don't sign, you're out of the Navy. I tolerated no exceptions."[21]

Like their male shipmates, the women had to learn to balance the competing claims of personal and professional life. Yeoman Second Class Deborah Cheek, mother of two, no doubt spoke for many when she explained why she wanted to go to sea: "I have to compete with my peers, and my peers are mostly men. And that's just a fact of life—this is the Navy." Her husband was an electronics warfare technician first class. Shipboard duty also figured prominently in his career, leaving Deborah with full child care in addition to her professional duties when he deployed. When she deployed, the situation was reversed: "I plan, I try to establish a lot of support factors and he's going to have to do the same thing. He's going to have to be father and mother, and it's the same thing I do."[22]

Many women also succeeded by taking advantage of every opportunity offered them. They could serve temporarily in other ships to gain experience that enabled them to compete for advancement with men who could serve in combatants. Radioman Second Class Heather McIntosh was assigned for sixty days to the aircraft carrier *Enterprise* while serving in the *Samuel Gompers*. She wrote to the editor of *Navy Times*,

> That experience I will remember for a long time. We were at sea for carrier qualifications. The flight deck was green [planes landing and launching] most of the time, and communications very, very busy. We had GQs [general quarters] every other day and mass conflagration drills several times a week to practice first aid/battle dressing. Though my duty aboard *Gompers* was good, I left *Enterprise* feeling like I was missing out on all the action. . . . My duty on board and on watch with the *Enterprise* crew enhanced my professional knowledge and performance. . . . I would jump at the chance to go to sea on a combatant ship, not as TAD [temporary additional duty] but as a permanent member of her crew.[23]

Beginning in 1980, enlisted women also had the opportunity to pursue the special qualifications of surface warfare. In 1989 Master Chief Janice Ayers became the first woman to assume the prestigious position of command master chief afloat. By 1990 four women had been named the same.[24]

Women Officers in Ships

The first women aiming to become fully qualified as surface warfare officers (SWOs) met with particularly frustrating circumstances. The Navy sent a quota of junior women officers to the SWO school each year, but completion of the school was just the beginning of a long and demanding process. It was usually on their first ship assignments that aspirants completed the long list of rigorous qualifications, and only after they demonstrated basic knowledge of all facets of naval warfare could they be designated SWOs and allowed to pin on the coveted "bow waves" insignia, comparable to the wings and dolphins worn by aviators and submariners. The ships to which women were first assigned did most of their work in port, offering little or no opportunity for experience in seamanship and warfighting, normally practiced and honed at sea in exercises with other ships. Moreover, billets in electronic warfare or missile and fire control, for example, simply did not exist in noncombatant ships. As a result it was difficult for women to prepare for and demonstrate the qualifications they needed. The male SWOs assigned to these ships may have been equally handicapped, but at least they *could* serve in combatants—it was a matter of competing for such assignments.

One way for both men and women to gain the qualification was to "crossdeck," that is, spend time in a combatant ship. The amended law permitted the Navy to assign women to combatant ships temporarily, so long as those ships were not expected to encounter hostilities. Women could and did do this, but it was not easy. One woman asking to leave the women-at-sea program said that her "opportunity to experience the full range of professional activities aboard combatants has been nil. . . ." Another woman explained that junior officers "are advised to crossdeck but are usually given no idea how to use such an opportunity. Women find it particularly difficult because of combatants' operational commitments and space constraints. And work demands do not always allow officers to leave their command for lengthy SWO training."[25]

Further frustrations awaited the women earliest qualified as SWOs. Their career paths were far from equivalent to those of male contemporaries, for, despite their best efforts, few could gain the same amount of shipboard experience. The number of billets at sea was slowly increasing but as yet included virtually no openings for women lieutenant commanders and commanders to serve as executive and commanding officers. To compensate, the Navy in 1984 attempted to assign the more senior women SWOs as executive officers of shore units closely related to the support of warfare communities, but these assignments offered none of the shiphandling experience they needed to compete for promotion and command. Stymied, many qualified women SWOs abandoned their sea-going careers. In 1987 the Navy reported that of 131 women who had qualified as SWOs, only 40 remained: 56 had returned to the Gen URL or some other nonoperational community, and 35 had resigned from the Navy. The reason most commonly cited for leaving was lack of a clear career path. The other great factor weighing in many of these decisions was the desire to have a family.

Although too late for some, help was on the way. In 1984, for unrelated reasons, destroyer tenders and repair ships began a cycle of periodic six-month deployments. Then in 1986 approximately 17 billets for women SWOs and 240 billets for enlisted women opened up in 17 replenishment ships and 3 maritime prepositioning squadrons under the control of the Military Sealift Command. In 1988, 24 ships assigned to the Navy's Combat Logistics Force opened to women, and the Navy announced its intentions to have women compose half of noncombatant ships' crews. The exact number of ships in which women were serving varied slightly from year to year as one or more ships were retired from service while alterations on others were completed; by 1990, it totaled 70 U.S. Navy ships and 37 assigned to the Military Sealift Command. No longer were women confined to USS "Seldomsail." Female SWOs now had a brighter outlook: Their command opportunities were excellent, their promotion opportunities compared to those of male contemporaries, and their retention rate was higher.

The performance of some women SWOs drew warm praise. For example, six months after Ens. Elizabeth Bres reported to the USS *Puget Sound*, fresh out of SWO school, her commanding officer recommended her for early promotion, saying that she was "as thoroughly impressive as any newly commissioned officer I've seen in 27 years." His successor described her as the ship's "most outstanding junior officer, male or female," with the "greatest all-around potential for promotion." Reports like these plus the tenacity of female SWOs who stayed on enabled the program to weather the early "dicey" period.[26]

Julia Roos: A SWO Who Stayed On

As Julia Roos sees it, the Air Force did her an enormous favor by turning her down when she went to enlist in 1969 right out of high school: "The Navy got me by default—best thing that ever happened to me." After completing one enlistment she returned to school, earned a bachelor's degree in education from the University of Missouri in 1978, and taught high school for two years. Meanwhile she remained a naval reservist and by late 1981 had become a chief petty officer. Almost simultaneously, the Navy accepted her as an officer candidate, and she reported to OCS in November 1981. "I was fascinated by damage control, navigation, engineering. It got me thinking about going to sea. At that time, there was one sea billet available for women in each class, and I determined to get it. I was the honor graduate—I got a free sword—and went to SWO school."[27]

In September 1982, in Barcelona, Spain, she reported to the *Puget Sound*, flagship of the Sixth Fleet. The ship spent a fair amount of time at sea.

My first job on *PS* was as deck division officer. I rotated through the four basic divisions and got my SWO qualification under a commanding officer who required his Officers of the Deck to know engineering inside and out. I kept extending, and so stayed aboard for five years—I was very lucky. I have more miles at sea than many men, most women. I just fleeted up to being Ops [operations] Officer, becoming a department head without having gone to Department Head School [the senior course at SWO school]. I finally got there after I left *PS*.

She was able to return to sea immediately, this time to the *Shenandoah*, again as operations officer and now determined to become an engineer.

The CO [commanding officer] was Captain Ray Sharpe, a really crusty guy who'd fired my predecessor, a woman, for incompetence. COs are reluctant to fire women. Sharpe wasn't. He'd fire *anybody* who didn't do it right. When I told him I wanted to be his engineer, he gave me the job—four months before a propulsion exam! I didn't let him down, or the ship.

Then after eight years of sea duty Roos had to go ashore. She wasn't able to get orders to graduate school, so she asked for a billet with the Propulsion Examining Board (PEB). That board had never had a woman member, partly because it was a hardship for some ships to find berthing space for a woman examiner for a night or two, and partly because there had been so few qualified women engineers. "But a few senior captains who knew me supported me 100 percent, and it helped that a senior PEB member had inspected *Shenandoah* and he approved of me highly. He said, 'If we're going to take a woman, this one should be it.' It was going to happen, but it couldn't until someone like me came along."

Roos emphasizes the need for patience, that it may be close to the turn of the century before the Navy will achieve its goal of having women make up 50 percent of noncombatant ships' crews, for first it must have enough women with enough sea time in all the rates needed. But she has no doubt the women will be ready. "I know one woman Boiler Technician who one day will be able to run the fireroom on any ship."

Now a lieutenant commander, Roos looks forward to command. She exemplifies the women officers who have walked up the gangway and never looked back. By single-minded pursuit of their goals, by hard work and perseverance, above all by consistently superior performance, they have proved that the Navy's confidence in them is well placed.

Problems at Sea

Every problem and issue that Navy women had met on shore went with them to the ships, where solutions proved neither more nor less difficult than before. All along the way, for example, women had to cope with a certain amount of male resentment, most of which melted as they proved their worth. Some problems, however, such as lesbianism, fraternization, and sexual harassment proved as troublesome in ships as they were ashore.

Early on, allegations of lesbianism aboard two ships momentarily distorted the picture of how successfully the overwhelming majority of women were living and working in the ships to which they were assigned. In 1980, twenty-four women serving in the USS *Norton Sound* were placed under investigation for homosexual activity after charges of lesbianism arose in the course of an inquiry into unrelated incidents. Several young women complained to investigators of being molested by lesbian crewmembers.[28] The case against the twenty-four received much publicity, especially after the ACLU cited irregularities in the investigation. Very shortly, the Navy withdrew charges against all but eight of the women, and eventually only two were discharged, both claiming innocence. When asked if these events would affect the women-at-sea program, a Navy spokesman, probably referring to the discharge of an enlisted woman aboard the *Samuel Gompers* earlier the same year, said that such problems were "not without precedent" and would be handled as in the past, that is, "routinely." This attempt to downplay the incident did little to allay suspicion that it had sprung more from resentment of women's presence in the ship than from their actual behavior. Indeed, the spokesman did not mention that homosexual men discovered aboard Navy ships were routinely removed and subsequently discharged, but almost secretively. That authorities had not found enough evidence even to hold hearings for two-thirds of the *Norton Sound* women originally investigated buttressed the suspicion.

In a later case, 11 women serving aboard the USS *Yellowstone* in the Mediterranean were ousted from the Navy after admitting their homosexuality. Once again, they were accused during an investigation of an unrelated incident. This echo of the *Norton Sound* episode raises a question: Why did the investigation lead to accusations against 11 of the 350 female crewmembers but against none of the 775 male crewmembers? Further, after some of the women, concluding they had not been given their rights, asked for a review of their cases, evidence against four of them was found to be insufficient.[29] In retrospect, much more appears to have been made of the cases than the facts warranted.

As for fraternization both on land and at sea, the basic and unresolved problem was inconsistent handling. In 1984 a number of such cases aboard the *L. Y. Spear* became notable only because some officers and enlisted crewmembers accused the commanding officer of dealing more harshly with accused women than with accused men. But little else regarding fraternization was reported, which tends to confirm one sailor's analysis addressed to the editor of *Navy Times*:

> The controlled and crowded conditions on board ships make it hard if not impossible to have private intimate relationships without being detected. The risk to career and reputation is too great for most responsible personnel to take. Good commands do not tolerate fraternization or adultery, and hand out stiff punishments for persons involved.[30]

Whether sexual harassment was more prevalent aboard ships is not known. In this area data of any sort are sparse; only recently has the Navy realized and tried to remedy this lack. Of the few cases that were publicly reported, the best known is that which occurred in the *USS Safeguard* in 1987, in which the commanding officer jokingly offered over the ship's radio to sell his female crewmembers to men on another ship.[31] He was stripped of his command. That incident shows the power, for better or worse, of command example. Where a commanding officer exemplifies deep respect for all personnel regardless of gender, respect becomes one of his command's governing mores. Such power is amplified aboard ships, where a crew is isolated from other influences.[32]

At least two rapes have been charged on board ships, with the Navy swiftly investigating the charges and court-martialing the accused.[33]

The *Acadia* Sails to the Persian Gulf

On May 17, 1987, in the Persian Gulf, an Iraqi jet fired two missiles at a guided-missile frigate, USS *Stark*, killing thirty-seven of her crew and damaging her so severely that she had to return to a U.S. shipyard for major repairs. First she had to be mended enough to make the trip home. By June 1 the USS *Acadia*, a destroyer tender, had left her homeport at San Diego and arrived in Bahrain to begin the necessary work. Probably no one would have noticed her arrival—repair and service ships rarely catch the public's attention—had the *Acadia*'s crew of 1,324 not included 248 women; for the first time the Navy was sending women to repair a ship damaged by hostile fire. According to a *Navy Times* story, Navy officials were "bracing for criticism" of the decision and already pointing out that the Persian Gulf was not a combat zone and the *Acadia* not a combat ship. What those officials did not brace for, because they knew there was no need, was any question as to whether the *Acadia* could accomplish the job. She did, then returned home and resumed her normal duties, to the surprise of hardly anyone.

Pregnancy and Ships

Three of the Navy's concerns about pregnancy became acute when women began serving in ships: the safety of the developing fetus; the availability of medical evacuation (medevac) should an emergency arise; and covering the loss of a pregnant crewmember who must leave the ship until well after delivery. Each issue could affect a ship's readiness.

Ships easily generate conditions that may be hazardous to a developing fetus and that can challenge the endurance of a pregnant woman, such as noxious fumes and long working hours. Current Navy policy removes a woman from her ship in the twentieth week of pregnancy. Most Navy women are healthy and fit, well able to fulfill their shipboard duties during the first half of pregnancy. The Navy has routine procedures for replacing crewmembers lost to accident, grave illness, or other emergency, thus the loss to the ship of a few women due to pregnancy would probably affect readiness only slightly more than the loss of a few men to a variety of other causes.

As the proportion of women in ships grows, the total number absent because of pregnancy is a mounting concern. While the number of women pregnant at any one time varies from one ship to another, the Navy estimates that approximately 5 percent of women serving in ships in 1989 and 1990 were pregnant at any given time.[34] In 1990 approximately eight thousand women were serving in about one hundred ships. If four hundred of these women were pregnant and distributed evenly aboard the ships, each ship would have four pregnant women. Their stages of pregnancy would vary, and not all would necessarily be absent at the same time. Currently the problem appears manageable. But if and when women constitute approximately half of the crews of those ships, the totals could be considerably larger. Of course the women are not evenly distributed; some ships would be much more affected by pregnancy than others. The Navy now requires that women return to their ships to complete their sea duty no later than four months after delivery.

Navy policy initially held that pregnant crewmembers had to be left ashore when a ship got under way. Later, they were allowed to stay aboard if they could be evacuated within three hours to a medical facility capable of handling obstetric emergencies. When fleet commanders pointed out that commanding officers of many ships, unsure of being able to meet such a time constraint, routinely left pregnant crewmembers on the dock when their ships sailed, medical authorities agreed to extend the time to six hours. Moreover, the Navy has developed more accurate diagnostic procedures for obstetrical emergencies and is giving more instruction in obstetrics and gynecology to senior hospital corpsmen who provide medical care in some ships and assist doctors and physician's assistants in others.

How great a challenge pregnant crewmembers present to readiness has yet to be determined. Some claim it is the single greatest problem associated with women aboard ships, while others say cases of shipboard pregnancy have been overpublicized and their import misconstrued. No one knows how well the Navy's policy regarding pregnancy and shipboard duty would actually work because it has not yet been consistently applied. The policy is cautious to begin with, and most commanding officers and other supervisors have interpreted it so conservatively that pregnant women are being overprotected and underutilized. This circumstance alone has given rise to many misperceptions and resentments that damage women's morale as well as that of their shipmates. The detailing procedures to replace lost crewmembers complicate the issue: Weeks and even months may go by before a replacement reports to a ship.[35]

Evidence strongly suggests that the pregnancy rate could be lowered. The Navy has sometimes failed to provide timely, adequate contraceptive counseling and to make available the means for birth control. Another, more hopeful finding is that on ships where strong leadership has aggressively enforced prohibitions against sexual activity on board and promoted education about sex and responsible parenting, pregnancy rates have declined. Unfortunately, some commanding officers prefer to avoid the issue.[36]

Command at Sea

As swiftly as possible in view of the obstacles, women climbed the ladder of responsibility aboard ships. In 1983 the first women SWOs were screened to become executive officers, that is, deemed qualified to be second in command of a ship. They were assigned as billets became available and put through a training "pipeline" of courses tailored for prospective commanding and executive officers. The first woman executive officer was Lt. Susan Cowar, who had graduated with distinction from the Naval Academy and entered a community known as special operations (SPECOPS) officers, who specialize in diving and salvage, mine countermeasures, disposal of explosive ordnance, and management of expendable ordnance. Physical qualifications to enter this community are rigorous and identical for men and women. SPECOPS officers also must complete SWO qualifications. Because most of their shipboard assignments are in small, noncombatant ships, they may attain command as lieutenant commanders. In 1984 Cowar became the executive officer of a fleet tug assigned to Naval Reserve forces.

By 1989 five women were serving as executive officers of ships, and one of them, Comdr. Deborah Gernes of the destroyer tender USS *Cape Cod*, was the first selected to become a commanding officer at sea. A 1971 graduate of the University of Massachusetts, she had been a research assistant at Harvard University before joining the Navy in 1973; she also earned a master's degree in computer-systems management from the U.S. Naval Postgraduate School. She was among the first women to serve at sea, as operations officer and navigator aboard the USS *Vulcan*, then as chief engineer of the USS *Hector*, both repair ships. In 1980 she was designated a SWO. A veteran of worldwide deployments, including three cruises to the western Pacific, Gernes described the *Cape Cod*'s work in the Indian Ocean as "exactly what this ship was designed to do—went to a forward area and tended units of the Seventh Fleet." Her commanding officer, speaking of the close relationship that must develop between commanding and executive officers, said he and Gernes were "able to shout at each other just like anybody else. She is very professional, very competent . . . not what you would call a shy flower, and she couldn't be." Early in 1991 she entered the training pipeline for prospective commanding officers and in November took command of the USS *Cimarron*, a fleet oiler with a crew of 230, including about 80 women.[37]

Before that happened, the commanding officer of the USS *Opportune*, a rescue and diving ship stationed with the Sixth Fleet in Naples, became ill and had to be relieved earlier than expected. Lt. Comdr. Darlene Iskra, a SPECOPS officer screened and in training for command, relieved him in December 1990, becoming the first woman to command a U.S. Navy ship. Like Gernes, Iskra had spent much time on sea duty, ten out of her twelve years in the Navy. A 1974 graduate of San Francisco State University, she was commissioned in 1979. After graduating from the

Naval School of Diving and Salvage in 1980, one of the first women to do so, she was in her fourth ship when she screened for command in April 1990. Her selection she attributed largely to sea time and performance at sea. That she got so much sea time was, in turn, owing largely to her determination. During her single tour of shore duty, she recalls, "I had to stomp on my detailer's desk and say 'I want a ship,' because I knew if I didn't terminate shore duty and get back to sea, I was never going to get where I am now." Iskra's responsibility was heightened because at the time she took command U.S. forces were engaged in Operation Desert Shield. Within weeks the operation became Desert Storm; the *Opportune*, in Iskra's words, "the closest salvage asset in the Mediterranean Sea," could have been called to conduct rescue and salvage in the Red Sea or Persian Gulf. Her husband of ten years, Lt. Comdr. Marc J. Thomas, stationed at the amphibious base in Little Creek, Virginia, said, "I'm feeling the same worries and anxieties that I have heard expressed by Navy wives in the past."[38]

The decision to put women in ships, the Navy's distinctive operational platforms, started them on a journey from the naval profession's periphery toward its heart. The ships were noncombatants, yet the long deployments some of them made exposed women to the realities of sea duty.

The decision in 1988 to increase the proportion of women in noncombatants from 25 to 50 percent represented a radical change in the attitude of Navy leaders. The matter-of-factness with which it was announced and received is noteworthy. Only a decade after the first women reported to the *Vulcan*, thousands of them were serving in ships, some for repeated tours of duty. The doubling of its earlier goal reflected the Navy's appraisal that women's service in ships worked. One after another, female personnel mastered tough, dirty tasks, assumed large responsibilities, and acquitted themselves well. Like many thousands of Navy women who had preceded them, they performed the job at hand and thereby readied themselves for further opportunities the Navy, in its need, might offer them. Their performance met the most pragmatic of Navy tests: They became valued shipmates. One commanding officer, addressing a civilian gathering, said that having been to sea with women, he wouldn't go back without them. Another reported that many of his department heads preferred a mixed crew to an all-male crew. These men are not alone in this judgment. Many other men who have served with women have become, in the words of one, "true believers."[39]

Issues that had long complicated the Navy's relationship with its women, such as sexual harassment and appropriate policy toward pregnancy, took on different dimensions now that women were at sea. These matters drew a disproportionate amount of attention within the Navy and from the media. Experience showed, however, that firm and enlightened leadership significantly minimized their occurrence and impact.

As sea duty became part of the fabric of life for more and more Navy women, neither recruitment nor retention suffered. Women who joined and stayed on seemed proud and pleased to take their place in ships, for going to sea was what the Navy was all about.

13

—

Women in Aviation

"*I* should be getting my wings on February 2 [1979]. . . . I'd love
to have you here, just to see how your girls in the world of naval
air are getting on. . . . I'm grateful I can do my job—fly!*"
— Ens. COLLEEN NEVIUS TO CAPT. JOY HANCOCK

The winds of the early 1970s that sent Navy women to sea also blew open
many doors to naval aviation. Admitting women to flight training was not
among the innovations of Z-116, but it certainly was a logical extension
of its spirit.

When the Navy announced in 1972 that it would accept women in its
flight training program, many had already proved their mettle aloft, and
a few had been internationally recognized as superb aviators. Among the
most prominent was Amelia Earhart, an aviation pioneer of the 1930s;
when she was lost in a flight over the Pacific in 1937, the world mourned.
Nearly as well known was Jacqueline Cochran, who created and led the
Women Airforce Service Pilots (WASPs) of World War II. Nonetheless,
the Navy set about training female officers as pilots and in other aviation
specialties so cautiously as to suggest it knew nothing of women's substantial achievements in aviation. Similarly, its conservatism in reopening
naval aviation to enlisted women suggested it had forgotten how ably
more than twenty-five thousand WAVES had already served in that field.
While it might have forgotten the past, however, the Navy could not
ignore three present realities. One was the climate of public and congressional opinion symbolized by Z-116. Another was that, without the draft,
finding and keeping the men to meet naval aviation's needs could prove
so difficult that opening the gates to women might be not only prudent
but exigent. The third reality was the attitude of men in naval aviation.
They needed to be reassured that combat flying was still their exclusive
prerogative. Consequently, policy regarding women's assignments would
at first be extremely limiting.

For female officers admitted into flight training, an entirely new range of career opportunities now appeared, most of them operational rather than administrative. To enlisted women too there now became available a greater range of training, billets, and rewards. After thirty years during which they had been all but banished, they now returned to the flight lines and hangars. Moreover, this time around, they flew in the aircraft.

Wings of Gold: Women Officers in Naval Aviation

Soon after the United States entered World War II, Lt. Joy Hancock recommended that approximately twenty WAVES who were also licensed pilots be trained to ferry Navy aircraft within the United States. Instead the Navy assigned ferrying to naval aviators who needed a respite from combat flying while keeping their aviation skills honed. Hancock dropped the idea "because I realized that a successful program for women must be based on a *need* for their services."[1] However, a small number of WAVES did fly and receive flight pay, notably those who taught navigation to fledgling pilots on flights between California and Hawaii (see chapter 5).

For nearly thirty years following World War II, few women served in naval aviation units, and women's extensive and varied contributions to "Navy air" were largely forgotten. Meanwhile, naval aviation shone ever more brightly. To earn the aviator's wings of gold was to enter an elite community whose claim to being the cream of the crop was challenged only by submariners. Only those with superb mental and physical conditioning need apply for flight training. Those who survived it and then qualified to fly on and off the great carriers stood at the very apex of their profession.

Thus when Secretary of the Navy John Warner announced in October 1972 that naval aviation training would soon be open to women, he was quick to add, "It's not likely they'll fly the fighter planes, but there are a number of opportunities with our transports, our helicopters, and other types of aviation for those girls that are up to it."[2] The secretary was referring to that large proportion of naval aviation designated as noncombat flying. It contributes significantly to the Navy's mission. Helicopter pilots, for example, conduct search-and-rescue missions and move people and supplies. Some pilots serve as flight instructors, while others test and evaluate new aircraft. Considerably more than half of naval flight operations consists of such tasks. Making clear that this was a test program (a pilot pilot program, so to speak), the Navy acknowledged two purposes: to promote equal rights and opportunity for women throughout the service and to see how women would perform as noncombat pilots. The latter suggested that soon the Navy might need women pilots. Retaining pilots on active duty was always a challenge, for commercial airlines were usually eager to lure them out of service with offers of more money, more safety, more time at home. In the absence of a draft, women eager to pin on naval aviators' gold wings could fill gaps left by men eager to put theirs aside.

To assure itself that "girls" would be "up to it," the Navy prevailed on Ens. B. A. Rodgers, a woman serving as public affairs officer for the Naval Aviation Schools Command, to undergo some of the more rigorous physical conditioning required. She paved the way for the first women naval aviators by extricating herself from a cockpit turned upside down under water, jumping from towers, being dragged through Pensacola Bay astern a Navy landing craft and picked up by a helicopter, and surviving a prisoner-of-war training course.[3]

It is difficult to understand why the Navy thought it needed such assurance, especially when it was already preparing to train women physicians for flight duties. Lts. Victoria Voge and Jane McWilliams, the Navy's first two women flight surgeons, graduated from the Naval Aerospace Medical Institute in December 1973. Furthermore, numerous women aviators, particularly the WASPs, had shown beyond question that women could not only fly, they could meet the standards of military aviation. Between September 1942 and December 1944 more than a thousand WASPs ferried 12,650 fighter and bomber planes all over the United States and Canada, and overseas when needed, towed targets for combat pilots to practice their shooting, and instructed hundreds of Army Air Corps pilots. They flew 7 days a week, a total of 60 million miles, and 38 of them lost their lives. Of them retired Maj. Gen. Jeanne Holm wrote, "They flew as regularly and as long as male pilots in the same jobs and showed no difference in physical, mental, or psychological capabilities. . . . The record shows that [their] accident rate was about the same as men's."[4]

The First Women Naval Aviators

The Navy embarked on its pilot program with the utmost caution. It intended to select for flight training only eight women officers already on active duty. But of the twenty-six who applied, only four passed the flight aptitude test and met the exacting physical requirements. Recruiters were then told to find four more candidates among civilian women. Only after they completed flight training and six months in flying billets would the Navy evaluate the program's success and decide how many more women, if any, it would train as pilots.

In March 1973, four women officers reported to the Naval Aviation Training Command at Pensacola to begin flight training, and four civilian women reported to OCS, with orders to enter flight training upon graduation. Navy flight training consists of three distinct phases and takes from twelve to eighteen months to complete, depending partly on the types of aircraft the student is expected to fly and partly on weather and the availability of planes. The first phase is ground school, about 170 hours of meteorology, aerodynamics, flight rules and regulations, aircraft systems, and navigation. The second phase is basic flight—how to get an aircraft up in the air, go from point A to point B, and land. After soloing, students learn formation and instrument flying. Thus far, all have taken the same training; now, in the third and final phase, they set out on different paths for advanced training in specialties: jets, propeller-driven aircraft, or helicopters. After advanced training, successful students receive their wings and are designated "naval aviators."

Six of the first women selected won their wings of gold: Judith Neuffer, Barbara Allen,* Rosemary Merims Conatser,* Jane Skiles,* Anna Scott,* and JoEllen Drag.* Allen was the first to be named a naval aviator, on February 22, 1974. Neuffer followed five days later, and Skiles, Drag, Scott, and Conatser all graduated by June. These were the first women pilots in any branch of the U.S. armed forces; the Army received its first women pilots later in 1974, the Air Force in 1977. In keeping with its intent first to evaluate their abilities and then determine how many women it could employ, the Navy assigned them to various aircraft engaged in various tasks. Two went into helicopters, four into fixed-wing, multiengined aircraft. Of the latter, two flew transport planes, one reconnoitered hurricanes, and the fourth did utility flying, such as towing targets for gunnery practice by crews of ships and combat aircraft.[5]

The backgrounds of these women suggest the reservoir of talent available to naval aviation. Barbara Allen Rainey had grown up in the Navy; at the time she entered flight training, her father was a retired commander. In high school she had distinguished herself as an athlete and member of the National Honor Society. She entered Long Beach

*Names after marriage: Barbara Allen Rainey, Rosemary Conatser Mariner, Jane Skiles O'Dea, Anna Scott Fuqua, JoEllen Drag Oslund.

College in California, where she consistently topped the dean's list, then graduated from Whittier College. Commissioned as an ensign in 1970, she had been a communications watch officer on the staff of the Supreme Allied Command, Atlantic, in Norfolk before selection to the flight program. She completed flight training with distinction, avoiding the ranks of those needing extra instructional flights. Her first assignment was flying C-1s with a transport squadron in Alameda, California. Within a year she became the first Navy woman to qualify as a jet pilot, flying the six-passenger, two-pilot T-39. She married Lt. (jg) John Rainey, a 1972 graduate of the Naval Academy then assigned to VP-46, a patrol squadron at Moffett Field in California.

Judith Neuffer's background was more aviation oriented than military. Her father had been an Army Air Corps pilot in World War II, then became an airport manager as a civilian. He started teaching his daughter to fly when she was fifteen, and at sixteen she soloed in a Piper Cub. Flight training was not open to women when she joined the Navy, nor did she have any idea that it would be. A graduate of Ohio State University, her first job in the Navy after being commissioned was programming computers at a fleet support activity in San Diego. When she heard that the flight program was being opened to women, she "jumped at the chance. I was in no way trying to be a pioneer, I was at the right place at the right time."[6] After earning her wings, she joined a squadron flying RP-3 Orions at Jacksonville, Florida. Its mission was to fly into the eyes of hurricanes and record their temperature and pressure so that forecasters could gauge more accurately their speed and direction.

Anna Scott came into the Navy with a pilot's license. A native of Williamsport, Pennsylvania, and the daughter of a civil engineer, she spoke Spanish fluently and had graduated from the University of California at Santa Barbara. She was already considering a Navy career when flight training for women opened up, and she promptly applied. For her first flying assignment, the Navy sent her to a helicopter transport squadron in Norfolk. She married another naval aviator, Lt. Harry Fuqua, also in a squadron at Norfolk.

Rosemary Conatser's father, an Air Force pilot, died in an aircraft accident when she was three years old. Growing up in San Diego, she was fascinated by the Navy jets flying out of the Naval Air Station at Mirimar. As a young teenager she cleaned houses to earn money for flying lessons, and later she washed airplanes at Lindbergh Airfield in return for flight hours. She had earned her pilot's license by age seventeen and at nineteen graduated from Purdue University with a degree in aviation technology. She entered the Navy's flight training program with 620 hours of flight time, together with FAA commercial and flight instructor certificates and flight instrument and multiengine ratings. In her first flying assignment at Oceana, Virginia, she applied to transition to jets along with other pilots in her squadron, although jet aircraft were still off-limits to women. Enlisting the help of the Navy's top-level aviators, she overcame bureaucratic footdragging and qualified in the A-4 and later the A-7E, both jet attack aircraft.

JoEllen Drag of Castro Valley, California, a graduate of California State College (Hayward) with a degree in political science, found flight training a sizeable challenge. "Learning the incredibly complicated controls with hundreds of switches, meters, and flashing lights was the toughest part, the acrobatics the fun part. I never got sick, but I got some of my instructors a little upset when it was my turn to bring the aircraft up smoothly from a crazy position."[7] She was the first Navy woman to complete helicopter training, and her father, a retired Navy commander, pinned on her wings. In her first assignment she flew transport helicopters in San Diego. There she married Lt. Comdr. Dwayne Oslund and left active duty to become a reservist, proud of her role as a "weekend warrior." There too, in 1976, she joined five other Navy women in a suit petitioning that Section 6015 of the 1948 legislation restricting women's duty at sea be declared unconstitutional (see chapter 12).

Jane Skiles was another daughter of the Navy. Both her parents had served in World War II: her father as a naval aviator, her mother as a Supply Corps officer. She too had a degree in political science, from Iowa State University. She was the first woman to qualify in the C-130 Hercules and later the first woman to qualify as a Navy flight instructor, a job she loved. "It's hard work, but very rewarding. . . . There's a great need for somebody to be doing the jobs women are doing. The Navy's hurting for pilots."[8]

In 1975, assured that the pilot program was succeeding, the Navy authorized a second group of eight women to enter flight training. Six earned their wings and went on to varied assignments. In 1976 the Navy took another cautious step forward. Heretofore, civilian women selected had all gone through OCS at Newport before reporting to Pensacola for flight training. Now some of the third group of candidates reported directly to aviation officer candidate training at Pensacola for a course that had previously been open only to men. Six women graduated from that course in February 1977, but not all went on to flight training. Three entered aviation specialties previously closed to women: Two became the first female naval air intelligence officers, while the third became the first female aviation maintenance duty officer.[9]

Life in the Squadrons

As these first women pilots entered the world of naval aviation, they were greeted with surprise, skepticism, and some resentment. To mark Judith Neuffer's arrival, her squadron commanding officer staged a poker game in his office, complete with clouds of cigar smoke and one player shoeless, another shirtless. Later on her first flight with the squadron, the crew said very little, a marked change from its usual bantering. Later when they saw that she was "not out there to prove anything, to pose a threat to them or to be better than them," they relaxed. Some of her fellow aviators believed that women had not had to pass the same physical requirements they had and wondered if she had the strength to handle the aircraft. "After the men have flown with me and realize that I've been trained just like any other pilot, they simply treat me like a member of the crew. . . . However, I do know that the language on my crew is not as colorful as it is on others . . . and I appreciate that, but I've never requested it." Even after her squadron took her presence in stride, she drew surprised stares from others. They would see her olive-drab flight suit and black boots and draw the wrong conclusion: "Nobody thinks I'm a pilot, they assume I'm a nurse." JoEllen Drag and Rosemary Conatser learned that the sound of female voices coming from Navy cockpits surprised many who first heard them.[10]

Old habits die hard. The admiral in charge of advanced aviation training where the first women finished the course so strongly opposed women being naval aviators that he refused to pin on their wings. A retired naval aviator later reported, "The Bureau of Personnel, rather ashamedly, had to send down another admiral to perform the ceremony."[11] But the skill of a pilot is quickly revealed, and the men in aviation squadrons soon saw that their female peers were capable. Further, as members of nondeploying squadrons, the first women aviators returned to their own homes or quarters when their daily duties were completed, thus avoiding the social, interpersonal challenges that were an inescapable part of life aboard ships with mixed crews.

The advent of women aviators opened another chapter in the old story of inappropriate uniforms. There were too few small helmets or foul-weather jackets available for them, and even the smallest were too big for some (as well as for smaller men). Torso harnesses also had to be modified to accommodate smaller frames. Even shoes presented a problem: Smaller aviation boots had to be specially procured.

Evidence that naval aviation was accepting women more or less calmly appeared when news of a naval aviator's pregnancy—that of Lt. (jg) Jane

O'Dea, on duty in Rota, Spain—caused little stir. The basic question was pragmatic: How long into her pregnancy could she be allowed to fly? The Navy's approach was strictly professional: She could continue "as long as pregnancy does not interfere either physically or psychologically with control of the aircraft." A flight surgeon and gynecologist would determine when that point was reached. Her immediate senior officer later emphasized that the impact of her pregnancy on her squadron was positive. After she reached the stage past which she could not fly, her share of flight hours was welcomed by other squadron pilots as the means to speed their advancement toward designation as aircraft commanders, the basic requirement for which was 1,500 pilot hours. Also, he reported, her grounding "provided tangible benefits to the maintenance department. . . . Many special projects requiring continued attention were completed much more quickly than [if they had] been constantly interrupted by flying duties." Recently, the Navy has grounded women pilots from the beginning of pregnancy until after delivery, returning them to flying status only after a flight surgeon certifies that they are fit to fly. The policy was changed in response to Federal Aviation Administration studies that raised questions about flying and possible damage to fetuses.[12]

At about the same time, Lt. Barbara Allen Rainey was also starting her family. Both women were able to combine motherhood with flying but in quite different ways. After marriage, O'Dea's husband traded a Navy career for that of a schoolteacher, which gave him more regular hours and more time at home; later, her mother joined the family circle. With child care assured, O'Dea was able to continue on active duty. Rainey chose instead to transfer to the Naval Reserve for four years, ferrying aircraft on weekends. In 1981, after the birth of her second daughter, she returned to active duty as a flight instructor. Within a year she was dead, killed when her turboprop crashed near Evergreen, Alabama, on July 13, 1982.[13]

Five days earlier, Ens. Cary Page Jones, a 1981 graduate of the Naval Academy, was killed in a midair collision of two training aircraft over Cabaniss Field, near Corpus Christi, Texas. Close to completing the advanced portion of the aviation curriculum when she was killed, she was posthumously designated a naval aviator. Naval aviation has always been a costly business; now that women were part of it, they too were paying the high price.[14]

Overall, women had made an impressive breakthrough in a field that emphasized brains, courage, and skill. Like women in ships, they demonstrated beyond argument females' ability to enter the Navy's operational arenas. Yet the inconsistency and unreasonableness of the restrictions imposed by law, custom, and policy frustrated them. Flying a helicopter, for example, JoEllen Drag Oslund, could not even *hover* over an aircraft carrier, even though civilian women or women from other services might temporarily be in that carrier. Women could not be assigned to patrol squadrons because patrol aircraft carried weapons, yet Judith Neuffer was flying the Orion patrol planes in far more dangerous conditions. Only with difficulty, as Rosemary Conatser discovered, could women gain access to tactical jets. In 1981 the Navy did open its jet-training pipeline, but to a maximum of only five women each year. They could not go into jet training directly, like men, but had to apply for a slot only after completing the propeller syllabus with high grades and receiving their wings. The Navy's first women aviators had known upon entering flight training about these restrictions and had enthusiastically seized their opportunities anyway. Yet one can almost feel Barbara Rainey's frustration at having completed all the training requirements and shown herself fully ready to fly out to the training carrier along with her male classmates, then having to remain ashore. To land on a carrier deck remained for her an unfulfilled goal.[15]

Widening Horizons

With little fanfare, opportunities for women officers in naval aviation began to expand after 1978, partly because their performance was earning the Navy's confidence and partly because the amended legislation allowed them to serve in ships. Although they could not be assigned permanently to aircraft carriers because these ships are combatants, they could be embarked for up to 180 days in any ship not expected to be engaged in hostilities during that time. Access to carriers enabled female pilots to show that they could master the techniques of carrier landings and takeoffs. In 1977, the first woman known to have done so landed her helicopter on a carrier, and in July 1979, Lt. Lynn Spruill became the first woman pilot of a fixed-wing aircraft to become carrier qualified.[16]

The Navy maintains its training carrier, a retired combatant, at Pensacola, Florida. In 1980, that carrier was the USS *Lexington,* an honored survivor of World War II. That year, 7 women officers and 130 enlisted women, the first to be assigned to the crew of an aircraft carrier, reported to "Lady Lex." Duty in the ship offered some excellent advantages to women officers. For example, seven months after reporting, Lt. Jean

Cackowski qualified as an officer of the deck under way, becoming the first woman officer to hold this position in a carrier. Women aviators especially valued carrier duty. As the *Lexington*'s communications officer in 1984, Lt. Comdr. Jane O'Dea was filling a major billet in one of the Navy's largest ships, experiencing a vital aspect of naval aviation not open to most women; yet the ship's operations schedule never required her to be separated from her two young daughters for longer than two weeks at a time. Another woman who made the most of her duty aboard the carrier was an aircraft controller named Jannine Weiss, who became the first woman to control aircraft approaching a carrier. When aviation's limited duty officer (LDO) program began in 1981, she was the first woman selected for it, and subsequently she returned to the *Lexington* as an aviator. In 1988 she completed training as a catapult officer, the first woman to do so. Her duties included responsibility for the crews that maintained and operated the carrier's giant catapults, which fling planes off the deck at a velocity sufficient to ensure that they achieve air speed. The *Lexington* was retired from service in 1991. A woman had the distinction of becoming the last aviator to land on her venerable deck. The larger USS *Forrestal*, the *Lexington*'s replacement, has twice as many billets available to women.[17]

Women pilots who became carrier qualified could now work in squadrons that ferried people, mail, and other cargo between shore stations and carriers at sea. For example, Lt. Patti Jedrey flew a 46,000-pound C-2A Greyhound with such an aircraft squadron stationed in Sigonella, Sicily. When interviewed in 1987 by a *Navy Times* reporter, she had landed on and been catapult-launched more than forty times from six different carriers operating in and near the Mediterranean Sea.[18]

The amended law clearly allowed women pilots to be assigned to noncombatant ships operating with task forces at sea, but what the law allowed and what Navy policy promoted were sometimes two different things. Lt. Wendy Lawrence, who graduated from the Naval Academy in 1981 and won her wings in July 1982, flies the H-46, a medium-size helicopter. In her first flying tour, her squadron's commanding officer actively cleared the way so that she could fly the same missions with fleet ships that her male colleagues did. But one of her contemporaries, a woman aviator in an identical squadron, had a less aggressive commanding officer and consequently was kept for almost three years from the same kind of flying Lawrence was doing. In 1983 the Navy stated explicitly that women helicopter pilots could be assigned to support ships operating with its forward-deployed fleets—the Sixth Fleet in the Mediterranean and the Seventh Fleet in the western Pacific. Even so, as late as 1989 some women helicopter pilots were kept off ships on which their male colleagues were landing. A Navy study released in 1990 concluded that fleet commanders interpreted the policy in widely differing ways, "generally tending to be restrictive."[19]

By the fall of 1990, Lawrence had completed two tours of duty with helicopter squadrons during which she deployed twice each to the Indian Ocean and the North Atlantic, once to Kenya, and several times to the Caribbean, for periods lasting from three weeks to more than four months. She described her fleet flying as "basically utility and support, your taxi and federal express service, flying around the task force—'You cry, we fly; you call, we haul.'" During her second tour she was the officer-in-charge of a detachment assigned to the USNS *Chauvenet,* engaged in oceanographic research off Kenya. To the already heavy responsibility of a pilot accountable for the safety of her aircraft and its crew was added that for the welfare and performance of the detachment's three other pilots and nine enlisted crewmembers. The *Chauvenet* depended on its helicopter to transport people and supplies back and forth to shore facilities, as well as for search, rescue, and medical evacuation if needed. In 1992, the National Aeronautics and Space Administration selected Lawrence, now a lieutenant commander, for its astronaut program; among her credentials to join this elite community was a graduate degree from the Massachusetts Institute of Technology. After learning of her selection, she acknowledged one price she would pay: "It removes me from any chance at squadron command."[20]

One highly prestigious area of naval aviation, test piloting, opened to women less than ten years after the first women won their wings. In June 1983 Lt. Colleen Nevius,a helicopter pilot, became the first woman to graduate from the Navy Test Pilot School at Patuxent River, a yearlong, grueling course in aeronautical engineering that all Navy test pilots must complete. The daughter of a retired Navy captain who had flown jets off carriers, Nevius had set her sights on naval aviation when she graduated from high school. She graduated from Purdue University four years later, one of the first women to win a full NROTC scholarship. Her father pinned on her wings in February 1979, and she went off to pilot helicopters out of Norfolk on replenishment flights. Benefiting from the legislation amended in 1978, she was able to make more than five hundred landings on more than a dozen ships. After graduating from test pilot school, she spent two more years at Patuxent River, responsible for testing and reporting on numerous modifications that would improve the safety, reliability, and maintainability of H-46 helicopters. Perhaps the most sincere compliment to her success was the Navy's decision to send other women pilots to the school. Before she left Patuxent, Nevius told an interviewer, "The people who deserve recognition are those who laid it on the line and selected me. They gave me the chance to stand or fall on my own."[21]

The success of female aviators led to women officers entering other fields in naval aviation. Ever since it began to use aircraft back in the 1920s, the Navy has trained flight officers for various tasks other than piloting, for example, as observers, bombardiers, navigators, or intelligence specialists. By the time women were entering the flight program, these personnel were known as naval flight officers (NFOs). The physical qualifications NFOs must meet are nearly as rigorous as those for pilots, and their training calls for the same degree of technical ability. They spend hundreds of hours in academic studies and familiarization with all aspects of flying. In June 1981, Ens. Mary A. Crawford, a 1980 graduate of the University of Washington, became the first woman NFO after completing six hundred hours of instruction during a six-month period. She was assigned as a navigator on C-130 Hercules aircraft flying with Operation Deep Freeze in the Antarctic. Since then, opportunities for women NFOs have burgeoned, especially in the large aircraft that provide tactical communications with nuclear-powered submarines.[22]

Crosswinds

By the end of 1990, the Navy had 173 women pilots and 80 women NFOs on active duty, flying more than a dozen types of aircraft and assigned to 20 kinds of aviation squadrons. The number of women taken into flight training each year had swelled to 52 pilots and 15 NFOs. In addition, more than 200 other women officers had been trained in aviation specialties such as air intelligence and aeronautical engineering and were serving in squadrons. In marked contrast to the women earliest qualified as surface warfare officers, a high percentage—nearly 90 percent—of women aviators and NFOs have remained on active duty and in aviation. One likely reason for this high rate of retention is that they have been able to keep flying throughout most of the 20 years it takes for naval officers to become eligible to retire. Women's career paths are in theory identical with those of male officers in naval aviation, but not always in practice. As of late 1992, the Navy does not allow women naval aviators to fly in combat squadrons, even though individual women have shown themselves proficient in several kinds of combat aircraft. Consequently, they are at a disadvantage as they compete with their male contemporaries for promotions and the choicest billets.

The success of women has secured and expanded their place in naval aviation. It has not necessarily made that place comfortable, for full acceptance has sometimes come slowly, grudgingly, or not at all. The infamous Tailhook incident in the fall of 1991 revealed that at least some male aviators completely lacked respect for their female colleagues.

The incident took place at the Hilton Hotel in Las Vegas, where about two thousand naval aviators and other aviation officers gathered for the thirty-fifth annual convention of the Tailhook Association. Named for the device that helps arrest aircraft landing on a carrier's deck, the association's convention provides a forum for frank and informal professional exchanges among all levels and components of the naval aviation community. Social festivities also play a large role at its conventions, which over the years have gained notoriety as occasions for lewd and drunken behavior.

The first distressing event of the 1991 convention occurred at a symposium on the morning of September 7, when Lt. Monica Rivadeneira asked the presiding panel of admirals when women aviators would be allowed to fly combat missions. Scores of male aviators greeted her question with jeers, catcalls and derisive comments. One admiral intervened mildly, reminding the men that some day women would fly combat missions; they should quit resisting and get on with other professional concerns. But not one member of the panel nor any other senior officer present rebuked the hecklers for their behavior.[23]

That evening, on the hotel's third floor, various aviation squadrons hosted "hospitality suites" where liquor flowed freely. In the thirty-foot hallway dozens and dozens of drunken males formed a "gauntlet," pawing and molesting women who passed through it. One of these women was Lt. Paula Coughlin, a helicopter pilot and aide to Rear Adm. John W. Snyder, commanding officer of the Patuxent River Naval Air Test Center. She was stunned and frightened by her assailants' refusal to desist despite her adamant resistance—she bit one man's arm as he groped inside her shirt—and was shocked that even those men at the scene to whom she appealed refused to help her. The next morning and twice more in the next few days, she told Snyder something of what had happened to her. When he took no action, Coughlin went to the next level of authority.

By this time, portions of the story had become public knowledge, and Secretary of the Navy Lawrence Garrett denounced the entire affair in the strongest possible terms. On October 10 the Naval Investigative Service (NIS) began a formal investigation, and on November 4, CNO

Adm. Frank Kelso transferred Snyder to a lesser post, saying that he questioned Snyder's "judgment in command."[24]

On April 30 the NIS reported its finding: twenty-six women, about half of them naval officers, had been assaulted in the gauntlet. However, no formal charges were brought against anyone, and only two suspects had been identified. Embarrassed at such a paltry result after such a lengthy investigation, NIS claimed its efforts were hamstrung by Tailhook Association members and other naval aviators who either refused to cooperate with Navy investigators or in some cases misled or lied to them. In a separate report released concurrently, the Navy's inspector general (IG) severely criticized the conduct in several of the hospitality suites for creating "an atmosphere demeaning to women." By resisting the NIS investigation as it did, the IG report continued, the aviation community displayed "a marked absence of moral courage and personal integrity." Even more damaging were the IG's conclusions that inappropriate sexual behavior in the hospitality suites and the abuse of alcohol throughout the so-called tactical aviation community had long been condoned or at least overlooked. The result of this failure of leadership, said the IG, was that some within the aviation community often conducted themselves in a manner distinctly "unbecoming an officer." Moreover, the participants apparently believed that such behavior was socially acceptable and that the allegations against them had been blown out of proportion.

Secretary Garrett consequently withdrew all Navy support from the Tailhook Association. He severed a thirty-five–year relationship that had included space for association offices at the Mirimar Naval Air Station, as well as time off and free transport for those attending Tailhook conventions.[25]

The NIS and IG reports, the published unsavory details of the assaults, and the fact that the NIS investigation had proved inconclusive led to further embarrassing publicity for the Navy. While most senior officials up to and including Secretary Garrett promised "zero tolerance" for sexual harassment, Navy women remembered that they had heard such promises before. Indeed, within weeks, another incident suggested that those Navy members inclined to demean women still believed they could do so with impunity: "Zero tolerance" might apply to others, but not to them. On June 18 men in combat aviation squadrons stationed at Mirimar put on skits at the Officers' Club. Two of these skits directed coarse, sexual innuendoes at Representative Pat Schroeder, who had often criticized the armed services while championing their members' rights. She had also been one of the first to find fault with the NIS report and call for more effective action. Although Navy officials apologized to

Schroeder promptly and profusely and three squadron commanding officers at the base were eventually relieved of their commands, the Navy's credibility was again severely damaged.[26]

The most regrettable aspect of these incidents may be that they belie the general goodwill and acceptance women have earned for themselves in naval aviation. Yet these incidents did not happen in a vacuum, and rather than being total aberrations, they are symptoms of old prejudices with which the Navy and women must still contend. Other legacies of Tailhook are described in chapter 14.

Having opened one aviation program after another to women, the Navy has done nothing other than increase the number it has admitted to each program, a tacit assessment of how successful those women who wear the wings of gold have been. Yet almost twenty years after the Navy first put women through flight training, women constitute only 1.5 percent of its pilots and NFOs.

Keep 'Em Flying: Enlisted Women in Naval Aviation

As the 1970s wore on, enlisted women returned to naval aviation in droves, thanks to the provision of Z-116 opening many ratings that had long been closed to them. In 1972 only 700 enlisted women were serving in aviation ratings; by 1987 there were more than 5,300, and by 1990 more than 7,700. To retired Capt. Joy Hancock it must have been a heartwarming resurgence, recalling the days of World War II, when 26,000 WAVES served in naval aviation.[27]

A major part of the expansion resulted from the Navy's decision in 1978 to assign enlisted women to some of the antisubmarine patrol squadrons on an experimental basis. These squadrons are based ashore, their aircraft being too large to operate off carriers. The experiment worked so well that in 1984 women were assigned to all the patrol squadrons.

The expansion of enlisted women in naval aviation has encountered its share of the growing pains associated with the increase of women in nontraditional ratings. Among recruits, fewer women than men score high enough on mechanical and technical aptitude tests to gain entry in a Navy "A" school. Graduation from such schools is usually necessary to be rated as a petty officer and to start up the advancement ladder. While waiting to enter A school, the enlistee is eligible only for unskilled, entry-level work such as washing airplanes. The Navy's term for such work is "general detail," and those not advanced beyond it are often referred to as GENdets. In addition, the Navy sometimes bars entry to A schools for ratings it deems overcrowded, so that a GENdet preparing to enter a particular A school may suddenly find it closed. Before 1987, the situation for GENdets was acute in both sea-intensive and aviation ratings and for both men and women, but it hit women in aviation hardest. Some, despite hard work, spent up to eighteen months before getting a chance to begin specialized training and compete for advancement. Then in 1987 women with low aptitude scores were encouraged to enter the Navy's remedial job-oriented basic skills (JOBS) program. Also, the Navy has somewhat simplified and stabilized advancement procedures, at the same time more vigorously publicizing the least crowded ratings.

Enlisted women in aviation work side by side with enlisted men on flight lines, fueling and servicing aircraft, and trouble-shooting engines in drafty hangars. Grease, noise, and irregular hours constitute their working environment; dungarees, their daily uniform. One new squadron chief asked a woman how many females were in it. "None," she told him, "until after working hours." In 1984, forty-three enlisted women serving in seven different aircraft squadrons were aboard the USS *Constellation* when she went to sea for the squadrons' routine period of carrier quali-fication. The women did the same jobs they did ashore, but now on the flight deck and in the ship's hangar bays, thus gaining valuable experience, an increased appreciation of what shipboard duty entails, and a fund of sea stories. They were the first to show that women could serve with their squadrons not only ashore but also where, in the Navy, service counts most—at sea.

To be in an aviation rating is one thing; to work in aviation squadrons, another; to become a flight crewmember, yet a third. Crewmembers receive special training and extra-hazardous duty pay (commonly called "flight pay"). Navy aircraft can require anywhere from one crewmember, the pilot, to thirteen personnel. Most of the additional crewmembers are enlisted men and women.

The Navy officially records Chief Photographer's Mate Clara B. Johnson as the first woman to be designated a flight crewmember. In 1964 she served as an aerial photographer with an aviation utility squad-ron on the East Coast. But long before 1964, a handful of Navy women were serving as crewmembers in roles pioneered by World War II WAVES. Designated as flight orderlies on transport planes, they were the Navy equivalent of civilian stewardesses. Petty Officer Third Class Patricia Beckman found herself filling this role in the early 1970s. She and a few other women in aviation ratings were assigned to serve in Navy transport planes that carried high-ranking officials in and out of Andrews Air Force Base, near Washington, D.C. She later said she had not asked for the job.

> They wanted women along to help serve female passengers and children. I'd rather have been a flight engineer, but they wouldn't allow that. I saw it mostly as an available opening for about three women to fly. I wondered why we didn't get wings and flight pay like the male crewmembers did. One day I asked why, and there was no good answer, so we got them. I don't want to say we were the first or the only, but I think I was one of probably a handful.

In 1974 Beckman was selected for the NESEP program and earned a degree in aerospace engineering from North Carolina State College in 1978. In 1980 she became one of the first women selected to enter the NFO program, and by 1983 she was serving in VQ-3, a squadron specializing in space surveillance. There she found enlisted women serving as crewmembers, and within a year or two one was assigned as flight engineer, the job she had aspired to in her enlisted days.[28]

H-46 helicopters and large C-130s that specialize in communications with submarines offer the most varied opportunities to women who are enlisted flight crewmembers. These women often operate the radios and other electronic equipment, the hoists used in rescues, and the reels used to extend antennae and other sensing equipment. They load cargo, direct its placement for safe and maximum use of space, watch over it in flight, and then unload it. For example, a crew composed of seven women flew a ski-equipped LC-130 to the South Pole from McMurdo Station in Antarctica to open up the science station for the 1991–92 season of Operation Deep Freeze. The two pilots and the navigator were officers. Of the four enlisted women, one was an aviation electrician's mate serving as flight engineer, another was a photographer's mate serving as utility crewman, and the two loadmasters were an aviation machinist's mate and an aviation electronics technician. They carried 39 passengers and 1,150 pounds of cargo to a smooth touchdown in temperatures of minus 55° Fahrenheit. They spent five hours repairing minor damage to the aircraft caused by the cold before returning safely to McMurdo Station. This flight was not the first noteworthy performance by an all-woman crew. Back in 1983, for example, two female pilots and four enlisted women— two aviation electrician's mates and two aviation machinist's mates— composed the crew of a C-9B transport belonging to a fleet-support squadron stationed at Alameda, California. They were the crew that topped the thirty thousand-hour mark of accident-free flying for their squadron. Despite the women's solid record of such accomplishments, some women crewmembers report being patronized, overlooked, or simply not trusted to do their jobs competently.[29]

The number of enlisted women qualified as aircrewmen remains minuscule. In 1989 it was only 69, reflecting the Navy's failure to seek out, inform, and guide women into the nearly 300 aircrew billets available to them. In the next year the number more than doubled, to 159, as the Navy intensified its efforts.[30]

Peggy Myers: Small Woman in a Big Job

Few as they are, the Navy's women aircrewmen nevertheless outnumber its women parachute testers. When Peggy Meyers was interviewed by a *Navy Times* reporter in February 1991, she was only the third woman to complete Navy test-parachute training and the only woman currently working as a test parachutist. She is an aircrew survival equipmentman; members of this rating normally stay on the ground, packing parachutes and maintaining aircrew equipment. But at the Naval Air Station in China Lake, California, an elite dozen of them learn free-fall parachuting, that is, falling for about a minute before releasing their chutes. In this way, they research, test, and evaluate different kinds of chutes and chuting techniques. For example, they can determine the descent rate of a given parachute or find the best way to jump with an M-16 rifle so that it does not become entangled in the lines.

At 108 pounds and its only woman, Meyers makes a special contribution to the testing team. As she explained, "There are female pilots and female astronauts and they're not all built like men. And there are guys my size and smaller. So how are they going to [be safe] if you've never tested somebody small?" Her twelfth jump dramatically demonstrated both the risks of testing and the rewards of safety precautions. Her main chute didn't open, and she fell 2,000 feet before the reserve chute blossomed above her—"the most beautiful thing in the world I ever saw—that reserve coming out." By that time she was 1,000 feet below the safety margin and headed toward a dangerous landing spot. To avoid it she had to land with the wind instead of against it, resulting in a bruising collision with the ground. At the time of the interview, she was 22 years old, a veteran of 154 military jumps, and still ready for more. She is married to Aircrew Survival Equipmentman Chip Myers, who also tests parachutes. Someday she wants to be an accountant and a lawyer—but not yet.[31] Like so many of the women whose stories are told in this chapter, she enjoys the excitement of naval aviation and responds with professional pride to its need for her service.

Squadron Command

Most female naval officers hold no formal warfare qualifications. A growing but still small number—in 1992, perhaps a few hundred—hold one. Rosemary Mariner, the first woman to command a squadron of Navy aircraft, holds two: In addition to her wings of gold, she is entitled to wear the bow waves of a surface warfare officer, earned while she served aboard the *Lexington*. In a profession where exceptional women are not the exception, Mariner stands out.

After fighting her way into the cockpit of an A-4 to become the first woman in the Navy to fly a tactical jet, she fought to remain in flying assignments. For two successive tours she flew the A-7E Corsair in squadrons dedicated to research, testing, and evaluation. During this time she met and married another A-7 pilot, Lt. Comdr. George Mariner. Then came her assignment to the *Lexington*, where she stood watches, flew passengers and cargo between ship and shore, and ran the combat information center. It was in this assignment, she told an interviewer, that "I really began to understand the Navy by going to sea."[32]

By 1988 she had logged thirty-three hundred flight hours in fifteen different kinds of aircraft. She became the executive officer of a squadron at Point Mugu, California, whose pilots fly A-6 Intruders, which simulate the electronic warfare that hostile forces might employ against U.S. forces. About ninety of the squadron's three hundred members, including some pilots, are women. In July 1990 she "fleeted up" to become the squadron's commanding officer, the very first Navy woman to hold command in a warfare specialty. Her next goal is command at sea, perhaps to command the training carrier, the USS *Forrestal*.

Mindful of the immense changes that have taken place since she earned her Navy wings, Mariner sees a bright future for women seeking operational roles in naval aviation. She can remember flight instructors who told her they would try to flunk her, but they were far outnumbered by those genuinely interested in helping her. She believes in "a bond amongst aviators that transcends sex or differences." Above all, she contends, women must hold the same high professional standards as their male colleagues, pursue the same career path, and accept the same risks. "You are in the service and that means sacrifice. Men have always made that sacrifice, you must be willing to make it too."[33]

The second woman to command an aviation squadron is Lt. Comdr. Linda Hutton, selected ahead of schedule for promotion to commander. In April 1992 she took command of a squadron at Norfolk, Virginia, whose pilots fly C-2s ferrying cargo and passengers both to ships and shore stations.

The opening of naval aviation to women officers has been highly reward-ing both for them and for the Navy. Although still excluded from combat flying, as pilots and NFOs they have advanced into all areas of noncombat flying. Moreover, a high proportion, close to 90 percent, have remained on active duty, justifying the Navy's investment in their training. Simi-larly, the skill, competence, and motivation of enlisted women in naval aviation have enabled the Navy to increase both their numbers and their places of deployment.

Yet both groups remain small, scarcely more than a token; the propor-tion of women to men in noncombat aviation is nowhere near that of women to men in noncombatant ships. Their presence seems rooted more in the Navy's sense that it must respond to the tenor of the times than in any perception of great or imminent need of their services. Although women pilots have received excellent press from which the Navy benefits, the accession and training pipeline for female aviation officers still produces only a trickle. Despite enlisted women's accom-plishments in naval aviation, female recruits have received only mini-mal information about how to enter the field. The Navy's exceedingly cautious pace suggests a failure of institutional memory, for women's historical contributions to military and naval aviation have been well documented.

Their token status, together with their exclusion from combat flying, has kept some of these women from receiving the full credit they merit. Yet their enthusiasm remains high as year after year they log hour upon hour of aviation experience, proving their capacity to compete with men. No longer can anyone responsibly ask, Can women meet the demands of naval aviation? They have done it. They are doing it.

14

Contemporary Currents

"*D*esert Storm is the shakedown cruise for the volunteer armed force."

—Brig. Gen. Evelyn P. Foote, USA (Ret.)

The Gulf War of 1990–91 focused the nation's attention on its armed forces, among other things presenting a new picture of the American military woman to the public. Many saw her as a hardy, skilled, disciplined person who served her country as part of a large armed force operating in a combat zone. Many applauded her loyalty and dedication and endorsed her desire for professional equity. Many, at the same time, were troubled by the thought of the family she left behind. Following the war, the Navy resumed the drawdown it began in the wake of the Soviet Union's collapse in the late 1980s. Our history concludes with a service deeply concerned about whom it should include in its shrinking forces and under what terms. Implicit in the concerns would be a reexamination of the role of women.

Operation Desert Storm: Navy Women at War

On August 2, 1990, the armies of Iraq invaded neighboring Kuwait and threatened to invade Saudi Arabia as well. U.S. naval forces already on station in and near the Persian Gulf went on immediate alert, and within days Operation Desert Shield, a vast military buildup, began. The United Nations placed an embargo on all shipping to and from Iraq, and on August 26 the UN Security Council agreed to back up the embargo with military force. The United States led a coalition of thirty-three nations committed to forcing Iraq out of Kuwait.

261

The U.S. Navy's long-established maritime superiority in the crisis area made possible the largest, fastest sealift ever undertaken. It was also the farthest, with voyages averaging nearly 8,700 miles. During the next five months, more than 240 ships carried more than 9 million tons of equipment and supplies to sustain the gathering multinational force. By March 1991, an average of 42,000 tons of cargo was arriving in Saudi Arabia each day, two and a half times the average daily amount delivered to U.S. forces in the Pacific during World War II.

As 1991 began, hopes for a peaceful withdrawal of Iraqi troops from Kuwait ended, and in mid-January Desert Shield turned into Desert Storm. More than a thousand Navy and Marine aircraft joined those of the U.S. Army and Air Force and of coalition partners to destroy Iraqi forces. Carrier-based naval aircraft flew about a fifth of all strike missions. In addition, Navy airborne refueling tankers, reconnaissance and patrol planes, and helicopters for search and rescue, medical evacuation, and resupply all played large roles. Desert Storm climaxed in the last days of February, when one hundred hours of combined ground, air, and naval operations succeeded in routing the Iraqis and liberating Kuwait. The Navy's job continued long after the combat ended, for much that was transported overseas had to be returned home. Some ships and sailors remained on station in remote areas, maintaining their vigil in routine deployments.

Of the approximately twenty-five hundred Navy women who took part in Operations Desert Shield and Desert Storm, most served with medical units and in support ships, while a much smaller number served in aviation units, construction battalions, and cargo-handling groups. The first women to take part were those already routinely deployed nearby in support ships—oilers, tenders, and ammunition and supply ships. In addition, Navy women were serving in communications and administration in the flagships of merchant marine squadrons under contract to the Navy and pre-positioned in forward areas. On September 5, 1990, the destroyer tender USS *Acadia* sailed from San Diego to the Persian Gulf, with a crew of 900 men and 360 women. She was hailed by the Navy as the "first war-time test of the combined male-female fighting force." The USS *Yellowstone* and *Cape Cod*, each with a complement of women, also took part in the operation, as did ships of the Combat Logistics Force and the Military Sealift Command, all with mixed crews. As early as September 30, the Navy reported at least 625 women in crews of ships already committed to Operation Desert Shield plus an unknown number who might also be aboard those ships on temporary assignments. By January

1991, the number had risen to 1,450 women serving in the ships involved, including 600 aboard hospital ships.[1]

The naval medical establishment put two hospital ships, the USNS *Comfort* and *Mercy*, to sea within weeks of the invasion. On August 11, 1990, the *Comfort* sailed from Baltimore to Norfolk with 385 personnel aboard, among them senior doctors, nurses, and enlisted hospital corpsmen pulled from their posts at the Navy Medical Center in Bethesda, Maryland. Ninety percent of them had never been to sea before, and they had to be drilled in fire control, damage control, and abandon-ship procedures. In Norfolk another 450 personnel came aboard. Then, with a 500-bed capacity, the *Comfort* sailed for the Gulf, arriving on September 8. Her capacity was doubled in January 1991, when 374 reservists came aboard. Overall, women constituted about a third of the crew, yet the ship lacked adequate gynecological equipment and specialists.[2]

In California, a similar story was unfolding for the *Mercy*. The Oakland Naval Hospital supplied 75 percent of her medical crew. She deployed on August 14 and days later picked up more crew who had been flown to meet her in the Philippines. On September 14 she arrived in the Gulf of Oman. By month's end she and the *Comfort* were steaming together in the Gulf of Arabia, making, as the Navy put it, "naval medical history." In addition, the naval hospital at Portsmouth, Virginia, supplied the staff for a fleet hospital established at Al Jubayl, Saudi Arabia. Expecting a far larger number of battle casualties than ever materialized, this was one of the units prepared to handle major surgery. Fortunately, sports injuries and auto accidents accounted for more patients than combat. Navy hospitals, afloat and ashore, provided more than two-thirds of the operation's medical capabilities in the first four months.[3]

A few women served in Construction Battalion ("Seabee") units that created the huge facilities required to sustain the operation. The two construction units that built the fleet hospital at Al Jubayl comprised one hundred men and six women. Two of the women were officers, and the four enlisted women included two equipment operators, one builder, and one yeoman. One of the officers later reported, "The local people were astonished to see our female bulldozer operator; in an area where women can't even drive cars, the concept of a woman driving heavy machinery was incomprehensible."[4] Also working heavy machinery in the brutal desert heat were the thirteen women and 167 men of a cargo-handling and port group, who were rushed in late July 1990 from their home base near Norfolk to Bahrain, a major port in the Persian Gulf, as the Iraqis threatened Kuwait. Among their first tasks was unloading the two nearby squadrons of ships, which carried enough equipment and stores to supply two Marine expeditionary brigades for thirty days. The cargo handlers subsequently unloaded all ships that came to Bahrain bearing supplies for the coalition forces. One of the women with the group, Boatswain's Mate Third Class Deborah Sheehan, a crane operator, later described her experiences:

> We worked 12 hours on, 12 off. What we were offloading mostly was ammo, vehicles, tents, supplies for the fleet hospital at Al Jubayl. We lived in American Camp, a westernized camp run by Indians that had previously housed civilian workers who'd now been evacuated. We wore T-shirts and pants, steel-toed boots, hard hats, then full body armor—flak jackets. You had to carry your gas mask, canteens, web belt at all times. If an attack came and you were up in the crane, or down in the hold of a ship, you had to be ready right then.
>
> While on the pier, we were under attack by Scuds [Iraqi missiles]. One blew up over the warehouse while we were unloading some ammo and we were training a reserve unit at the time. If it had hit us, it would have blown up everything within a radius of 70 miles. Iraqi death squads had mapped our route to and from the piers, and there were a lot of drive-by shootings. In the camp down the street from us they lost two people. Women served as security, stood guard, manned machine guns. I drove a truck to and from the pier with another woman riding shotgun next to me. We had M-16s, M-60s, small caliber hand guns.
>
> After the ground offensive started, we went to Ras Al Mishab, about 25 miles from Kuwait. There we stayed in tents, took some howitzer rounds. The Iraqis were trying to blow up the oil refineries. When they missed, they hit the beach where we were.[5]

Only a handful of women in naval aviation, both officer and enlisted, are known to have participated in Desert Shield and Desert Storm, most of them being in two helicopter combat-support squadrons. Their wartime duties were essentially the same as in peacetime—replenishment and search and rescue—but performed in a combat zone. One woman pilot, for example, flew the first Navy logistic helicopter into Kuwait after it was liberated, carrying demolition experts ordered to defuse explosives left by the departing Iraqi troops. Another woman pilot, Lt. Kelly Franke, earned national recognition when the Naval Helicopter Association named her its Pilot of the Year in 1991, primarily for her exploits during the 105 combat-support missions she flew in Desert Storm. These included the transport of Iraqi prisoners of war and numerous logistic flights before Iraqi gun positions had been cleared from sea-based oil platforms. Her most notable exploit was a rescue. With nowhere to land, she hovered her aircraft 75 feet above the water in a 20-knot tail wind while her crew hoisted aboard an injured Navy diver clinging to a dive platform. On another occasion, she brought her helicopter and its crew to a safe landing after a severe in-flight emergency.[6]

Meanwhile, Navy women back home were serving much as their predecessors had in every war from 1917 on: taking up the tasks left by those now deployed to the combat zone, meeting the increased tempo of wartime, putting special skills into use. One woman helicopter pilot, for example, stationed on the West Coast had just learned she was pregnant when Operation Desert Shield began and when many members of her squadron were required to deploy. She was among those remaining who had to fly and work extra hours in training exercises to prepare pilots, ships, and elite sea-air-land commando teams for their deployment. She flew until the seventh month of her pregnancy. Another woman, a reservist who studies the earth's atmosphere for the National Aeronautics and Space Administration, reported for duty every weekend during the operation to predict weather patterns for the coalition forces, including carrier groups, in the combat zone.[7]

The Gulf War, as it soon came to be called, was a turning point for women in the Navy. For the first time they were in operational units in a combat zone, many of them exposed to hostile fire. The Navy's experience in the war provided some data on how the increased number of women in operational units affected readiness. Official reports showed that 1.5 percent of Navy men and 5.6 percent of Navy women could not deploy with their units. A Navy spokesman said, "We know that pregnancy is the underlying reason why the women's rate is higher. Pregnancy continues to be a concern but to date it has been a manageable one."[8]

Legacies of the Gulf War

Much as television had thrust live images of war into American living rooms some twenty-five years earlier during the Vietnam War, so now it brought into American homes pictures of military women at work. For the first time, it seemed, the American public became aware not only that there were many thousands of women serving in the armed forces but that, like men, they must go wherever ordered, even to a combat zone. As the war progressed and a number of women were killed and two captured, the American public seemed to awake with a start. Women in combat? Was this not prohibited by law? The answers to both these questions were yes, no, and maybe. The ambiguities of the combat issue now began to become as evident to the general public as they had long been to policy analysts, lawmakers, and men and women in uniform. The Gulf War brought the question of women in combat front and center.

The reality of women called to war and leaving their children behind aroused the American public even more strongly than did the images of women in a combat zone. The sight of a toddler clinging to his uniformed mother as she kissed him goodbye and turned him over to his father, or his grandmother, or his aunt, or a friend, wrenched hearts that had never felt one way or another about children separated from their uniformed fathers. To the surprise of many observers, the idea of mothers leaving their children was far more troubling than the idea of women killed or captured in combat. The two issues were separate, but so closely related that to address one was, inevitably, to raise the other. Almost immediately, Congress began to examine both.

Women in Combat

By May 1991 members of both houses of Congress were acknowledging that the time had come to reexamine and perhaps amend that portion of the 1948 legislation that kept women from combat. The intent in 1948 appeared to be clear: no combat for women. How that intent was achieved varied among the services. For the Navy and Air Force, the answer was simply to bar them from combat ships and aircraft. Army women were kept out of combat by Army policy alone, which was as effective as a statute. In 1978, as we have seen, Judge John Sirica handed down a decision stating that restricting Navy women from serving in ships and aircraft did in fact abridge their constitutional rights. In reviewing the debate that had led to these restrictions, he noted that they were imposed

> over the military's objections and without significant deliberation. . . .
> Instead, the sense of the discussion is that Section 6015's bar against
> assigning females to shipboard duty was premised on the notion that
> duty at sea is part of an essentially masculine tradition . . . more related
> to the traditional way of thinking about women than to military pre-
> paredness.[9]

In 1978 Congress amended the legislation so that the Navy could put women in noncombatant ships and planes and even temporarily in combatants under certain conditions. By retaining the authority to determine what was and was not a combatant platform, the Navy had the flexibility to put women where it needed them while appearing to conform to congressional intent as well as, presumably, the public's will.

For a long while, many women in the military and their supporters had questioned the logic of restricting women from combat. If it was to keep them out of harm's way, then why had military nurses served in combat zones, some of them dying or being wounded or captured as a result? If it was because they could not fight, then why did history offer examples of successful women warriors? If it was because they could not do the job, then why did so many men who served with them testify otherwise? Where could safety be guaranteed: in the salvage ship commanded by Darlene Iskra? In boiler rooms tended by Julia Roos? In an experimental plane flown by Colleen Nevius?

Throughout the 1980s, Army, Air Force, and Navy women were more than once in combat or quasi combat. Over Libya, for example, Air Force women were in flying tankers that refueled the fighter planes, and in Grenada they landed cargo planes before the shooting stopped. In the Middle East, Navy women pilots flew supplies to besieged Marines in Beirut and flew on and off carriers in operations against Libyan terrorists. In Panama an Army woman led her unit into hostile fire.

The U.S. Army, Air Force, and Marine Corps had a total of nearly thirty-one thousand women serving in the combat zone during the Gulf War. Eleven Army women lost their lives, five of them killed in action. Two women, a truck driver and a flight surgeon, were among the twenty-five U.S. personnel taken prisoner of war by Iraq. Demonstrably, the restrictions do not guarantee safety to women: They allow women to be shot at but not to shoot. In light of this and the fact that serving in combat units enhances military and naval careers, one can understand that many women have grown increasingly skeptical about just who is being protected from just what—or whom.[10]

For many years DACOWITS was divided over the issue. It had questioned service-assignment policies resulting from combat restrictions but never recommended their repeal. At its semiannual conference in April 1991, however, at least fifteen women who had served in the Gulf War gave its members firsthand accounts of their experience and noted the barriers affecting their careers. Their testimony was credited for the committee's vote in favor of asking the secretary of defense to urge repeal of the restrictions. The House of Representatives was already considering repeal. On May 22, 1991, the House passed a bill removing the legal barrier against women serving as pilots, navigators, or crewmembers in

Air Force, Navy, or Marine combat aircraft; but it did not require the services to assign women to such aircraft. By opening the door but not pushing anyone through it, the House's action aroused little controversy. Not so in the Senate, whose Armed Services Committee had widened the debate to encompass all policy that related assignments to gender. Rank-and-file soldiers, sailors, and airmen as well as service leaders testified, revealing deep divisions of opinion. The scope of the debate was now so wide that little could be concluded.

In December the Roth-Kennedy Amendment emerged, a compromise whereby women officers were no longer legally barred from combat aircraft, but the president would appoint a commission to study combat restrictions before any further action was taken. In November 1992 the commission recommended, by a seven-to-six vote, that Congress reverse its decision and once more prohibit assigning women to combat aircraft. Yet it voted, eight to five, to recommend allowing women to serve on all ships except submarines and amphibious ships.

Parents in Combat

In February 1991, Pentagon officials said that the Navy had 2,765 single parents in the combat zone. An unknown number of those parents did not have legal custody of their children, although they claimed them as dependents because they paid child support to the custodial parent. As for dual-career military couples with children, the Navy is estimated to have twelve thousand to fifteen thousand of them, of whom fewer than twenty-five (both mother and father) were sent to the combat zone. That so few couples were sent may be attributed to the Navy policy that prohibits deploying husband and wife simultaneously unless they request the deployment in writing. Another Navy policy of recent years is that all members with children must file, as part of their official records, a certificate of worldwide availability; that is, they certify that they have arranged for alternative child care so that they can be deployed anywhere in the world. However, the Navy reported in 1990 that only 60 percent of the women and 44 percent of the men required to file certificates had done so; about one-fourth of the women and almost half of the men had not been told by their commands to do so. At many locations, junior officers without dependents knew little or nothing about the certificate policy and so failed to advise their subordinates. Also, commands viewed the certificates as a "labor-intensive administrative burden which, in the final analysis, may not reflect planning that will prove executable."[11]

Obviously, such a policy cannot ensure adequate care for children. All it can do is put the responsibility for arranging care squarely on the shoulders of the parents and make clear that being parents in no way releases them from their service obligations. The Department of Defense has acknowledged that circumstances sometimes arise beyond the control of service members so that they cannot provide adequate child care. As these cases are put forward, policy among all the services is either to reassign or to discharge. The tax-paying public that supports the armed forces knew little or nothing about these numbers and policies. All they knew was that during the Gulf War women in service uniforms were going off to a combat zone and leaving their children behind them, and they—the public, that is—did not like it. As one editorial writer put it, "The tug at our hearts feels something like a triple bypass."[12]

Congress's response was to consider legislation that would allow exemptions. The question was, For whom? While it was the sight of *mothers* leaving their children that first raised the issue, Congress and the public soon learned in a crash course on the realities of the all-volunteer force that thousands of children (the Pentagon estimated 17,500 families were involved) were being separated from their custodial parent or both parents. The problem extended to both sexes and to both married and single persons. It even extended beyond overseas deployment; one proposed bill would have given single parents and dual-career service couples with children the right to turn down assignments to combat zones and peacetime assignments to remote areas where family support facilities were inadequate.[13]

Opposition to these proposals arose immediately, in Congress and in the Department of Defense. First, opponents raised the question of equity. Should the burden of deployment rest only on single members or on service members married to civilians? Second, the services publicized their policies in an attempt to show that the problems were minimal. An assistant secretary of the Navy said that fewer than twenty sailors had child-care problems so severe that they had to be discharged. A final objection was that the proposed exemptions did not in fact serve the best interests of those exempted. In a letter addressed to the Senate, Secretary of Defense Richard Cheney and Chairman of the Joint Chiefs of Staff Colin Powell said, "Our single parents and military couples across the board have been meeting their obligations both as members of the military and as parents."[14] The implication is a lesson from the history of women in the armed forces: Those exempted from pulling their weight are also exempted from full respect. Indeed, objections to the proposed exemptions came from service parents, who declared that they had signed on to do a job, and while it was hard to leave their families, they were not about to renege on their agreement to carry out orders.

Lt. Stephanie Oram's daughter, Danielle, for example, had just turned two when her mother, an aviator, was deployed to the Gulf in January 1991. Oram served as the assistant officer-in-charge of a two-helicopter, forty-person detachment whose primary mission was to fly people, mail, and cargo to fleet units in the Gulf. Her husband assumed full responsibility for their daughter at the same time he was going to law school. Oram says her husband is "the main reason I can continue to actively pursue a naval career," but she concedes that "it does take quite a balancing act to handle the demands of a child and those of a military career." Another couple, parents of three children, were both deployed to the Gulf shortly before the invasion of Kuwait with the expectation that they would be returning to their children within a few weeks. When it became clear that this would not be the case, first the mother was returned for several weeks to work at the unit's home base, while the father remained deployed. Then they switched places, an example of their commitment to their unit and the Navy's willingness to accommodate parents.[15]

The upshot of the debate about military parents was that Congress pulled back from exemption legislation, and the services' current policies were more or less vindicated. With the return of the deployed U.S. forces, the issue faded from public view, but not before the nation had been reminded of two important realities. First, war and deployment are painful for families; second, the all-volunteer force is a family force.

Legacies of Tailhook

As of July 1992, nine months after the infamous Tailhook convention, the Navy still had not punished any of the seventy Navy and Marine Corps officers who had committed assaults, been present where they occurred, or hindered the ensuing investigation.

Frustrated that none of her assailants had been brought to account and angered that many of her fellow officers believed it was her fault she was attacked, on June 24, 1992, Lt. Paula Coughlin went public. She told her story to the *Washington Post* and to Peter Jennings, anchorman for a nightly, national television newscast. Two days later she told *Navy Times* reporter Tom Philpott that she believed it was time "to put a face" on the Tailhook incident. So long as she remained anonymous, Coughlin said, she was sending to other mistreated women the wrong signals, that is, that they should keep quiet.

> I had an obligation as an officer to stop what was going on in that hallway. I have an obligation as a human being to let everyone know you have to come forward when something bad like that happens. People I don't even know have called and said, "You did the right thing. . . ." But there are a lot of guys out there who still don't get it.[16]

At about the same time, the Navy asked for an independent review by the Department of Defense, for accusations about cover-ups and scape-goating kept the story alive and eroded morale throughout the Navy. On June 24, the Defense Department inspector general ordered that all disciplinary proceedings against the officers involved in Tailhook be put on hold while he completed his investigation. On June 26, Secretary of the Navy Lawrence Garrett resigned, dramatic testimony to the power of the currents unleashed by Tailhook.

Navy Responses to Tailhook

Well before these startling events of early summer 1992, the Navy attempted to get back on course. On March 1 it announced a strength-ening of its zero-tolerance policy toward sexual harassment. As before, acts of sexual harassment short of assault were punishable, but now individuals found guilty of sexual assault would be discharged. Also, hereafter formal evaluations of service members' professional perform-ance would include a comment on how well they supported the zero-tol-erance policy.

Following Garrett's resignation in June, J. Daniel Howard, temporary acting secretary, ordered a Navy-wide "stand down": By September 1, every Navy member and civilian employee would have to have attended a day-long seminar on sexual harassment that included discussion, a video presentation, and a taped message from Howard. In addition the office of the secretary of the Navy established a standing committee chartered to focus attention on and improve the treatment of Navy women. To underscore its importance, the committee is headed by an assistant secretary and reports directly to the secretary.

Meanwhile, some Navy members failed to take the lessons of Tailhook to heart. For example, some aviators stationed at Mirimar added to their uniforms patches that show cartoon character Bart Simpson wearing a

Navy flight suit, holding a beer can, and proclaiming, "I didn't do it! Nobody saw me do it—you can't prove a thing." Admiral Kelso ordered the patches removed, but some pilots merely moved them to the inside of their flight jackets, making them easily visible when the jackets are flashed open.[17]

Heavy consequences of the Tailhook scandal fell on officers at higher levels. Two senior officers nominated for promotion—one slated to head the Navy's aviation community, and one proposed for command of the Third Fleet—saw their nominations revoked. The former was criticized for originating in 1991 a newsletter with distasteful jokes about women, while the latter had been charged with lack of leadership in the 1989 case of the Naval Academy female midshipman who had been chained to a urinal. The Navy withdrew these nominations in July 1992, fearing that the requisite Senate Armed Services Committee's hearings would be long and embarrassing and perhaps end in refusal to confirm. In September 1992, the Defense Department's inspector general released the first of two reports on Tailhook. It blasted the Navy investigation. Among its major criticisms were that former acting Secretary Howard had limited the scope of the Navy report and that the Naval Investigative Service and the Navy inspector general failed to cooperate with one another. The new acting secretary, Sean O'Keefe, asked two admirals—the head of the investigative service and the judge advocate general—to resign. According to the Defense Department report

> The principals in the Navy investigations erred when they allowed their concern for the Navy as an institution to obscure the need to determine accountability for the misconduct and the failure of leadership that had occurred. In our view, the deficiencies in the investigations were the result of an attempt to limit the exposure of the Navy and senior Navy officials to criticism regarding Tailhook 91.

The second report focusing on criminal assault and misconduct would be released later in 1992.[18]

Wider Repercussions

Coughlin's disclosures led to further repercussions. In June 1992 the Senate Armed Services Committee declined to confirm the promotions of more than five thousand naval officers until the Navy could show that none had been involved in the Tailhook incident. Each candidate had to state whether he or she, or any subordinate, had attended the convention.

The promotions of those who had answered yes were delayed. Ironically, some of these officers were women, at least one of whom had suffered through the gauntlet.

In August the House of Representatives began to consider new legislation intended to reduce sexual harassment in the military and ensure better treatment of its victims. The Senate was considering establishing an independent agency to investigate all cases of sexual harassment and assault in the Department of Defense.

As for the Tailhook Association, change was imperative to reestablish its official ties with the Navy. In August the association formally apologized to the women who said they were molested. In addition, it banned alcohol at future conventions, established a toll-free hot line to report harassment, and announced that aviation squadrons would no longer be allowed to host hospitality suites. The association must find new sites for future Tailhook conventions, for Hilton Hotel executives canceled reservations the association already made through 1996.[19]

Drawdown

The size, speed, and climactic fury of the Gulf War temporarily diverted attention from another international development of equal or greater significance: the dissolution of the Soviet Union. By the time Kuwait was liberated and the coalition forces began dispersing, it was clear that the era of the cold war had passed into history, together with the need for the large standing armed forces the United States had maintained since World War II. In fact, a drawdown of forces had begun even before the invasion of Kuwait, with the paradoxical result that even as great numbers of reservists were being selectively called up for Operations Desert Shield and Desert Storm (such as medical units, construction battalions, and Middle Eastern language experts), some regular members were being retired early and involuntarily.

As the drawdown resumed, earlier fears that it might halt the expansion of career opportunities for women subsided somewhat, largely as a result of the excellent account women gave of themselves during the Gulf War. Furthermore, ongoing Navy plans and programs appeared to confirm a growing role for women even in a reduced Navy. In March 1992, OP-01(W) reported that the present number of women at sea—8,900— would increase to about 11,000 by 1996, even though the Navy would have fewer ships. Three developments would account for this increase:

As previously scheduled alterations being performed on noncombatant ships were completed, more sea billets would open for women; the *Forrestal* had 600 more billets for women than her predecessor, the *Lexington,* had; and eight frigates assigned to train reservists would open almost 130 more sea billets.[20]

As the number of people who want a Navy career begins to exceed the number who can be kept, women may do well in the competition. The Navy announced that a complex ranking system would begin in April 1992 for enlisted members seeking their first reenlistment. Several factors, in descending order of importance, would determine each member's ranking: commanding officer's recommendation, seniority, advancement potential and recommendations, good conduct, specialized job skills, warfare qualifications, speed of advancement, and sea duty. Historically, women have compared well with men in terms of advancement, conduct, and mastery of specialized job skills. These attributes have generally earned them good standing with their commanding officers, whose recommendations play the most important role in deciding which sailors make the "quality cut." In contrast, a higher proportion of men will be senior and warfare qualified and have more sea duty. All who fail to make the cut will have to leave the Navy when their enlistments expire unless they can switch to another rating. Willingness to switch and ability to qualify for nontraditional ratings will be particularly important for women. The Navy continues to seek them for those ratings, especially as it increases the numbers of women in ships and aviation squadrons. The drawdown may motivate more women to consider switching, an outcome that will benefit both them and Navy planners.[21]

What Lies Ahead?

This narrative ends late in the summer of 1992, a time when the future of women in the Navy is subject to much discussion and, quite possibly, to serious change. The authors can offer no predictions; they can only weigh those factors that will shape the role of women in the U.S. Navy into the next century and survey the problems especially relevant to Navy women.

Historically, the force that brought women into the Navy was the need for their services. When that need abated, the Navy neglected or rejected them. While this was the case for the past seventy-five years, it is not likely to be for the future. Women have been serving for fifty consecutive years, and their right to serve in standing, peacetime forces is no longer a question; a two-gender force has become the norm. At issue then is the extent of the role they will be allowed to play.

It seems unlikely that they will once more be relegated to the periphery of the profession. At least three currents converge to ensure that the tide of advancement set loose by Z-116 is in no immediate danger of being reversed. First is the Navy's plan, discussed earlier, to increase the number of women at sea. Second are all the congressional and judicial decisions of the past twenty years, as well as public opinion in the wake of the Gulf War, which supports a woman's right to train for and serve in operational roles. Third is the stance of women themselves. As we have seen, enlisted women can ably compete for the declining number of jobs available. For the moment, at least, the Navy wants to keep them in service and is encouraging their expansion into nontraditional ratings. More generally, modern Navy women will not be so easily shoved aside as their predecessors were after World Wars I and II. They have flown planes, commanded squadrons and ships, worn admiral's stripes, formed professional associations, tested parachutes, and been shot at. One of them told us, "We won't let [the Navy] do it; there are too many of us and they need us too much to get rid of us."[22]

Finally, technology will play a role, for it will continue to change the practice of warfare and probably at an increasingly rapid pace. For a long time the Navy has needed more brain than brawn in its sailors. Much combat today is conducted by pushing a button to destroy an enemy far over the horizon. The old hand-to-hand contest of brute strength is rare today, as the Gulf War so recently and vividly demonstrated. The attributes of the modern warrior belong to women as well as to men. Many past and present struggles over woman's role, such as the early 1990s' debate over repealing combat restrictions, may be interpreted as the services' inability to adapt their thinking as swiftly as they improve their weapons.

In a smaller force, flexibility of assignment may be more important than at present, for overall there will be fewer and smaller facilities, giving detailers fewer options. To the extent that they are less flexible, single parents and dual-career couples may become a luxury the services cannot afford. Congress and the courts may not allow them to bar these categories of people completely, but the services may still try to limit their numbers. If they should succeed, a larger proportion of women will be affected than men because a larger proportion of women are single custodial parents than men. As is customary when such policies change, those on active duty would not be immediately forced out of service. But their chances for advancement could well be reduced, if not completely ended—an unfortunate outcome for some excellent service members who have managed to surmount the difficulties of being single parents. Most of these would be women.

The Navy is committed, as we have seen, to collocating its dual-career couples, which allows it fewer options in assigning them. When these couples are also parents, flexibility may be further impaired by their need for adequate child care. If maximum assignment flexibility justifies limiting the number of or barring altogether those parents, then the Navy could also justify removing the combat restriction for women. The trade-off would be a smaller service with fewer women who would serve on equal terms with men, resulting in decreased male prejudice and resentment. If a smaller Navy is successful in limiting the number of dual-career couples and parents it will accept, some wives will drop out of the service so that their husbands may remain. One way or another, fewer women may seek Navy careers, and as in the 1940s, 1950s, and 1960s, those who do may choose to bypass motherhood entirely. Because medical advances have made childbearing feasible through a woman's thirties and into her forties, Navy women could defer motherhood until at or near the end of their careers. Solutions to family issues will cut many ways, some of them quite unforeseen.

While questions about parents in the services bubble away, an older issue smolders in the background—how the services treat homosexuals. The long-standing military antipathy toward this group has so far not been decisively confronted. Current judicial and congressional perspectives seem to cast the issue in terms of equity and individual rights, giving short shrift to the services' insistence that it hinges instead on discipline and morale. One outcome may be that the services will have to accept homosexuals, which will bring about further adjustments.

The Gulf War clearly revealed just how extensively the Navy had integrated women into the heart of the profession, that is, into ships and aircraft. This was the result of Z-116, which from 1972 to 1990 was the strongest direct influence on the history of Navy women. Even today, Z-116's energy may not be fully spent, for the number of women in ships and planes continues to rise. Perhaps overtaking Z-116 today as influences on Navy policy are the reduction of the armed forces and concerns over sexual harassment, women in combat, and the deployment of parents.

The sexual harassment scandals of the early 1990s forced painful self-examination within the Navy. Out of the turmoil, one inescapable fact emerged: Navy women *matter*, and improper or ineffective handling of issues regarding them can have serious political consequences, as evidenced in the resignation of the secretary of the Navy in 1992.

The issues of women in combat and the deployment of parents are so closely related that decisions about either hold implications for the other. It now appears that the former question will be confronted first, but that is not to say it will be decided earlier. Even if Congress repeals statutory restrictions, service policy may keep them in effect until a successful legal challenge puts an end to them. Until that time, the history of women in the Navy is likely to unfold much as it has in the past. Within the Navy, obsolescent attitudes will collide with women's insistence on parity. At the same time, public opinion outside the Navy as reflected in Congress and the courts, along with developing technology, will continue to affect what the Navy can or may do.

Once restrictions fall away in fact as well as by law, a new era for women in the armed forces will begin. The energies unleashed by this new current will pervade every aspect of the Navy and profoundly affect all who serve in it, for there exists a historic link between defense of the country and the privileges of citizenship. In other words, for women to serve in combat units on a par with men is a logical extension of their equal citizenship, which carries both obligations and privileges.

Such was the notion of the woman from New York who wrote to Josephus Daniels in 1917; she perceived a link between women's acceptance into an armed service and the right to vote. Such is the notion that runs through this history. It is often a hidden current, this drive of women to accept the burdens of service, for it appears first as a demand for equal privileges. From their history, today's Navy women may draw a clearer understanding of the relationship between the obligations and privileges of service and a conviction that they are called to share both.

NOTES

1. America's First Enlisted Women

1. "Philadelphia Woman Enlists in the Navy," *New York Times,* March 22, 1917, p. 2.

2. Navy Department, "Memo to the Press," June 30, 1942, "Personnel Surveys, 1955–1968," folder 76, box 11, series I, ACNP(W), Navy Operational Archives.

3. Press release, March 27, 1917, subject file 1911-27; "Women in the USNR, Employment as YN(F)," folder NA3, Record Group 45, National Archives.

4. *The Notebook,* September 1939; Navy Department historical section memo, April 19, 1923; and Bureau of Navigation Circular Letter, March 19, 1917, subject file 1911-27, "Women in the USNR," folder NA3, Record Group 45, National Archives.

5. *The Notebook,* passim; Estelle Richardson Ruby interview; Phyllis Kelley Peterson interview.

6. Navy Department Correspondence to the Bureau (of Navigation), March 27–April 12, 1917; letters from Bureau, April 15–16, 1917; Bureau of Medicine and Surgery letter, March 24, 1917; Bureau of Navigation general correspondence, 1913-25, subject file 9878, folder 9879-1313, Record Group 45, National Archives.

7. Phyllis Kelley Peterson interview; "Women Besiege Censor," *New York Times,* July 19, 1917, p. 11.

8. Postcard to Daniels, March 21, 1917, subject file, "Correspondence, Secretary of the Navy, 1913–1921," Josephus S. Daniels Collection, Manuscript Division, Library of Congress.

9. Dolly Purvis Grumbles interview.

10. Navy Department, historical section memos, April 19, 1923, "Women in the USNR," folder NA3, and June 1, 1921, "General Information, Enlisted Personnel," folder NA3, subject file 1911-27, Record Group 45, National Archives.

11. Eunice C. Dessez, *The First Enlisted Women, 1917–1918*, p. 19 (Dessez was a former Yeoman [F]); "Historical Narrative of Activities of Navy Yard and Thirteenth Naval District, April 1917–March 1919: Register 13 Book I," p. 33, "Thirteenth Naval District (F.F.13)," folder ZPN13, subject file 1911-27, Record Group 45, National Archives.

12. Speech by Daniels, date and place not given, subject file, "Correspondence, Secretary of the Navy, 1913–1921," Josephus S. Daniels Collection, Library of Congress.

13. Two historians have stated that this number includes black women. Jack D. Foner states that a group of about thirty black women was enlisted as "yeomanettes" and employed in a segregated office in the Navy Department (*Blacks and the Military in American History* [New York: Praeger, 1974], p. 124). Morris J. MacGregor states that twenty-four black women reservists served in World War I (*Integration of the Armed Forces, 1940–1965*, Defense Studies Series [Washington, D.C.: Center for Military History of U.S. Army, 1981], p. 5).

In reviewing Foner's and MacGregor's sources, the authors were unable to substantiate that black women served in the Navy in World War I. One reference was cited by MacGregor: a letter from Chester A. Nimitz (then acting chief of the Bureau of Navigation) to Representative Hamilton Fish of New York, June 17, 1937. Nimitz wrote:

I desire to acknowledge your letter of 7 June 1939, requesting statistics relative to the number of men and women of the colored race who served with the Navy during the World War. . . . You are advised that the exact figure is not available, but by applying the ratio determined as of 30 June 1918, to the total number served, a figure of 6,751, including 24 women, of the colored race is approximated. [Folder A 9-10(A)mm(93), box 73, General Correspondence of the Bureau of Navigation, Record Group 19, National Archives, Washington, D.C.]

Apparently, the only information Nimitz had regarding blacks was that on June 30, 1918, 5,328 of the Navy's 435,398 members on active duty were black, or 1.22 percent. Nimitz apparently took 1.22 percent of the total number of those who had served during the war to arrive at an approximation of 6,751 blacks. Since approximately 2,000 Yeomen (F) served in Washington, D.C., where most if not all black women would have served if any served at all, by applying the ratio of 1.22 that he derived (of black men to total force) to 2,000, one arrives at a figure of 24. This does not show that a certain number of black women *did* serve, only that if they served, and if their number was in the same ratio to white women serving in Washington, D.C., as the ratio of black men to the total force, then that number would be twenty-four.

The authors examined Washington newspapers of the period—the *Washington Post* and the *Washington Bee* (a weekly newspaper of Washington's black community)—but found no reference to black Yeomen (F). An examination of other histories of blacks in the armed forces, and of women, as well as journals and other materials held at the Martin Luther King Library, Washington D.C., and at Howard University, met with similar results. Finally, none of the former Yeomen (F) interviewed recalled knowing or hearing of black Yeomen (F).

14. Navy Department, "General Information: Enlisted Personnel Strength," folder NA3, box 277, Record Group 45, National Archives, gives enlistments by state; Bureau of Naval Personnel, *U.S. Naval Administration in World War II: Fourteenth Naval District,* vol. I, p. 142, describes the work of Yeomen (F) in Hawaii during World War I; letter regarding enrollment of women in Panama, April 26, 1918, subject file 2896, Records of the Bureau of Naval Personnel, Record Group 45, National Archives; Dessez, *The First Enlisted Women,* p. 62, notes Yeomen (F) working in San Juan, Puerto Rico; *The Notebook,* June 1960, for British subjects' enlistments.

15. Joy Bright Hancock, *Lady in the Navy,* p. 25.

16. Navy Department press release, March 27, 1918, "Women in the USNR," folder NA3, subject file 1911-27, Record Group 45, National Archives.

17. *The Notebook,* September 1939.

18. Dessez, *The First Enlisted Women,* pp. 13, 22–23.

19. Ardelle Humphrey letter, July 12, 1983; memo from Bureau of Yards and Docks, May 14, 1917, and letter to Daniels from W. A. Dromgoole, June 12, 1917, subject file, "Correspondence, Secretary of the Navy, 1913–1921," Josephus S. Daniels Collection, Library of Congress; photographs of P. Greaves recruiting in Corvallis and Spokane, Washington, Pauline Greaves Collection, Southern Oregon Historical Society, Jacksonville, Oregon; assorted press clippings, Will Allen Dromgoole, "Women in the USNR," folder NA3, subject file 1911–27, Record Group 45, National Archives; Bureau of Naval Personnel, *Fourteenth Naval District,* vol. I, p. 142.

20. Dessez, *The First Enlisted Women,* pp. 61–62.

21. *Report of the Secretary of the Navy, 1918* (1919), p. 494. For a brief account of the munitions factory at Newport and for Daniels's quote, see Eileen Warburton, *In Living Memory,* pp. 59–60.

22. Hancock, *Lady in the Navy,* pp. 24–25; Bureau of Naval Personnel, "Navy Women," *All Hands,* Navy bicentennial issue (August 1975):70; Dessez, *The*

First Enlisted Women, p. 62, names Pauline Bourneauf of Boston as "among those" who served in Paris, France.

23. Letter from Daniels, September 3, 1918, roll no. M1052, General and Special Indexes, "General Correspondence of the Secretary of the Navy," Record Group 80, National Archives.

24. Josephus Daniels letter, December 17, 1917, roll no. M1052, General and Special Indexes, General Correspondence of the Secretary of the Navy, Record Group 80, National Archives; Josephus S. Daniels, *The Cabinet Diaries of Josephus Daniels, 1913–1921,* p. 253.

25. "Will Navy Commission Women?" *Army and Navy Journal* 55 (June 8, 1918):1569; Meriwether, "The Many-Sided Naval Reserve: Plumber's Helpers, Naval Architects, College Professors and a Corps of Able Women," *Sea Power* (March 1918):199; press release, February 4, 1918, and Navy Department historical section memo, April 19, 1923, "Women in the USNR," folder NA3, subject file 1911-27, Record Group 45, National Archives.

26. Hancock, *Lady in the Navy,* p. 25.

27. *The Notebook,* passim; Butler, "I Was a Yeoman (F)," p. 9; "Navy Women," *All Hands* (August 1975):70; Navy Department, historical section memo, October 16, 1925, "Naval Personnel Losses," folder NC1, subject file 1911-27, Record Group 45, National Archives.

28. Helen O'Neill interview.

29. Helen O'Neill interview.

30. *The Notebook,* September 1939, March 1944, March 1981, and June 1982.

31. Helen O'Neill interview.

32. Helen O'Neill interview.

2. Once Again, a Time of Need

1. Virginia Gildersleeve, *Many a Good Crusade,* p. 267.

2. Treadwell, *U.S. Army in World War II: Special Studies—The Women's Army Corps,* pp. 15–16.

3. Treadwell, *Women's Army Corps,* pp. 45, 115–18, 221.

4. Joy Bright Hancock oral history, pp. 49–50.

5. Bureau of Naval Personnel, *U.S. Naval Administration in World War II: Women's Reserve,* vol. I, p. 2.

6. Hancock, *Lady in the Navy,* p. 52; quoted material, Bureau of Naval Personnel, *Women's Reserve,* p. 6.

7. Letter from L. E. Denfeld, assistant chief of the Bureau of Navigation, April 20, 1942, and replies, entry 90, folder QR8, box 2328, Record Group 24, National Archives.

8. Bureau of Naval Personnel, *Women's Reserve*, pp. 9–10.

9. Joy Bright Hancock oral history, pp. 61–62; *Lady in the Navy*, p. 54.

10. Albion, *Makers of Naval Policy*, p. 453; Hancock, *Lady in the Navy*, pp. 55–50.

11. Gildersleeve, *Many a Good Crusade*, pp. 268–70.

12. Gildersleeve, *Many a Good Crusade*, pp. 273–74; Mildred McAfee Horton oral history, p. 5.

13. Max R. Grossman, "Life Story of Wellesley's New College President," *Boston Sunday Post*, May 24, 1936, p. A3.

14. Grossman, "Life Story of Wellesley's New College President, Continued," *Boston Sunday Post*, June 14, 1936, p. A4.

15. Margaret Hamilton, "The Ruler of the W.A.V.E.S." *Kansas City Star*, August 9, 1942, pp. 1C, 3C; Patrick Sullivan, "'Miss Mac' Rules the Waves," *Boston Sunday Post*, August 2, 1942, p. A3; S. J. Woolf, "She Rules the WAVES," *New York Times Magazine*, August 16, 1942, pp. 15, 26.

16. Gildersleeve, *Many a Good Crusade*, p. 270.

17. Woolf, "She Rules the WAVES," p. 15.

18. Bureau of Naval Personnel, *Women's Reserve*, pp. 12–13.

19. Gildersleeve, *Many a Good Crusade*, quotes of Elizabeth Reynard, p. 272.

3. The Navy's First Women Officers

1. Mary Daily, address to a group of Navy women in Seattle, November 17, 1983, copy sent to authors, quoted with permission.

2. Jean Palmer oral history, pp. 3, 11–12.

3. Mildred McAfee Horton interview; "Suggestions and Recommendations Resulting from District Directors Conference," Bureau of Naval Personnel memo, folder 14, box 2, series I, ACNP(W), Navy Operational Archives.

4. Mildred McAfee Horton interview and oral history, p. 51.

5. Bureau of Naval Personnel, *Women's Reserve*, p. 49; Joy Hancock oral history, p. 60.

6. Etta Belle Kitchen oral history, p. 7; Margaret Disert and Mary Daily interviews.

7. Hancock, *Lady in the Navy*, pp. 75–76; letter to Elizabeth Reynard, Bureau of Navigation from C. Mildred Thompson, Vassar College, April 29, 1942, folder QR8, box 2328, Record Group 24, National Archives.

8. Bureau of Naval Personnel, *Women's Reserve*, pp. 230–33.

9. Marguerite Higgins, clipping from *New York Herald Tribune*, August 28, 1942, WAVES general folder, World War 1939–45, War Service Collection,

Smith College Archives; Bureau of Naval Personnel, *Women's Reserve,* p. 239; Edwin Smetheram interview.

10. Marguerite Higgins, quoting Captain Underwood, clipping from *New York Herald Tribune,* August 28, 1942.

11. Edwin Smetheram interview.

12. Edwin Smetheram interview.

13. Dorothy Stratton oral history, p. 2; Edwin Smetheram interview.

14. Elizabeth Crandall oral history, p. 5.

15. Bureau of Naval Personnel, *Women's Reserve,* pp. 247–49.

16. Mildred McAfee Horton interview; Dorothy Stratton oral history, p. 13; Bureau of Naval Personnel, *Women's Reserve,* p. 246.

17. *The Notebook,* December 1980.

18. Bureau of Naval Personnel, *Statistics Yearbook, 1944,* p. 80; Hancock, *Lady in the Navy,* p. 79.

19. Hancock, *Lady in the Navy,* pp. 80–90.

20. Hancock, *Lady in the Navy,* pp. 80–81.

21. Hancock, *Lady in the Navy,* p. 80.

4. Recruitment and Training of Enlisted WAVES

1. Mildred McAfee Horton oral history, p. 74.

2. Mary Josephine Shelley oral history, pp. 19–20.

3. Bureau of Naval Personnel, *Women's Reserve,* pp. 338–46 (appendix: U.S. NTS, Stillwater, Okla.).

4. Copy of talk given by Ensign Quait before the Cedar Falls High School Girls Reserve, February 9, 1943, Gladys Hearst Collection, University of Northern Iowa Archives.

5. "The Navy at Cedar Falls, 1942–1945," a history, probably written by Gladys Henderson, p. 6, document 13312, Gladys Hearst Collection, University of Northern Iowa Archives.

6. "The Navy at Cedar Falls, 1942–1945"; Margaret Disert interview.

7. Margaret Disert interview.

8. Bureau of Naval Personnel, *Women's Reserve,* vol. II, pp. 46, 53; oral history Eleanor Rigby, pp. 13–14; Marie Bennett Alsmeyer, *The Way of the WAVES,* p. 17.

9. Bureau of Naval Personnel, *Women's Reserve,* vol. II, pp. 27–29.

10. Bureau of Naval Personnel, *Women's Reserve,* vol. II, pp, 31–33; Gildersleeve, *Many a Good Crusade,* pp. 277–78; Hancock, *Lady in the Navy,* p. 105.

11. Patricia G. Morgan, unpublished memoir, copy sent to Jean Ebbert on May 14, 1983. Quoted with permission.

12. Alsmeyer, *The Way of the WAVES,* pp. 15–16.

13. Gildersleeve, *Many a Good Crusade,* pp. 284–86.

14. Alsmeyer, *The Way of the WAVES,* p. 24.

15. Bureau of Naval Personnel, *Women's Reserve,* vol. II, p. 56.

16. "Training Program for Members of the Women's Reserve," folder 29, box 4, series I, ACNP(W), Navy Operational Archives; Bureau of Naval Personnel memorandum, June 24, 1943, folder QR8/NC, box 2330, Record Group 24, National Archives.

17. History of the Women's Reserve, folder 29, box 4, series I, ACNP(W), Navy Operational Archives.

18. Alsmeyer, *Way of the WAVES,* pp. 29–30.

19. Hancock, *Lady in the Navy,* pp. 128–42 (Hancock gives numbers for each school, total derived by summing numbers); letter from the chief of naval personnel to officer-in-charge, Navy Recruiting Bureau, June 29, 1943, folder QR8, box 2330, Record Group 24, National Archives.

20. Mary Josephine Shelly oral history, p. 10.

21. La Verne Bradley, "Women in Uniform," *National Geographic* (October 1943):454.

22. Joy Bright Hancock oral history, pp. 109–10.

5. A Maturing Relationship

1. Mary Daily, address to a group of Navy women, Seattle, November 17, 1983; Louise Wilde oral history, p. 15; Bureau of Naval Personnel, *U.S. Naval Administration in World War II: Administrative History of the Twelfth Naval District,* vol. I, p. 457; Joy Bright Hancock oral history, pp. 84–88.

2. Mildred McAfee Horton, "Women in the United States Navy," *American Journal of Sociology* (March 1946):450.

3. Mildred McAfee Horton oral history, pp. 72–73; letters regarding working conditions for Hospital Corps WAVES (June 7, 1944; June 29, 1944; June 30, 1944; August 30, 1944), "District Director Reports (1944)," folder 16, box 3, series I, ACNP(W), Navy Operational Archives.

4. Veronica Mackey Hulick interview.

5. Joy Bright Hancock oral history, pp. 87–88.

6. Oral histories of Jean Palmer (p. 35) and Joy Bright Hancock (pp. 73–74).

7. Mildred McAfee Horton interview.

8. Jean Palmer oral history, p. 12.

9. Hancock, *Lady in the Navy*, p. 117, states that only one WAVE was convicted of a felony and "sentenced by a general court martial to a federal prison for the crime of forgery."

10. Bureau of Naval Personnel, *U.S. Naval Administration in World War II: The Bureau of Ships*, vol. II, p. 134.

11. Mildred McAfee Horton oral history, p. 80.

12. Bureau of Naval Personnel, *U.S. Naval Administration in World War II: The Negro in the Navy*, p. 15; letters and telegrams dated August 25, 1942, folder QR8, box 2329, Record Group 24, National Archives.

13. Bureau of Naval Personnel, *The Negro in the Navy*, pp. 1–8, 15.

14. Morris J. MacGregor, Jr., *Integration of the Armed Forces, 1940–1965*, p. 86.

15. Mildred McAfee Horton oral history, p. 46.

16. Bureau of Naval Personnel, *The Negro in the Navy*, pp. 15–16. Also petition urging integration, subject file QR8/MN(N)B, box 2331, Record Group 24, National Archives; letter, July 13, 1943, from Women's Auxiliary of Congress of Industrial Organizations, to Secretary Knox; two letters to Knox from Alpha Kappa Alpha and Phi Delta Kappa, sororities for black women; and memo from Women's Advisory Council to McAfee, August 6, 1943—all from subject file QR8, box 2330, Record Group 24, National Archives.

17. MacGregor, *Integration of the Armed Forces*, p. 88; Navy press release dated October 19, 1944, folder 29, Historical Data Concerning Women's Reserve (1942–62), box 4, series I, ACNP(W), Navy Operational Archives.

18. Mary Josephine Shelly oral history, p. 32; document P14-2 records the rushed activity within the Bureau of Naval Personnel to find black women qualified to enter WAVE officer training at Northampton, subject file QR8, box 2330, Record Group 24, National Archives; "Sounding Off," September 31, 1944, publications folder, "WAVES," War Service Collection, World War 1939–45, Smith College Archives; Bureau of Naval Personnel, *The Negro in the Navy*, p. 98.

19. Mildred McAfee Horton oral history, p. 48.

20. Department of the Navy, *Final Report of the Navy Manpower Survey Board to the Secretary of the Navy*, June 28, 1944, p. 7.

21. Bureau of Naval Personnel, *Women's Reserve*, p. 146; report dated October 29, 1944, Fourteenth Naval District (1943–53), folder 50, box 7, series I, ACNP(W), Navy Operational Archives.

22. Letter to port director of Twelfth Naval District from assistant to operations officer of Twelfth Naval District, January 16, 1945, Fourteenth Naval District (1943–53), folder 50, box 7, series I, ACNP(W), Navy Operational Archives; Hancock, *Lady in the Navy*, p. 199.

23. Eleanor Rigby oral history, p. 41. Rigby recalled, "Here is this lieutenant commander sitting on the back seat of this big limousine [with Senator Margaret

Chase Smith], and on the two jump seats in front of us, Admiral Spruance and Admiral Nimitz."

24. Memo from the commandant of the Fourteenth Naval District to Bureau of Naval Personnel, February 14, 1945, Fourteenth Naval District (1943–53), folder 50, box 7, series I, ACNP(W), Navy Operational Archives.

25. Memo from Louise Wilde to McAfee, February 23, 1945, Fourteenth Naval District (1943–53), folder 50, box 7, series I, ACNP(W), Navy Operational Archives.

26. Department of the Navy, *Annual Report of the Secretary of the Navy, 1946*, p. 23.

27. Navy Department press release, July 21, 1945, "Press Releases on WAVES (July 1942–December 1947)," folder 3, box 18, series II, ACNP(W), Navy Operational Archives.

28. Typescript of an article by McAfee intended for the *Army-Navy Journal*; "Speeches, Statements and Articles of Captain M. M. Horton (1943–1945)," folder 2 of folder 101, box 16, series I, ACNP(W), Navy Operational Archives.

29. Memo from chief of communications to chief of naval personnel, January 25, 1946, "Post-World War II WAVES (1945–1947)," folder 80, box 12, series I, ACNP(W), Navy Operational Archives.

30. Elder, "Demobilization of Women's Reserve," pp. 22, 38–39, 58, 72, 179.

31. Mary T. Gore interview.

32. Alsmeyer, *Way of the WAVES,* pp. 181–82.

33. Mildred McAfee Horton, "Women in the United States Navy," *American Journal of Sociology* (March 1946): 450.

6. Setting a New Course

1. Secretary of the Navy, message August 1, 1945, "Policies for the Administration of Women's Reserve (1943–1969)," folder 79, box 12, series I, ACNP(W), Navy Operational Archives; Hancock, *Lady in the Navy,* p. 214.

2. ALSTACON 05234, January 5, 1946, and ALSTACON 172109, January 17, 1946, "Letters, Memoranda to District/Air Command Directors (1943–1948)," folder 35, box 5, series I, ACNP(W), Navy Operational Archives.

3. Letter from Jean Palmer to Winifred Quick, January 20, 1946, "Overseas (1944–1946)," folder 69, box 10, series I, and letter from Jean Palmer to district directors, February 19, 1946, folder 35, box 5, series I, ACNP(W), Navy Operational Archives.

4. Bureau of Aeronautics memo to Bureau of Naval Personnel, July 18, 1945, "Post-World War II WAVES (1945–1947)" folder 80, box, 12, series I, ACNP(W), Navy Operational Archives.

5. Memo from chief of communications to chief of naval personnel, January 25, 1946; memo from OP-20 to chief of naval personnel, February 13, 1946; memo from Bureau of Medicine and Surgery to Bureau of Naval Personnel, February 13, 1946; memo from Bureau of Supplies and Accounts to chief of naval personnel, June 12, 1946; and memo from Office of Public Information to Bureau of Naval Personnel, February 21, 1946—all in "Post-World War II WAVES (1945–1947)," folder 80, box 12, series I, ACNP(W), Navy Operational Archives.

6. ALSTACON 14455, March 14, 1946, "Post-World War II WAVES (1945–1947), folder 80, box 12; memo from Jean Palmer to deputy chief of naval personnel, May 24, 1946, "Historical—Women's Reserve," folder 28, box 4; and *Annual Report of the Women's Reserve for the Fiscal Year Ending 30 June 1947*, "Reports Recurring (1943–1954)," folder 88, box 14—all in series I, ACNP(W), Navy Operational Archives.

7. Billings, *Grace Hopper: Navy Admiral and Computer Pioneer*, pp. 13, 28–32, 36–39, 47–53, 82; quote, p. 39.

8. Navy Department, *Annual Report of the Women's Reserve for the Fiscal Year Ending 30 June 1947*; memos from Joy Hancock to district directors, January 13, 1947, and April 14, 1947, "Letters, Memoranda to District/Air Command Directors (1943–1948)," folder 35, box 5, series I, ACNP(W), Navy Operational Archives.

9. Hancock, *Lady in the Navy*, pp. 220, 222.

10. Hancock, *Lady in the Navy*, pp. 223–24.

11. Report of Louise Wilde, November 8, 1946, on visit to Naval Air Training Command and to Ninth Naval District, "Reports on Trips (1945–1947)," folder 89, box 14, series I, ACNP(W), Navy Operational Archives.

12. Winifred Quick Collins interview and letter, July 1992.

13. Hancock, *Lady in the Navy*, p. 224.

14. Joy Bright Hancock interview.

15. Hancock, *Lady in the Navy*, p. 26.

16. "Hearings on WAVE Legislation and Public Laws (1942–1948)," folder 10, box 33, series IV, ACNP(W), Navy Operational Archives.

17. Memo to the undersecretary of the Navy from the chief of naval operations, January 1, 1949, "Women in the Regular Navy: Official Correspondence (1946–1948)," folder 113, box 18, series I, ACNP(W), Navy Operational Archives.

18. Hancock, *Lady in the Navy*, p. 227.

19. Smith, *Declaration of Conscience*, pp. 85–87.

20. Winifred Quick Collins interview.

21. Joy Bright Hancock oral history, pp. 123–25.

22. Smith, *Declaration of Conscience*, pp. 96–97.

23. Smith, *Declaration of Conscience*, pp. 96–97.

24. Hancock, *Lady in the Navy*, p. 232.

7. A Nucleus Is Launched and Tested

1. Hancock, *Lady in the Navy*, p. 235.

2. Joy Bright Hancock interview; Hancock, *Lady in the Navy*, p. 157; chronology of Nurse Corps history, Office of the Director of the Nurse Corps, Navy Department.

3. Almira B. Davis, "WAVE Recruit Training," *Training Bulletin*, Navy Department, pp. 3–4.

4. Davis, "WAVE Recruit Training," p. 8.

5. Lt. Robert A. Rodgers, "These Boots Wear Skirts," U.S. Naval Institute *Proceedings* (September 1949):1027.

6. *The News*, Newport, October 14, 1950, p. 5, copy found in Naval Station Library, Newport, RI.

7. Bureau of Personnel memo, 153-rb of July 6, 1948, "Utilization (1948–1966)," folder 106, box 17, series I, ACNP(W), Navy Operational Archives.

8. Memo from director of research division to director of plans and policy, July 27, 1950; and memo from Capt. Joy Bright Hancock to chairman of Working Group on Human Behavior Under Conditions of Military Service on employment of women by U.S. Navy, February 27, 1951, "Utilization (1948–1966)," folder 106, box 17, series I, ACNP(W), Navy Operational Archives.

9. Memo from deputy chief of naval personnel to assistant chief for personnel control, Pers A1-M9, July 27, 1950, "Utilization (1948–1966)," folder 106, box 17, series I, ACNP(W), Navy Operational Archives; Kathleen Amick-Temple interview.

10. Proposed pamphlet for Naval Historical Foundation by Lt. Claire Brou, forwarded to Captain Lenihan, December 19, 1966, "Historical Matters (1944–1968)," folder 33, box 5; memo from director of naval intelligence to chief of naval personnel, June 24, 1949, "Overseas (1946–1953)," file 69, box 10; "History," chronology of Navy women, "Past to Present 1919–1970," folder 4, box 30—all in series III, ACNP(W), Navy Operational Archives; letter to chief of naval personnel from president, Reserve Line Selection Board to Lieutenant from Lieutenant (junior grade), February 16, 1950, "Naval Reserve Correspondence (January 1948–December 1949)," folder 55, box 8, series I, ACNP(W), Navy Operational Archives.

11. Mueller, *War, Presidents, and Public Opinion*, p. 48.

12. Navy Department, Bureau of Medicine and Surgery, *The History of the Medical Department of the U.S. Navy, 1945–1950*, NAVMED P-5057, pp. 159, 181.

13. Field, *History of United States Naval Operations in Korea*, pp. 73–77.

14. Letter to Capt. Joy Bright Hancock from women's representative at Jacksonville, May 17, 1951, "Chief of Naval Air Reserve Training Command (1943–1952)," folder 5, box 1, and Bureau of Naval Personnel circular letter 102-51, June 25, 1951, and Eighth Naval District questions in response to letter from chief of naval personnel to all district commandants and chief of Naval Air Reserve training, August 4, 1950, "Naval Reserve (1948–1955)," folder 53, box 7—both in series I, ACNP(W), Navy Operational Archives.

15. Letter from chief of naval information to commandants of naval districts and Potomac River Command, May 24, 1951, "Recruiting and Procurement Policies 1951–1952 (1947–1952)," file 85, box 13, series I, ACNP(W), Navy Operational Archives; Brou pamphlet.

16. Letter from Capt. Louise Wilde to director, Naval Reserve Division, April 7, 1955, "Naval Reserve (1948–1955)," folder 33, box 7, series I, ACNP(W), Navy Operational Archives.

17. Memo for the record, September 8, 1952, "Utilization of Enlisted Women," file 9, OP-01(W) files, Bureau of Naval Personnel, Navy Department.

18. "Women Recruits Sign up Faster," *Navy Times*, December 13, 1952, p. 3; Holm, *Women in the Military*, pp. 152–3.

19. Dorothy Council interview; Bureau of Naval Personnel memos, March 5, 1951, and August 31, 1951, "OCS(W) Policy," file 8, OP-01 Files, Bureau of Personnel, Navy Department; Brou pamphlet. A significant exemption in this offer foreshadowed later attempts to deal with the difficult issue of admitting or retaining women with dependents under eighteen. If a woman was the step-parent of a child under eighteen, she could qualify if the child lived with her no more than thirty days a year. It is not known how many Navy women had recourse to this exemption.

20. Brou pamphlet; Office of the Assistant Secretary of Defense, Manpower and Reserve Affairs, "Utilization of Military Women (A Report of Increased Utilization of Military Women, FY 1973–1977)," p. B-20, Department of Defense Library, the Pentagon.

21. Navy Department, Bureau of Medicine, *The History of the Medical Department of the U.S. Navy*, pp. 102, 105.

22. Katherine Keating letters, October 13 and November 11, 1989.

8. 1953–63: Surviving the Peace

1. Louise Wilde oral history; biography of Wilde, "Past to Present (1919–1971)," folder 4, box 30, series I, ACNP(W), Navy Operational Archives.

2. Holm, *Women in the Military*, pp. 162–64.

3. Memo from Capt. Louise Wilde, January 14, 1957, "Utilization of Enlisted Women," file 9, OP-01(W) files, Navy Department.

4. "Service Gal's Husband Ruled Independent Though Jobless," *Navy Times*, March 14, 1953, p. 17; Julie DiLorenzo letter, January 3, 1986.

5. Lois Berman Brown interview; Kathleen D. Bruyere interview.

6. Mary Gore interview; Dorothy Council interview; Marie Kelleher letter, February 26, 1986; Viola Sanders letter, March 18, 1986.

7. Memo for the record, October 20, 1955, shows eight women commanders, "Utilization of Enlisted Women," file 9, OP-01(W) files, Navy Department; "Bill to Relax WAVE Grade Curbs OK'd," *Navy Times*, March 31, 1956, p. 6, reports nine.

8. "Navy to Screen 2,500 for 800 Comdr. Slots," *Navy Times*, September 9, 1961, p. 10; memo for the record, October 18, 1968, "Promotion Plans," file 12, OP-01(W) files, Navy Department.

9. Arbogast, "The Procurement of Women for the Armed Forces: An Analysis of Occupational Choice," p. 48; Office of the Assistant Secretary of Defense, Manpower and Reserve Affairs, "Utilization of Military Women: A Report of Increased Utilization of Military Women, FY 1973–1977," pp. B-21 and B-22, citing U.S. Department of Labor study, "Womanpower: An Underutilized Resource?" 1968, p. 296, Department of the Defense Library, the Pentagon; "The Woman's Touch," *Navy Times*, January 22, 1969, p. 24, and "WAVE CT's on Way Out," November 20, 1963, p. 1.

10. All information in this section is based on Kathleen Amick-Temple and Sidney Temple interview, plus biographical summaries provided by Kathleen Amick-Temple.

11. Winifred Quick Collins interview.

12. Winifred Quick Collins interview; Etta Belle Kitchen oral history, pp. 1–18.

13. Male officer candidates were commissioned only after completing the sixteen-week course; a similar arrangement considered for women was rejected as likely to hamper recruitment ("History of the Women Officers School," entry dated June 1954, collection 33, box 1, Naval War College Historical Collection); Elizabeth G. Wylie interview; Anne Aoki interview.

14. "History of the Women Officers School," entry dated August 1963; report by Lt. Comdr. Jean Smith and Comdr. Ann Ducey, "Survey of Performance, Learning Ability and Background Information of Junior WAVE Officers in the United States Navy," folder 34, "Justification: Officer/Enlisted, January–May, 1963," box 5, series I, ACNP(W), Navy Operational Archives.

15. "Maybe She'll Become 'Jill of All Trades,'" *Navy Times*, October 10, 1953, p. 15; correspondence of assistant chief of naval personnel (W) with chief of naval personnel and with chief of naval education and training, from April 10, 1957 to March 21, 1958, "Officers: Plans and Policies (Advanced Schools) (1955–1958)," folder 60; letter from personnel officer of Armed Forces Staff College, May 12, 1958—all in box 8, series I, ACNP(W), Navy Operational Archives; Rita Lenihan interview.

16. Memo from Capt. Louise Wilde to chief of naval personnel, July 31, 1955; letter from Eleanor Sower to chief of naval personnel, April 11, 1957; list found under "1958" in "Officers: Plans and Policies (Advanced Schools) (1955–1958)"—all in folder 60, box 8, series I, ACNP(W), Navy Operational Archives; Ann Ducey letter, May 25, 1986.

17. "Cornell to Graduate First WAVE NESEP," *Navy Times,* February 10, 1965, p. 7; Brou pamphlet (citing ALNAV 4, November 16, 1958); Navy Internal Relations Activity memo, April 30, 1987, re: NESEP program, in response to query by Jean Ebbert.

18. All information in this section is based on Lucille Kuhn interview.

19. For example, in 1951 Margaret Dunn was one of the original four women hospital corpsmen who served aboard the converted LST 1134, which ferried service members and their families from Oahu to other Hawaiian islands on overnight trips (questionnaire completed by Margaret Dunn Mead in September 1982 and provided to authors); *Navy Times:* "MSTLant WAVE Could Put Travel Braggers to Shame," July 14, 1956, p. 42; "Four WAVES Assigned to Duty on Transports," September 12, 1953, p. 3; "Telfair Adds WAVE to Crew to Make History Third Time," April 21, 1956, p. 48.

20. "Mann's Woman Is Navy First," *Navy Times,* July 15, 1961, p. 2; Ann Ducey letter, June 12, 1986; Dale F. Garlock letter, March 13, 1989. Ducey, as detailer for women officers, was responsible for assigning Suneson to the *Mann*; Garlock was Suneson's department head and immediate superior in the ship.

21. Ann Ducey letter, June 12, 1986.

22. Winifred Quick Collins interview.

23. *Navy Times:* "All Weather Pleases PAX WAVE Chief," September 29, 1956, p. 12; "WAVE Is Honor Grad," July 5, 1952, p. 2; "WAVE Earns Ph.D. Degree," July 29, 1961, p. 11; and JO1 Ely M. Orias, "WAVE Has a Physical Fitness Plan All Her Own," December 2, 1961, p. 4.

24. *North Islander,* San Diego, April 6, 1962, "Publicity Press Clippings (1961–1962)," folder 23, box 21, series II, ACNP(W), Navy Operational Archives.

9. Upheaval: Vietnam and Its Legacy

1. Holm, *Women in the Military,* pp. 260–65; Department of Defense, Office of the Assistant Secretary of Defense, *Utilization of Military Women,* table 7, p. B-20; *Annual Report of the Secretary of Defense, 1965,* table 11, p. 394; *Annual Report of the Secretary of Defense, 1968,* table 17, p. 515.

2. Letter dated January 11, 1967, file "Vietnam Officer Assignments"; Pers-K newsletter, April 1967, file "Pers-K Bulletins"; memo to deputy assistant chief for personnel control, enclosure dated May 19, 1971, file "Enlisted Assignments Policy (1961–1973)"—all in OP-01 files, Navy Department.

3. Elizabeth G. Wylie interview.

4. Elizabeth G. Wylie interview; Donna Weatherly, "How's This for Spending a Year Abroad," *Virginian-Pilot*, August 1, 1968, p. 23.

5. Information supplied by the staff of the Naval Historical Center, Washington Navy Yard, compiled from documents held in the Navy Operational Archives; "Second WAVE Officer Assigned to Vietnam," *Navy Times*, February 14, 1968, p. 2; "2 More WAVES Get Vietnam Duty," *Navy Times*, August 11, 1971, p. 2; "First Woman U.S. Navy Advisor Aids Dependents of Vietnamese Navymen," *All Hands* (July 1972):53; "Te Deum for WAVES from 31-Knot Sailor Admiral Arleigh A. Burke, USN (Ret.)," *Defense Management Journal* 6, no. 1 (Winter 1970): 27.

6. Edith M. Lederer, Associated Press, dateline Saigon, *The Press* (Atlantic City), March 22, 1973, p. 14; "The Expanding Role of Navy Women," *All Hands*, April 1973, p. 23.

7. Lt. Elizabeth G. Wylie, letter to Capt. Rita Lenihan, August 5, 1967, file "Vietnam Officer Appointments," OP-01 files, Navy Department.

8. Holm, *Women in the Military*, pp. 214–28; Richard S. Christian, director of Environmental Support Group, Office of the Adjutant General, Department of the Army, letter to Senator Alan Cranston, March 27, 1984, copy supplied by Navy Operational Archives.

9. Holm, *Women in the Military*, pp. 209–10.

10. Viola Sanders letters, March 18, 1986, and December 7, 1987.

11. Binkin and Bach, *Women in the Military*, p. 12; Holm, *Women in the Military*, pp. 196–200 and quote on p. 200.

12. Marie Kelleher letter, February 26, 1986.

13. Zumwalt, *On Watch*, p. 262, and quote from unclassified message from NO (Z-116) to NAVOP, August 7, 1972, OP-01 files, Navy Department.

14. Robin Quigley oral history, p. 177.

15. Robin Quigley oral history, pp. 2–16, 36–46, and quote on pp. 36–37.

16. Robin Quigley oral history, p. 219; Pers-K memo no. 5, February 23, 1972, p. 1, OP-01 files, Navy Department.

17. Pers-K memo no. 5, p. 2.

18. Pers-K memo no. 5, p. 4.

19. Robin Quigley oral history, pp. 231–34; Fran McKee interview; Elizabeth G. Wylie interview, Carolina Clair Wylie interview.

20. Robin Quigley oral history, pp. 249–50, 279–82.

10. Sustaining a Volunteer Force

1. Navy Department, Bureau of Naval Personnel, "FY-88—Annual Report of Navy Military Personnel Statistics," pp. 5–6, and 1990 Navy Women's Study

Group, "An Update Report on the Progress of Women in the Navy" (1990), pp. I-B-1, -5, and -6.

2. Navy Department, "Navy Study Group Report on Progress of Women in the Navy" (1987), pp. 1–35; "Update Report on the Progress of Women" (1990), pp. I-49, -50, I-B-1, -5, -6.

3. Veronica Froman interview; Elizabeth Wylie interview.

4. Holm, *Women in the Military*, pp. 290–91.

5. Holm, *Women in the Military*, pp. 296–97.

6. Winifred Hamerlinck, letter to the Bureau of Personnel, September 29, 1969; letter to Jean Ebbert, March 26, 1986; Capt. Marie Kelleher letter; Capt. C. E. Stastny, commanding officer, U.S. Naval Station, Long Beach, to chief of naval personnel, October 1, 1969.

7. Holm, *Women in the Military*, p. 298.

8. Jordine Von Wantoch letter, April 9, 1989; Von Wantoch letter to chief of naval personnel, June 3, 1970; Commanding Officer Amphibious School, Coronado, endorsement, June 3, 1970; commander, Amphibious Training Command, Pacific Fleet, endorsement, June 8, 1970.

9. Bureau of Naval Personnel, letter to Jordine Von Wantoch, July 29, 1970; Von Wantoch letter to chief of naval personnel, August 10, 1970.

10. Robin Quigley oral history, pp. 179–96, quote, p. 193; Von Wantoch letter to chief of naval personnel, November 16, 1971; Von Wantoch letter, August 3, 1992.

11. William Matthews, "Unmarried Pregnancy Concern," *Navy Times*, February 1, 1988, pp. 1, 14; "Navy Study Group Report on Progress of Women in the Navy" (1987), p. 2-50; "Update Report on the Progress of Women" (1990), p. II-72.

12. *Minerva* (Fall 1991):1–32; "Update Report of the Progress of Women" (1990), p. II-68.

13. *Navy Times*: Rosemary Purcell, "No More Automatic 'Outs' for Pregnant Navy Women," June 7, 1982, p. 19; William Matthews, "Navy Turns to Civilians to Transfuse Medical Care," January 23, 1989, p. 11; Rick Maze, "House Panel Votes More Child Care Centers," July 10, 1989, p. 7; Grant Willis, "Child Care Improvement Brings New Kind of Turmoil," May 13, 1991, p. 18; and Grant Willis, "Child Care Centers Can Hire 1,700 New Workers," August 26, 1991, p. 4.

14. Molly Moore, "When Soldiers Have Babies," *Washington Post*, April 29, 1988, p. 19; Grant Willis, "Navy Extends Working Post-birth Leave by 12 Days," *Navy Times*, February 6, 1989, p. 6.

15. *Navy Times*: James Longo, "More Navy Family Support Needed: Edney," December 12, 1988, p. 4; Brian Mitchell, "MCTON Bushey Gets His Licks in for the Fleet," February 13, 1989, pp. 8–9; Karen Jowers, "Single Parents, Ready or Not," December 4, 1989, pp. 53, 58, 62; Lucille Kuhn interview.

16. *Navy Times*: Rick Maze, "Lone Parenthood in Military Getting New Look," January 9, 1989, p. 4, and Rick Maze, "Panel Orders Single Parent Study," July 17, 1989, p. 2; Schneider, *Sound Off*, p. 217.

17. Rick Maze, "Written Fraternization Policy Halted by Top Navy Officials," *Navy Times*, September 5, 1983, p. 8.

18. *Navy Times*: Mel Jones, "Affair May Cost Cmdr. His 19-Year Navy Career," May 13, 1985, p. 2; Mel Jones, "Wyatt Not Bitter After Fraternization Conviction," May 20, 1985, p. 2; Capt. R. L. Kline, "Slap on the Wrist," June 3, 1985, p. 23; John Burlage, "Officer Guilty of Adultery," March 10, 1986, p. 38; James Longo, "Familiar Rules on Relation Among Ranks Put in Writing," February 20, 1989, p. 3.

19. Grant Willis, "2 Lawmakers Want Fraternization Rules Re-evaluated," *Navy Times*, October 17, 1988, p. 19.

20. *Navy Times*: James Longo, "Coast Guard to Issue First Fraternization Policy," January 16, 1989, p. 16, and James Longo, "Familiar Rules," p. 3.

21. *Navy Times*: Longo, "Familiar Rules," and James Longo, "NAS Mirimar CO Fined in Fraternization Case," May 13, 1991, p. 8.

22. OPNAVISNT 5300.9, November 6, 1989, OP-01 files, Navy Department.

23. "Sex Harassment Called Widespread in Military," *Washington Post*, February 12, 1980, quote on p. A6; *Navy Times*: Andy Plattner, "Panel Hears Sexual Harassment Testimony," February 25, 1980, p. 2, and E. C. Grayson, "Navy Women: How They Have Performed," June 7, 1982, quote on p. 19.

24. *Navy Times*: Tom Burgess, "Adm. Narmi Charged in Sexual Harassment Case," January 28, 1985, quote, p. 24, and "Admiral Narmi Will Retire," February 4, 1985, p. 1; United States Naval Academy, "The Assimilation of Women in the Brigade of Midshipmen" (July 1990), p. 23, OP-01 files, Navy Department.

25. *Navy Times*: John Burlage, "Salvage Ship's CO Draws Allegations of Harassment," September 14, 1987, p. 3, and John Burlage, "Complaints Spark New Policy Review," September 21, 1987, pp. 1, 28–29; Molly Moore, "Pentagon Unit Finds Sexual Harassment," *Washington Post*, September 18, 1987, p. A20.

26. "Navy Study Group's Report of Progress of Women" (1987), pp. 3-15, 3-17 through 3-20.

27. *Navy Times*: John Burlage, "Skipper Leaves Navy after Harassment Reprimand," August 28, 1989, p. 9, and Elizabeth Donovan, "Women Try to Handle Harassment Problems by Themselves, Report Says," September 24, 1990, p. 4; Molly Moore, "Navy Failed to Prosecute in 6 Rapes," *Washington Post*, October 25, 1990, p. A4.

28. U.S. Senate, Committee on Expenditures in the Executive Department, Subcommittee on Investigation, 1975, cited in Adam, *The Rise of a Gay and Lesbian Movement*, pp. 58–60; Allan Berube and John D'Emilio, "The Military and Lesbians During the McCarthy Years," *Signs* 9, no. 4 (1984):759;

Lucille Kuhn interview; Lois Berman Brown interview; and Sarah Watlington interview.

29. Sarah Watlington interview.

30. "Update Report on the Progress of Women" (1990), pp. IV-27 through IV-29; Lucille Kuhn interview.

31. *Navy Times*: Grant Willis, "More Women than Men Discharged as Homosexuals," February 29, 1988, p. 2, and Brian Mitchell, "Disciplinary Discharges Drop Within Navy's Enlisted Ranks," September 19, 1988, p. 6.

11. Professional Advances: A Matter of Equity

1. Chief of naval education and training, *Tra Navy: The Magazine of Naval Training* (November 1973):5; Lucille Kuhn, Mary Gore, and Sarah Watlington interviews.

2. Marc Zolta, "Together!" *Navy Times,* April 20, 1992, pp. 12–14.

3. Rosemary Purcell, "Adm. Hazard Tells Women to Expect to 'Do It All,'" *Navy Times,* August 24, 1987, p. 4.

4. Elizabeth P. Donovan, "Men's Work," *Navy Times,* July 9, 1990.

5. *Navy Times*: J. H. Smith and R. D. Carr, "Women Fight Fires on Aleutian Island," August 11, 1986, p. 48, and Donovan, "Men's Work," p. 14.

6. Gregg Stallworth, telephone conversation; Lynn MacDonald, telephone conversation; Melissa Lefler, "Ens. Lynn Schrage," *All Hands* (June 1988):28.

7. Elizabeth Wylie interview; "History of the Women Officers School," entries dated October 1972 and November 2, 1973, Naval War College Archives.

8. Quote from Lucille Kuhn interview; "Cdr. Kuhn Makes History," *All Hands* (June 1975):30.

9. Enclosure 1 to memo from CNO to secretary of the Navy, "NROTC College Program for Women," November 30, 1972; memo to secretary of the Navy from vice CNO, "Women in the NROTC," February 5, 1973; memo for CNO and commandant of the U.S. Marine Corps, "Women in the NROTC," November 15, 1973—all in "NROTC" file, OP-01 files, Navy Department; C. J. Stein letter.

10. Lt. Comdr. William Hoover, "The Disadvantaged Navy Woman," U.S. Naval Institute *Proceedings* (July 1977):118–21; Lt. JoAnne Stone and Comdr. Arthur J. Tuttle, telephone conversations.

11. Rick Maze, "Top Navy Officials Paint Bright Manpower Picture," *Navy Times,* February 23, 1982, p. 3; Stiehm, *Bring Me Men and Women,* pp. 10–14.

12. Stiehm, *Bring Me Men and Women,* pp. 32–38.

13. Stiehm, *Bring Me Men and Women,* pp. 132–35; Bill Peterson, "Academy Plans for Female Invasion," *Washington Post,* February 28, 1976, p. 1.

14. Women Midshipmen Study Group, "The Integration of Women in the Brigade of Midshipmen" (1987), p. 5.

15. Lts. Barbette Henry Lowndes, Maureen Foley, Pamela Wacek Svendsen, Tina d'Ercole, and Sandy Daniels oral histories. Except where otherwise noted, material in the following four paragraphs is drawn from these accounts.

16. Art Harris, "The Women Take Charge and Plebes Shudder," *Washington Post,* July 25, 1979, pp. A1, A6.

17. Women Midshipmen Study Group, "Integration," pp. i–ii.

18. Women Midshipmen Study Group, "Integration," pp. 21, 33, 36, 42, 61, 88–89, 102–5; Wendy Lawrence interview, April 30, 1991.

19. Midshipman First Class Stephanie Schollaert, "Nobody Asked Me Either, But. . . ," U.S. Naval Institute *Proceedings* (August 1988): 94; Women Midshipmen Study Group, "Integration," pp. 15–16; Anne Murphy, "Midship-women Make Waves at Naval Academy," *The Fairfax Connection,* May 26, 1988, p. 31; Desda Moss, "Sister Keeps Naval Academy All in the Family," *USA Today,* May 26, 1992, quote on p. A2; John Burlage, "Fleet Sailors Enhance Academy Class of '95," *Navy Times,* July 22, 1991, p. 8.

20. *New York Times,* Associated Press, "Taunted Woman Quits Academy," May 14, 1990, p. B9; Felicity Barringer, "Harassment of Women Shakes Naval Academy," May 20, 1990, p. 22; Molly Moore, "Navy, Congress Open Probes of Harassment at Annapolis," *Washington Post,* May 18, 1990, pp. A1, A4; John Glionna, "Southland Woman Tells of Her Annapolis Ordeal," *Los Angeles Times,* May 23, 1990, pp. A2, A12; Kathleen Bruyere interview, May 1991; Naval Academy Alumni Association, "The Supe's Perspective," *Shipmate* (July/August 1990):8, 10.

22. Juliane Gallina telephone interview.

23. Navy Department, "Navy Study Group's Report on Progress of Women" (1987), p. 1-A-2; Naval District of Washington, "Navy Puts Faith in New Chaplain," *Navy News,* August 17, 1973; Claire Cox, "The Problems of Women Chaplains," *Oakland Tribune,* July 8, 1973, p. 7.

24. Kelsey Stewart letter.

25. Barbara Nyce interview; "They've Come a Long Way from Typewriter to. . . ," *Navy News,* August 17, 1973, p. 12; *Navy Times*: "First Woman Named NFSSO Head," July 25, 1973, p. 2, and "Behind the Lines," April 24, 1974 (Family insert, p. 30); "Navy Study Group's Report on Progress of Women" (1987), p. 1-14; "Cdr. Kuhn Makes History," *All Hands* (June 1975):28.

26. Fran McKee interview; Department of Defense, "Women in the Navy," *Women in Defense* (October 1984), p. 13, states that thirty-three women were in command of naval shore activities. Of this number no more than three could have been nurses, as the first three nurses selected for command were chosen in 1983; Jean Ebbert, "Military Sealift Plays Vital Strategic Role," *Navy Times,* April 28, 1986, p. 26.

27. "Update Report on the Progress of Women" (1990), p. II- 41.

28. Kelsey Stewart letter; Veronica Froman interview and letter.

29. James Watkins interview.

30. Fran McKee interview.

31. Fran McKee interview.

32. *Navy Times*: Ted Bush, "President Gives Hopper Star, Navy Quickly Finds Number," January 2, 1984, p. 17, and Sharon B. Young, "Hopper Won't Retire, She'll Just Fade into Another Computer Job," August 11, 1986, pp. 6, 10.

12. Women at Sea

1. Bureau of Naval Personnel, "Women in the Navy Information Book," NavPers 15516A, pp. 33–50, and "Report on the Evaluation of the Assignment of Women to the USS Sanctuary, 1 October 1972 to 1 October 1973," pp. 15-1, p. 13-2, OP-01 files, Navy Department; *Navy Times*: Suzanne Viau, "Lack of Women's Clothing Strides Chided," October 1, 1979, p. 14, and "Female YP Skipper 'Can Do the Job,'" May 3, 1976, pp. 16, 32; B. G. Allen, telephone conversation.

2. "Three Navy Women Explain Reasons for 'Sex Bias' Suit," *Navy Times*, November 29, 1976, pp. 4, 58.

3. "'Sex Bias' Suit," *Navy Times*, November 29, 1976, p. 58.

4. Holm, *Women in the Military*, pp. 329–31.

5. *Navy Times*: Rosemary Purcell, "4 Sue to Lift Distaff Ship Ban," November 22, 1976, p. 3, and "'Sex Bias' Suit," November 29, 1976, pp. 4, 58; Kathleen Byerly interview, March 4, 1986.

6. "Drag, Woman Fighting to Go to Sea," *Navy Times*, September 5, 1977, pp. 4, 26.

7. Kathleen Bruyere (formerly Byerly) interview, May 6, 1991.

8. Kathleen Bruyere interviews, quote: March 4, 1986.

9. James Watkins interview; "Women in the Navy Information Book," p. 25; CNO memo to all flag officers, unit commanders, commanding officers, and officers-in-charge, November 27, 1978, "Women in Ships, 1978," file D-118, OP-01 files, Navy Department.

10. Capt. Robin Quigley, "Women Aboard Ship: A Few Observations," *Sea Power* (May 1977):17; Lt. Comdr. Dimity Graichen, "Some Drawbacks to Women at Sea," *Navy Times*, April 11, 1977, pp. 15, 32.

11. Rosemary Purcell, "McKee Tells Wave Convention Sea Duty for Women Is Coming," *Navy Times*, August 15, 1977, p. 2; Capt. James F. Kelly, Jr., "Women in Warships: A Right to Serve," U.S. Naval Institute *Proceedings* (October 1978):44–52; Vice Adm. Samuel Gravely to Rear Adm. H. G. Rich, Pers-6, July 14, 1977, Bureau of Naval Personnel.

12. Kelly, "Women in Warships," p. 46; "Navy's Point Loma to Receive Women," *Navy Times,* December 25, 1978, p. 20; "Women on Sea Duty," *All Hands* (November 1978):8.

13. Kelly, "Women in Warships," p. 50; "Navy Study Group Report on Progress of Women" (1987) p. 1-A-5.

14. Karlyn Barker, "Women at Sea: Navy Traditions Being Rewritten," *Washington Post,* February 26, 1979, pp. A1, A21; "Women Sailors Mark First Foreign Landing," *Washington Star,* November 25, 1979, p. B2; "Vulcan's Coed Deployment a Success," *Navy Times,* March 24, 1980, p. 43; "Navy Study Group's Report on Progress of Women" (1987), p. 1-16; *San Diego Union,* September 29, 1979, p. A12.

15. John Burlage, "Navy Confident It Will Get Enough People for 605 Ship Fleet," *Navy Times,* March 18, 1985, p. 3; "Update Report on Progress of Women" (1990), p. I-25.

16. James Watkins interview.

17. "Update Report on Progress of Women" (1990), p. I-25; secretary of the Navy, memorandum to secretary of defense, March 8, 1982, OP-01 files, Navy Department.

18. Lt. Comdr. Katherine S. Buchta, "Women at Sea: A Female Physician's Viewpoint," *U.S. Navy Medicine,* pp. 8–11.

19. Memorandum for the deputy CNO, July 6, 1984, "Women in Ships, 1983," file D-11E, OP-01 files, Navy Department.

20. David Masci, "ET2(SW) Leith Regan," *All Hands* (June 1988):27.

21. Raymond Sharpe, telephone conversation.

22. Robin Barnette, "YN2 Deborah Cheek," *All Hands* (June 1988):26.

23. RM2 Heather McIntosh, letter to the editor, *Navy Times,* July 17, 1987, p. 22.

24. "Navy Study Group's Report on Progress of Women" (1987), p. 1-A-7; "Update Report on Progress of Women" (1990), p. I-A-3; *Navy Times,* September 24, 1990, p. 4.

25. Lt. (jg) Pamela Rodgers, USNA, letter to OP-01(W), July 10, 1982, "Surface Warfare," file A-7, OP-01(W) files, Navy Department; Lt. Sheila Scarborough, "Noncombatants SWOs Can Be Warriors," *U.S. Naval Institute Proceedings* (October 1985):151.

26. "Navy Study Group's Report on Progress of Women" (1987), pp. 1-21 and 2-35; "Update Report on the Progress of Women" (1990), pp. I-22 through I-24, II-45, and II-47; James Longo, "Lt. Unger Faces Court-martial for Refusing Drug Test," *Navy Times,* October 24, 1988, p. 6; Capts. R. J. Kerrigan and G. W. Stewart, messages and memos to OP-01(W), reports submitted August 24, 1979, July 31, 1980, and February 28, 1981, OP-01 files, Navy Department.

27. This and the following quotes are from the Julia Roos interview.

28. Robert Lindsay, "Navy Sends More Women to Sea, Despite Problems," *New York Times,* June 29, 1980, p. 2.

29. Margaret Hornblower, "Female Sailors Asked to 'Red Pencil' Names of Lesbians, ACLU Says," *Washington Post,* June 14, 1980, p. A7; Beth Ann Krier, "None of Your Business Uncle Sam," *San Francisco Chronicle,* August 6, 1980, p. 2; James Longo, "11 Who Admit Homosexuality Face Separation," *Navy Times,* September 5, 1988, p. 12; William J. Bartman, "Straight and Gay Service-women Battered in Wave of Witch Hunts," *Minerva's Bulletin Board* (Spring 1989), pp. 1–3.

30. *Navy Times:* Tom Burgess, "Some in L.Y. Spear Crew Question Handling of Fraternization Cases," March 5, 1984, p. 4; "Comments on Spear," letters to the editor, April 2, 1984, p. 19; quote, RDCS Barry S. Gee, letter to the editor, September 4, 1989, p. 22.

31. John Burlage, "Salvage Ship CO Draws Allegations of Harassment," *Navy Times,* September 14, 1987, p. 30.

32. "Update Report on the Progress of Women" (1990), pp. III-1 through III-47; Rosemary Purcell, "Former CO Punished for Sexual Harassment," *Navy Times,* October 5, 1987, p. 2.

33. James Longo and Elizabeth Donovan, "Officer Charged with Rape of Shipmate," *Navy Times,* June 18, 1990, p. 4.

34. "Update Report on the Progress of Women" (1990), p. II-77.

35. "Update Report on the Progress of Women" (1990), p. II-78.

36. "Navy Study Group's Report on Progress of Women" (1987), p. 2-49 and "Update Report on the Progress of Women" (1990), p. II-76.

37. "Navy Study Group's Report on Progress of Women" (1987), pp. 1-16 and 1-25; "Update Report on the Progress of Women" (1990), pp. I-31 and I-32; *Navy Times:* "Navy Assigns 1st Female XO," October 8, 1984, and Deborah Schmidt, "First Female SWO Takes Command of Ship," December 9, 1991, p. 8; Ronald Bayles, "Lt. Cmdr. Deborah Gernes," *All Hands* (June 1988):33; JOC(SW) Terry Briggs and JOCS(SW) James Giusti, "Women at Sea on Course," *Surface Warfare* (March–April 1991):24.

38. Briggs and Giusti, "Women at Sea on Course," p. 26; Larry Bonka, "Navy Wife Has One-up on Spouse: She Commands a Ship," *Virginian-Pilot,* January 26, 1991, p. B1.

39. Julia Roos interview; Capt. Raymond Sharpe, letter to the editor, U.S. Naval Institute *Proceedings* (October 1987):14; Raymond Sharpe, telephone conversation; Kathleen Bruyere interview, May 1991.

13. Women in Aviation

1. Joy Hancock, letter to retired Master Chief Helen Suddith, March 23, 1974, copy supplied to authors by Captain Hancock.

2. Chief of naval information, weekly newsgram (41-72), October 18, 1972, OP-01 files, Navy Department.

3. "Women Take the Hurdles," pp. 28–31 from unidentified periodical, copy given to authors by Captain Hancock; Helen F. Collins, "From Plane Captains to Pilots," *Naval Aviation News* (July 1977), p. 9.

4. Holm, *Women in the Military*, pp. 314–15.

5. The information on the original six women aviators is taken from the following sources: Rosemary Purcell, "Behind the Lines," *Navy Times* (Family insert), April 24, 1974; *All Hands*: "Women With Navy Wings," (April 1975):25, 32–37, and "The Expanding Role of Navy Women" (April 1973):25; *Naval Aviation News*: Collins, "From Plane Captains to Pilots," (July 1977):12, 18, and Sandy Russell, "High Flying Ladies" (February 1981):8.

6. Sandy Nye, "Up Front with Judy," *Naval Aviation News* (July 1977):19.

7. "Ens. Joellen Drag," *All Hands* (April 1975):36.

8. Russell, "High Flying Ladies," p. 8.

9. Collins, "From Plane Captains to Pilots," pp. 13–14.

10. Nye, "Up Front with Judy," quote on p. 20; Pam Proctor, "The Stormy Life of Judy Neuffer," *Parade*, October 13, 1974, quote on p. 20; "Women with Navy Wings," *All Hands* (April 1975):36; Elizabeth Donovan, "Woman's Uprising," *Navy Times*, July 30, 1990, p. 16.

11. Capt. John Lacouture, USN (Ret.), "Nobody Asked Me, But . . .," U.S. Naval Institute *Proceedings* (July 1989):84.

12. *Navy Times*: "Impending Motherhood Keeps Naval Aviator on the Ground," July 12, 1976, p. 62; Comdr. D. A. Hafford, "CO Says Pregnancy Didn't Hurt Squadron," December 20, 1976, p. 17; "Taking Action," May 11, 1992, p. 18.

13. "First Woman Designated Naval Aviator Dies in Plane Crash," *Naval Aviation News* (October 1982):48.

14. Naval Academy Alumni Association, "Last Call, Cary Page Jones," *Shipmate* (September 1982):119.

15. "Navy Study Group's Report on Progress of Women" (1987), p. 1-30; Lt. Chrystal Lewis, USN, "Becoming a Female Naval Aviator," U.S. Naval Institute *Proceedings* (October 1986):105–6; "Women with Navy Wings," *All Hands* (April 1975):33.

16. Douglas Payne interview.

17. Russell, "High Flying Ladies," pp. 13, 46–47; "Mom at Sea," *Wifeline* (Spring 1984):1; "Larger Horizons and Brighter Sunsets," *All Hands* (December 1983):5–6; *Navy Times*: "Woman Trains as Catapult Officer," January 25, 1988, p. 37; Deborah Schmidt, "Lt. Kathy Owens Flies into History," April 18, 1991, p. 4; Deborah Schmidt, "Women's Role Expected to Expand in Military," January 6, 1992, p. 16.

18. Edward Lundquist, "Sigonella-Based Aviator Lands in Man's World," *Navy Times*, February 16, 1987, p. 36.

19. Wendy Lawrence interview, April 30, 1991; "Navy Study Group's Report on Progress of Women" (1987), p. 1-30; "Voices," *Washington Post*, Sep-

tember 25, 1989, p. A16; "Update Report on the Progress of Women" (1990), p. II-39.

20. Wendy Lawrence interviews; David S. Steigman, "17 Officers Win Privilege to Blast Off," *Navy Times,* May 4, 1992, p. 10.

21. Timothy J. Christmann, "Navy's First Female Test Pilot," *Naval Aviation News* (November–December 1985):24–26.

22. Navy Department, *Campus* (October 1981), p. 18; Cheryl Sullivan interview.

23. Melissa Healy and James Bornemeier, "For Women in the Navy Rough Waters Run Deep," *Los Angeles Times,* June 28, 1992, pp. 1, 4.

24. John Lancaster, "Admiral Punished in Abuse Probe," *Washington Post,* November 6, 1991, p. A1.

25. *Navy Times*: James Longo, "No Moral Integrity," May 11, 1992, p. 3, and James Longo, "Navy Probes Tailhook Party," November 11, 1991, p. 4.

26. "Here Are the Skits that Cost Squadron Leaders Their Jobs," *Navy Times,* August 3, 1992, p. 10.

27. "Navy Study Group's Report on Progress of Women" (1987), p. 1-28; "Update Report on the Progress of Women" (1990), p. I-37.

28. Patricia Beckman interview.

29. "Scan Patterns," *Naval Aviation News* (March–April 1992):33–34; "High Flying Safety Mark," *Navy Times,* April 11, 1983, p. 3; Marie Bernard interview.

30. "Update Report on the Progress of Women" (1990), p. I-37.

31. Elizabeth Donovan, "She Falls Through the Air with the Greatest of Ease," *Navy Times,* February 25, 1991, p. 36.

32. Donovan, "Woman's Uprising," *Navy Times,* July 30, 1990, p. 16.

33. JO2 Milinda D. Jensen, "Women Military Aviators 1989 Convention," *Naval Aviation News* (November–December 1989):10; Donovan, "Woman's Uprising," *Navy Times,* July 30, 1990, p. 16; Nora Zamchow, "Navy Pilot Blazes a Trial for Other Women," *Los Angeles Times,* June 25, 1990, pp. B1, B5–B6.

14. Contemporary Currents

1. Navy Department, "The United States Navy in 'Desert Shield' 'Desert Storm' " (1991), quote on p. A-5; Eric Voge interview; *Navy Times*: Elizabeth Donovan, "Over 600 Navy Women in Effort," September 3, 1990, p. 6, and Deborah Schmidt, "Women's Role to Expand," January 6, 1992, p. 16.

2. Medicine in the Gulf War," *U.S. Medicine* (August 1991):28–32.

3. "U.S. Navy in 'Desert Shield' 'Desert Storm,' " pp. A-6, 63; "Medicine in the Gulf War," pp. 22–23, 98, 106.

4. Susan Globokar interview.

5. Deborah Sheehan interview.

6. Stephanie Oram letter; Jane Stevens interview; "Lt. Kelly Franke Selected as the Naval Helicopter Association's 1991 Pilot of the Year," WOPA Newsletter, March 1992.

7. Linda Evans-Wackerman letter; "People, Planes, Places," *Naval Aviation News* (May–June 1991):33.

8. Rowan Scarborough, "Women Fall Short on Battle Readiness," *Washington Times,* July 28, 1992, pp. A1, A6.

9. Association of the Bar of the City of New York, "The Combat Exclusion Laws: An Idea Whose Time Has Gone," reprinted in *Minerva* (Winter 1991), quote on pp. 4 and 8.

10. "The Combat Exclusion Laws," pp. 17–18; Carolyn Becraft, "Women in the U.S. Armed Services: The War in the Persian Gulf."

11. Navy Department, "Update Report on the Progress of Women" (1990), p. IV-21.

12. *Navy Times*: Rick Maze, "Pentagon Balks at Change in Parent Assignment," February 25, 1991, p. 3, and "Message to Parents," March 4, 1991, quote on p. 19.

13. Dana Priest, "Parent Debate Goes Beyond Sex of GI," *Washington Post,* February 19, 1991, p. A10; Maze, "Pentagon Balks," *Navy Times,* February 25, 1991, p. 3.

14. *Navy Times*: "Message to Parents," March 4, 1991, p. 4, and Maze, "Pentagon Balks," p. 3.

15. Stephanie Oram letter; Deborah Sheehan interview.

16. Tom Philpott, "Her Story," *Navy Times,* July 6, 1992, pp. 12–14.

17. Gregory Vistica, "Some Fliers at Mirimar Wearing Tailhook Patch," *San Diego Union Tribune,* August 14, 1992, p. 18.

18. Department of Defense, Office of Inspector General, "Tailhook 91: Part 1-Review of the Navy Investigations," September 1992, pp. 31–32, and John Lancaster, "Pentagon Blasts Tailhook Inquiry," *Washington Post,* September 25, 1992, pp. A1, A10.

19. "Hilton Bars Aviator Group Tied to Scandal," *New York Times,* August 1992, p. 15.

20. *Navy Times*: Grant Willis, "Force Cuts May Jeopardize Military Women's Gains," May 7, 1990, p. 6; Schmidt, "Women's Role to Expand," January 6, 1992, p. 16; and Capt. Martha Whitehead, "Women's Sea Billets Afloat," March 23, 1992, p. 35.

21. John Burlage, "Surviving the 'Quality Cut,'" *Navy Times,* March 9, 1992, p. 6.

22. Jane Stevens interview.

REFERENCES

⚓

Archives

Aviation History Office, Naval Historical Center, Washington, D.C.

Department of Defense Library, Pentagon, Washington, D.C.

Library of Congress, Washington, D.C., Josephus S. Daniels Collection, subject file, "Correspondence, Secretary of the Navy, 1913–1921."

National Archives, Washington, D.C.: (1) Record Group 45: subject file 1911–1927, folder NA3, "Women in the USNR, Employment as YN(F)"; folder NA3, "General Information, Enlisted Personnel"; folder ZPN13, "Thirteenth Naval District (F.F. 13)"; and subject file 9878, folders 1313, 2763, and 2422, "Bureau of Navigation General Correspondence, 1913–1925"; folder NC1, "Naval Personnel Losses."
　(2) Record Group 80, roll M1052, general and special indexes, "General Correspondence of the Secretary of the Navy."
　(3) Record Group 24: box 2328, folder QR8; box 2329, folder QR8; box 2330; QR8/MN(N)B, box 2331.

Naval War College Library, Newport, R.I., Naval History Collection, "History of the Women Officers School" and "Changes in Uniform Regulations, No. 15."

Navy Department, Bureau of Naval Personnel, OP-01(W) files.

Navy Operational Archives, Washington, D.C., Series I, Assistant Chief of Naval Personnel for Women ACNP(W).

Schlesinger Library, Radcliffe College, Cambridge, Mass., papers of Elizabeth Reynard.

Smith College Archives, Northampton, Mass., War Service Collection.

Smithsonian Institution, Museum of American History, Washington, D.C., Division of Naval History, *The Notebook* (quarterly newsletter published by the National Yeomen [F] from 1926 through 1985).

Southern Oregon Historical Society, Jacksonville, Oreg., Pauline Graves Collection.

Stanford University Archives, Palo Alto, Calif., *The Stanford Illustrated Review,* January 1919 and *1891–1920 Alumni Directory and Ten Year Book.*

University of Northern Iowa Archives, Cedar Falls, Iowa, Gladys Hearst Collection.

Books and Other Publications

Adam, Barry D. *The Rise of a Gay and Lesbian Movement.* Boston, Mass.: Twayne Publishers, 1987.

Albion, Robert. *Makers of Naval Policy.* Annapolis, Md.: Naval Institute Press, 1982.

Alsmeyer, Marie Bennett. *The Way of the WAVES.* Conway, Ark.: HAMBA Books, 1981.

Arbogast, Kate Avery. "The Procurement of Women for the Armed Forces: An Analysis of Occupational Choice." Ph.D. dissertation, George Washington University, Washington, D.C., 1974.

Becraft, Carolyn. *Women in the U.S. Armed Services: The War in the Persian Gulf.* Washington, D.C.: Women's Research and Education Institute, March 1991.

Billings, Charlene W. *Grace Hopper, Navy Admiral and Computer Pioneer.* Hillside, N.J.: Enslow Publishers, Inc., 1989.

Binkin, Martin, and Bach, Shirley S. *Women in the Military.* Washington, D.C.: The Brookings Institution, 1977.

Butler, Mrs. Henry F. "I Was a Yeoman (F)." Naval Historical Foundation Publication. Series 2, no. 7. Washington, D.C.: Naval Historical Foundation, 1967.

Campbell, D'Ann, *Women at War With America: Private Lives in a Patriotic Era.* Cambridge, Mass.: Harvard University Press, 1984.

DACOWITS Secretariat, Pentagon. Ten-page historical summary. Washington, D.C.: DACOWITS, 1976.

Daniels, Josephus. *The Cabinet Diaries of Josephus Daniels, 1913–1921.* Edited by E. David Cronon. Lincoln, Nebr.: University of Nebraska Press, 1963.

Department of Defense. *Second Annual Report,* 1949; *Semiannual Report of the Secretary of Defense, January 1, 1951–June 30, 1951; Annual Report of the Secretary of Defense,* 1965, 1968; *Utilization of Military Women,* 1977; *Women in Defense,* Washington, D.C., October 1984.

Dessez, Eunice. *The First Enlisted Women, 1917–1918.* Philadelphia: Dorrance & Company, 1955.

Elder, Robert. "History of the Demobilization of the United States Navy's Women's Reserve, 1945–1946." Ph.D. dissertation, University of Chicago, 1947.

Field, James A., Jr. *History of United States Naval Operations in Korea.* Washington, D.C.: Government Printing Office, 1962.

Gildersleeve, Virginia. *Many a Good Crusade.* New York: Macmillan Company, 1954.

Hancock, Joy Bright. *Lady in the Navy.* Annapolis, Md.: Naval Institute Press, 1972.

Holm, Jeanne, Maj. Gen., USAF (Ret.). *Women in the Military.* Novato, Calif.: Presidio Press, 1983.

Katz, Jonathan. *Gay American History.* New York: Thomas V. Crowell, 1976.

MacGregor, Morris J., Jr. *Integration of the Armed Forces, 1940–1964.* Washington, D.C.: Defense Studies Series, Center for Military History, U.S. Army, 1981.

Marolda, Edward J., and Pryce, G. Wesley, III. *A Short History of the U.S. Navy and the Southeast Asian Conflict, 1950–1975.* Washington, D.C.: Naval Historical Center, Department of the Navy, 1984.

Miller, Nathan. *F.D.R.: An Intimate History.* Garden City, N.Y.: Doubleday, 1983.

The Ministry of National Defense. *The History of the United Nations Forces in the Korean War,* Vol. VI. Seoul, Korea, 1977.

Morison, Samuel Eliot. *History of the United States Naval Operations in World War II.* Vol. 1, *Battle of the Atlantic.* Boston: Little Brown and Company, 1957.

Mueller, John E. *War, Presidents, and Public Opinion.* New York: John Wiley and Sons, Inc., 1973.

Navy Department, Bureau of Medicine and Surgery. *The History of the Medical Department of the U.S. Navy, 1945–1950,* NAVMED P-5057.

Navy Department, Bureau of Naval Personnel. *U.S. Naval Administration in World War II: The Bureau of Ships; Administrative History of the Twelfth Naval District; Eleventh Naval District; Enlisted Personnel; Fourteenth Naval District,* Vol. 1, *Naval Communications; The Negro in the Navy; Office of Naval Operations, School of Oriental Languages; Officer Personnel; Women's Reserve,* Vols. I and II. Washington, D.C., 1947.

Navy Department, Bureau of Naval Personnel. *Secretary's Report to Congress, 1941,* 1941; *Statistics Yearbook, 1944,* 1944; *Final Report of the Navy Manpower Survey Board to the Secretary of the Navy,* June 1944; *Annual Report of the Secretary of the Navy, 1945,* 1945; *Annual Report of the Secretary of the Navy, 1946,* 1946; *Annual Report of the Women's Reserve for the Fiscal Year Ending 30 June 1947,* 1947; *Training Bulletin,* December 1949; SEC-

NAVNOTE 1900, August 30, 1982; *Navy Study Group's Report on Progress of Women in the Navy,* December 5, 1987; *FY-88—Annual Report of Navy Military Personnel Statistics,* September 30, 1988; OPNAVINST 6000.1A, February 1989; OPNAVINST 5300.9, November 6, 1989; 1990 Navy Women's Study Group, *An Update Report on the Progress of Women in the Navy,* March 1991; *The United States Navy in "Desert Shield" "Desert Storm,"* May 15, 1991; all, Washington, D.C.

Navy Department, Office of the Director of the Nurse Corps. "History of the Nurse Corps, U.S. Navy, 1811–1985." Chronology of Nurse Corps History, Washington, D.C., 1986.

Navy Department, "Uniform Regulation, United States Navy," Chap. 2. Washington, D.C., 1913.

Public Papers of the Presidents: Harry S Truman, 1945. Washington, D.C.: U.S. Government Printing Office, 1961.

Schneider, Dorothy, and Schneider, Carl. *Sound Off.* New York: E.P. Dutton, 1988.

Smith, Margaret Chase. *Declaration of Conscience.* Garden City, NY: Doubleday and Company, 1972.

Stiehm, Judith Hicks. *Bring Me Men and Women.* Berkeley and Los Angeles: University of California Press, 1981.

Treadwell, Mattie B. *U.S. Army in World War II: Special Studies—The Women's Army Corps.* Washington, D.C.: U.S. Army, 1954.

U.S. Congress. Senate. *Hearings Before the Committee on Naval Affairs on S. 2527.* 77th Cong., 2nd sess., 1942.

U.S. Congress. House. *Hearings Before the Committee on Ways and Means.* 68th Cong., 1st sess., March 3–5, 1924.

Warburton, Eileen. *In Living Memory.* Newport, R.I.: Newport Savings & Loan Association/Island Trust Company, 1988.

Wieand, Harold T. "The History of the Development of the United States Naval Reserve, 1989–1941." Ph.D. dissertation, University of Pittsburgh, Navy Department Library, 1952.

Women Midshipmen Study Group. *The Integration of Women in the Brigade of Midshipmen,* report to the superintendent. Annapolis: U.S. Naval Academy, November 1987.

Zumwalt, Elmo. *On Watch.* New York: Quadrangle Books, The New York Times Book Company, 1976.

Newspapers and Magazines

All Hands, July 1972; April 1973, December 1983; April, June, August 1975; June 1988.

American Journal of Sociology, March 1946: Mildred McAfee Horton, "Women in the United States Navy."

Defense Management Journal, VI, no. 1 (Winter 1970).

Minerva, Fall 1991; Winter 1991.

National Geographic, October 1943: La Verne Bradley, "Women in Uniform."

Naval Aviation News, July 1977; February 1981; October 1982; November–December 1985; November–December 1989; March–April 1992.

The Notebook, December 1980.

Parade Magazine, October 13, 1974: Pam Proctor, "The Stormy Life of Judy Neuffer."

Pers-K Newsletter(s), Bureau of Naval Personnel.

Sea Power, March 1918.

Shipmate, USNA Alumni Association, September 1982; July/August 1990.

Signs, 1984: Allan Berube and John D'Emilio, "The Military and Lesbians During the McCarthy Years."

Tra Navy: The Magazine of Naval Training, Chief of Naval Education and Training, November 1973.

U.S. Medicine, August 1991: "Medicine in the Gulf War."

U.S. Naval Institute, *Proceedings*: Lt. Robert A. Rogers, "These Boots Wear Skirts" (September 1949); Lt. Comdr. William Hoover, USN, "The Disadvantaged Navy Woman" (July 1977); Lt. Chrystal Lewis, USN, "Becoming a Female Naval Aviator" (October 1986); Midshipman First Class Stephanie Schollaert, USN, "Nobody Asked Me Either, But. . ." (August 1988); Capt. John Lacouture, USN (Ret.), "Nobody Asked Me But. . ." (July 1989).

Oral Histories

Interviews by John T. Mason, Jr. (typed transcripts, U.S. Naval Institute, Annapolis, Md.)

Capt. Joy Bright Hancock, USN (Ret.), November 12–13, 1969, and March 11, 1970, Annapolis, Md.

Mildred McAfee Horton, August 25–26, 1969, Randolph, N.H.

Comdr. Etta Belle Kitchen, USN (Ret.), November 30, 1983, Annapolis, Md.

Capt. Jean Palmer, USN, May 19, 1969, New York, N.Y.

Lt. Comdr. Mary Josephine Shelly, USNR, February 9, 1970, New York, N.Y. (later, colonel, USAFR).

Capt. Dorothy Stratton, USCGR, September 24, 1970, New York, N.Y.

Capt. Louise Wilde, USN (Ret.), December 2, 1969, Washington, D.C.

Interviews by Etta Belle Kitchen (typed transcripts, U.S. Naval Institute, Annapolis, Md.)

Comdr. Elizabeth Crandall, USNR, July 18, 1970, Palo Alto, Calif.

Comdr. Tova Wiley Peterson, USNR, September 28, 1969, San Francisco, Calif.

Capt. Robin Quigley, USN (Ret.), June 15, 1976, San Diego, Calif.

Lt. Comdr. Frances Rich, USNR, September 6, 1960, Palm Springs, Calif.

Comdr. Eleanor Rigby, USNR, July 19, 1970, Palo Alto, Calif.

Interviews by Susan Sweeney (typed transcripts, U.S. Naval Institute, Annapolis, Md.)

Lts. Sandy Daniels, Tina d'Ercole, Maureen Foley, Barbette Henry Lowndes, and Pamela Wacek Svendsen, USN, 1984–1988.

Interviews, Letters, and Conversations

With Jean Ebbert

Comdr. Jan Adams, USN (WOPA 1991 membership chairman), telephone communication, September 6, 1991.

Ms. Terry Allen, Navy Uniform Material Office, telephone communication, May 7, 1990.

AFCM Kathleen Amick-Temple, USN (Ret.), and AFCM Sidney Temple, USN (Ret.), interview, October 15, 1990, Norfolk, Va.

Lt. Comdr. Anne Aoki, USN, interview, July 30, 1986, Springfield, Mass.

Lt. Comdr. Patricia Beckman, USN, by telephone, March 4, 1992.

YNC Lois Berman Brown, USN (Ret.), interview, March 6, 1987, Annandale, Va.

Capt. Kathleen Bruyere (formerly Byerly), USN, interview, March 4, 1986, Philadelphia, Penn.; interview, May 6, 1991, Alexandria, Va.

Capt. Winifred Quick Collins, USN (Ret.), interview, June 12, 1985, Washington, D.C.; letter, June 21, 1992.

Capt. Dorothy Council, USN (Ret.), interview, July 22, 1986, Newport, R.I.

Mary Daily, interview, July 30, 1982, Seattle, Wash.; also papers supplied by Daily to authors.

Capt. Julie DiLorenzo, USN, letter, January 3, 1986.

Margaret Disert, interview, November 30, 1983, Chambersburg, Penn.

Capt. Ann Ducey, USN (Ret.), letter, May 16, 1986.

Lt. Linda Evans-Wackerman, USN, letter, May 12, 1992.

Midshipman First Class Juliane Gallina, USN, by telephone, October 8, 1991.

Lt. Comdr. Dale F. Garlock, USN (Ret.), letter, March 13, 1989.

Capt. Mary T. Gore, USN (Ret.), interview, March 18, 1985, Washington, D.C.

Master Chief Personnelman Winifred Hamerlinck, USN (Ret.), letter, March 26, 1986.

Mildred McAfee Horton, interview, April 12, 1984, Randolph, N.H.

Gertrude French Howalt, and Walter Howalt, letters and papers, November 1986–January 1987.

Veronica Mackey Hulick, interview, May 19, 1983, Alexandria, Va.

Ardelle Humphrey, interview, May 4, 1983, Gaithersburg, Md.; letter, July 12, 1983.

Lt. Comdr. Dorothy Joyce, USN (Ret.), interview, July 28, 1986, Bethesda, Md.

Capt. Katherine Keating, USN (Ret.), letters, October 13 and November 11, 1989.

Capt. Marie Kelleher, USN (Ret.), letter, February 26, 1986.

Capt. Lucille Kuhn, USN (Ret.), interview, May 6, 1986, Richmond, Va.; telephone interview, June 13, 1991.

Harold D. Langley, curator for naval history, conversation, November 3, 1986, Washington, D.C.

Lt. Comdr. Wendy Lawrence, USN, interviews, March 19, 1991; April 30, 1991 (with Marie-Beth Hall), Annapolis, Md.

Capt. Rita Lenihan, USN (Ret.), interview, March 4, 1986, Washington, D.C.

Lynn MacDonald, Naval Academy Admissions Office, telephone communication, October 2, 1991.

Rear Adm. Fran McKee, USN (Ret.), interview, March 18, 1982, Annandale, Va.

Margaret Dunn Mead, questionnaire supplied to Jean Ebbert, September 21, 1982.

Naval Internal Relations Activity, Navy Department, Washington, D.C., memo in response to query, April 30, 1987.

Capt. Barbara Nyce, USN (Ret.), interview, January 10, 1986, Alexandria, Va.

Lt. Col. Helen O'Neill, USMCR (Ret.), interview, May 13, 1982, McLean, Va.

Lt. Comdr. Stephanie Oram, letter, April 14, 1992.

Capt. Douglas Payne, USN (Ret.), telephone interview, February 20, 1992.

Lt. Marjorie Rawhouser, USN, and Lt. Timothy Lombardo, assistant training officer, U.S. Naval Academy, telephone communication, June 27, 1989.

Lt. Julia Roos, USN, interview, May 17, 1991, Virginia Beach, Va.

Estelle Richardson Ruby, interview, July 12, 1982, Washington, D.C.

Capt. Viola Sanders, USN (Ret.), letter, March 18, 1986, and December 7, 1987.

Capt. Ray Sharpe, USN, telephone interview, October 8, 1991.

Boatswain's Mate Third Class Deborah Sheehan, USN, telephone interview, April 27, 1992.

Edwin Smetheram, interview, July 30, 1982, Seattle, Wash.

Gregg Stallworth, Public Affairs Office of the chief of naval education and training, telephone communication, September 25, 1991.

C. J. Stein, assistant director, Resources, Plans, and Analysis, NROTC Program, chief of naval education and training, letter, July 11, 1991.

Lt. Jane Stevens, USN, telephone interview, March 13, 1992.

Lt. JoAnne Stone, USN, and Comdr. Arthur J. Tuttle, USN, NROTC Program, chief of naval education and training, telephone communication, July 7, 1989.

Yeomen (F) interviews at U.S. Naval Home, including Dollie Purvis Grumbles, Phyllis Kelley Peterson, and Marjorie Slocum, Gulfport, Miss., April 6, 1983.

Capt. Jordine Von Wantoch, USN, letter, April 9, 1989, and August 3, 1992.

Adm. James D. Watkins, USN (Ret.), interview, June 9, 1988, Washington, D.C.

Capt. Sarah Watlington, USN (Ret.), interview, September 15, 1989, West Lafayette, Ind.

Comdr. Carolina Clair Wylie, USN, interview, October 1, 1982, Arlington, Va.

Capt. Elizabeth G. Wylie, USN, interview, July 29, 1982, Seattle, Wash.

With Marie-Beth Hall

Petty Officer Marie Bernard, interview, July 1, 1991, Burke, Va.

Capt. Veronica Froman, USN, interview, June 11, 1991, Fairfax, Va.; letter, June 27, 1991.

Lt. Susan P. Globokar, USN, telephone interview, September 6, 1991.

Capt. Kelsey Stewart, USN (Ret.), letter, April 18, 1991.

Lt. Cheryl Sullivan, USN, interview, January 22, 1992, Lexington Park, Md.

Lt. Eric Voge, USN, interview, April 25, 1992, Newport, R.I.

Letters

Supplied by Winifred Hamerlinck

Letter to the Bureau of Personnel, September 29, 1969; Capt. C. E. Stastny, commanding officer, U.S. Naval Station, Long Beach, Calif., to chief of naval personnel, October 1, 1969 [re: Hamerlinck].

Supplied by Jordine Von Wantoch

Jordine Von Wantoch, letter to chief of naval personnel, June 3, 1970; commanding officer, Amphibious School, Coronado, Calif., endorsement, June 3, 1970; commander, Amphibious Training Command, Pacific Fleet, endorsement, June 8, 1970; secretary of the Navy, letter to Jordine Von Wantoch, July 16, 1970; Bureau of Naval Personnel, letter to Jordine Von Wantoch, July 29, 1970; Jordine Von Wantoch, letter to chief of naval personnel, August 10, 1970; Jordine Von Wantoch, letter to chief of naval personnel, November 16, 1971.

INDEX

⚓